G6/27

JM Swinton
1957

Alderley Edge
Christian Fellowship
For a Lecture on
Worship.
March 1997

TRADITION AND EXPLORATION

Tradition and Exploration

Collected Papers on Theology and the Church

by

HENRY CHADWICK

The Canterbury Press
Norwich

Collected papers © Henry Chadwick, KBE, 1994

First published in book form 1994 by
The Canterbury Press Norwich
(a publishing imprint of Hymns Ancient & Modern Limited,
a registered charity)
St Mary's Works, St Mary's Plain,
Norwich, Norfolk NR3 3BH

British Library Cataloguing in Publication Data

A catalogue record for this book is available
from the British Library

ISBN 1-85311-082-5

Typeset by Chansitor Publications Limited, Beccles, Suffolk

*Printed and bound in Great Britain by
St Edmundsbury Press Limited
Bury St Edmunds, Suffolk*

Contents

Introduction   *page* vii

1. Episcopacy in the New Testament and Early Church   1
2. Ministry and Tradition   12
3. The vindication of Christianity in Westcott's thought   19
4. 'Ego Berengarius'   33
5. The Lambeth Quadrilateral in England   61
6. Truth and Authority   75
7. Full Communion with other Episcopal Churches   84
8. Justification by Faith: a perspective   93
9. Lima, ARCIC, and the Church of England   135
10. Ecumenical stocktaking: Unfinished business   143
11. Newman, a man for our Time   154
12. Newman's doctrine of justification   170
13. Newman's Sacramental Faith   188
14. Paul VI and Vatican II   194
15. Why Music in Church?   203
16. Romanticism and Religion   217
17. Royal ecclesiastical supremacy   229
18. The Status of Ecumenical Councils in Anglican Thought   258
19. Making and Remaking in the Ministry of the Church   270

Notes   285

Sources   320

Index   321

ABBREVIATIONS

ACO	Acta Conciliorum Oecumenicorum (Berlin, de Gruyter, 1914-1992)
ARCIC	Anglican Roman Catholic International Commission
CIC	Codex Iuris Canonici
CDF	Congregation for the Doctrine of the Faith
CT	Concilium Tridentinum (edition of the Acts of the Council of Trent)
DS	Denzinger/Schönmetzer, *Enchiridion Symbolorum Definitionum et Definitionum*, 36th edition (Freiburg, Herder, 1976)
DTC	*Dictionnaire de Théologie Catholique*, 15 vols.
EP	Richard Hooker, *The Laws of Ecclesiastical Polity*
Jfc	J. H. Newman, *Lectures on Justification* (1838)
MGH	Monumenta Germaniae Historica
PG	J. P. Migne (ed.), Patrologia Graeco-Latina
PL	J. P. Migne (ed.), Patrologia Latina
PS	Parker Society
STC	Short Title Catalogue
WA	Weimar Edition of Luther's works
WABr	Weimar Edition of Luther's letters

Introduction

THIS COLLECTION of papers brings together a miscellany of pieces, widely scattered in a diversity of places and by this volume provided with rescue from obscurity. Although diverse in their character, the majority converge on themes which impart a degree of coherence and unity. Several of these essays are strictly academic attempts to clarify dark places in the history of Christian thought. Some, while not less rigorous (I hope) in the application of proper criteria, are more obviously directed towards issues raised by recent ecumenical dialogues. Many of the pieces were originally composed because an authority or a Church committee or an international congress specifically asked for a paper on a particular problem. Even the most academic of the papers here, though written with detachment, has a bearing on questions which are alive for the contemporary Church.

Ecumenical dialogues have lately suffered discouragement. The second Vatican Council's decree on Ecumenism transformed the long frost into a massive thaw in relationships, which would perhaps still prevail had not the aftermath of that great assembly also brought with it an unhappy loss of nerve among priests and religious who felt that the Roman Catholic Church had almost lost its identity by ceasing to be authoritarian and juridical in its ways. The seventies saw remarkable progress which astonished the participants, especially in the Lima document of the World Council of Churches on 'Baptism, Eucharist, and Ministry', and the closely parallel movement in the report of the first Anglican – Roman Catholic International Commission of 1982. The near-euphoria surrounding these two carefully thought-out texts has been replaced by disappointment and disillusion, as the separated bodies have reasserted attitudes and propositions which are not only distinctive but even divisive. There has been a subconscious feeling that what divides imparts a specific identity, and that to lose the negative condemnations and rejections of the past is to engage in a kind of treachery to one's tradition.

Nevertheless, brief reflection suffices to convince any thoughtful person that the pause in progress cannot mean that the cause has to be abandoned as hopeless. There are sharp words in the New Testament about the Christian duty to foster unity. And the steady growth of secularism and atheism owes not a little to the repellent effect of the dissensions between Christians which, when exported from the West to the Third World engender further bewilderment.

The essay on 'Episcopacy in the New Testament and early Church' was written for the Lambeth Conference of 1978. 'Ministry and Tradition' originated in a Spanish lecture at the University of Burgos. The lecture on Bishop Westcott was given in 1961 for Westcott House, Cambridge. The paper on Berengar and his place in the history of eucharistic doctrine (1989) arose out of some weeks in the great library at Wolfenbüttel, providing the opportunity to consult the unique manuscript of Berengar's reply to Lanfranc, and from the occasion of Professor Huygens' new edition for Corpus Christianorum. The study of the Lambeth Quadrilateral was limited, by the plan of the volume, to the English scene. 'Truth and Authority' was a lecture at Westminster Abbey in a series examining the context of ARCIC's statements.

'Full Communion' was a paper commissioned in 1981 by the Secretary-General of the Anglican Communion. The examination of 'Justification by Faith'—the most intricate of all matters of faith—emerged from the early stages of ARCIC's discussion, and was designed to clarify for members unfamiliar with the European and western terms of reference what the issues have been understood to be. The ninth paper on 'Lima and ARCIC' was in origin an invited address to the General Synod of the Church of England on 13 July 1983. The Vatican's response to the report of the first ARCIC of 1982 appeared in December 1991, and has occasioned some sadness among ecumenists generally. At the invitation of the editor of *The Tablet* I attempted a cool analysis of the Vatican's reasons and arguments, which have been interpreted to be more negative than the Vatican claimed them to be.

Of the two papers on Newman the first was a lecture at Oxford commissioned by Oriel College and Trinity College for the centenary commemoration in 1990, while the second sought to analyse the central theme of Newman's most important single theological work, his *Lectures on Justification* (1838).

The review-discussion of the part played by Pope Paul VI in directing the discussion at Vatican II on the Church (Lumen Gentium) and Ecumenism (Unitatis Redintegratio), in face of the deep misgivings of the large minority, appeared in the *Journal of Ecclesiastical History* for July 1990, and was able to make use of the recently published working papers of Gerard Philips of Louvain, the principal drafter of Lumen Gentium.

A lifelong passion for music in general and Church music in particular lies behind the lecture, for the Church Music Society in 1981, on why Christians like to use music as a vehicle of worship. Parts of this lecture have affinity with a much earlier lecture (1960), given to the Modern Humanities Research Association, on the nature of Romanticism and the religious ingredient which is constitutive of what we mean by this elusive word.

The commemoration in Cambridge of Cardinal John Fisher, martyred under Henry VIII, brought out how important a part he played in the high culture of the university during Henry VIII's reign. An invitation to contribute an essay on the notion of royal ecclesiastical supremacy (the issue which brought him to his death) provoked a wider consideration of the idea, to which it is far from easy for twentieth century Christians to assent.

Finally, the honouring of a great theologian of the Russian Orthodox tradition, Georges Florovsky, occasioned an examination of the treatment of ecumenical councils in Anglican theologians, especially of the classical age of the seventeenth century. The volume of essays *The Heritage of the Early Church* (1973) gathered a chorus of admirers of Fr Florovsky from several traditions.

For the generous good will of societies, editors of journals, and publishers in raising no objection to the reproduction of these papers now collected I have to thank in particular, Oxford University Press, Cambridge University Press, SPCK, the Church Music Society, the Modern Humanities Research Association, the Sisters of Turvey Abbey, Forward Movement Publications, Cincinnati, the editors of *The Tablet* and the *Churchman*, The Faculty of Theology of the University of Burgos, and the Pontifical Institute of Oriental Studies.

HENRY CHADWICK

46 St John Street
Oxford

1

Episcopacy in the New Testament and Early Church

ALL CHRISTIAN ministry is a gift of the Spirit, a charism. It is neither an end in itself, nor an entity independent of the community, but rather a service for the building up of the Church (Eph. 4 : 7-16). As a supernatural call, a charism belongs to the transcendent, divine order. As a service within the community, its action is seen in the visible historical order, in the society grounded in the discipleship of Jesus Christ and rooted in the continuing life of the Church. This society is ever vulnerable to temptations and to secularising pressures; the treasure may be contained in very earthen vessels. Nevertheless, if the revelation of God in Christ is rightly seen not only as a word of justifying grace in mercy to the ungodly, but also as a sanctifying power mediated in, with and under the means of grace in word and sacrament and shared worship, the role of an ordered ministry in relation to these means of grace is of essential importance to the maintenance of the Church in the truth of the gospel and the life of the Spirit. For in these words and acts, done in obedience to the Lord's command, the presiding minister is called to act in the name of Christ, the head of the body. He is not merely carrying out a function which the community delegates to him. Himself a man under obedience, he calls those whom he serves to a like obedience.

Charisms differ (I Cor. 12 : 4-13). The ordained ministry is one of the Spirit's gifts to the Church, by which ministers are specially appointed to an office and authorised both for the proclamation and guarding of the word and for the due administration of the sacraments. They are not to lord it over the community they serve (I Peter 5 : 3), but to protect the means of grace upon which the community as a whole depends for its life. Among the Spirit's gifts this ministry is called to ensure that the very diversity of charisms does not endanger the essential unity of the one fellowship of Christ's flock. Accordingly, the oversight given by the ordained ministry always has a dual role or relationship—on the one hand in service to the local Christian community; on the other hand, in relation to other churches in the federation of local communities

1

bonded together in love and constituting the visible universal Church.

The New Testament does not show a precise form or single structure of ministry which can be seen to be there from the day of Pentecost and can in the simplest sense be claimed as a direct and express institution by Jesus. The primary ministry in the apostolic age is that of the apostles themselves; and we have to look partly beyond the first century documents to see what forms of ministry the Church developed as and after the apostles passed from the scene. In fact the later books of the New Testament provide a substantial body of historical evidence for the earlier stages of this development. One essential principle, however, remains constant from the start through all variations of form, namely that the pastoral ministry is not a human invention but a gift of God to his Church to enable it to be what he intends in mission, unity, and holiness.

The *Apostolate* was strictly no doubt neither a charism nor an office in so far as the latter concept would imply a more constitutionally structured society than the earliest Christians possessed. The apostles are witnesses to the resurrection of the Lord and from their glorified Master receive a commission to preach the gospel. But they are not an authority only in the sense of good historical testimony for the events of Christ's coming and triumph. In the communities which their mission founded they also become a source of contemporary jurisdiction. The power of the keys is a dominical commission to decide points in dispute as well as a discretion to give rulings concerning the position of erring individuals within the society of disciples.

In respect of their witness to Jesus Christ (both of his words and deeds 'in the days of his flesh' and as to the fact of God's triumph in his rising again) there is an obvious sense in which the apostles had and could have no successors. What they said and did in their generation no one else can say or do at a later time. The refusal of the Church to add to the canon of the New Testament (i.e. to admit later Christian writings to the lectionary) is a way of making this point, that in the apostolate certain essential functions are not transferable or transmissible, and that primary apostolic authority is permanently contained in the written records of apostolic literature. At the same time the historical continuity of the Church means that in another sense there are responsibilities and powers of the apostolate which have not died with them. Not only does the Church as a whole have an apostolic mission and character. The authenticity of the tradition about Jesus needs to be preserved in the process of transmission. The local families of Christians gathered in scattered communities need pastoral leadership for decisions on questions of right training and practice in obedience to the revealed will of God. As the early Church came to understand that history was not coming to an immediate end, they also came to see that some permanent structure of ministry was required.

In the earliest stage of pioneer missionaries, the ministers will often have been itinerant 'prophets' or teachers, not tied to any single congregation, but going about from place to place encouraging and correcting, and receiving hospitality (according to the Didache, up to a limit of three days). But the congregations will also require resident shepherds to guide and protect the flock. Accordingly there come to be those 'set over' the congregation whose position of authority (I Thess. 5 : 12f; Heb. 13 : 17) derives sanction and lifelong tenure from the sacred nature of their functions.

During the first century some diversity in structure between different regions and local churches seems to have been characteristic. In some churches spiritual leadership was in the hands of a group of elders or 'presbyters', as at Ephesus (Acts, 20 : 17), under the overall authority of the apostle. On the other hand, the mother church at Jerusalem had a single head in the person of James, the Lord's brother. This 'monarchical' and apparently earliest form of pastorate could easily be fused with a presbyteral council, in which it would be natural for one man to be held as first among equals if he possessed special charismatic powers or seniority in years and wisdom, or, like Stephanas at Corinth (I Cor. 16:15-16), was the first convert who then devoted himself to forming a community round him.

At Philippi Paul sends greetings to the 'bishops and deacons' (Phil. I : 1). This reference is the only Pauline allusion, outside the late Pastoral Epistles to Timothy and Titus, to permanent ministerial offices in a local church. In Paul's letters the overwhelming emphasis lies upon the Spirit as the creator of both vitality and order in the Church (as in I Cor. 12-14, order at Corinth being less evident than vitality); and the only controversy about 'office' revealed in the epistles concerns Paul's own standing as an apostle. The Gentile churches he has founded are themselves the living vindication of the Lord's call to him to be apostle to the Gentiles; and their membership and acceptance in the one universal Church, with its focus and touchstone of communion in the mother church of Jerusalem (Gal. 2 : 1-10), depend upon the authenticity of his apostolate (I Cor. 9 : 1-2). While Paul has much to say of the principles and nature of Christian authority, e.g. that its function is to set free, not to enslave (II Cor. 1 : 24; 10 : 8), he has nothing to say about the practical provision of a formal constitutional structure for his missionary churches, for whom he himself, through his letters and his helpers such as Titus, is the focus of loyalty under Christ. The reference in Philippians 1 : 1 shows that in time the general itinerant care exercised by Paul and his helpers is being supplemented by resident officers. Although one cannot be sure just what functions the Philippian bishops and deacons had, the subsequent development suggests that the deacons helped on the administrative side, while the spiritual leadership of the community would be in the hands of the 'bishops' with pastoral oversight, subject to Paul himself. The Didache (15) shows how there was a natural tendency for local churches at first to value their resident bishops and deacons much less than itinerant prophets and teachers, perhaps not only because they seemed less obviously charismatic, but also because of the limited and local character of their responsibilities.

The twofold designation of 'bishops and deacons' attested in Philippians 1 appears both in the early (probably first-century) church order, the Didache (chap. 15) which never mentions presbyters, and also in the epistle written by Clement in the name of the church of Rome to the church of Corinth about the end of the first century (I Clement 42). In the Rome of A.D. 100 the name 'bishop' may be applied to church leaders who are also called 'presbyters'. At least, therefore, the presbyterate is a function and office in which bishops also have a full share. A similar pattern of terminology appears in the Pastoral Epistles to Timothy and Titus, where presbyters are generally plural, the bishop is singular, suggesting the probable conclusion that already among the college of presbyters exercising *episkope*, or pastoral oversight, one is the commonly accepted president. Of the bishop the highest qualities are required, and they are not only spiritual or supernatural but

4

include natural qualities of leadership and common sense (I Tim. 3 : 3-7; Titus 1 : 6-9). The likelihood is that in some local churches an initially single pastor subsequently became joined in authority by a council of presbyters, while in others the development went the opposite way; i.e. among a group of equal 'presbyter-bishops', one became distinct as presiding bishop without losing the sense of fully sharing a common pastorate and liturgical duty with his presbyteral colleagues, sitting with them in common council much like the 24 elders of the Revelation of John of Patmos (Rev. 4 : 4). In a relationship of primacy among equals, it is likely enough that in some places the primacy was more apparent than the parity, and elsewhere the other way round. In the first epistle of Peter addressed to the Gentile churches of Asia Minor the 'presbyters' are instructed to be shepherds after the pattern of Christ who is the Chief Shepherd, and are therefore to be living examples to their flock (I Peter 5 : 2-4). The author of the second and third Johannine epistles, 'John the Presbyter', exercised authority not only as a local teacher but as a shepherd of a region in which there were a number of churches. Like Timothy and Titus in the Pastoral Epistles, John the Presbyter probably had special responsibilities in ordinations of local clergy, since at ordinations the choice of local congregations would need to be guided and even in some measure controlled to maintain the fellowship of churches with each other. As the local churches grew in strength and independence, the authority of the ministry of local congregations became more securely recognised. It was then natural for the presiding minister in each local church to play a principal role in, and to bear ultimate responsibility for, ordinations of presbyters and deacons in his church, though always with the consent of the people. Likewise this presiding 'bishop' or 'presbyter' was responsible for correspondence with other churches, for hospitality to travellers, for going to represent his own people at the ordination of the ministers of neighbouring churches. He was therefore the person through whom the local church realised its links with others in the worldwide fellowship of churches.

Each local church is to be a self-sufficient fellowship, in which all the elements of the universal Church are present. Yet its independence is simultaneously limited by the mutual care that local churches have for each other or by the leadership given particularly by prominent churches looking back to an apostolic foundation (a feature exemplified in the epistle of Clement of Rome to Corinth).

The synodical idea imposes a restriction on what any individual bishop or church may do. At the same time the second century Church found in churches of apostolic foundation (in the West, in Rome as the city where St Peter and St Paul died) a touchstone of authentic communion. Accordingly, frequent contacts between churches act as a check upon private idiosyncrasies in teaching, at the same time as they help the realisation of catholicity. Through their fellowship with one another, at first expressed in informal ways and without formalised patterns of conciliarity, the presiding clergy of local churches are a living embodiment of the sacred tradition about Jesus Christ. This special ministerial responsibility for safeguarding what is taught in the churches goes back to an early stage. In Paul's discourse to the presbyters of Ephesus (who are called 'bishops': Acts 20 : 24-28) these leaders of the church are warned to be guardians of the true tradition against the false doctrine that threatens the very existence of the Church of Christ's redemption. (It is not thereby implied that laymen have no responsibility to interpret the faith.) This protective, guarding role comes to be especially carried out by synods, in which the bishop is the sacramental representative of his local community.

Of the manner of the making of clergy in the New Testament period, the Pastoral Epistles and Acts 13 : 3 mention the laying on of hands, the rite associated with the giving of the power of the Spirit in the sacrament of baptism: 'Do not neglect the spiritual endowment you possess, which was given you, under the guidance of prophecy, through the laying on of the hands of the elders as a body.' (I Tim. 4 : 14 N.E.B.) 'I now remind you to stir into flame the gift of God which is within you through the laying on of my hands' (II Tim. 1 : 6). Ordination is here understood to be a sacramental act conferring a charismatic gift of grace appropriate to the office. There is or should be no antithesis of office and charism, because the laying on of hands with prayer, in a solemn act by the council of 'presbyters', is at the same time a recognition of the prophetic call and a sign of the Spirit's gift. The gift can be nullified, or Timothy would not need to be warned to take good care to act according to the charism bestowed (I Tim. 1 : 18-19; II Tim. 4 : 10). At the same time the gift and call in ordination are to be the ground of his confidence as a minister, and the commission of ordination is apparently accompanied by a most solemn charge to keep 'the good confession' (I Tim. 6 : 11-16). So also St Paul

6

tells the presbyters of Ephesus that their appointment to exercise episcopal oversight comes from the Holy Spirit (Acts 20 : 28). Hence the ancient Church's conviction that in ordination God's call is irrevocable; the shepherd of the flock is to represent the Chief Shepherd whose constancy is unfailing.

The ancient Church understands ordination as more than a local authorisation limited to the local community where the ordination has taken place. The orders of episcopate, presbyterate, and diaconate are universally extended orders; that is to say, a presbyter ordained at Corinth needs only a letter of recommendation by his own bishop to be accepted, without reordination, in, say, Rome or Ephesus, and allowed to officiate there with the agreement of the local bishop. The priesthood in which he shares belongs to the universal Church and at his ordination other presbyters join the bishop in the laying on of hands. A newly elected bishop, chosen by his flock, is duly entrusted with the charism of episcopal office by other bishops, who represent, therefore, this universal recognition. This is in line with the New Testament records in which all those commissioned to exercise pastoral oversight are appointed by those who themselves have previously received such a commission. Nevertheless, the ancient Church had a deep sense of the intimate bond between a bishop and his own flock. He is, or ought to feel himself, married to his church. Hence their censures of episcopal translations from a small see to a greater as a secularising concession to worldly ambition.

This bond was inevitably weakened by the success of the Christian mission, which so enlarged the size of local churches that at least in large cities it soon became impossible for the bishop to know each of his sheep personally. It then became common to assign suburban or rural parishes to one or, in Rome, two presbyters. This increase in the number of presbyters, and the growth during the fourth century of the notion of grades of ordained ministers constituting a ladder of honour, like a civil service, came to erect a barrier between the laity and the president of their diocesan family. By the fourth century the clergy came to play a more prominent part than the laity in the election of a new bishop. Even so the rule (expressed by Cyprian and enacted at Nicaea, 325) that each city may have only one bishop, continued in force.

The early Church learnt by experience that the diocesan family needs to have one man rather than a committee as the focus of unity both in the local Church and in his fellowship with the college of bishops. Despite the strong language of Ignatius of Antioch, the 'monarchical' character of the episcopate is not, as such, a matter of fundamental juridical or dogmatic principle, essential to the Church in the sense that if the episcopate were shared and not monarchical the Church would be amputated, but is a practical need for the expression of unity. Nevertheless, Ignatius is surely right in seeing the bishop's central authority as linked to his presidency at the eucharist, in which he stands in a sacramental relation to Christ. He is there a focus of 'harmony' (Ignatius does not say unison) in the family of God. Ignatius never alludes to a historic succession as the ground of episcopal authority. But he simply assumes that what orthodox bishops are teaching is what the apostles taught; he holds office in a society that is continuous with that of Peter and Paul.

Ignatius is the earliest writer to attest a three-fold ministry in which bishop, presbyters, and deacons are distinguished as separate grades, 'without which a community cannot be called a church' (*Trall.* 3). This three-tiered structure is well attested (and taken for granted) by later writers, and must quickly have become universal without trace of controversy. The three grades were seen to correspond to the three grades of Old Testament ministry, high priest, priest and levite. It cannot, however, be this correspondence which made it seem natural to use the Greek *hiereus* or the Latin *sacerdos* of the Christian minister (attested from the beginning of the third century in both East and West), since these words were already being traditionally used of the bishop rather than of the presbyter. The Old Testament hierarchical typology did not create the threefold Christian ministry, a structure which owes its origin to the second century Church's inheritance from the sub-apostolic generation in which an originally two-tiered local ministry, under general apostolic oversight, passed into a three-tiered ministry, with the presiding bishops representing apostolicity. The earliest deacons were needed primarily for administrative duties; male deacons gradually acquired limited liturgical functions, especially reading the gospel (power to celebrate the eucharist being expressly denied to them), but remained the bishop's personal staff. As the congregations grew in size and number, presbyters also acquired wider duties. From being a council, sharing the pastoral and teaching responsibility with the bishop, they began to look after suburban parish churches for which they performed all functions shared with the bishop other than ordination and (except in Egypt) confirmation; these the bishops kept in their own hands, ordinations being among their most solemn responsibilities, and confirmations being a direct link with the lay members of their flock. In the fourth century the extension of presbyteral duties was given a theological justification by the presbyter Jerome (letter 146) who argued from New Testament texts that bishops and presbyters belong to a single order of ministerial priesthood, sharply distinct from the diaconate. Jerome regretted the performance by deacons of certain liturgical functions as obscuring their distinction from the pastoral and priestly order of presbyters and bishops, and so encouraging mistaken pretensions.

In the conflict with gnostic dualism, perhaps the gravest crisis of the Church's history, the early Church found the centralising of authority in the bishop a necessary safeguard against centrifugal forces, whether heretical or schismatic. Formal institutions in the ministry, in the pattern of baptismal confessions of faith, and finally in a fixed canon of the New Testament were developed in the course of the second century. Clement of Rome sees the duly ordained ministry as the embodiment of the principle that God wills order in his Church, so that a local church like Corinth cannot simply get rid of its clergy without satisfying other churches in the universal fellowship that the deposed clergy have been unworthy of their holy office. This principle of order is linked for Clement with the idea of apostolic succession. The fact of a succession in ministerial commission is not asserted by Clement in controversy, but an agreed datum from which he argues for the security of tenure of worthy ministers. Against the Gnostics' claims that their bizarre theosophical speculations represent a secret tradition handed down from the apostles, the second century Church pointed to the publicly verifiable succession of bishops in the churches, especially in those of known apostolic foundation, and to the consensus of all the churches that authentic Christianity does not include these gnostic fantasies. The second century bishops stand in the apostolic succession not merely (or even mainly) because of those who laid hands on them, but because the churches over which they preside do so in universal communion with each other. There is no question in the early period of an authentic ministerial succession having a career apart from the one holy catholic and apostolic Church and being

9

empowered independently to minister the word and sacraments according to the mind of the Spirit. The local churches together with their clergy are authentic because they stand in the true and universal succession, which is accordingly a transmission of faith together with that recognized order of ministry which serves it. So Irenaeus excludes from the apostolic succession heretics, schismatics, and orthodox bishops of evil life.

The Donatist schism in fourth century North Africa moved Augustine to find reasons to dissent from the general patristic view that outside the catholic Church there can be no authenticity; but his argument that if valid baptism can be received outside catholic unity, the same holds good for orders, was not generally accepted and acted on in the West until medieval times. The generous intention of Augustine's doctrine was to make reconciliation with the Donatists easier by allowing the unconditional validity of their orders. The form of his argument, however, had an obverse side. It unhappily encouraged men to think of ordination by a bishop in apostolic succession as if this were the exclusive and sole test of ministerial and ecclesial validity. The early Church did not think in this way. When the Council of Nicaea in 325 decreed that a bishop should be consecrated by the metropolitan with, if possible, all the bishops of the province or, if not all, a minimum of three, the Council understood its minimal three to be representing the wider fellowship. The Nicene bishops would never have thought that a person consecrated by any three bishops in any circumstances whatever had claims to catholic recognition.

The recognition of the orders of separated ecclesial bodies is invaluable as one element in a total reconciliation but useless if taken in isolation. When it becomes treated as a technical way of 'foot-faulting' other communions, argument about ministerial validity quickly comes to look trivial and pedantic, and can carry more than a suggestion (which would be alien to the thought of the early Church about apostolic succession) that the transmission of sacramental grace through the apostolic ministry is mechanical. On the contrary, for the early Christians the participation of bishops of other local churches in the consecration of a bishop is a sign and instrument of the continuity of both the new bishop and his church with the apostolic communion extended through time and space; and this is the nerve-centre of the concept of apostolic succession. It is a positive doctrine which has also a negative side in that it presupposes the presence of some defect of order in a separated ministry which is 'self-made' or is dependent on the private enterprise of a particular congregation. Such an independent pastorate may indeed be blessed by God as an efficacious means of proclaiming the gospel; but if it rejects communion with the apostolic and catholic tradition, something is lacking; it may assume a radical disjoining of charism and office which is out of line with the New Testament and the early Church; its authority and recognition are restricted; and ultimately the comprehension of the faith becomes one-sided and partial. Accordingly, the defect is one of universality: that is, it is not a technical fault of pedigree, but an isolation from the organic spiritual life of the one holy catholic and apostolic Church, in which the pastoral ministry has received its commission in a succession of order that goes hand in hand with a succession in faith and life.

2

Ministry and Tradition

THE TERM 'ministry' is one which Christians associate with ordination. That association was already fixed for Latin-speaking Christians by the time of Augustine. In one of his sermons on St John's Gospel (51 : 12-13) he warns his people against supposing that only bishops and presbyters are Christ's ministers. All lay people who live rightly, who are generous in alms to the poor, who proclaim the name and teaching of Christ to everyone, are ministers of Christ. Every paterfamilias exercises a kind of episcopal office in his own household. And the majority of martyrs in the calendar are lay people, men and women, old and young. Clergy are a minority.

Spiritual discernment is given by God to both the clergy and the laity; it is no monopoly of the clergy (*Confessions* 13, 23, 33). The evangelists of the Church are laity: 'Because of the witness of lay people, many with whom I have had no contact are coming to me wishing to become Christians' (*Enarr. in Ps.* 96 : 10).

More than one passage in Augustine speaks of the priesthood of the entire body of the Church. A clericalised conception of the Church seemed to him characteristic of the Donatist community, for whom the authenticity of the Church was exclusively located in the episcopal succession. So, in his stress on ministry as an activity shared by the laity, there may be an underlying anti-Donatist motive. However, the passage from the sermons on St John's Gospel makes it certain that his people ordinarily associate ministry with the functions and offices of bishop, presbyter, and deacon.

In this lecture I shall assume that the term 'ministry' primarily concerns the ordained members of the Church, but without forgetting Augustine's warning.

The gift of Christian ministry is a spiritual charism for the building up of the Church (Ephesians 4 : 7-16). Because it is rooted in the continuing life of the Church, it is deeply related to tradition.

Tradition is a word with many meanings, and with many implicit evaluations. Sometimes we speak of 'mere tradition', meaning a conventional way of thinking or acting which has not been subjected to scrutiny. Unexamined theology is not worth doing. During the baptismal controversy of the third century between Stephen bishop of Rome and Cyprian bishop of Carthage, one of the questions at issue was precisely whether immemorial tradition is or is not binding. To Cyprian and the African bishops, there was no force in the Roman principle 'Nihil innovetur nisi quod traditum est'. That was nothing more than 'consuetudo', custom or convention which was to be contrasted with *veritas*; and the 'truth' for Cyprian is that all sacramental acts performed by heretics or schismatics are not only invalid but the devil's deceit, a counterfeit for the divine reality. Cyprian's sacramentology was not accepted in Rome, but was welcomed in the East by Greek bishops.

The consequent debates on the relation of ministry and sacraments have remained a lasting source of divergence between East and West. The Orthodox Churches of the East are deeply resistant even today about the possibility of recognising the baptism of any Christian community which does not wholly share the right faith, orthodoxia: Baptism is initiation into the Church, and no heretic can admit anyone to the Church. At the first ecumenical Council of Nicaea a distinction was drawn. The followers of Novatianus were schismatics but orthodox in the doctrine of the Trinity and of the Person of Christ. Their baptism could stand, but individuals returning to the Catholic Church must be admitted by imposition of hands. On the other hand, the adherents of Paul of Samosata at Antioch must be baptized in water. Later Greek canons tend to become more rigorist. The Apostolic Canons (46-50) eliminate all distinctions, and declare heretical baptism to be invalid without distinction. In accordance with the rigorism, at Constantinople in 1755 it was decreed that the baptism of the western Churches is null and void (Rhalles-Potles, *Syntagma* 5, 614-616), and, although the decree did not receive unanimous support, it was printed and diffused[1]. It has remained a difficulty in ecumenical conversation that the Greeks do not recognise Catholic baptism, while the Russians accept it. From the baptismal controversy of the third century there flows the difference between East and West in attitude to the ecumenical movement. If the Roman Catholic Church, the Anglican Communion, and the Lutherans recognise each other's baptism, which also implies recognition of right faith concerning Christ and the Holy Trinity, then they are in a state of imperfect communion. And this partly positive appreciation of the Churches from which one is separated goes with a western attitude of continual striving after a not yet attained truth, a not yet attained grasp of salvation. The continuity of tradition in the West is intensely important, as also in the East.

But unlike the Orthodox Churches of the East, the West characteristically wishes to be for ever questioning, for ever seeking to get back to first principles.

We speak of tradition, first, in the sense of the Gospel, the word of God which is the content of what is transmitted. But the Gospel requires a preacher who is a primary organ of the process of transmission. Moreover, the context in the community within which he transmits the Gospel provides an interpretation of the text which the preacher is expounding. The Biblical text, the interpretation in the community (which may be contrasted with that found among the Rabbis), and the interpreting preacher are all included in the transmitting of tradition. The ministry of ordained bishops and priests is never independent either of the sacred text or of the community within which the text is received.

We often speak of 'tradition' in the sense of the way in which we worship, or of the characteristic ethic of the Church, that is 'our moral tradition'. Not all of these features of Christian liturgy and action are explicit in scripture. Nevertheless it is not today controversial to say that tradition is not really a second source besides scripture from which we can produce truths of a different kind and content. At the same time, the principle that definitions of dogma need to be consonant with scripture is not to be understood to mean that scripture is the sole source or means by which we can know anything of the will of God. The divine will is also mediated and declared to us through the glory and wonder of the created order and through the experience of the worshipping community in the fellowship of the mystery. Tradition, then, means the memory of the community which gives the people of God their self-understanding.

We feel deeply sorry for elderly people who have lost their memory. It is a rich treasury of experience for them and for all who have conversation with them. Augustine liked to say that the memory is the stomach of the mind (*Conf.* 10:14, 21 and elsewhere). The tenth book of the Confessions is a study of the way in which the memory of the past is decisive for interpreting the present. In the community, tradition is the memory of the Church's foundation and origins, and a continuing story to determine the present. To speak of tradition is to recognise that the prophetic and apostolic witness of the biblical record can become revelation for us now because of the experience of grace in and through the Church which

14

is Christ's Body. In the life of the Church we are anchored to the past because, by faith and baptism, we are members of a society with a continuing history, linking us to St Peter, to the Twelve, to Mary the mother of Jesus, to St Paul and the Gentile mission, to the emerging ministry with apostolic commission which would become the visible and concrete sign and instrument of continuity and of the links in a historic chain. The concept of a sacred tradition of teaching antedates the concept of an apostolic succession of pastors, but the second became necessary to safeguard the first. This should not mean that the visible succession of ordinations is the only factor to be considered. In the course of history the Church has observed groups of bishops and individual bishops whose juridical succession could hardly be faulted. Yet they have not been reckoned to share in the apostolic succession because they have not been seen to share in the tradition of Catholic teaching and in the universal communion of the local churches. Teaching and communion are not less significant than the visible manifestation by which legitimation is put beyond controversy.

If the juridical succession is regarded as providing everything necessary and sufficient, the normal and natural consequence is to produce individualism among bishops. Because the sharing in a common inheritance of doctrine and universal fellowship has not been stressed as having no less importance, each bishop can easily come to think that he can disregard his colleagues. He may come to have little respect for the exhortation in the Pastoral Epistles (2 Timothy 3 : 14) that he should 'teach what he has been taught'.

Transmitter of a sacred trust, the mediator of a tradition, the bishop shares in a common pastorate whose commission lies in the past.

Nevertheless, this does not mean imprisonment in the past. A Church which is imprisoned in its own past will end by betraying the deposit of faith entrusted by God. A society 'without the means of change is without the means of its conservation' (Edmund Burke, 1790). 'To live is to change' (John Henry Newman, 1845). And so the ordained ministry with apostolic commission does not exist exclusively to mediate and to transmit faithfully what has been received from a sacred past. It is also called to proclaim, to utter prophecy in the Spirit, speaking to a changing situation. It must teach; and that teaching must imply far more than an unreflective repetition of formulas of a distant past shaped in utterly different

15

circumstances and with philosophical presuppositions that later generations cannot share. The ministry exists to serve the pastoral needs of the community, some of which are astonishingly unchanging, but others (especially in our modern world) change fast, and somehow we have to move at the same speed to stay in the same place.

In the second century Irenaeus of Lyon pronounced orthodoxy to be unchanging, while it was a characteristic of heretics that they were continually changing. To Irenaeus orthodoxy is uniform, heresy marked by variations. Eighty years before his time, during the generation which followed the death of the last of the Twelve Apostles and which had to come to terms with the fact that the Lord had not returned and so the Church would have a historical future, the Church experienced a degree of diversity which was traumatic. There was near-anarchy, whether in ministerial order or in moral practice or in central matters of faith. Therefore, at a very early stage as the apostles passed from the scene, the Church found it necessary to establish frontiers and standards, criteria of authenticity. Three norms of reference appeared, very familiar to every elementary student of the subject: first, a ministry in visible and tangible continuity with the apostolic community and possessing an apostolic commission; secondly, a baptismal confession of faith, structured round the affirmation of belief in God the Father, Maker of heaven and earth (by familiarity we forget how contentious and controversial these words were early in the second century); belief in Jesus his unique Son, so truly human that he was born and crucified, yet experiencing both in such a way that the birth and the crucifixion were divine wonders; and belief in the Holy Spirit in the Church. Thirdly and last in chronological order, but greatest in weight, the formation of the biblical canon.

In much later debate the formation of the canon became a sensitive issue. Were the books admitted to the lectionary because their content was self-evidently authoritative and apostolic, so that the acknowledgement of their inherent quality of authority was a purely passive act of submission by the community? Or did the Church have an active and creative role in forming the canon in response to Marcion and Montanism? The historian finds it easier to give a positive answer to the second question than to the first. But in the formation of the canon of scripture, the second-century churches were right to discern in these books the record of the oldest and most original witness to their faith and practice. Until the middle years of the second century, Christians appear to have drawn more upon oral tradition than upon authoritative books. The words of Papias about the superiority of oral tradition are famous. Irenaeus is the first to possess a canon of the New Testament.

It is a safe generalisation that there is friction in the Church when someone wishes to modify or even discard one of the three norms which evolved in the second century. The continuing Church on earth needs to affirm its faith, needs to acknowledge the witness of scripture, needs to admit to its community by baptism in the name of Christ, and, in obedience to his command, to renew its life by the eucharistic memorial. Moreover, for the sake of its own coherence, it needs a ministry generally accepted as possessing a commission, given by Christ in his Church, to serve and to safeguard the word and the sacraments. In these areas of Bible, Creed, Sacraments and Ministry, the Church understands itself to have received divine gifts (as in Ephesians 4), *dona data,* touching the deepest roots of Christian existence, and therefore needing to be handled with sensitivity.

Uniformity in respect of the canon of Scripture, the apostolic ministry, the essentials of the faith, and the sacraments, does not necessitate uniformity in liturgy. In forms of worship the tradition allows for wide diversities, at least between different regions. The desire for liturgical uniformity has pastoral roots. But such uniformity has normally been imposed more by secular than by ecclesiastical authority, more by Charles the Great than by medieval Popes.[2]. In the time of Augustine, there were different translations of the old Latin Bible in Africa and Italy, and different customs. One letter complains of the bewilderment caused to congregations when the clergy introduced liturgical customs which they had seen abroad (Ep. 54, 3; 55, 35). He recalled the advice given by Ambrosius to his mother Monnica to keep Roman customs in Rome, but not when not in Rome (Ep. 36, 32; 54, 3). Liturgical variety is compatible with one faith (Ep. 36, 22). Admittedly, Augustine was in favour of reasonable uniformity in a single region, and warns his correspondent Januarius (who seems to have been confronted by people wanting total uniformity in a single rite) that there are limits to diversity (Ep. 55, 35). The Lord imposed certain minimum obligations; these are whatever is commanded in the Bible, baptism, eucharist, what has apostolic sanction or is agreed by plenary councils of the Church; but there can be regional diversity beyond these (Ep. 54, 1). Tolerable diversity does not, however, include heretical prayers (Bapt. vi, 25, 47).

One of the grounds on which Cardinal Humbert excommunicated the ecumenical Patriarch Michael Kerullarios in the year 1054 was that by using leavened bread the Greeks rendered their mass invalid. A dissenting view was recorded by St Anselm of Canterbury. Anselm thought the Greeks wrong not to use azyma, unleavened bread; and that mistake was for him no adiaphoron. Nevertheless what they used was bread. Therefore, *substantialiter* there was agreement. (*Ep. de sacrif. azymi* 1, Schmitt II 224). The passage is the earliest instance known to me of a claim that in ecumenical conversation there can be differences of language or custom within an essential agreement. Anselm was writing to a man who thought that all recognised Catholics must use a single eucharistic rite. Uniformity in rite was for that man a mark of catholicity.

In the Church of our own time, the link between Ministry and Tradition has become problematic because of the question precipitated by the feminist revolution in the West. In antiquity priestesses were associated with the temples of goddesses. Epiphanius (Panar. 78, 3; 79, 1-8) rejected priestesses because he rejected goddesses, and argued that the first could lead to the second. Outsiders would mock the Church if it had women as priests or bishops. In the West of the twentieth century, outsiders mock the Church because it has none.

3

The vindication of Christianity in Westcott's thought

THERE ARE many good reasons why it is right that we should look back to consider the work of the distinguished scholar and theologian to whom Westcott House owes its name and inspiration. To Westcott, Lightfoot and Hort Cambridge theology owes perhaps one thing above all—its standards of critical scholarship. Lightfoot and Hort established a standard of pure learning such as the University had hardly seen since the time of Pearson in the seventeenth century. In an age when the traditional connection of the University with the Church of England was undergoing profound modification, it would have been fatally easy for the University's theologians to have identified themselves with the forces of conservatism and reaction, with the inevitable consequence that to their secular colleagues they would have appeared not as men who owed their supreme allegiance to the truth, but as orthodox partisans. That this has been signally avoided is due to the providential appearance of the right men at the right time in the right place. Each of the three friends had his own marked individuality, and one might compare the massive ruggedness of Lightfoot's mountainous erudition with the refinement, perfectionism and *esprit* of Hort. Westcott is perhaps more elusive than the other two. He was an energetic personality with intense feelings on the numerous subjects to which he addressed his mind, a man of strong emotions held in control by the force of an iron will. The descriptions of him that we have from his friends and contemporaries go far to explain the remarkable influence which he exercised not only upon his friend and pupil Lightfoot, or upon the group of undergraduates and young dons (including Inge and Ryle) who used to meet in his rooms in King's on Sunday afternoons, but also upon the University at large. He possessed a rare power of winning confidence. Yet perhaps the influence is surprising when we think of his essential loneliness of spirit. He was in himself a reserved person; and that reserve we can sense in the attractive but curiously disturbing portrait of him by Richmond now in the dining hall at Westcott House. Arthur Benson remarked of him that he did not need people, though he suffered them gladly; that though he was warm-hearted by temperament and immediate in sympathy to

19

anyone in need, yet he was happier giving himself to work and duty than in personal relations with others. He was given to ideas and principles in general rather than to individuals in particular. But, Benson adds, 'there remains a spirit which for energy, highmindedness, purity, and devotion, was one among ten thousand'.[1] And in Cambridge he left a mark that has extended far beyond the circle of his immediate friends and pupils—one of whom, Charles Travers Wood, is happily among us, full of years and honour, in his sixty-first year as Fellow of Queens'. Whether in the Divinity School or in Westcott House, the generous legacy of Brooke Foss Westcott is still to be discerned. Perhaps there is no figure in the history of Victorian Cambridge of whom it is more true to say that he being dead yet speaketh.

To his contemporaries Westcott was often a puzzling person. He had a love of being provocative and unexpected. Once when Lightfoot and Archbishop Benson disagreed on a point, Lightfoot said, 'We will appeal to Westcott; he will agree with me'. 'Yes,' said Benson, 'but for my reasons.'[2] He delighted in paradox, in setting side by side two incompatible propositions and insisting that they are complementary truths. He shared with F. D. Maurice a horror of theology that was too self-confident and clear-cut. Rigid, hard outlines distressed him. He believed that this kind of clarity was achieved at the expense of truth. Inevitably, this way of thinking provoked criticism. Those who are fortunate enough to think of truth and error as white and black, and as no less easily distinguishable, do not take kindly to people who seem to believe in varying shades of grey. The story is well known that, when there was dense fog in London, Liddon remarked that 'it is commonly attributed to Dr Westcott having opened his study window in Westminster'.[3] If at Oxford Westcott's reputation did not stand as high as in his own University, perhaps that may be traced to Liddon's influence. Scott Holland, who owed an equal debt to both Liddon and Westcott, observed that to Liddon 'Westcott was a type of what he suspected and distrusted in the Cambridge mind'.[4] In 1881, it is true, Oxford conferred on Westcott the high honour of D.C.L.; we learn that on this occasion he stayed happily at Christ Church with the Margaret Professor, Dr Heurtley. But he never felt himself in close intellectual sympathy with the leading Oxford figures of the age before Driver and Sanday.[5] They in turn regarded his dominance of the Cambridge scene as at least as much a source of weakness as of strength to the sister University. To the historian William Bright, Westcott, 'like Clement of Alexandria, seemed to take his reader through a golden Platonic mist' so that he was 'not sure where he stood or what definite objects were within view'. And Bright regretted that under Westcott's influence doctrinal theology had yielded place to historical criticism in the Cambridge divinity school.[6]

Perhaps the sense of belonging to no party did something to increase Westcott's isolation and reserve. Churchmen who liked quick answers to what they imagined to be straightforward questions could be disappointed and irritated by his apparent vagueness. He stood poles apart from the old Tractarian concept of ecclesiastical authority represented by Liddon, Pusey, and Bright; and, although there was much to make the socialist bishop of Durham join hands with the young Charles Gore, whom he had taught in the sixth form at Harrow, he was quite out of sympathy with ordinary Anglo-Catholicism. The language of conventional Evangelicalism was not much more congenial to him; and he declared openly his deep distrust of all exact definitions of the Atonement. All who looked to him for snap answers delivered with certainty based on super-naturally guaranteed authority found that, like Ixion, they were embracing a cloud.

There is much truth in Bright's observation that under Westcott's aegis Cambridge divinity passed from dogmatics to historical criticism. But the change of emphasis did not mean that Westcott was somehow afraid to ask questions of fundamental doctrine and took refuge in the study of ancient manuscripts. It corresponded to his view of the very nature of Christian doctrine that it should be studied historically. The history of doctrine is that of an organic growth, not a catalogue of given, static propositions. Christian doctrine he defines as 'the partial and progressive approximation towards the complete intellectual expression of the Truth manifested to men once for all in the Incarnation'.[7] And because it consists of approximations, because it is a process of advance, it belongs to the essence of the study of theology that it should be historical in its emphases and in its methods. The fullness of the truth lies beyond the human language of creeds and conciliar declarations. 'Not by one way but by many must we strive to reach the fullness of truth.'[8] 'My desire', he wrote in *The Gospel of Life*, 'has been to encourage patient reflection, to suggest lines of enquiry, to indicate necessary limits to knowledge, and not to convey formulas or ready made arguments. Thoughts cannot be transferred; they must be appropriated.'[9]

This was a theological principle which he put into practice as a matter of educational method. When Herbert Ryle was elected to the Hulsean professorship, he went to call on the Regius Professor to ask if he had any advice to offer him. It was a difficult interview; Westcott was strangely uncommunicative, and no advice whatever was forthcoming—until, just as he was leaving, there came the bewildering words: 'Never tell the undergraduates anything.'

Obscurity is not numbered among the theological virtues, and Westcott could be exceedingly opaque. The this-worldly philosophers of our own day, with their brisk tendency to set aside anything that cannot be said clearly and concisely, are even more likely than Westcott's contemporaries to inquire how he might have proposed to verify some of his statements. Let it be said in fairness that in Westcott Platonism joined forces with Christianity to make him suspicious of all systems of thought with an exclusively this-worldly reference. He was deliberately setting himself, in certain respects, against the stream of his time. In an age of advancing materialism he was impelled to emphasise transcendental ideas. In face of the prevalent complacent rationalism he loved to insist upon the mysteriousness of things, upon the inconclusiveness of our thinking and experience, just because this very inconclusiveness points us beyond this temporal order to a higher realm apprehended by faith and insight. *Omnia exeunt in mysterium.*

The fastidious scholarship in which he had been trained by Prince Lee made Westcott constant in his striving for exactitude in the use of words. He never tired of observing that attention to the precise force of Greek tenses and prepositions is the foundation of true exegesis, and without that Christian theology cannot begin. In one remarkable lecture he urges the paradox that by meticulous precision in the use of words we are brought to recognise the inadequacy of human language to express infinite truth. Nothing for Westcott could be more important than that recognition. 'Unless the student of Christian doctrine is vividly conscious at all times of the difficulty, the mysteriousness, the inexhaustible fullness, the practical significance of the subject with which he deals, nothing but half-truths and barren formulas can result from his labours, and these may soon become in his hands the perilous instruments of a lifeless dogmatism.'[10] And in *The Gospel of Life* he writes: 'The

22

world is not clear or intelligible. If we are to deliver our message as Christians we must face the riddles of life and consider how others have faced them.' 'Christianity is in life and through life. It is not an abstract system but a vital power, active through an organized body. It can never be said that the interpretation of the Gospel is final. Absolute in its essence so that nothing can be added to the revelation which it includes, it is relative so far as the human apprehension of it at any time is concerned.'

Admittedly this way of regarding our experience has certain limitations. Westcott's theology was not able easily to speak to those who stood quite outside the Christian society. Henry Sidgwick said that Westcott and F. D. Maurice had 'the common characteristic of continually offering to their opponents an intellectual sympathy which the latter, with the utmost gratitude, are quite unable to accept. The difference is that Westcott is orthodox in his conclusions, and only paradoxical in his arguments, whereas Maurice was to some extent paradoxical in both.'[11] To many who already believed in God Westcott spoke words of gold. He was interpreting an experience in which they shared; and even if he was not always fully comprehensible, they knew that at least he was genuinely trying to express something very important. There was no mumbo-jumbo, no mystification for its own sake. But to materialists, pantheists, and atheists, and to anyone who did not intuitively understand his passionate sense of the mystery of life and of the inconclusiveness of our space-time existence, Westcott's words could never be effective in the same way. He was somehow at a loss when confronted by a coldly detached onlooker, analysing and dissecting the logic of his words without mercy or sympathy. He was almost as baffled in this situation as he was when faced with terrible viciousness. Malevolent and gross wickedness was not so much shocking to Westcott as inconceivable. There is an optimism in his doctrine of man which no doubt had its influence upon his understanding of Atonement and Redemption. It certainly influenced his socialism, so profoundly scandalous to the conservatives of the age who thought socialism in a bishop tantamount to treachery to his cloth. Westcott firmly believed that the divine purpose was to be worked out in human society, and that brotherhood and fellowship in industrial relations must be brought by the Gospel. He did not think much about the radical evil, the grasping motives, the ferocious conflicts of interest, which appear so terrifying and intransigent when large groups and classes are in dispute. Optimistic, open-hearted and charitable, Westcott was not at ease with enemies. But his optimism also meant that, in the undertaking to defend the Christian faith from attack, one of the prime tasks was the presentation of correct information about the faith, unvarnished, unadorned. This conviction lay at the back of much of his textual and historical labours. Accurate scholarship was all a part of the business of the vindication of Christianity.

Westcott's reputation as a theologian depends upon four related but distinct aspects of his work. First and most obvious, there is his laborious work on the text of the New Testament in collaboration with Hort. Secondly, there are his commentaries of which Professor Barrett spoke two years ago,[12] and which remain a mine of instruction for the student. Thirdly, there is his doctrinal teaching, best seen perhaps in those remarkable books, *The Gospel of the Resurrection* and *The Gospel of Life.* The fourth aspect is that of Westcott the church historian, represented by his studies in the Christian Platonists of Alexandria and by his book on the New Testament canon. It is to this latter book that I now wish especially to invite your attention. As a piece of scholarship it stands beside his work on Clement and Origen in its quality and depth, and may justly be claimed to be the best book Westcott wrote. 'Solid and thorough' are the epithets applied to it by Hort. Though open to correction in detail, it remains today a work of high value 105 years after its first publication; and, although written with a considerable interest in vindicating a particular point of view, it is not seriously open to the charge of special pleading to which the enormous work of Zahn is so painfully vulnerable. Westcott could hardly help looking over his shoulder at the German critics who seemed to undermine the traditional basis of the faith by their extreme scepticism regarding the authenticity and antiquity of the New Testament writings. From time to time Westcott may protest too much; but it is not often. Moreover, the book is not merely of interest to the harmless drudges who collect historical information; it contains virtually all the principles of his dogmatic position.[13]

A General Survey of the History of the Canon of the New Testament was first published in 1855, written while Westcott was still a schoolmaster at Harrow and dedicated to his old headmaster, the bishop of Manchester, Prince Lee. It is an attempt to amass the salient facts and to order them so as to tell a coherent story. So far as the facts go, he was able to draw upon the labours of Nathaniel Lardner, whose *Credibility of the Gospel History*, written over a century before in reply to the Deists, supplied a rich store of learned information. Westcott's chief foreign debt is to Karl August Credner (1797-1857) of Giessen, whose contributions to the subject were marked by singular objectivity and impartiality. Credner's reputation as a scholar was unhappily somewhat diminished by a posthumous history of the New Testament canon edited in 1860 by Volkmar and marred by mistakes. But in the middle of the nineteenth century it was not easy to keep a clear head when writing about the canon. The subject was a veritable minefield; for the fundamental issue was the correctness of the entire Tübingen theory of the origins of early Christian literature.

It may be well if we remind ourselves of the essentials of this theory. According to Ferdinand Christian Baur, professor at Tübingen from 1826 to his death in 1860, the documents of the New Testament must be understood as a part of early church history. They belong to a process. They are not merely the initiating cause of all that followed, but are themselves the product of a highly controversial situation in the life of the primitive church. The historian can discern tendencies in his documents reflecting their interest in the controversy. The four epistles, I and II Corinthians, Galatians and Romans, disclose that St Paul's apostolic status was the object of violent attack from Judaising agitators who appealed to St Peter and to the rest of the Twelve as superior authorities. The battle royal between St Peter and St Paul at Antioch, described in the second chapter of Galatians, is crucial evidence of the true state of things. Out of the original conflict between Gentile Christianity and Judaistic or Ebionitic Christianity there gradually emerged the Hegelian synthesis, the compromise of Catholic Christendom which, though Gentile in its composition, used the Old Testament as a sacred book and acknowledged its debt to Judaism. Every early Christian document must be fitted into some niche in this historical development. Thus the Judaic strain is represented by the Johannine Apocalypse, with its stern anti-Pauline attack on those who say that they are apostles and are not and its exaltation of the Twelve as the foundation of the New Jerusalem; by the lost Gospel according to the Hebrews; and by the Epistle of James. The stage of synthesis and conciliation is represented by the Epistle to the Hebrews, written perhaps about 100, which, in claiming Christianity to be the fulfilment of the Old Testament, marks a coming to terms between a developed Paulinism and Jewish Christianity. A similarly irenic position is presupposed in Acts and I Peter, according to which St Peter rather than St Paul is the true apostle to the Gentiles. The next generation sees the production of works reflecting a more advanced Catholicism: the Pastoral epistles, Colossians, Ephesians and the correspondence ascribed (according to Baur, falsely) to Ignatius of Antioch. By about 150 the final stage of evolution has been reached, and this is reflected in the Fourth Gospel and the Johannine epistles written about this time.

The Tübingen account of the Synoptic Gospels ran thus. St Matthew's Gospel, being the most strongly Judaic, must use the earliest traditions of all, and may be taken to be an embroidered Greek recension of the lost Aramaic Gospel according to the Hebrews, made perhaps about 130. St Luke is essentially a Gentile gospel; but probably its original text was even more anti-Judaic, for the probability must be considered high that Marcion's text was not a censored Luke with the Judaic bits cut out, but the original text. Our received text is a radically modified form in which the anti-Judaic passages are drastically softened. The modifications were probably carried out by some mediating figure, a disciple of the Pauline tradition who, with certain safeguards, was ready to compromise with Jewish Christianity. The Gospel which Baur found it hard to place with plausibility was St Mark. It is neither specially Judaic nor obviously Gentile, and it is not easy to see how there could be room for a document so neutral within a Christendom passionately divided by controversy. Baur decided that it must be a patchwork, a late selection dependent on Matthew and Luke and intended to eliminate the contradiction between them by the happy expedient of omitting everything controversial. The Marcan ideal is to be as colourless as possible and to leave out everything, such as the Sermon on the Mount or the Parable of the Prodigal Son, which might conceivably hurt somebody's feelings.

The colossal improbability of Baur's theory about St Mark was one of the factors which led Albrecht Ritschl to break with the Tübingen school and to strike out on his own on the basis of Lachmann's theory that St Mark was the first of the evangelists. There are also other points where Baur's judgement was at fault. The treatment of the epistle to the Philippians at the hands of the Tübingen school must rank as one of the outstanding monuments of professorial absurdity. The epistle is taken to belong to the stage of reconciliation, and the key to the whole lies in the greeting sent to Clement who, for Baur, is a mythical character symbolising the synthesis of the Petrine and Pauline parties. Schwegler developed Baur's theory further: the ladies Euodia and Syntyche turn out to be symbols of the two church parties of whose happy union Clement is the representative. The climax of this nonsense is reached with a pamphlet of amazing erudition from the pen of Hitzig, who argued that Euodia and Syntyche are derived from the patriarchs Asher and Gad who, *en route* from Hebrew to Greek, changed their sex and stand for the Greek and Roman elements in the church. Hitzig added to this suggestion the hypothesis that the Philippian epistle was a plagiarism of Tacitus's *Agricola*.[14]

All this is merely additional evidence of a fact amply illustrated in the history of scholarship: there never fails a supply of persons whose learning is rivalled only by their own folly. Nevertheless, the Tübingen theory as a whole had certain merits. It provided a total historical framework within which the documents could be fitted, and it perceived that the New Testament writings themselves are part of early church history. Baur did not set the history of the apostolic age on a pedestal. He did not think of it as a golden age altogether set apart from the history which succeeded to it. He absolutely rejected the orthodox view that the primitive church was a happy and harmonious body, into which the apple of discord was thrown only after the apostles had died. The early church was racked with dissensions, and the whole conception of the apostolic age as an era of halcyon peace and concord was mere mythology resulting from the conciliation between the warring elements introduced during the second century.

The orthodox conception of the unity of the primitive church corresponded with its conception of the unity and uniqueness of the biblical canon. Once the church came to think of the New Testament writings as a closed canon of inspired documents containing timeless truths designed to instruct the church for all time, the diversity of the documents was lost to view, submerged by the requirements of dogmatics. It was a direct consequence of the rise of historical criticism that it brought into high relief the individualities of the separate books; it stressed differences and discovered not only that the personalities of St Paul and St John are distinct but also that their theologies are not simply to be identified.

Such considerations help us to understand why the Tübingen theory was so formidable to answer. It might be possible to puncture it here and there by negative criticism, and a great deal hung upon the date and authenticity of the Ignatian letters. But the theory could only be effectively answered by an alternative framework which saw the evolution of the early church as a whole. The days were over when a commentary could be content to explain what the gospels and epistles said; it was now necessary to explain why they said it.

Westcott's *History of the Canon* is aware that the unity of the New Testament has become a central issue, and that a total view of the evolution of the early church is required. In fact he comes to terms unreservedly with Baur's principles, while absolutely rejecting his actual reconstruction. What Westcott provides is not a refutation but something much better—an alternative hypothesis. He is as fully persuaded as Baur that the New Testament writings have to be understood not merely as creative of the future, but as being themselves created by pressures within the life of the ancient church. His criticism of the Tübingen reconstruction is that it is altogether too abstract, remote from any imaginable sequence of actual events, in short, psychologically incredible. And in matters of detail it deals violently with certain crucial pieces of awkward evidence; denying, for example, that Justin Martyr shows knowledge of the Synoptic Gospels, and rejecting the Ignatian correspondence which it could not admit without the entire construction collapsing in ruins.

Westcott concedes so much in the way of principle to the rights of free criticism that one is left with the question, How did he succeed in being so conservative? We are reminded of Sidgwick's judgement on him: paradoxical in argument, orthodox in conclusion. The *History of the Canon* is a highly orthodox book which, except for a suspension of judgement concerning the second Epistle of Peter ('which on purely historical grounds cannot be pronounced certainly authentic', p. 501), upholds tradition at all points. The answer to the question is (I think) that, like Lightfoot, he looked at the second century through the spectacles of Irenaeus. Irenaeus confidently took for granted the continuity of the church from the time of the apostles, his mind was that of a traditionalist, and he possessed a New Testament nearly identical with ours. He took much pains to assure his readers that, for example, John the son of

28

Zebedee wrote both the Gospel and the Apocalypse, and was confident that the other apostolic writings were written by the authors to whom they are traditionally ascribed. To the unity and continuity of which Irenaeus is the fundamental witness Westcott constantly appeals. The casual and fragmentary nature of the second-century evidence makes it easy to erect hypotheses that are plausible but false. 'The strength of negative criticism lies in ignoring the existence of a Christian society from the apostolic age, strong in discipline, clear in faith, and jealous of innovation.' The Tübingen method takes the separate pieces of evidence in isolation. If we put all the fragments in the context of the continuing life of the church, extravagant theories are superfluous. In short, Westcott's answer to the Tübingen school is substantially identical with Irenaeus's refutation of the Gnostics. To Irenaeus he adds his own characteristic individuality when he hints that in this contrast between the fragmentary evidence and the latent unity which gives coherence and meaning to all the separate pieces we may discern a quasi-Platonic symbol of the nature of all our earthly knowledge.

On the historical plane we may doubt whether Westcott allowed enough for the apologetic interests of Irenaeus himself. The reader of the book on the canon is given the feeling that in the mind of the author there is unconscious tension between two distinct questions. The historian of the second-century church is confronted by certain documents and institutions. Is he to ask what is the most probable explanation of them? Or is he to ask how much of the traditional view can be maintained? Westcott unreservedly believed that Irenaeus' account, that is, the traditional account, was the most probable. The two questions became fused in his mind.

Westcott's book was not allowed to pass uncriticised. Walter Richard Cassels (1826-1907) was a Bombay merchant noted for his knowledge of commercial law who, having made his pile by the age of thirty-nine, retired to England in 1865 to devote himself to collecting Flemish pictures, Chinese porcelain, and German theology. In 1874 he published the fruits of his reading in an anonymous work in two volumes entitled *Supernatural Religion: An Inquiry into the Reality of Divine Revelation* (a third volume followed in 1876). The reviewers, including eminent agnostics like John Morley,[15] were corybantic with enthusiasm. Speculation about the author's identity began at once. Some attributed the book to a nephew of Dr Pusey. A widely credited rumour said it was the work of no less a scholar than Connop Thirlwall, lately retired from the see of St David's. The reported conversion of a most learned bishop to positivism and free thinking was enough to ensure the book a gigantic success, and it quickly ran through six editions. Thirlwall denied the rumour as soon as he heard of it, but it was too late. Another probable candidate was believed to be Sir John Seeley.[16] Cassels kept his secret well, and the cat was only let quietly out of the bag in 1895, after Seeley's death.

The first part of the book briefly argues that on philosophical grounds miracles are antecedently incredible. The second and third parts are devoted to a lengthy examination of the evidence for the date and authorship of the Gospels and Acts, and reach the conclusion that there is no certain trace of the Synoptic Gospels and Acts before Irenaeus near the end of the second century, nor of St John's Gospel before Theophilus of Antioch at about the same date. These conclusions are supported by impressive footnotes, giving voluminous references to German and Dutch scholars.

In the course of his argument Cassels had frequent occasion to refer to Westcott's book on the canon, and his references are hostile. He speaks of Westcott's 'discreet reserve', 'clever evasion', 'apologetic partiality', and 'disingenuousness'. He could have made no greater tactical mistake. His sneers at Westcott's academic integrity stung Lightfoot to a fury of righteous indignation; and in a series of articles in the *Contemporary Review* Lightfoot launched a succession of torpedoes at the book which completely stripped it of all pretensions to serious scholarship. Giving chapter and verse, Lightfoot patiently convicted Cassels of the stupidest blunders in dealing with the ancient texts, and then turned his guns upon the intimidating footnotes, 'those exhibitions of learning which have made such a deep impression on the reviewers'. After analysing some in minute detail, he observes that a considerable number of the secondary authorities mentioned expressed opinions opposed to that for which they were cited. The reader is left to draw the inevitable conclusion. Lightfoot is careful neither to say nor to insinuate that the author of *Supernatural Religion* is a rogue. Indeed his attack is the more formidable for its serene assumption that the right explanation for this extraordinary farrago of error is the author's incredible incompetence. When Cassels replied in the *Fortnightly*, angrily demanding an apology of Lightfoot for having been so offensive as to remark that he could not possibly have read one of the works to which he refers, inasmuch as it provided a complete refutation of the view expressed, Lightfoot sardonically answered that he would apologise if desired, but with reluctance, since, if Cassels really had read the work in question, he laid himself open to a more damaging charge.

In Lightfoot's *Essays on the Work entitled Supernatural Religion*[17] there is much that still repays study: the restraint in controversy, the detachment, the irresistible weight of historical arguments marshalled by a master-hand, the refrigerating blasts of common sense. Harnack said of Lightfoot that there was never an apologist who was less of an advocate.[18] Where Cassels's tone is that of a captious prosecuting counsel, Lightfoot's is that of a judge. Wisely he does not attempt to discuss the theological and philosophical issues. These formed a relatively small part of Cassels's book. Moreover, Lightfoot (like Duchesne) was not much interested in such matters anyway. Hort once said that 'Lightfoot's mental interests lay almost exclusively in concrete facts or written words. He never seemed to care for any generalisation. No one can with advantage be everything; and he gained much by what was surely a limitation.' Among other things Hort felt that Lightfoot had gained ready access to the English mind which in general shared his mistaken view that the difficult questions of theology are a barren cloudland.[19]

Westcott's own reflections on Cassels's book appeared in the form of a long preface to the fourth edition of his book on the canon (1874). At a few points Cassels's criticisms led him to make minor modifications in the text. But for the rest Westcott could find in the book only mistakes in detail, a complete absence of historical method, and the strange superstition that a ton of German opinion is somehow worth more than an ounce of evidence. At the end Westcott goes to what is perhaps the heart of the matter. We are familiar today with those exclusive claims to a monopoly of candour which are the favourite weapon of the academic terrorist. No weapon was dearer to Cassels. Again and again he claimed that as a sceptic he could write about Christian beginnings with an impartiality and detachment denied to a Christian scholar like Westcott who could not help being an 'apologist'—a word which to Cassels meant an ingenious advocate trying to make the best of a poor case. Westcott freely admits that at times writers in defence of the faith may have overrated the force of the evidence in support of their position. They have had their human failings, but, as the present case shows, such failings are not peculiar to Christian writers. Above all, the fault is not inherent in the Christian position. If apologists have erred in this respect, they have failed in their allegiance to the very thing for which they are striving. Westcott absolutely rebuts the notion that only a sceptic can give an unbiased opinion on the nature and value of early Christian literature. If a man is committed to an antecedent decision that there is no God and no revelation, it is hard to see that his inquiry can be wholly dispassionate in dealing with the miraculous element. In a word, it is false to think 'that it is necessary to cease to be Christian in order to judge of the meaning of Christian documents'.

To conclude: the modern reader of Westcott's writings is likely to think that his vindication of Christianity would have been stronger if his conclusions had been as paradoxical as his arguments. Here it is necessary to remember the contemporary climate of ecclesiastical opinion. The fact that Westcott and Lightfoot generally ended by upholding the traditional story enabled them to do much to make the church safe for critical methods in theological study. No doubt it is for this reason that Westcott's influence during his lifetime was altogether remarkable in a way which came to seem surprising and disproportionate to critics of the succeeding generation who found him indefensibly conservative. I venture to think that a more strictly historical view of his achievement will increasingly tend to correct the recent inclination slightly to under-value him as a scholar. The history of the New Testament canon remains the best general study of the subject that we have, and it is a typical product of Westcott's mind with all his characteristic strength and weakness. If we today have neither the desire nor the power to occupy some of the positions that seemed secure to him, he would not, I believe, disapprove. For it would provide additional evidence for his view of the nature of Christian doctrine as 'the partial and progressive approximation towards the complete intellectual expression of the Truth manifested to men once for all in the Incarnation'.

The Bishop Westcott Memorial Lecture 1960

4

'Ego Berengarius'

(For Luise Abramowski)

IN THE long history of Christian debate about the relation between symbol and reality, and the siting of the concept of sacramentality within this relation, the study of Eucharistic controversy brings three names in particular before the mind's eye of the historian. Central to the story are Berengar of Tours, archdeacon of Angers in the eleventh century (the nine-hundredth anniversary of whose death on 6 January 1088 has lately been commemorated, notably at Wolfenbüttel Ducal Library, possessor of the unique manuscript of Berengar's irate *apologia pro vita et doctrina sua*),[1] John Wyclif in fourteenth-century Oxford, and Martin Luther in sixteenth-century Wittenberg. It has long been conventional to reckon these three theologians, representatives of France, England, and Germany respectively, to stand in a single straight line of consciously chosen deviation from an unchanging and timeless Catholic orthodoxy. All three are presented as distancing themselves from an accepted dogma of transubstantiation.[2] Moreover, all three shared an enjoyment of vituperative invective, notably when speaking of some of the bishops of Rome, and therefore they appeared in their time and since to constitute a threat to authority in the western Church and so to the coherence of the believing community. Long after their death Berengar and Wyclif were bogies whom the orthodox feared to find under their beds. For that fear there was the reinforcement that, despite all censures and condemnations, their principal theses commanded some perennial sympathy within the Catholic community. The threat has been from within, not without.

Yet the historian has to record that they were not in line with each other. At Pope Nicholas II's council in Rome of 1059, the redoubtable Cardinal Humbert of Silva Candida extracted from Berengar a reluctant assent to a roughly worded confession of belief in physical Eucharistic change. The text was emphatic that this change occurs in the realm of the five senses *(sensualiter)*; therefore it is no mere symbol of Christ's body which is broken at the liturgical fraction and crushed by the teeth of communicants, but the actuality. Fearing for his life Berengar was impelled to accept, and the Pope distributed the text widely and enthusiastically.

It became incorporated in canon collections under its opening words 'Ego Berengarius'.[3]

Berengar soon disavowed his assent and in an attack on the pope's synod argued with cogency that the formula was in any event internally self-contradictory.[4] His critics conceded. They found themselves in the surprising situation of having to uphold a papal council and of simultaneously surrendering to the force of Berengar's arguments against it.

Among the minor paradoxes of the Berengarian controversy is the fact that for at least four centuries after his time there was debate in the schools of Catholic theology whether *'Ego Berengarius'* is or is not orthodox. One could not abandon it without slighting papal authority. It must be all right if Pope Nicholas II said so; and yet Berengar's critique was formidable and perhaps the council of 1059 had been one-sided and incomplete. Naturally the anti-Berengarians were strong for Roman authority. The brilliant Cardinal Humbert figures among the earlier exponents of the opinion that Roman primacy is the divinely given organ through which an all too human Church, prone to limitless error and threatened by centrifugal force, is granted its one effective guarantee of abiding in the right path. But even those who thought Berengar dangerously mistaken to emphasize the non-literal, non-physical understanding of the sacrament of the altar, had deep reservations about Humbert's formula which Pope Nicholas II had blessed.

John Wyclif and Martin Luther are prominent among those who voiced criticisms of the doctrine of transubstantiation—Wyclif far more than Luther, since he was perturbed by the incomprehensibility of a notion of detached accidents floating in air or whatever, having been deprived of the 'substance' that alone could give them existence. One might at first sight expect these two theologians to look back on Berengar as a precursor, perhaps even a persecuted martyr for the truth, a heroic confessor harassed by uncomprehending or tyrannical bishops of Rome. Was he some kind of Protestant *avant la lettre*, or indeed a Liberal Protestant born out of due time, patron of more modern Christians sympathetic to Christian tradition if interpreted symbolically but not as describing what is the case?[5] The actuality is totally different.

Both Wyclif and Luther assented to Humbert's *'Ego Berengarius'*. Luther in particular enthusiastically welcomed it as a wholly correct statement of true Eucharistic faith, a vindication of his own inflexible stand against Zwingli and Oecolampadius.[6] Luther was not the only late medieval theologian to dislike the intrusion of technical Aristotelian terms into the defining of articles of faith, and was sensitive to the accusation (already brought against western scholastic theology by Greek divines at the Council of Florence) that the West had made theology all Aristotle, and neglected Peter, Paul, Basil, Gregory Nazianzen, and John Chrysostom.[7] But his Eucharistic language put him far closer to Thomas Aquinas (despite all his discourtesies to him) than to Zwingli or Calvin or Bucer— though the slippery character of Calvin's expositions in this area makes it hard to be sure what he thought.

Inasmuch as the term transubstantiation was not coined until many decades after his death, there is a technical anachronism in speaking of Berengar as rejecting it; moreover, the matter had been the subject of no formal definition. After the term became generally current, it is unclear that everyone understood it in the same sense. 'Substance' is an ambivalent word: it answered the question, What kind of change? It implied that this question be answered in terms of objective actuality. But the more Aristotle was called in aid, the less material this actuality became. Tough logical problems haunted the theologians for centuries to come: Is the substantial change one that has any analogies in the natural order? To bring in Aristotle might suggest that it had, since the *Categories* were a classification system for speaking coherently about things in this world, not in the divine realm. And then there were deeply troubling questions about the way in which the substance of bread and wine (the medieval philosophers and theologians were able to assume that they had one) passed away to yield place to the accident-free substance of Christ's body and blood. Berengar was sharp against the notion that the Creator could annihilate his own handiwork and that there could be a destruction of that without which the bread and wine must wholly cease to be. Moreover, if after consecration the Eucharistic species are mere 'accidents', and if it remains self-evident that accidents must be 'in' a substance, what can these accidents be said to be in? Air seemed an unpersuasive answer. One could not say that the accidents of bread are transferred to the human body of Christ if only for the obvious reason that the qualities of bread are not possessed by human bodies. To locate bready qualities in the glorified body of the Redeemer was unfitting. Berengar has the distinction of having seen these questions looming over the horizon to rack the brains of the theological teachers and their pupils for generations to come.

The impetus that led people to speak of a change of substance took its energies from the existential necessity of discovering a rational way of answering and perhaps absorbing his disturbing contentions.[8] The dogma of transubstantiation is sometimes represented as a toughminded and extreme statement of Eucharistic 'realism' in antithesis to the 'mere symbolism' of Berengar. It would surely be more accurate to see it as the product of an attempt to discover a *via media* between mere symbolism and impanation (or the doctrine that there is by consecration a total union between the body of Christ and the natural bread, fully analogous to the complete divinity and complete humanity united in the one person of Christ). How far that attempt can be reckoned successful is a question in itself, since it has never been easy to show that even transubstantiation does not eliminate all elements of 'sign' by leaving exclusively the 'reality' which is being signified.

At the heart of Berengar's campaign (it was nothing less, and in his own part of France it met with remarkable support at the time) was a concern to recognize that the change brought about by consecrating the appointed elements of bread and wine need not and should not entail the corollary that the species wholly cease to be bread and wine, because that would be incompatible with the Augustinian concept of the sacrament as sign.[9] Berengar owed much to Augustine, especially to the texts which had been important to the arsenal of Ratramnus in the ninth century (whose work Berengar, unhappily for his own cause, mistakenly attributed to the already suspect John the Scot, Eriugena)[10]. Certainly Augustine used much symbolist language about the Eucharist, and his doctrine is not entirely easy to state in positive terms. At least it is beyond controversy that Augustine's doctrine of Eucharistic Presence is not merely symbolist. He certainly believed that a change is wrought by the consecration, and that the reality and the sign are concomitant to the believer. At the same time his homilies (especially *Tract. in Joh.* 26-7) were not to establish the supernatural character of the sacrament, which his people did not doubt, but rather to remind his congregation that in receiving the sacrament they should bring penitent and believing hearts and discerning minds alert to the unicity of the Church expressed in the Eucharist. His question concerns not God's gift but human response.[11]

Nothing in Augustine presented a problem for Berengar; it was Lanfranc who had to find a way of interpreting Augustine compatible with his own contentions. On the other hand, Ambrose offered more obstacles to Berengar, especially through his closely related works, *De mysteriis* and *De sacramentis*, and Lanfranc was reduced to splutters of rage as he contemplated Berengar's confident claim that Ambrose, even in *De sacramentis*, should be numbered among his supporters.[12] For Ambrose is emphatic about the miraculous character of the change wrought by the consecration, and roundly declares that what was bread is now 'something else', namely the body of Christ. Did Ambrose believe the bread and wine ceased to exist?[13]

Berengar never questioned the authenticity of *De sacramentis*. That query was left for the Zwinglians at Zürich in the sixteenth century, for whom the document was gravely embarrassing. The dispute achieved the dignity of becoming a minor issue at the Colloquy of Marburg (1529), at which Melanchthon was frankly outraged at the Zwinglian claim to regard the work as a medieval forgery and urged that, if not by Ambrose himself, *De sacramentis* was unquestionably a work of his age, and excellent evidence for the mind of the ancient Church on the Real Presence. The doubts about Ambrosian authorship came to be shared by Catholic historians, notably by the Maurists. It is only in recent times that the convergent studies of R. H. Connolly and O. Faller have convinced the learned world that the work is by Ambrose, with whose idiosyncratic biblical text *De sacramentis* exactly coincides (an agreement scarcely thinkable in a medieval forger).[14]

Although Ambrose's observations about the sacrament of the altar attest, beyond a peradventure, his belief (and that of the Church of his time) in a change by consecration, Berengar was not guilty of sophistry or twisting of the evidence when he remarked that the illustrations used by Ambrose to illustrate the possibility of such a supernatural change did not necessarily imply that the elements entirely ceased to be what they were before consecration. Something of the deepest significance was indeed *added* to them, but Berengar saw no ground for thinking that the senses are deceived in supposing the bread to be bread and the wine wine even after the prayer of consecration is complete. To suggest otherwise, he urged, might make God open to the charge of being less than frank with believers. How could Christ, the truth, be so misleading?[15] Yet Berengar repeatedly affirms the actuality of a change. Lanfranc wanted him to concede a change of *essentia*.[16] Berengar appealed to Ambrose to support the position that the change was an addition of entirely new dignity to the elements. If it were to be conceded that the Eucharist is prefigured in the bread and wine offered by Melchizedek to Abraham,[17] then Berengar felt confident of being in possession of the field. Moreover, Ambrose had spoken of 'an unbloody sacrifice', *incruenta hostia*; such language excludes any possibility that he can have thought of the consecrated liquid in the cup as being blood.[18]

Berengar could use figurative language for the Eucharistic Presence, but to classify him a '*mere* symbolist' would be misleading. For him the bread before consecration does not bring the recipient to eternal life; after consecration it is 'efficax'.[19] It is not thereby made clear whether the efficacity lies only in the reminder it gives to the believing memory, but elsewhere Berengar repeatedly affirms change: 'panem et vinum per consecrationem converti in altari in verum Christi corpus et sanguinem' (i, 750, Huygens p. 57), insisting that this is enforced by evangelical and apostolical authority, not as the opinion of either Berengar or Lanfranc. Later in his rejoinder to Lanfranc, he declared that what is sustained by Christ's sacramental body is the soul, while the physical body is naturally fed by the 'panis sensualis qui tamen post consecrationem est corpus Christi et in ea valet etiam ad vitam aeternam fideli' (i, 2255-7, p. 98 Huygens). The passage, written on an inserted leaf in the Wolfenbüttel codex, was evidently an afterthought. Likewise of Ambrose's conversion doctrine: 'Non enim sine competenti conversione panis in altari consecratus factus dicitur Christi corpus' (ii, 54, p. 102). At the council of Tours, spring 1054, Berengar had declared on oath: 'Panis atque vinum altaris post consecrationem sunt corpus Christi et sanguis' (I, 627, 646), and he vehemently disavowed the notion attributed to him that between consecrated and unconsecrated bread there is no significant difference. Naturally, Lanfranc regarded such orthodox utterances as additional evidence of the corruption of a heretical heart. Nevertheless, one cannot mistake the passion of his reply, the sincerity of a man protesting at misrepresentation. He certainly believed in change. But what kind of change?[20]

He did not believe that to put the consecrated bread in one's mouth and bite it is without more ado to receive the glorious body of the Redeemer, born of Mary, crucified for our salvation. The Lord's glorious body is in heaven, incorruptible and impassible. To talk with Lanfranc of the hosts at a thousand masses[21] being 'little bits' of the body of Christ, created by the celebrant (de novo?),[22] presumably adding to the total sum, seemed to Berengar not merely prosaic but irreligious. For Berengar the communicant receives the whole, not a little fragment. And it is abhorrent to speak of the communicants' teeth slicing up the impassible body, now at the Father's right hand, immune from human violence and bites.

Cardinal Humbert of Silva Candida was Leo IX's right-hand man, possessed of great energy, competent in canon law, capable of reorganizing the papal library. He was a zealot for tidiness and precision; perhaps it is fitting he is the first to speak of seven sacraments—long before canonistic glossators had begun to count—in his denunciation of simony (ii, 20). For him simoniac orders were not doubtful but utterly null. The Greek use of leavened bread in the Eucharist was no tolerable diversity (as it was for Anselm) but insufferable heresy. He would deliver a papal excommunication to an admittedly offensive patriarch of Constantinople in such a manner as to inflict a wound capable of being healed only after 900 years and even then with relatively little effect in restoring communion. Anything he touched long bore the mark of his hand. He was an integrist, sure that if ever he failed to be totally uncompromising he would be a traitor to God and his Church. His last great battle was to be the crushing of Berengar.

In the confession of faith demanded at the Roman council of 1059 Berengar was forced to deny (a) that after consecration the bread and wine are 'only the sacrament and not the true body and blood of the Lord', and (b) that it is impossible except[23] in the sacrament alone for them to be handled or broken by priests' hands or crushed by the teeth of the faithful, *sensualiter*—in the realm of the physical senses. The formula echoed terms already current at the earlier council of Vercelli (1050) under Pope Leo IX, at which Berengar had not been present. But Berengar consistently speaks of the Roman formula as the work of Humbert.

Berengar accepted on oath, but subsequently published his highly critical account of the Roman synod. He recoiled in horror from the earthy crudity of Humbert's language; it confused the *sacramentum* with the *res sacramenti*, and was deficient in *spiritualitas*, a quality which he valued, above all in *mysterium*.[24]

However, the awkward wording of the formula conceded Berengar's essential point. He believed neither that after consecration there is only *sacramentum* without *res*, nor that there is *res* without *sacramentum*. To assert that the consecrated bread and wine are Christ's body and blood necessarily implies that they exist to be so. *X* cannot be *Y* if no *X* exists to be *Y*. Berengar triumphantly echoes a sentence taken from Augustine's reply to the Donatist Petilian (i, 10) that like Goliath his opponent dies by his own sword (cited by Lanfranc 412C; Berengar, *Rescr.* i, 161).

The logically slippery word 'only' plays a part in the argument here. Berengar interprets Humbert to condemn the proposition that the bread and wine are only the true body and blood; that is, one may not say 'only' either of the sacramental sign or of the divine *res* which that sign conveys and represents. One must affirm both.

The second clause, with *sensualiter*, caused Berengar more difficulty. Its natural exegesis must be that Christ's body is physically present, broken at the fraction, crushed at communion by the teeth. For Berengar only the sacramental species can be broken and chewed. Lanfranc might complain of his perjury in withdrawing his assent to the second proposition of Humbert's formula; but in fact Lanfranc himself is only one of a long line of interpreters of *Ego Berengarius* who glossed it in a sense very different from that intended in 1059.

This observation brings up Lanfranc's interpretation of Humbert's formula. If Lanfranc was present at the Roman council of 1059 (which Montclos has contested), he is nevertheless not likely to have been responsible for the actual drafting of the text. Ego Berengarius has too many ambiguities and loose ends to be the natural product of a mind with a certain pride both in dialectical skill and in an avowed policy of expressing logical points within the familiar vocabulary of ecclesiastical tradition (417A explains that he liked to use 'equipollent propositions'). Moreover, although Pope Nicholas II seems to have gone out of his way to give personal encouragement, that fact in itself suggests that Lanfranc was not trusted by all. He expressly mentions that his past correspondence with Berengar made people ask if perhaps he also was at heart a Berengarian, so that suggestions by him for greater care in formulation could easily have confirmed existing suspicions.[25] By 1063, the year of his move from Bec to Caen, Lanfranc composed his treatise 'On the Lord's body and blood', making a direct and frontal attack on a tract by Berengar justifying his disowning of his oath of assent extorted by duress. That warded off remaining anxieties about Lanfranc's own orthodoxy.

Berengar's tract survives only through Lanfranc's quotations, which Lanfranc expressly designates as a selection of sentences to which exception may be taken; for in Berengar's work he also found 'roses among the thorns' (409C). Lanfranc's strongest argument was the alarm caused by Berengar's threat to acknowledged authority in offensive remarks about recent Popes, and the implied arrogance of a man who, on his own admission, had only come late to the study of scripture and yet thought fit to criticise accepted devotional language. Lanfranc put into Berengar's mouth an assertion that physical change *(mutatio materialis)* does not occur at consecration, and that the notion is an innovation unsupported by Augustine, Ambrose, and the patristic tradition;[26] and therefore that if a Pope had taught any such doctrine, then his chair had become Satan's seat (415B, 426A, cf. 410B). Berengar denied that his view was being correctly represented: he agreed that consecration brought a change affecting the bread and wine, but not that the change is an annihilation of the 'substance', the intangible underlying reality 'in' which the accidental qualities can exist. He sharply attacked the idea that the eternal, glorious body of Christ can descend from heaven to the altar, there to be broken and chewed into bits (421B, 422A). The Augustinian synonyms—sacrament, species, likeness, figure, sign, mystery—imply a relation, and therefore a distinction, between sign and reality. Consecration makes the species holy and effective signs communicating the body and blood of Christ to the believer; but they are not so absolutely and totally the body and blood as to eliminate the sign (436A). To remove the sign was to annihilate the sacrament as sacrament. In Berengar's terminology there is always a strict observance of the Augustinian distinction between *sacramentum*, the external visible sign, and the *res*, inward invisible grace (echoing Augustine, *De catechizandis rudibus* 50 and *Ep*. 105, 11). For him what makes the bread and wine a sacrament is the presence of and relationship to the *res* or inward grace.

But the sacrament cannot cease to be a sign, and therefore must retain its nature as distinct from the *res* of which it is a sign and means. The earthly elements can be broken, bitten with teeth, burnt, consumed by animals, or even putrefy; but the glorious body of the Lord remains eternally incorruptible in heaven. Nevertheless, Berengar was keen to affirm that the union of *sacramentum* and *res* is parallel to the union of the human and divine in the incarnate Lord.[27]

Lanfranc's riposte is to reassert with force the strong terms of Humbert's formula to which Berengar had declared his adherence on oath, and had then repudiated. But Lanfranc then associates himself with propositions which Berengar himself asserted by way of critique of Humbert. Berengar is right, Lanfranc agrees, to deny that in holy communion we divide the body of Christ into parts (422A). He is entirely right that Christ's glorified body remains in heaven, and therefore while in one sense we receive the very body taken from the Virgin, in another sense we do not: we receive 'ipsum corpus et tamen non ipsum' (430C, 434A).[28] We believe that Christ can be eaten by worthy persons who perceive his body even on this earth, while we hold him to be incorruptible in heaven (427C). True communion is both physical and spiritual simultaneously (435C 'corporaliter, spiritualiter'). 'The material bread feeds the body, while the spiritual and invisible body of Christ feeds the soul' (438D). In a passage to be gratefully quoted by Alger of Liège in the next century, Lanfranc affirms the simultaneity of physical and spiritual manducation (429B, cited by Alger, PL 180, 797CD 798A paraphrastically).

Accordingly Lanfranc agrees with Berengar that the sacrament (a word which is rightly noted to have many senses, 437D) must here retain signification (418D). The symbolic element in the mass must be recognized because the sacrifice of the Church is no repetition of the suffering and death of Christ. The 'immolation' of Christ's flesh in the hands of the celebrant is not concrete actuality but a mystery acted out in ritual form (425A). 'We so eat and drink the immolated Christ on earth that he remains for ever whole and living in heaven at the Father's right hand' (422A). By the broken bread and poured out wine his death is symbolized (*figuratur*, 424A).

But the *figura* of the sacrifice is contrasted with the *veritas* of the presence. Ten years before Lanfranc wrote, an alarmed opponent of Berengar, Durandus of Troarn, is found using *substantia* to express concrete reality in contrast to imaginative fantasy, subjective image. But it is first in Lanfranc that *substantia* is used with Aristotelian overtones. He knew of the distinction in the *Categories* between primary and secondary substances (418B). The change in the bread and wine is not therefore in the accidents or qualities, but in the inward essence.

It is a question whether this is a 'material change' or an immaterial one. Aristotle's substance is metaphysical. The word answers the question, What is it? Therefore to speak of the 'substantia' being altered is but another way of saying, in Aristotelian language (but not in a framework of Aristotelian metaphysic), that after consecration the question, What is that?, receives a different answer from that given before the consecration.

Berengar in no way disagreed with Lanfranc that consecration required a different answer to the question. His great mentor Augustine had written that 'not all bread but that which receives Christ's blessing becomes Christ's body (*Sermo* 234, 2; *c. Faustum* 20, 13).

Berengar's reply to Lanfranc's attack, commonly known as *De sacra coena*, the title inscribed on the first folio of the codex in the hand of Matthaeus Flacius Illyricus (who surprisingly made no use of it in the piece on Berengar in the Magdeburg Centuries), was probably never widely diffused. The old opinion that the manuscript at Wolfenbüttel (Weissenburg 101), found by Lessing in 1770, could be the autograph must now be abandoned; but the codex stood close to the author's archetype. The beginning is lost and there are lesser lacunae; but, if only because Berengar was relentless in repetition, the central arguments are clear.[29]

Both Berengar and Lanfranc were part of a revival of the liberal arts in the schools of Touraine and Normandy, familiar with Donatus' grammar and Boethius' logic.[30] Lanfranc was scornful of Berengar's resort to dialectic in discussing articles of faith, where the only proper criterion is authority. Yet his own use of the distinction of accidents and substance showed that logic could not be kept out. Berengar saw this move as a gross misuse of Aristotle. Aristotle could not imaginably have understood the proposition that after the underlying metaphysical substance is removed, the accidents can remain. That impossibility was an axiom not merely obvious in the light of reason; it had the support of authority, being neatly stated by St Augustine in the second book of his *Soliloquies* (ii, 12, 22).[31] Philosophical reflection on coming to be and passing away could never have envisaged the possibility of change in Lanfranc's sense. Berengar identified himself with Boethius, the professional logician who found himself lonely and bewildered at a meeting when ecclesiastical persons were discussing intricate questions of Christology, and discerned little but dialectical confusion.

In the *Categories* (2b 6) Aristotle had stated the axiom that if the primary substance is removed, it is impossible for the accidents to exist. The text was well known in Boethius' translation and commentary. Destruction of the substance, combined with the assertion of the retention of the qualities or accidents of the bread and wine, is for Berengar incoherent and intrinsically absurd.

In regard to the sacrifice offered in the mass, Berengar discerns no difference between himself and Lanfranc. Both accepted as authoritative a commentary on the epistle to the Hebrews, compiled from various sources by Alcuin, but in the eleventh century current under Ambrose's name. Both quote an excerpt incorporated in this commentary from the sixth-century Latin translation of John Chrysostom's homilies on the epistle. 'Ambrose' is incisive in affirming that the sacrifice of the Church is a memorial of Calvary, not a repetition.[32]

In 1070 Lanfranc became Archbishop of Canterbury and had more to do than to combat Berengarian replies to his book. Towards the end of that book he had rested his case on the consensus of the universal Church which, for him, included not only the West but also Greeks and Armenians (441A). Thereby Lanfranc could suggest that Berengar's all too well-founded appeal to numerous texts in Augustine was one-sided. No theme is louder in Augustine than the binding authority of the unique Catholica. To set oneself up against the agreement of all the faithful world-wide is to be self-condemned. Berengar's unhappy remarks about successive bishops of Rome from Leo IX to Nicholas II confirmed the dissidence of his personality and of his theology.

Admittedly Berengar was to receive markedly sympathetic treatment from archdeacon Hildebrand, soon to be Pope Gregory VII (1073-85), to an extent which brought embarrassment and necessitated the action of 1078-9 (below, p. 48). To Lanfranc, however, it betrayed Berengar's case that he could describe Peter's see as Satan's seat (426D). That was to undermine the very principle of unity in the Catholica.

In the 1070s the battle against Berengar and his not inconsiderable number of admirers was taken up by Lanfranc's pupil, Guitmund, sent from Normandy to strengthen the Norman presence in south Italy by becoming bishop of Aversa. His treatise 'On the truth of the body and blood of Christ in the eucharist' reads at times as an attempt to cover weaknesses and indiscretions in Lanfranc. At one point (PL 149, 1443C f.) Guitmund approaches the awkward question of changes in substance—'mutationes substantivae sive efficientes'. The Creator creates things out of nothing. Moreover, what is made out of nothing can return to nothingness. Accidents can remain only in their underlying 'subject', and must pass into nothingness unless they can be said to undergo transmutation. Black ink on white parchment changes it. Other substantial changes occur in nature as a seed grows into a plant, or as food and drink are changed into flesh and blood by digestion, or in miracles as when Moses' rod becomes a snake. Guitmund grants that these kinds of change are less than the change which occurs on the altar, but at least the latter kind is not more incomprehensible in a world where all such changes are wonderful; and in the consecration we are dealing with a change wrought 'through solemn prayers and the very words of Christ himself'. Guitmund does not discuss the survival of the accidents of the bread and wine, but is content repeatedly to declare that the change takes place *substantialiter*. This seems to mean 'in concrete reality'.

When Berengar's followers were pressed by Guitmund that the Eucharistic species must be more than a mere *figura* (a figure of speech, perhaps), they answered that their master's real meaning was more subtle: he held that Christ's body and blood lie, imperceptible to the five senses, somehow hidden within. By this subtle doctrine, Guitmund allows, Berengar 'was in some way with us' (*aliquo modo nobiscum*, 1430D); but the analogy of the incarnation suggested belief in impanation, as if the bread and wine were united to the divine Word and his glorified humanity in the way the flesh was once united to the Word. Guitmund does not explain his exact objections to such notions; he is content to express horror. Does the Word become bread to dwell among us?

Guitmund did not accept Berengarian language about the body and blood being 'hidden' within the species, nor that they 'come into' the elements (1484D). His verb for the change is *transire* (1452D) or *transmutari* (1440B).

For the rest Guitmund is found to agree with much that Berengar said in criticism of Humbert's formula: the Lord's glorified body is incorruptible and indivisible. Guitmund's defence of the formula largely consists in explaining it away. He could not entirely abandon it, without betraying not merely his master Lanfranc but also the high papal authority of Nicholas II who had endorsed Humbert and distributed *Ego Berengarius* around the western Church as a correct statement of belief. Where Lanfranc had formulated Roman authority in terms of a special case of the Petrine office entrusted to all bishops, Guitmund expressed it in terms of the authority attaching to *Romanum imperium*, to the dignity attaching to a council with the pope as president held in the palace of Constantine the Great (1486D).

With some artifice Humbert's formula could be softened by Guitmund's unction. 'To grind with the teeth' need mean no more than to subject to friction. But 'we and the Berengarians' agree that the communicant receives the whole Christ, not a little chunk broken off at the fraction when, 'as the proper way of celebrating requires', the priest splits the host into three parts (1434B). A thousand masses do not mean any dividing or distributing. 'In every mass there is the entire body of Christ, and the Berengarians are right to deny that the Lord's body is divisible' (1434A, 1435A).

The awkward weapon in Berengar's arsenal was that the reserved sacrament, kept for the sick and dying (in the eleventh century, normally in the sacristy), eventually putrefies. Current canon law forbade keeping the host so long that it became mouldy, and conciliar canons directed renewal at intervals of 7 days (1446C).[33] Nevertheless, Guitmund was reduced to trying to meet Berengar's formidable argument by asserting that the consecrated host can never putrefy, and cannot be corrupted by being eaten by mice or other animals (1448C). Such arguments illuminate Anselm's distaste for the Eucharistic debate (*ep.* 20, iii 127 Schmitt).

Berengar's followers observed that if Christ's body is bitten by the teeth of the communicants, it will also be digested; and it is unseemly and unsavoury to suppose that anything so holy can pass out of the body with other body-waste. Guitmund again had to concede that Berengar was right on this. 'We also so believe' (1451A). But he sought to save Humbert by arguing that just as the body absorbs 'the subtle parts' of food and discards the rest, so also the body and blood of Christ are separated out within the body which receives them, and are not passed out. As for the stories in the lives of saints that for years they lived exclusively on the sacramental gifts, one must deduce that nothing was ever passed out by them (1452B).

A century or more later Caesarius of Heisterbach can tell of a devout woman who decided to live exclusively on the body of Christ, and accordingly obtained special leave from her priest to receive communion every Lord's day (ix, 47).

Berengar was stridently insistent that the sacramental body of Christ is received not by mere physical eating (though he did not suggest that that was unnecessary) but by faith. Guitmund himself, strongly conscious of Ambrose's words about the 'operative force' of the consecrating words of Christ, nevertheless conceded that the miraculous Eucharistic change only occurs to those who believe that Christ's words possess this power (1452D). Consecration is therefore a response to the prayer of faith, and not magic.

Yet Guitmund could not entirely surrender Humbert's 'crushing by the teeth'. If doubting Thomas could put his hand into the Lord's side, surely the faithful could bite his body with their teeth? What hands can touch teeth can chew—and indeed teeth are normally much cleaner (1433A). Berengarian reserve before Humbert's tough language is merely a form of rationalism, denying the omnipotence of the Creator who made the world out of nothing and presumably finds the Eucharistic change a simpler matter (1431A). But here again Guitmund yields to Berengar's critique of the notion that Christ's body is created by the celebrant's act of consecration. 'When we say the bread is changed, it is not into flesh which did not exist as flesh before'; that is no addition to the body of Christ (1440C).

Although Berengar appealed to the accepted rules of grammar and logic, confident that 'to fly to logic is to fly to reason which is God's image in man', and that Augustine had described logic as the 'art of arts',[34] nevertheless he placed the greatest weight on patristic authority. He rested on not only Augustine which was easy, but also on Ambrose, Jerome, Hilary, a catena of prayers from the Latin sacramentaries, and even select citations from Gregory the Great. The supreme art in polemical skill is always to be able to quote one's opponents' authorities in support of one's own case. The texts were largely collected already. In the alternative Eucharistic theologies offered in the ninth century by Ratramnus and Paschasius Radbertus, many of the same texts occur; they reappear too in a florilegium made to support 'realism' against

47

'symbolism' gathered by Heribert of Lobbes (d. 1007).[35] But Paschasius and Lanfranc invoked Eucharistic miracles from the Lives of the Fathers, stories such as those soon to be gathered by Caesarius of Heisterbach, or apocryphal Acts of Apostles.[36] The Berengarians explicitly scorned such evidence.

Patristic proof texts answered the dangerous charge of innovation. To have a new idea was heretical in itself. Towards the end of his work Guitmund affirms a change of the bread and wine into the substance of Christ's body and blood, with the ringing declaration: 'This is the Church's faith; it is not recent, it is not the opinion of this or that individual but of the entire world. It alone is reasonable, alone true, alone valid . . .' (1489D).

Guitmund met with success, especially for his favourite adverb 'substantialiter'. The long drawn-out story of successive councils censuring Berengar culminated in Gregory VII's council at Rome in 1079. Gregory VII had played a remarkably protective role towards Berengar. Condemnations might hinder the concord in the Church which was at the top of his agenda, and it might not have been clear that censure of Berengar was not also a rejection of the patristic and liturgical authorities to which he appealed. Granted that the Eucharist is mystery, might Berengar's interpretation be a legitimate option within the broad river of Catholic tradition, much as the use of leavened bread by the Greeks might be deemed tolerable diversity not affecting fundamental faith? Gregory VII had enemies who exploited his hesitations about Berengar and even accused him of being a disciple.[37] How, they might ask, could the official guardian of Catholic faith compromise with a man whose symbolist doctrines threaten the salvific power of the sacrament of the altar?

At Rome in 1078-9 Guitmund was present. The probability is high that he was among the drafters of the new confession of faith, similarly beginning 'Ego Berengarius', which Berengar was brought to Rome to accept. Guitmund's adverb *substantialiter* was inserted into the text. Nothing was now said about breaking or biting Christ's body and nothing of *'sensualiter'*. It sufficed to affirm that by the mystery of the prayer of consecration and the words of Christ[38] the bread and wine on the altar are substantially changed into the lifegiving flesh and blood of Christ by which humanity is redeemed, so that they are Christ's body and blood 'not merely in the symbol and virtue of the sacrament but in their proper nature and substantial truth' (*non tantum per signum et virtutem sacramenti sed in proprietate naturae et veritate substantiae*).[39]

This last phrase looks like an echo of Durandus of Troarn, writing about 1053 to alert Normans to the danger of Berengar's teaching. In his tract against 'modern dogmaticians', whose 'head' is Berengar (*PL* 149, 1378B), he had insisted that the Eucharistic change occurs *substantialiter* (1386D, 1405A), wrought by the Lord's words (1381D, 1397C) to change the nature, not the appearance (1380A). So the species are the true body and blood 'not only by the effect of their virtue and spiritual power but also in the complete truth of nature' (1387C). What lies on the altar is 'veritas in proprietate substantiae' (1413B). Repeatedly, Durandus contrasts substance with what is not really the case, with 'an empty image of the imagination' (1405A). The word asserts reality, not dreams.

Yet Durandus had to grant to the Augustinians that the terms sign, likeness, or pledge are also correct; that the mass is a 'representation' of the Passion of the Son of God (1392B, 1401B), the unique sacrifice by which God is propitiated to the world (1381A) in which Christ is both priest and victim (1381B). So believers 'have the very flesh of the glorious deity *in pignore*' (1384A), the *pignus gratiae* (1384B), a token or pledge of grace. Moreover, the substantial reality is given in response to faith. In a bold and surprising sentence Durandus explained that believing reception completes the transformation of the elements which has been partly achieved by consecration (1379B). Because what is received is *res divina*, there can be no question of a divine reality being liable to destruction through physical digestion. Durandus disowned entirely the obscene questions asked by 'Stercoritae' (1382AB, 1389D). A somewhat obscure observation shows that some were asking awkward questions about the transformation of the drop of water added to the wine at the consecration (1389C); did that also become the blood of Christ? Durandus did not have everything clear in his mind. It is certain that he must affirm the objective reality of the divine presence received under the forms of the consecrated species, but also that he must safeguard himself against any suggestion that the divine *res* is eaten and drunk to be digested as ordinary food and drink and thereby to impart 'the substance of eternal life'.

It may be suggested that the drafters of Berengar's confession of 1079 turned to Durandus to help them because he offered a case against Berengar which antedated Humbert's awkward formula. He had said nothing about the fraction or the teeth of communicants. The moderation of his terms could offer a way of reconciling the warring parties in Gregory VII's synod.

At the assembly of bishops in Rome under Gregory VII, Berengar had friends and supporters, though they were a minority as the record of the synod in Gregory's Register insists. But on the third day a lightning strike was understood to decide the issue against Berengar and in favour of the formula confessing that the bread and wine are changed 'substantialiter'. Berengar's own account of the proceedings, preserved in a Gembloux manuscript now at Brussels, shows that the insertion of this adverb distressed him. He had to offer an elaborate justification for signing with mental reservations (with an appeal to John 7: 8 as in his *Rescriptum contra Lanfrannum*, ii. 1918 ff.). He was unmoved in his conviction that after consecration both *sacramentum* and *res* retain their proper being, since to lose the *sacramentum* is to lose access to the *res*; that to speak of consecrated bread and wine must imply that they survive to be consecrated, which is to be elevated to something better, *in melius*, a phrase Berengar borrows from Augustine on the incarnation, *Tract. in Joh.* 52, 3 ('hominem in melius commutavit'). And surely God would have mercy on him for having been compelled to compromise with ignorant and dangerous fools. Sadly he had found the Pope weak, despite Gregory's expression of trust in Berengar's legitimate place within the Augustinian tradition and a vision in which the Blessed Virgin had instructed the Pope not to require of Berengar any dogma going beyond authoritative *scripturae*.

The new Ego Berengarius seems not to have been distributed by Gregory VII with a fervour equal to that shown in 1059 by Nicholas II. It is twice recorded in the contemporary manuscript of Gregory's Register and, as Z. N. Brooke showed in his classic study *The English Church and the Papacy* (1931), turns up in a few canonistic manuscripts probably going back to a model prepared under Lanfranc's eye at Christ Church, Canterbury. Nevertheless, the new formula was remarkably little known.[40] Except for a minor contribution to Ivo of Chartres' fifth book of his *Decretum* on papal primacy (v. 36), Gregory VII was not drawn upon by Ivo.

In the early fifteenth century the English theologian combating Wyclif, Thomas Netter, records discovering Gregory VII's Ego

Berengarius 'in an old codex of papal decretals'.[41] Netter supposed that Gregory VII's *substantialiter* was intended to close a loophole for Berengar left open by Nicholas II, so that the second formula was less moderate than the first. This seems an unlikely reading of the story. Except for the adverb, the new formula of 1079 was altogether simple for Berengar to accept. In fact, therein lay the problem for him: it was eminently reasonable. It did not assert with Humbert that the Eucharistic change occurs in the realm of the five senses (*sensualiter*). There was no inherent inconsistency between its propositions such as had enabled Berengar to deliver damaging attacks on Humbert's formula 20 years before. Moreover, it was not open, as Humbert's formula was, to being interpreted to enforce impanation. Whatever glosses Berengar might put upon *substantialiter*, the document would not need to be explained away.

Long before Berengar faced Cardinal Humbert, he had exchanged important letters with Adelmann of Liège, a fellow student at Chartres under Fulbert and later bishop of Brescia (d. 1061). Adelmann had been perturbed by reports and sought reassurance about Berengar's belief in Christ's presence in the eucharist. Berengar's reply survives only in fragments, and one cannot estimate how much of the original text has been lost. But the main lines are clear. Berengar expressly affirmed that the bread and wine are by consecration changed into the body and blood of Christ, with the proviso that this is to be understood to be no kind of change in physical space. The change occurs 'not in the realm of the senses but in that of the mind, not by the removal of something but by the taking up of the bread and wine' (*non sensualiter sed intellectualiter, non per absumptionem sed per assumptionem*). Bread and wine are not, therefore, annihilated, but assumed by Christ to become his body and blood. Moreover, Berengar added, the host is not a little piece of Christ's body, but the whole.[42]

Mabillon's Life of Berengar, prefixed to the second part of the sixth volume of his history of the Benedictine order (1701), held Berengar's position to be free of serious ambiguity: the archdeacon believed Christ to be truly present in the consecrated species but denied the annihilation of the bread and wine. He affirmed change but denied that it occurred in the physical realm. He believed that the body of Christ is received and eaten by the believing communicant. He did not want to say that after consecration what lies upon the altar only looks like bread and wine, tastes and feels like bread and wine, satisfies hunger and thirst like bread and wine, while in reality the senses (notoriously fallible, Guitmund argued) are deceived, and what is there is nothing but the body and blood of Christ, whether brought from heaven or created *de novo* by the celebrating priest.

Mabillon thought it certain that Berengar should not be described as a mere symbolist. He believed in what much later theologians called Real Presence, but not in what theologians a century after his time would call Transubstantiation in which the bread and wine cease to be what they appear to be. He believed that the consecrated species are changed to be quite distinct from unconsecrated bread and wine, but the change must not be the destruction of the substance, or the sacrament itself ceases to be a sign.

To Mabillon one might add that Guitmund's report of Berengar's inclination to 'impanation' should be taken seriously, in the sense that he sought to defend the reality of the bread and wine after consecration by the analogy of the reality of Christ's humanity, which is not annihilated by union with the divine nature. But Humbert's formula added notable reinforcement to impanation. Its aggressive language satisfied the devotion of the impassioned ascetic in the monastery, and caused qualms only to secular priests who had to try to explain the Church's faith to enquiring minds, glad to believe so as to understand, but finding it impossible to believe what they could not begin to understand. Humbert, on the other hand, spoke for those who deeply felt that authentic faith must defy reason.

Two or three decades after Berengar's death in 1088, his questions surfaced again in the exchanges between Rupert of Deutz and Alger of Liège.[43] Rupert excluded any merely metaphorical interpretation of Eucharistic presence. He opposed 'the great and magnificent teachers of the young' who used terms 'more redolent of Plato than of the Lord's Table' and spoke of the consecrated bread and wine as figurative in the same sense as the manna of the Exodus (*PL* 169, 463D). He felt it indispensable to affirm that the consecration changes bread and wine into the 'substance' of Christ's body and blood, 'the external physical accidents remaining unchanged' (494A). But Rupert juxtaposes this language with terms suggesting impanation: the bread is by consecration made one with the body of Christ, as the human nature born of Mary is one with the divine Word. Moreover, as he made emphatic in his commentaries on Exodus (ii, 10) and on John 6-7, the incarnation cannot mean that Christ's humanity lost anything essential to its nature, and in the same way one cannot suppose that 'the effect of the Holy Spirit in the Eucharistic consecration is to destroy or corrupt the substance which he assumes for his own uses'. So the substance of the species does not suffer loss. 'There is an invisible addition which it did not previously possess.' 'Sic substantiam panis et vini, secundum exteriorem speciem quinque sensibus subactam, non mutat aut destruit' (*PL* 167, 618A). Moreover, 'the bread once consecrated never subsequently loses the virtue of its sanctification or ceases to be Christ's flesh' (on John 6, *PL* 169, 470B). Rupert's disavowal of those who think of the sacrament of the altar in merely figurative terms makes him scathing about 'incautious adulators of Augustine' (469B) who take the great Church Father to be a mere symbolist. The absurdity of their position is shown by the fact that some among them take the Augustinian stress on inward faith so far as to make physical participation in Eucharistic communion entirely superfluous (469D), a notion at variance with scripture and tradition and not in the least compatible with Augustine.

Sad at discord in the Church on the sacrament of unity (*PL* 169, 491D), Rupert set out to bring peace by a statement of Eucharistic belief intended to reconcile all thoughtful believers. A merely symbolist doctrine of Christ's presence must be felt inadequate. The principle of his coming to his people at the altar makes the Eucharist a kind of reenactment of the incarnation. Moreover, the Eucharistic sacrifice is no independent offering; it is none other than the once for all offering of the Cross. 'It is contrary to all orthodox faith to think that Christ suffers and dies as often as this bread is broken on the Lord's Table' (491A). 'The body of Christ sacrificed, broken, and eaten does not suffer, just as the divine nature did not suffer in the Passion' (495C). But 'in the bread and wine the Son of God is immolated in the truth of his flesh and blood' (491B). Because Christ joined the bread to his body and united the wine to his blood, he made one sacrifice. When the priest puts the consecrated elements into the mouths of the faithful, the bread and wine are transient, whereas Christ's body, both in heaven and in the communicants, remains complete and unconsumed. The unbeliever—like Judas (whose non-participation in the Last Supper seemed important to Rupert)—receives only natural bread and wine, kills Christ, and has no share in the sacrifice (*De divinis officiis*, ii, 9).

Rupert's early work on the rites and ceremonies of the Church (*De divinis officiis*, supplementing the Carolingian work by Amalarius of Metz) first appeared in 1111 and was published with no note of the author's name. That was soon known. A reissue in 1126 was explicitly dedicated to his friend Kuno, newly consecrated bishop of Regensburg. It is instructive that the work was well known to Wyclif under St Ambrose's name, though Wyclif doubted the ascription and attributed it to a pupil of the saint. The Oxford theologian found the work congenial. As late as the 1590s, Bellarmine felt it necessary to compose a refutation.

Rupert's covering letter to Kuno attached to his commentary on St John of 1115 shows an explicit awareness of Berengar's error that the sacrament is only a sign of the *res* and of Berengar's appeal to Augustine. Rupert intended to show that Augustine's sermons on St John failed to support Berengar, and he knew that to be a difficult undertaking.

It is therefore striking that there is in Rupert's writings no direct allusion to or quotation from Humbert's formula of 1059, other than a subtle and indirect reference to the question whether Christ's body is broken in the fraction or cut with teeth when Rupert expounds the Jews' difficulty in John 6 : 63. He thinks such questions presuppose that Christ's body is received as a corpse rather than as united to the glorified Lord. In communion 'we leave nothing over which can be consumed by the solid tooth of faith; but if anything remains, we burn it with fire, i.e. we commit it to the Holy Spirit' (on John 7, 495D). Rupert's opposition to the notion that at the Last Supper Judas received the sacrament of Christ's body shows that he did not believe Christ to be received by those without faith. The bread and wine are changed 'not carnally but spiritually, *non secundum crassitudinem carnis sed secundum mentis nostrae spiritum*'. Moreover, the Word of God is not changed into bread, but assumes the visible bread into unity with his person (463C, 481C). Rupert did not wish to say that God is bread.

Rupert wrote while a monk at St Laurence, Liège. His colleague Alger of Liège[44] experienced some alarm on reading him, and feared that Rupert's language would encourage the heresy of impanation (*PL* 180, 765B, 761B) with foul inferences about the digestive processes, and with awkward consequences from the thesis that the union between the bread and the body of Christ is permanent or perpetual. Alger affirmed a change of the substance of the bread and wine, while the accidents remain; he was much influenced by Lanfranc. But he also felt the force of points urged by Berengar. He denied that in the consecration the body of Christ is created *de nihilo* (768AB). The body of Christ, whether in heaven or on the altar, is 'integra' (782C), by divine omnipotence able to be both at the Father's right hand and on any altar where mass is being celebrated. Many masses do not mean many bodies of Christ in different places (785A). The Eucharistic sacrifice is no repetition of the dying of Christ which was once for all, but is not thereby superfluous (786B) but identical with that of the Cross, and is not other than that; for here on the altar it is present 'in figura et imitatione' (786D). On this last point Alger found support in Alcuin's commentary on Hebrews. So, in the mass, Christ 'does not suffer but is represented as if he suffered' (787D). The immolation is not actual but in image (789C *imaginaria*).

Alger received Humbert as a writer of authority to be circumvented. In dealing with the Latin/Greek dispute over unleavened/leavened bread he subtly juxtaposed sentences from Humbert's wholly negative treatment of the Greek position with sentences drawn from Anselm's treatise where the Greeks are mistaken but tolerated, and Alger's verdict clearly agreed with Anselm's.[45] So also with the *Ego Berengarius* of Nicholas II, Alger explained it away, using every concession he could find in Lanfranc, to reach the doctrine that in the Eucharist there is a twofold eating of Christ's body, physically by mouth, spiritually in the heart. Alger's anxiety to discourage Rupert's ideas about impanation ran parallel with his wish to retain the distinction important to Berengar between the *res* as the body of Christ and the *sacramentum*. 'The sacraments are not Christ's body and blood, but contain it' (753CD), and the reason for rejecting impanation is that the distinction between sign and *res* is obliterated.

Similarly, Rupert's friend and critic, William of St Thierry (*c.* 1085-1148), was alarmed at the suggestion that Christ is incarnate in the host. That was not for him the meaning of the change of substance while the accidents (through divine omnipotence) remain intact. Augustine he knew to have disturbed people (*PL* 180, 345-6);

but that was no good reason to abandon the clear position that the Eucharistic food 'is not of the stomach but of the mind' (a quotation from the ninth-century Florus of Lyon),[46] 355B. Without naming Berengar or his confession of 1059, William utterly opposes Humbert's terms. The sacrifice of the mass is for him no repetition of the Passion, but linked to the Lord's heavenly intercession (358C).

The Berengarian controversy bequeathed questions that reverberated through the twelfth century and beyond. If monks had insufficient employment, here was an issue to exercise their minds. The questions raised had a catalytic effect in mobilizing the resources of the liberal arts, especially dialectic, in the service of theology with lasting consequences. But to the early schoolmen Humbert's formula of 1059 remained intensely problematic. *Quaeritur an corpus frangitur*, asked Roland Bandinelli, later Pope Alexander III and our earliest witness to the term *transubstantiatio*: Berengar's sworn confession required by the Roman Church would say it can be broken; but the objections require one to be more qualified—'frangitur sacramentaliter et non essentialiter.'[47] Robert of Melun's commentary on I Corinthians preferred to juxtapose the irreconcilables: 'Even if Christ's body is crushed by the teeth, as Berengar's confession has it, yet miraculously it remains unhurt.'[48] Peter Lombard (*Sent.* iv, 12, 5) attempted a compromise: it is *in veritate* that Christ's body is handled by the priest's hands, but only *in sacramento* that it is broken and ground by teeth.[49]

To read twelfth-century schoolmen is to discern Berengar's questions at almost every turn of their Eucharistic argument. His initiative in insisting that the communicant receives not a bit of Christ but the whole will lead to the doctrine of concomitance, that the blood is received with the consecrated bread and the body with the consecrated cup; a doctrine laying the foundation for defending communion in one kind (though already by 1100 it was customary to communicate children only with the cup, and crowds of peasants only with bread).[50] On the other hand, if with Berengar one places intense stress on the signification of the sacrament, that is on the symbol as that indispensable medium without which the 'res' is not attained, then communion in both kinds will be felt important, since the symbolism is no mere concession to human frailty or even some kind of optical illusion (as Guitmund would have it) but the one effective path to communion with the lifegiving source of salvation.

The theologians explaining away the bold words of *Ego Berengarius* did not escape uncriticized. About 1130 abbot Abbaudus entered vigorous protest:

If the Lord could bless, he could break; if we can offer his body, why cannot we break it? They say, But he is *integer* at the Father's right hand. Do they imagine that the apostle had forgotten that when writing I Cor. 10, 16? To deny that Christ's body on the altar is broken is bluntly to deny 'totam fidem tanti sacramenti'. He who denies the Lord's body is broken should be asked if he believes Christ's body is on the altar.[51]

Abbaudus shared Humbert's view that authentic faith will be uncompromising to the seductions of reason. He resented clever theologians diluting the ringing challenge of faith. One may wonder what he would have made of the Eucharistic treatise by the most eminent of those who systematically explain away Humbert's text, Innocent III.

Although he may have known of Gregory VII's formula of 1079, Innocent III never mentions it. In his book on 'The Sacred Mystery of the Altar'[52] written before his election to be pope, he deals only with the *Ego Berengarius* of 1059, not that of 1079. He unambiguously took it to condemn a merely symbolist understanding of Christ's presence, as if 'This is my Body' could be on a par with 'That rock was Christ', and as if 'est' could mean only 'significat'. (iv, 10). *Figura* may be a proper term for Old Testament sacrifice, but in the Eucharist we have *veritas*, and the believing communicant truly receives Christ. But let there be no idea that by daily consecration and daily reception the sum of Christ's body is being added to or diminished; nor that in the fraction or the bites of the faithful Christ's body is divided and lacerated. He is received complete and intact (iv, 7-8). For Innocent there are admitted problems for the intellect about the accidents surviving the cession of the underlying substance, and he does not try to solve them. But the belief in change of inner substance offers a way of averting the gross and physical crudity of the *Ego Berengarius*. It meets, in short, the religious demand for 'spiritualitas' (voiced by Berengar) and the equally religious revulsion from the 'crassness of the flesh' feared by Rupert of Deutz. For transubstantiation means that 'Christ passes from the mouth to the heart' and 'the food is not of the body but of the soul' (iv, 15).

Humbert's text achieved recognition from the canonists Ivo and Gratian, and surprisingly retains its place in Denzinger's

standard collection of authoritative Catholic documents. In consequence it has commonly been taken by those of more Protestant
sympathy to be an acknowledged statement of the grossness they
like to associate with transubstantiation.[53] There might be a touch
of paradox in the suggestion that the doctrine of a change of
metaphysical substance emerged out of the necessity to avert
Humbert's materialistic and naturalistic interpretations of Eucharistic change and reception, and that no popes contributed so much
towards a safeguarding of a truly spiritual Eucharistic belief as
Hildebrand and Innocent III—both popes who (because of their
excessive claims for papal monarchy) have commonly enjoyed a
distinguished place in Protestant demonology and myth. That,
however, is the most probable account.

The mass of medieval commentators on *Ego Berengarius* (1059)
explained it in terms that validated Berengar's objections. So it was
easy for John Wyclif to appeal to the confession as vindicating his
belief that the sacramental signs survive consecration. His appeal
enraged Thomas Netter, who stands almost alone among medieval
theologians in trying to defend Humbert's formula as meaning
almost what it says. Yet even he had to add a qualification. For
Netter the body of Christ is broken 'in its essence under the sacrament or through the medium of the sacrament'; and yet it is not
broken 'in its pure essence in itself' (*secundum se*).[54] Berengar
could no doubt have felt him to be using words without intelligible
meaning.

The least reserved of all defenders of *Ego Berengarius* turns
out to be, of all people, Martin Luther, whose defence of it was
militant. Luther would have no truck even with the anxious note in
the *glossa ordinaria* on Gratian, that 'Unless you understand
Berengar's words prudently (*sane*), you will fall into a heresy worse
than his.'[55] For Luther there must be no weasel words about double
manducation, of the body eating common bread while the thought
of Christ feeds the soul. 'There is only one body of Christ which
both mouth and heart eat, each in its own way.' The one gloss on
Ego Berengarius allowed by Luther is that believers do not receive
Christ in communion in the identical manner in which ordinary
food is consumed, but in faith.[56]

With the deep cleavage between Luther and Zwingli, Berengar's
Confession became a divisive issue between Reformers of the right
and those of the radical left. To Zwingli, Calvin, Peter Martyr and

his English disciple John Jewel,[57] Berengar ranked as a persecuted
hero resisting papal tyranny, forced by coercion into professing a
formula from which the true, offensive grossness of transubstantiation stands revealed to all the world, and was alined with
Waldensians and Wyclif as providing the radical protestant answer
to the question, Where was your Church before Luther? Among the
seventeenth-century Anglicans, however, more cautious estimates
appear, especially among the Laudians who rejected any notion
that the Eucharistic Presence is merely figurative and who asserted
change without seeing that to require the cessation of the natural
elements as sign.[58] Some among them were hesitant or negative at
the proposal to see in Berengar a liberal Anglican in advance of his
time.

   Berengar asked questions that have shown deep reluctance to
die. The perennial problems remain. At Laon about 1150 Zacharias
of Besançon observed that in the Catholic tradition many condemn
Berengar with the Church, but are quietly of the same opinion
as he. His observation is illustrated by a story in Caesarius of
Heisterbach of Peter, a learned canon of Cologne, who suddenly
came to realize that, despite the condemnation of the Church, for
years he had been unwittingly holding symbolist views of the
Eucharist.[59] But what was it to hold Berengarian opinions? To
Walter of St Victor the wish to gloss *Ego Berengarius* in such a way
as to deny that Christ's actual body can be broken and chewed in
the Eucharistic action was ipso facto to declare oneself to be
'another Berengar'.[60] He was writing perhaps a decade or two
before the future Innocent III would set out to canonize precisely
the ideas to which he most deeply objected. Walter of St Victor
represented that more tough-minded alternative which in effect
understood transubstantiation to be virtually indistinguishable
from impanation and which wished to affirm, without the least
qualification, that in the mystery of the Eucharist Christ is incarnate
in the bread and wine consecrated on the altar, broken at the
fraction, bitten in reception at communion.

   Transubstantiation was foreseen by Berengar to entail insoluble
logical problems (of which Alexander III and Innocent III were not
unaware, but for which they offered no alleviation). It had the
disadvantage of tying the formulation of an article of faith to
Aristotelian terminology and concepts; but no fairminded historian
could deny that the Chalcedonian definition of AD 451 had similarly

called in some terms of Neoplatonic logic to help its formulation, so the canonization of transubstantiation at the fourth Lateran Council of 1215 was not the first major occasion when the vocabulary of the philosophical schools was used. In the context of the twelfth-century post-Berengarian debates transubstantiation was a term offering a way of escape. On the one hand, it had the merit of affirming Christ's presence in the Eucharist to be more than a metaphorical or subjective way of speaking. Although Berengar would not have conceded that he intended no more than metaphor, he had certainly scared many into supposing that in the end his programme for the reform of Eucharistic theology by getting back to Augustine would mean this. On the other hand, transubstantiation met the necessity of explaining away Pope Nicholas II's *Ego Berengarius* of 1059. It went hand in hand with a quest for a via media between affirming the present *spiritualiter* and affirming it *corporaliter* or *sensualiter*, and encouraged the adverb *sacramentaliter*, thereby conveying the simultaneity of sign and *res*. To affirm that Christ's presence in the Eucharist is 'sacramental' was felt to offer a middle path between a representative symbolism and Humbert's too gross physicality. Transubstantiation was not actually a long way from Berengar's *conversio intelligibilis* and anxiety to safeguard *mysterium*.

Journal of Theological Studies, NS, Vol. 40, Pt. 2, October 1989

5

The Lambeth Quadrilateral in England

THE CHICAGO-LAMBETH QUADRILATERAL from its earliest beginnings played a significant part in the formation of Anglican policy toward ecumenism. The Lambeth Conference of 1888 saw it as supplying a basis on which approach may be made toward 'Home Reunion.' By Home Reunion the English bishops meant the reconciliation of Protestant Nonconformists to the ministry and liturgy of the Church of England, or, in other words, the old ideal of a 'national' church with essential marks of Catholic continuity but including all Christians in one Christian nation in allegiance to the Crown. The necessary condition was to acknowledge the royal ecclesiastical supremacy, formed under Henry VIII to scourge English Christians who did not feel sure of the Catholic orthodoxy of the Church of England if it broke communion with Rome as the historic safeguard, but then transformed under Elizabeth I into a force to prevent the Puritans from turning the Church of England into a radically Protestant body without bishops or priests, without the sign of the cross in baptism, without an ordinal hardly distinguishable at the crucial points from the Roman pontifical, without provision for private confession and absolution in its late medieval form (*Ego te absolvo* . . .).

Although many seventeenth-century Puritans in England were vehemently Erastian, vesting supremacy over the church in Parliament itself, the Independent tradition wanted a church free of secular ties, and naturally this had profound influence in America. Both in England and in America the Quadrilateral of 1886-88 seemed to offer a path toward peace and communion between English-speaking 'protestants'. The growing presence in America of a powerful Roman Catholic population imparted impetus to the dream of a united Protestant 'front'. In England the immigration of many Irish people meant that the same dream was dreamt there too. But there were other factors in the 1880s. Squabbles about the character of religious education to be allowed in church schools if they were subsidised (as they had to be to survive) by general taxation had been bitter and sharp only a few years previously. Could teachers in tax-supported church schools instruct children in the prayer book catechism, as Anglicans wished, or must religious instruction be limited to Bible stories, as the Protestant Non-conformists desired? The latter view prevailed, but the resentment survived into the twentieth century and played a central political role in the British general election of 1906. The acrimony of the debate gave impetus to the desire to end ecclesiastical rivalry.

The Quadrilateral stated minimum conditions for establishing even partial and imperfect communion, and stripped things down to that skeletal structure which perhaps a moderate Nonconformist might think possible as a basis for discussion. The bishops at Lambeth in 1888 may have included some Liberal Protestants, but among them were certainly many who believed ordination by a bishop in due succession to be a sacramental action, marriage to be indissoluble, confirmation (though not necessary to salvation) an edifying and apostolic rite, and absolution by a priest, entrusted with the power of the keys in his ordination, an assurance of which the laity ought not to be deprived. Nevertheless, the Quadrilateral affirms none of these things, but only the minimum. No one would quarrel with the proposition that the Bible is indispensable to the church; some Nonconformists did not much wish to tie themselves to the Apostles' and Nicene creeds, on the ground that they are ancient documents, and the notion that Christianity ought to have visible links with anything in antiquity other than Holy Scripture was not natural to them. Creeds looked to some Nonconformists like 'tradition', of which they were conditioned to be suspicious. However, the majority would not have dissented from the evident truth that, apart from the Nicene 'consubstantial', the two great classical creeds can be easily supported from Scripture. Biblical authority underpinned the affirmation of the necessity of baptism and Eucharist. The Quadrilateral offered no theological interpretation to explain the significance of these two sacraments, without which there might be the possibility of someone treating them almost as a fetish.

Similarly the clause concerning the episcopate does not ask anyone to believe that the succession in apostolic order is a requisite sign and instrument of unity and continuity in the community. It is asserted only that it is 'historic', a proposition standing beyond any possibility of refutation: the episcopal order has been around for a very long time, attested in the New Testament itself, and it would be a breach of decent order to be without it. This last phrase perhaps adds a little gloss on the wording of 1888, but every Nonconformist knew that this was indeed the position of Anglicanism from which it had never shifted. And in England the commemoration in 1862 of the exclusion in 1662 of ministers unwilling to accept episcopal ordination, even as a supplementary act just in case anything were felt to be lacking, had been an occasion for much anti-Anglican resentment. The Church of England had at an early stage felt some common bond with the Protestant churches of the European continent. But the Act of Parliament of 1662 was very un-Protestant. It required 'unfeigned assent and consent to all and everything' in *The Book of Common Prayer*, and made it an absolute condition of ministry in the Church of England that a minister must be episcopally ordained.

So the Chicago Quadrilateral seemed to offer the Church of England terms of reconciliation which dripped moderation, and could surely cause not the least sense of offence to Nonconformists anxious that their ministry was not being fully recognised. To the Anglicans of 1888 the Quadrilateral seemed to offer welcome help toward that ever-to-be-desired but endlessly elusive goal: comprehension within a national church in England and shared worship, including mutual recognition of both baptism and Eucharist.

The Quadrilateral had merit as an instrument for furthering the cause of comprehension, nationally or (within English-speaking churches) internationally. Though it said not a word of either appreciation or regret about the Reformation of the sixteenth century (and therefore could not altogether satisfy strongly Protestant groups, such as the Church of Scotland among others, which have tended to sacralise the Reformation), yet it asserted nothing that a Protestant of honest and good heart could not on the face of it accept. Therefore it offered the balm of reassurance to the many Nonconformists in Britain and America who had been distinctly alarmed by some of the negative evaluations of the Reformation that, since Hurrell Froude in the 1830s, had been articulated by followers of the Tractarians—by Tractarian laity at least as much as by clergy. People were accustomed to having Reformation texts, such as those reprinted in the still indispensable volumes of the Parker Society, edited by scholars who were enthusiasts for the Protestant cause. It was surprising and disturbing when one Tractarian priest at Oxford, Nicholas Pocock, began producing immensely learned editions of Reformation documents and sources, such as Gilbert Burnet's great *History* or the muniments of Henry VIII's divorce proceedings in the matter of Catherine of Aragon, despite the known fact that Pocock's sympathy for the Protestant cause was distinctly cool, and that his work destroyed Protestant myths. At a time when an increasing number of influential members of the Church of England seemed to be voicing misgiving about the sixteenth-century breach with Rome (though it was rare for them not to uphold the necessity of a vernacular liturgy, the error of imposing celibacy on the clergy by canon law, and the dominical authority for communion in both kinds), Protestant Nonconformists were astonished and, in a few cases, made to feel that perhaps even the 'establishment' of the Church of England under parliamentary authority, against which their principles rebelled, had practical merits in somehow keeping a bulwark against the gathering revival of Roman Catholic strength in British society.

Against this backcloth one can more easily understand why the Chicago text offered the Lambeth Conference of 1888 a programmatic formula that seemed to offer hope of ecumenical progress. Protestant Nonconformists, whose traditional opposition to the Church of England continued to rest on the well-founded suspicion that Anglicanism was not really a reformed church polity, could surely feel reassured to see the bishops of 1888 endorsing four articles which invited them to share communion with the bishops of the Anglican Communion at what was obviously a bargain-basement price. For here was not a word of baptismal regeneration, of eucharistic presence and offering, of priesthood and apostolic succession, of the catholicity of the one apostolic church to which the continuity of an episcopal ministry imparted visible and concrete form. With this programme they were being invited to accept only the external forms of catholic tradition in the shape of bare bones without catholic flesh and blood, without a theological statement of their traditional content, without much that was characteristic of, and to Nonconformists (as to some Anglican Evangelicals) objectionable in, *The Book of Common Prayer* and Ordinal.

It is inherent in the nature of any success attending a formula for ecumenical rapprochement that the proposed basis will contain nothing, or almost nothing, to which anyone can reasonably object. (It is instructive that a recent Protestant onslaught on ARCIC took the form of accusing its work of being 'theologically innocuous'.)

The Quadrilateral was minimal and therefore offered a bridge that might be crossed even by liberal Protestant theologians to whom liberty has always been far more highly prized than unity and individual freedom something never to be submitted to the authority of the community's collective mind. But was the text too minimal? In Britain at least, the Nonconformists were likely to feel that the Lambeth Conference was proposing an affectionate hug which was likely to turn into an uncomfortable squeeze under which they would feel robbed of breath. They were sharply aware, perhaps more so than many of the Anglicans, that the requirement of episcopal ordination could not easily be put on a par with an attachment to the Bible and the two sacraments of the gospel unless the episcopal succession also shared in those marks of authenticity in the church of Christ which Anglicans felt bound to regard as non-negotiable. To place bishops and baptism and Bible in parallel was to arouse fear that non-episcopal ministry was at best thought second-class, at worst null and void, and that by implication the episcopal ordering of the ministry was being regarded (in an ingeniously covert way) as possessing a right conferred by 'history' if not actually and literally by the apostles. The Anglicans seemed to be saying, or were readily heard as saying, that what has been given us by the development of the ancient church in the age when the apostles were passing from the scene is there by divine providence, virtually *iure divino*, and that it would be either a misfortune or, more culpably, carelessness to be without it.

The notion that episcopacy possessed a divine right comparable with that of the New Testament canon or the Apostles' creed presupposed an evaluation not so much of history as of the living tradition of the church. This could not come naturally to the mind of a Protestant reformed theologian, accustomed to thinking of the 'church' as a merely human institution in which authority is liable to be a polite name for naked power, and of the ordained ministry as a convenient human arrangement in which God played little part. To the radical Protestant mind the entire history of the church from the death of the last of the Twelve to the day when Martin Luther attacked the church door at Wittenberg with an antipapal hammer and ninety-five theses (if, as is now gravely doubted, that is what he did) was a sad story in which human error and superstition are more prominent than truth; in which none of the great thinkers and churchmen, not even St Augustine of Hippo, really

65

understood and proclaimed the glorious gospel of justification by faith alone; and in which 'the church of the pope and his bishops' was prefigured by the people of God in the Old Testament, denounced by the prophets for their ineradicable propensity for apostasy, not by the church built on the foundation of the apostles. The Protestants read the Epistle to the Galatians as a charter for rejecting a mingling of the gospel with 'ceremonies.' (The Epistle to the Ephesians made less comfortable reading.) The apostolic succession seemed to them a following of Annas and Caiaphas, priesthood a revival of Levitical ideas utterly abolished by the high priesthood of Christ (as proclaimed in the Epistle to the Hebrews), the mass an idolatrous travesty of the Lord's Supper infected with the rags not of Judaism but of paganism and magic, and the papacy the subject of those terrible warnings of the Apocalypse against the harlot of Babylon enthroned on the city with seven hills. To the hard-line Protestant the Church of England's preservation of bishops, its ordinal which for technical reasons might look dubious to a Roman Catholic canonist, but to a reformed theologian seemed to have a deplorably close resemblance to the Latin Pontifical, and the failure of the Thirty-Nine Articles to have the courage of the Westminster Confession in frankly labelling the papacy Antichrist, all created an atmosphere and a social tradition in which the episcopal order was almost as much a bogy as Roman Catholicism. Even to Nonconformists who did not wish to use lurid apocalyptic language about the Catholic tradition, episcopal church government seemed unattractively centralised. And the Independents thought it of the essence of the matter that the local congregation should be decentralised, free of direction from some distant bigwig of a bishop or indeed from the tight-knit Presbyterian system of Scotland and Geneva.

In the Britain of the 1880s the Church of England was not always popular. The high church ritualists bewildered and angered people accustomed to the simplest of ceremonial, and their very Gallican attitudes to the royal supremacy, given expression in Pusey's important book of 1850 at the crisis of the Gorham Judgment, were incomprehensible to old-fashioned Erastians like Archbishop Tait and many lay anticlericals. The Benthamites had little respect for old and venerable institutions and required secular utility as a criterion for survival. The quarrels about religious education in schools developed with a ferocity and resentment that in 1988 is hardly imaginable.

The Lambeth Conference of 1888 did not help the Quadrilateral along its ecumenical path by adding resolutions to explain or qualify the nature of the theology and ecclesiology underlying the four articles. The prominence of concern for the Old Catholics at the conference of 1897 may evidently reflect a deeper realisation of the truth that Anglican ecumenism could not hope for much success if it were constructed on the basis of liberal Protestant ecclesiology; and the committee of the 1908 conference roundly declared "there can be no fulfillment of the Divine purpose in any scheme of reunion which does not ultimately include the great Latin Church of the West, with which our history has been so closely associated in the past, and to which we are still bound by many ties of common faith and tradition"—remarkable words when one recalls the abrasive exchanges about the validity of Anglican orders eleven years before. The committee noted with encouragement the freer participation of Roman Catholic theologians into the general field of modern scholarship, the tendency of many non-Roman Catholics to look with sympathy to Rome as embodying a catholicity defective in sectional Christianity, and a growing interest on the part of Roman Catholic theologians in non-Roman theological work. On the other hand, they were well aware that no proposal for inter-communion with Rome could be entertained except on impossible conditions of total submission, and therefore concluded that the best hope for the present was mutual courtesy, combined with candour about the objectionable nature of Roman canon law regarding mixed marriages.

The Quadrilateral was given a new vitality by the movement in the American church which in 1910 issued in the World Conference on Questions of Faith and Order, and then by the Lambeth Conference of 1920 with its Appeal to all Christian People. In 1920 the Quadrilateral's fourth article on episcopacy was reworded to declare that the visible unity of the church required "a ministry acknowledged by every part of the Church as possessing not only the inward call of the Spirit but also the commission of Christ and the authority of the whole body." This was immediately followed by the words "May we not reasonably claim that the Episcopate is the one means of providing such a ministry?" The question introduces a paragraph illustrating the evident awareness of the bishops that their aspiration was to reconcile the non-episcopal churches rather than the divided episcopal bodies of Rome, Canterbury and the Orthodox churches. The appeal adds that "bishops and clergy of our Communion would willingly accept from these authorities (i.e. of other communions) a form of commission or recognition which would commend our ministry to their congregations. . . . It is our hope that the same motive (i.e. of attaining unity) would lead ministers who have not received it to accept a commission through episcopal ordination, as obtaining for them a ministry throughout the whole fellowship. In so acting no one of us could possibly be taken to repudiate his past ministry. . . . We do not ask that any one Communion should consent to be absorbed in another. We do ask that all should unite in a new and great endeavour to recover and to manifest to the world the unity of the Body of Christ for which He prayed."

The 1920 conference did not, however, approve of general intercommunion or exchange of pulpits, on the ground that the preface to the Anglican ordinal made episcopal ordination a prerequisite for the celebration of a Eucharist at which Anglicans could properly receive. Since the preface to the ordinal was in itself deeply objectionable to the Protestant Nonconformists, an invocation of its authority was bound to be felt as an offence against the spirit of the Appeal. Internal differences within the Anglican Communion are no doubt the prime reason for the weakness of the Appeal as also of the Quadrilateral which it takes up. The Lambeth Conference could not clothe the dry bones of the Quadrilateral with much flesh and blood without finding that it had lost some of its own brethren. The reader of the various reactions to the 1920 Appeal, very conveniently assembled by G. K. A. Bell in his *Documents on Christian Unity 1920-4* (Oxford 1924), cannot escape the deep impression that almost all the fundamental theological questions were formulated not by the Anglicans but in the various responses that the Appeal evoked from non-Anglican bodies. The report of the Federal Council of the Evangelical Free Churches of England of 22 May 1921 (Bell, no. 41) provided a welcome to the Appeal, tempered, however, by some basic Protestant concerns for the priority of the gospel to the church, for the recognition that any structure or organization that the church might have developed could only be secondary, for the acknowledgement of the direct charisms of the Spirit (rather than succession in a society founded in history by Jesus Christ) as the originating source of life in the church. The Nonconformist theologians correctly perceived that the commission or authorisation that their authorities were being invited to confer on Anglican clergy would differ in kind from episcopal ordination, and with infinite delicacy inquired why the Lambeth scheme gave such prominence to episcopal ordination when, in its Anglican form, the orders conferred are 'not accepted by the majority of Episcopalians' (i.e. by the Roman Catholic Church since the bull *Apostolicae Curae* of 1896). The Nonconformists were stating in a tactful sentence that they did not really want a Catholic ministry, but that, if ever they did, they would prefer to go to Rome for it. The Anglican halfway house was not attractive to them.

The Free Church Federal Council of England was in effect restating the abhorrence expressed by Puritan writers of the 1560s that the Church of England, as in process of being formed in the first decade of Queen Elizabeth I, was 'a miserable compound of popery and the gospel.' The Nonconformists found it incomprehensible that the authors of the warm and fraternal Appeal should in the next breath express disapproval of general intercommunion and exchange of pulpits. They were glad that the Anglicans recognised Nonconformists' ministry as 'real' and 'efficacious,' but only gradually came to ask the telling question whether this was a synonym for 'valid,' the very concept of a juridical validity being in principle alien to the charismatic mind.

In July 1923 at a joint conference with the Nonconformist divines held at Lambeth Palace, the representatives of the Church of England, all but one of whom were bishops, declared that they could not declare non-episcopal ministries to be 'invalid,' and that the very concept of validity was one they found unhelpful when they were dealing with an unquestionable spiritual reality. On the other hand, they immediately went on to say that even 'real ministries of Christ's Word and Sacraments' could be 'irregular or defective'; they did not regard the preface to the ordinal of 1662 as formulating no more than a local rule of discipline for the Church of England, but rather as enshrining a principle of order that Anglicans could not break without painful consequences both for relations with Rome and orthodoxy and for the internal coherence of the Anglican Communion. They envisaged the real possibility of an internal Anglican schism if the ordinal's requirement of episcopal ordination were to be set aside or made optional.

The text is a significant expression of the view that the Anglican Communion does not possess freedom to treat essential matters of order with any more liberty than could be applied to the doctrines of the creed or the use of the two sacraments of the gospel and the Bible.

The study of the documents produced in reaction to the 1920 Lambeth Appeal illustrates the deadlock that resulted in part from the jejune theological content of the Quadrilateral. The courtesy which the Lambeth Conference of 1908 regarded as the effective limit of realistic hopes for conversations with Rome turned out to be also the limit attained in Anglican conversations in England with the non-episcopal churches. Attention began to move elsewhere. The Malines conversations, unofficial as they were and an immense distance from reaching anything that could be called an agreed statement, at least showed that there were Roman Catholic theologians in Europe who did not think talking to well-informed Anglicans a waste of time. It is extraordinary now to realise what alarm bells were rung by the revelation that the conversations were taking place at all. Until the late 1950s conversations continued on a cloak-and-dagger basis between Roman Catholic and Anglican theologians, meeting normally on the European continent under circumstances which were immune from the pursuit of journalists or fire-eating Protestants fearful of the Reformation being sold down the river. The Vatican and Lambeth always knew just what was going on, and who was talking to whom. But the sharp reactions of the mid-1920s imposed an extraordinary degree of caution. The record of Malines and of the private conversations afterwards shows that a little bridge was deliberately being kept open.

Then there was the Bonn Agreement of 1932-33 with the Old Catholic Churches of the Union of Utrecht. The text of that agreement was even more laconic and less theological than the Quadrilateral; but then it was not offered as basis for reunion with non-episcopal Protestant bodies, and a great deal could simply be taken for granted. The Bonn consensus statement was a notable step forward, though it omitted to say anything about the desirability of Old Catholic and Anglican bishops taking common counsel so as to avoid creating difficulties for one another or for their respective laity. It is to be noted that in a toughly Protestant publication by three Anglicans of 1977 (*Across the Divide*, by R. T. Beckwith,

G. E. Duffield, and J. I. Packer) the Bonn Agreement is regarded as the best of all possible models for establishing full communion, if consensus on essentials were to be reached with Rome or orthodoxy, the reason being that it safeguards the churches' freedom to differ on secondary matters.

The traumas of English discussions of the Quadrilateral in the early 1920s had long-term effects of a lasting kind upon the study of the questions raised by the reunion scheme in South India which eventually took the Anglicans there out of full communion with the see of Canterbury, and by that in North India and Pakistan, which was accepted by the Lambeth Conference of 1958 after important revision, though it was not until further changes had been made that full communion with Canterbury was achieved (1972). The thorny problems to be resolved were partly the consequence of having learnt the hard way that reconciliation requires serious theological work, and were partly inherent in the process of integrating ministries. It is impossible to bring together two ecclesial communities, one having bishops in apostolic succession, the other content perhaps to have bishops *provided that* no one thinks the succession to be of the least significance in imparting a sign and instrument of continuity and unity in the Christian community and in assuring the faithful of the authenticity and validity of the sacraments celebrated by the clergy who have received ordination within the communion. The proviso is one that can never be satisfied. Any number of protestations that the giving of episcopal ordination to ministers who have not previously received it can add nothing whatever to them other than a merely human recognition, and that if God is doing anything in such an act no one can know or have an inkling of what that might be, will always sound hollow to non-episcopal ministers who would not be non-episcopalians if they thought apostolic succession valuable and important.

In the 1960s the conversations between the Church of England and the English Methodists succeeded in clarifying many issues, but the consummation desired by Archbishop Michael Ramsey was defeated by a combination of forces among the Anglicans between those who were certain that God requires episcopal ordination and those who were certain that it is an irrelevance to the reality and quality of evangelical ministry. Neither party could contentedly accept a reconciliation of ministries which was in effect a conditional episcopal ordination with a most unusual condition, namely

71

that it did not say 'If you are not already validly ordained, then I now ordain you' but rather 'If God's will for his Church is that the episcopal succession be the safeguard of ordinations and of the sacraments, then this prayer and imposition of hands will provide whatever is lacking.' A reconciliation in this form could not avoid offending those who felt that it introduced uncertainty and hesitation in an area where they had none, either because they were certain that ordination by a bishop in due succession is needed or because they held the opposite opinion; and indeed, if militantly charismatic, they might take umbrage at the very notion that in the rite of ordination the Lord conferred any spiritual gift.

Behind the minimal formula of the Quadrilateral there lay a long Anglican history. In the seventeenth century a liberal Anglican divine like the famous Stillingfleet could defend episcopacy against Nonconformist attack by appealing to the authority of the magistrate: the upholding of the episcopal order fell within the royal supremacy, not merely as a sheer fact of what had taken place but as a proper exercise of the state's responsibility to uphold true religion. But Stillingfleet had not defended bishops as performing a necessary function in the church in respect of unity or sacramental authority or the preservation of true doctrine. By the late nineteenth century it could not sound plausible to anyone but the most dyed-in-the-wool Erastian to talk of bishops as deriving their authority from the Crown of England. The Crown in England might nominate. Medieval Catholic monarchs had done so, centuries before the time of Henry VIII. The head of state in France retains vestigial powers under the old Concordat even today; vestigial, because they are wisely exercised only after consultation with the Vatican. But to have a right of nomination is wholly different from claiming (as Henry VIII did) that bishops derive their right to exist, their power of order and of jurisdiction, from the secular power.

The emergence of the secular state, implemented in England by the parliamentary reforms of 1828-32, inevitably undermined the Erastian thesis.

Yet why did the Anglicans attach importance to bishops so as to make the order an indispensable condition for even imperfect communion? In the sixteenth century Richard Hooker (*EP* VII, v 10) could regard the institution of bishops as 'from heaven, even of God, the Holy Ghost was the author of it,' the form of church government that best agrees with Scripture (III, xi 16), and even

Wesley used the early Stillingfleet.

72

Whitgift could say the same in his controversy with Cartwright: episcopacy is 'an order placed by the Holy Spirit in the Church' (Parker Society, II, 405). The Puritans hated such language. For William Ames (admittedly a divine of such rigorous Calvinism and of so strong desire to change the Church of England that he had to make his home in the Netherlands) the episcopal order was one among a number of possible and equally valid ways of structuring the ministry. The form of ministry was to this strong Calvinist an adiaphoron. It was not prescribed in Scripture as the one proper form, though one could not say (as some Calvinists did) that the order must of itself obscure the lordship of Christ over his church. In short, the Puritans tended to claim citizenship rights in the Church of England provided that bishops were thought no more than a convenience. One could happily do without them if they became inconvenient. To claim that the episcopate is a matter of indifference to the continuity and unity of the church deprives the anti-episcopal dissenter of much of the ground for its objections to it. Only overheated brains become excited about matters of indifference. On the other hand, the contention equally invalidates the claim that the episcopate performs a necessary function in the continuing life of the Christian community which cannot really be carried out by a ministry resting for its authority on the charism of the local congregation.

The English Reformers of the sixteenth century had passed through various stages in their thinking about authority. At first they, or at any rate some of them, were attracted by the stark *sola scriptura* language of those who wished to rubbish the authority of the church in any form. But they soon found themselves reaffirming the authority of the church in its responsibility for forming the New Testament canon and in the great ecumenical councils of antiquity such as Nicaea and Chalcedon. They did not wish the Church of England to be infected by the anti-Trinitarians and Socinians and by some of the more hot-headed notions found among the Anabaptists. With Whitgift and especially with Hooker, they were under pressure to oppose the radical, exclusive biblicism of Puritanism. To affirm the authority of the ancient ecumenical councils was by evident implication to adopt a positive view of the bishops who participated in those councils, whatever troublesome faction may at times have attended those assemblies. It was in effect to affirm that not all the understanding of truth that God wills his people to know for their soul's health can be adequately safeguarded and transmitted if divine truth is thought to be *exclusively* contained in writing. The Scripture needs an expositor, a living community to proclaim the gospel contained in it, and the succession of expositors has also been that of the presidents of the eucharistic community.

The Quadrilateral states facts, and in relation to the episcopal order lays stress on the historicity of the fact. But this fact is also asserted to be a norm for life and unity because, for the Anglicans who first drafted the four articles, it seemed self-evident that the church of the patristic and medieval period was not lost in total darkness. It produced Anselm and Bernard and Thomas Aquinas, from whose pages Anglicans (especially in the sixteenth and seventeenth centuries perhaps) have drawn much illumination. The episcopal order is important, then, because to keep it as the guarantee of sacramental authenticity and due succession is also to make a statement about the continuity of the church in history. The Anglicans have normally been very ready to acknowledge the presence of grace and holiness among those who have not the same sense of the continuity of Christian history, of which the episcopate is the sign. But is it 'fundamental'? Hooker strongly denied that the church of Rome was mistaken in the fundamentals of the faith; it was the Roman superstructure towards which he was critical. William Laud much offended William Prynne by his statement that Rome had erred not *in fundamentalibus*, only *circa fundamentalibus*. Hooker expressed a characteristic Anglican conviction that the church is not merely the creation of individuals as they respond to the Word of God, but that prior entity through which the Word of God is mediated by God's merciful grace, making it possible for the individual to be authentically Christian.

In a word, the Quadrilateral would have been more telling if the Lambeth Conference of 1888 could have said more about its reasons for thinking the episcopate in apostolic succession one of the God-given norms. By leaving the matter as an unadorned fact they opened the road for the Nonconformist criticism that Anglicans seem to regard the episcopate as a fetish or amulet. It is no accident that theology has been far more prominent in recent Anglican ecumenism, that there has been full Evangelical participation in it, and that bishops are not treated as merely a historical accident.

6
Truth and Authority

'WHAT IS TRUTH? asked jesting Pilate, and stayed not for an answer.' Our reflections on the place of authority in the apprehension of religious truth must presuppose that in faith what is apprehended by the believer, or rather that which apprehends him, is truth—the truth that God gives to illuminate the nature and destiny of man. Yet truth is an elusive thing in any department of human life and inquiry, and in relation to the ground and mystery of our being it will not be easy to pin down. Christians believe that God was in Christ who is to us the way, truth, and life. Truth, therefore, is not just a matter of collecting a great number of particular statements that we discover to be the case. If Jesus Christ is the truth, he gives the cardinal clue to the meaning of human existence. To confess one's faith in him is also to affirm that in him there is given to us that which we could not have found for ourselves, and something is done for us which we could not do for ourselves. The confession Jesus is Lord is the heart of the Christian faith.

When we accept something on authority, we are accepting it from outside ourselves. Authority is therefore a word easily contrasted with three aspects of what human beings naturally do for themselves. First, we contrast authority with reason; that is, with a process of inference and argument leading to a conclusion which we have thought through, using methods and assumptions that conform to our inferences and arguments in more familiar areas. Secondly, we contrast authority with the judgment of the individual conscience; that is, we set our personal and private sense of a moral imperative over against the pressures of surrounding society. Here authority often represents the claim of the community upon the individual; and there are moments when the individual feels that the community is pushing him around so that he must make a stand against it. Thirdly, we contrast authority with personal experience and feeling. Here tension arises when authority seems to prescribe assent to propositions which seem at variance with what you as an individual feel. In this case again authority comes to look like a source not of liberation but of constriction. In each of these three cases—reasoning, moral judgment, and innermost feeling, authority can be in tension with the freedom of the individual.

On the other hand, none of us enjoys the freedom to do as he pleases. The world would be an insufferable place to live in if we were to do so. Each of us would then need his own private world, the rules of which were bent to conform to one's private convenience or advantage. But it is no accident that human beings fear anarchy even more than they fear tyranny, and those who want to introduce tyranny often set about it by first trying to generate anarchy as the condition most likely to bring about the end they seek. Football would not be a good game if played without rules, touchlines, or referee and linesmen to give decisions.

None of us is as self-determining and autonomous as we would like to think. All manner of personal influences and social pressures impinge upon us, often in ways we positively welcome. Personal influence is an obvious form of authority. Taking some hero as a moral ideal is a recognition of authority. A sense of loyalty towards, and pride in, the institution one serves is also an acknowledgement of something greater than and external to oneself. We are glad of that 'greater than'. In religion authority stands for that response of loyalty to our Master and to the community of his disciples, the Church.

In the first Epistle to the Corinthians the apostle Paul speaks of the Church as the body of Christ, indeed as being Christ himself, with all its diversity of members still constituting a single body. The eye cannot say to the foot, I have no need of you. In the Church we need one another. Separation from one another is an injury to the body. The earliest Church is an ordered society focussed upon the one glorious Lord through whose Word and sacraments its life is sustained. To ensure the pastoral care of the people the Church knows that a ministry of oversight is given. It does not invent its ministry but receives it as God's gift. The functions initially performed by mobile apostles, evangelists, and teachers continue in the resident, permanent pastors of the congregations, bishops, presbyters, and deacons. A special responsibility is understood by the ancient Church to lie upon the shoulders of bishops presiding over their local dioceses. Once the mission moved out into the pagan world of Gentile polytheism, the authentically Christian character of what was being taught in the churches came under immediate threat from gnostic theosophy. Strong centrifugal forces threatened disruption and division. Out of this crisis emerge the principles of emphatic adherence to the succession of authorized teachers presiding over the churches, to the apostolic writings read in the community's worship side by side with the ancient prophets of the Old Testament, and to the rule of faith formulated in the baptismal creed. By the end of the second century the Church had largely established a fixed list of apostolic writings of the new covenant, that is the New Testament canon; and that process of canonization implies that the Church is not in itself a simply self-sufficient body able to decide in controversies of faith without reference to its primary sources and records. Its foundation documents retain a constitutive role as a witness to the apostolic testimony. Scripture is the principal written, publicly accessible part of the sacred tradition of the community. To believe in the Holy Spirit speaking to his people through Holy Scripture is simultaneously to confess belief in the Holy Spirit through Holy Church, and vice versa.

We are thus brought to our first proposition concerning Truth and Authority in the Christian society: Holy Scripture is where we find the faith of the Church written down, declared by the community to be a criterion and standard of authenticity in teaching; and because it represents the apostolic witness to Christ, it occupies a position to which no other norm of authority within the Church aspires.

But of course we at once need the guidance of the community in the understanding of Scripture, or we shall quickly become ranters. The Church has never believed that bishops have, by virtue of the gifts of the Spirit in their ordination and consecration, a hot line to heaven. But by the end of the second century the bishops found that they needed to meet regularly in synod for the mutual encouragement of each other, and for reaching decisions on diversities of discipline and of faith. Initially, however, their discussions concern such matters as the date of Easter and rules of procedure for the pastoral care of those who are blown off course in marriage, or in compromise with paganism. In gatherings of bishops in council the individual bishop represents his people. With the large council assembled by Constantine the Great at Nicaea in 325 there begins the series of councils which sought to transcend local and regional boundaries, and tried to express the faith of both East and West in a common confession of faith. Through the ancient ecumenical councils the Church said No to the assertion that the Son of God is not identical in being with the Father; or that our

77

Lord's body was not formed in his mother Mary but brought with him from heaven; or that the divine and human are so loosely conjoined in Christ that it is only in a Pickwickian sense that we can speak of him as one person. These and other such verdicts have become taken for granted as irreversible, as having permanently and lastingly deflected the course of the river.

Councils, even very numerous councils, are not problem-free. All assemblies of numerous high-minded people are vulnerable to faction; and you do not hold a large council unless there are weighty matters to resolve. In time of dissension councils are painful experiences, and if the decisions are not universally accepted you may have a schism resulting. The Church of England has accepted as authoritative the decisions of the ancient ecumenical councils concerning the doctrines of the Trinity and the Person of Christ. These councils said No to what is erroneous; that is, to what is seen by the tradition of the community to be not consonant with Scripture, and appears to threaten some element of great importance in the Christian understanding of salvation. At the same time the Church of England has occupied wholly non-controversial ground in saying that the correctness of a council's decisions is not necessarily automatic. Even ecumenical councils may in some respects err, say the Thirty-Nine Articles; but it is an illusion to suppose that this is a Protestant proposition which would be denied by Roman Catholic theologians. No one has ever supposed that everything said or done in an ecumenical council is automatically free of error and binding on the consciences of loyal believers. There is also an indispensable process of reception by the faithful, which is not simply a matter of passive obedience but an active critical entering into the intention of the conciliar definition.

Obviously it would be absurd to say that the ultimate reception by the faithful is that which *first* confers authority on the decision of a council. If the council reached the right decision, then, we believe, the authenticity of its definition, even its preservation from any leading of the Church along mistaken paths, is given in the very act of defining; and the reception by the faithful is the recognition and sign that this is the case, and therefore that through which the rightness of the decision is known. The Holy Spirit who gives truth to the council gives the charism of recognition to his people. Their reception clarifies the definition.

I may seem to some of my hearers to be labouring a rather technical point. In fact it is precisely in this area of the proper understanding of reception that Roman Catholics and Anglicans have most frequently talked at cross-purposes. I hope and trust that in what I have said both Anglicans and Roman Catholics will be able to recognize their faith, and in time come to recognize it together.

However, let us not exaggerate the importance of councils. S. Augustine once turns on the Pelagians, who were asking for an ecumenical council to review their case, with the double-barrelled rejoinder, first that only very arrogant people could think their opinions of sufficient importance to justify the calling of a world-wide council, and secondly that the great majority of grave heresies have been so obviously heretical that the faithful have not needed a council to discuss them. There are some risks in the proposition (congenial to canon lawyers) that only matters expressly defined by authority are binding and the rest is a free-for-all.

In any event it is not always possible to convene a council, for political or other reasons. The Thirty-Nine Articles wisely remark that councils drawn from many nationalities are impracticable without the consent of governments—'without the will of Princes' and their immigration controls.

A council needs a president of acknowledged authority to make it work, and this brings me to the question of primacy. Primacy is hardly worth having if one is talking about a nominal figurehead with hardly a function to perform other than to grace a festive occasion. The Church expects a primate to give a lead; often, too often for his comfort, to be the court of last instance to which an awkward controversy may have to be referred; and from time to time, when there is division and debate, to articulate the convictions of the faithful on matters of essential faith or morals.

The practice of a centralized bureaucratic control is in no sense necessary to the notion of primatial authority; that is rather a matter of discipline and custom. But a real primacy must imply responsibility for some kind of jurisdiction and also a teaching authority in safeguarding the maintaining of truth in the Church. The essential proviso is that the authority of the primate must be seen to support and not to destroy that of the local bishop in his diocese; and that will be seen to be the case when the leaders of the Church are not regarded as separate from the body they lead. Then

79

the primate's jurisdiction and his teaching authority are within the body, not an external assertion of authority asking for unconditional obedience and blind assent. The decisions are those of the Church, not of an isolated individual, even though the Church's verdict may be voiced by a single voice and not by a committee.

Religious belief takes in a very wide diversity of expression. Modern Biblical studies have brought out the rich diversity of theology comprehended within the one communion of the New Testament Church. An examination of all creeds and confessions of faith will quickly show how the most important of them not only give a verdict but also allow the legitimate options to be kept open. The role of authority in the Church is often not simply to say No to deviation (Here, not there; This, not that), but also to assert and safeguard the legitimate freedom of a position which may be under fire. The definition of the Council of Chalcedon, the fourth ecumenical council, in the year 451 is a case in point, familiar to undergraduate students of the subject. In other words, the role of authority in maintaining the Church in the truth ought not to be, and, when working properly, is not, an instrument for constraint which narrows the stream. Its calling is to hold together something rich, full, and universal.

The Lord of the Church has promised to be ever with his people, that the gates of hell would not prevail against it, and that the Spirit will guide his disciples in all truth. Yet the Church the world sees may look less exciting: claiming to present an unchanging truth, but sometimes seeming all too flexible to compromise with the secular; claiming to lift men's eyes to spiritual things, but seemingly concerned to the point of obsession with the cost of keeping the roof on and the new organ built, with social status and power, with capturing good seats in the theatre of life. There is a powerful stream of Biblical exegesis in both the Catholic and the Protestant traditions which sees the Church as continuous with the ancient people of God in the Old Testament. They were continually being denounced by the prophets for their extraordinary genius not for religion and truth but for apostasy, always needing to be drastically recalled to the right paths. It is not easy to maintain that the Church cannot get things wrong, even in pretty important matters. It is a saddening fact (but one we have no right to forget) that for some centuries in the late Middle Ages and into the Reformation period Christians (both Catholic and Protestant) could think it right, indeed a duty, to inflict burning on heretics: a belief in extraordinary contrast with the earlier age of the Church Fathers for whom any form of capital punishment was in principle unacceptable. Let us say candidly that mistakes of considerable gravity can be made, especially if some security in the community is felt to be threatened. Men who are frightened can long persist in a paralysis of their rational judgment.

Yet when all has been said, to be a Christian believer is sooner or later to make the affirmation of faith that, because of God's faithfulness, the true gospel will not cease to be found upon the earth, the Church will not succumb to exhaustion, and so cease to be. Only, the Church is continually needing purification under the Word of God. An essential part of the proper role of authority in the Church is to seek to encourage every possible means of that purification.

The power to bind and loose is entrusted not to Peter alone or in isolation but to the whole Church in which Peter is the rock-apostle and of which he speaks as representative. (I adapt a sentence from S. Augustine's commentary on S. John, 50 : 12.) I must speak as a presbyter in communion with the see of Canterbury and say that there are two points that seem especially necessary qualifications to claims that have been made in the past for the see of Rome: the first is that if authority is thought to be concentrated in one man above all else, difficulties will be felt because of the limitations inherent in a single individual's background, nationality, and culture. His office is to be a service to the universal Church; but it is hard for him to become a universal man. The second qualification is closely related. It is not in dispute between Roman Catholics and Anglicans that the Church may and must judge in controversies of faith, and that its judgment must be consonant with Scripture. It is not in dispute also that at moments of crisis authority is, we believe, assisted by the Spirit and protected from leading the Church into serious and irremediable error. For it inheres in our faith in the faithfulness of God that the Church will not be irrevocably committed to error in an essential matter of the faith. But Anglicans do not wish to use language which suggests either that the Church possesses absolute truth in an absolute degree, or that a privilege of certainty in teaching so uniquely attaches to the office of the universal primate that truth is ensured in the Church just in so far as it obediently submits to centralized authoritative guidance from

81

Peter's see (and from its civil service in the curia). If (as we believe) the Church is corrected by the Spirit and prevented from departing from the truth, that is God's gift to the whole Church rather than to one particular office within the Church.

Although the points I have just mentioned are important to Anglicans, there is no implication that the words I have been using would be unacceptable to Roman Catholics today. Since the Second Vatican Council theologians have looked for the source of objective confidence first in the universal faith of the whole Church. Within this body faith is articulated and guided by a teaching office and authority which has its presiding focus in the Roman see, but whose authority is nevertheless secondary or subsidiary to the former.

Between Canterbury and Rome there are two particular areas where divergent conclusions have been reached, in part because of different ways of thinking about authority, and especially Biblical authority. One of these concerns the Blessed Virgin Mary. A glance at the calendar of festivals in the old English Prayer Book will show that Anglicans have enjoyed a rich tradition of honour to our Lord's mother. Besides owing our best hymns on the communion of saints to that great dissenter Richard Baxter, our congregations gladly sing that, in that company of saints, the bearer of the eternal Word is 'higher than the Cherubim, more glorious than the Seraphim'. We take it for granted that the mother of our incarnate Lord was prepared by divine grace for her indispensable role; that whatever be her glory in heaven, it will accord with the unique honour God gave her on earth; that in the Annunciation we see a model to the Church in faith, obedience and holiness. Because we think Holy Scripture's testimony a very important matter, we do not need to prescribe too exactly how these things are so. But we are not so perverse as to hold that the inner theological content of the two Roman Marian definitions is at variance with the general Biblical understanding of grace and salvation. We share the judgment of Roman Catholic theologians themselves that there are dangers if popular devotion transfers to Mary what is done for our redemption by our Lord's humanity. All are agreed that between God and man there is but one mediator, Jesus Christ.

The second area of differing style is the application of the principle of consonance with Scripture in the discussion of the admission of women to the presbyterate. Roman official statements have in part rested a negative verdict directly on New Testament texts, whose plain meaning is discouraging. Anglicans have put the question in another form, whether such admission of women is excluded by those general principles of ministry given in the sacred tradition of Scripture, particular texts being perhaps culturally conditioned by the assumptions of ancient society.

We are held apart partly by fear, partly by group rivalry. Anglicans fear too grandiloquent a statement of the authority given to the visible Church on earth, and dislike excessive, centralization in an ecclesiastical bureaucracy. Roman Catholics fear that, in Anglicanism, authority is all theory and talk, and no practice, with the consequence that we appear amorphous and inarticulate. The sixteenth century dream of incorporating every Englishman within the Church of England has had the consequence of making it more difficult to be precise in doctrine. Anglicans think Roman Catholics do not need quite so much firmness as they get, and that the distinction between unity and uniformity is crucial. But such attitudes cut across all boundaries. Group rivalry can be overcome only if we can learn to live together and grow together, if by God's grace we can be delivered from static immobilized positions, from the mud and blood of sixteenth century trench warfare. For we seek one communion of the Spirit in faith, hope, and love which is realized in shared sacramental forms. Problems such as orders are rooted in group rivalry, and could be solved if we could learn to grow together as brothers.

In this lecture I have in a word tried to submit that, provided the questions are correctly stated, there is nothing in the nexus of truth and authority that must necessarily keep us apart, that must prevent honest believers from seeking convergence in Christ.

7

Full Communion with other Episcopal Churches

[1981]

1. 'Full Communion' normally means a relationship between two distinct and autonomous ecclesial communities, generally located in different geographical areas, of such a nature that

a) each communion recognizes the catholicity and independence of the other and maintains its own, and each believes the other to hold the essentials of the Christian faith;

b) subject to letters of recommendation or such other safeguards as local discipline may properly require, members of the one ecclesial body may receive the sacraments of the other;

c) bishops of the one church may take part, if invited, in the consecration of bishops of the other;

d) subject to provincial canon and episcopal licence, a bishop, presbyter, or deacon of one ecclesial body may exercise liturgical functions in a congregation of the other body if invited to do so. (In such cases commendatory letters from the home diocese and metropolitan would be expected as customary in case of doubt, and visiting clergy are not understood to possess rights in respect of liturgical functions.[1] On the other hand, it is also normal for such an invitation to be given.)

If the full communion established on these understandings is to be fruitful for the churches concerned, and not only for individuals on their travels, then it is also a desirable addition and complement that

e) there should be recognized organs of consultation with a view to common action, both for mutual aid and also lest one body needlessly embarks on a course which causes embarrassment or pain to the sister church.

To be in communion with others is necessarily both an enhancing of the corporate strength of the churches in love, and also a restraining of individualism or subjectivism. But it inheres in the relationship of full communion that

i) the two bodies remain autonomous and fraternal, without elevation of the one to be judge of the other and without mutual insensitivity;

ii) the two bodies remain themselves without either being committed to every secondary feature of the traditions of the other, and without necessarily embarking on conversations directed towards establishing organic union. (Organic union would be appropriate and necessary if the ecclesial bodies already in full communion are, or come to be, immediately adjacent in the same geographical area and speak the same language, in which case they should seek to become a single visible fellowship and eschew the indulgence of parallel episcopal jurisdictions.)

2. The churches and provinces of the Anglican Communion are in simple unqualified communion with one another in the one, holy, catholic and apostolic church of Christ through the communion of the bishops of each province with the see of Canterbury. In this respect (not always in his juridical authority) the Archbishop of Canterbury exercises functions that can be described as 'patriarchal', inasmuch as the see's position as touchstone of communion transcends the boundaries of the province of which the Archbishop is metropolitan. In the 1860s this mutual relationship between churches of the Anglican Communion was usually described by the word 'intercommunion'. But by the end of the nineteenth century this last term was undergoing a modification of its meaning, and was coming to be employed of the possible future relationship between the Anglican Communion and churches which do not look to the see of Canterbury as their centre or touchstone of fellowship and sacramental sharing. Today we would simply use the unadorned noun 'communion' to describe the mutual relations of the various churches and provinces of the Anglican Communion with one another and with the see of Canterbury.

3. At the present time (1980) full communion exists between churches of the Anglican Communion and the Old Catholics, the Polish National Catholic Church, USA, the Philippine Independent Church, the Spanish Reformed Episcopal Church, the Lusitanian Church, the United Churches of North India, South India, Pakistan and Bangladesh, and the Mar Thoma Syrian Church. However, with the acceptance of the application by the Lusitanian Church and the Spanish Reformed Episcopal Church for full integration into the Anglican Communion, these churches will cease to be distinct and independent bodies and it will now be more correct to

speak of them as being 'in communion' rather than in full communion with the see of Canterbury and the Anglican Communion.

4. Full communion implies the distinctness of the ecclesial bodies which enter into this relationship. On the other hand, the relationship is much closer than that implied by the ambiguous term 'intercommunion'.[2] Today intercommunion is often found to be a word capable of generating misunderstandings, and proposals to establish it can have the reverse effect to that intended. In many contexts (not all) the word now signifies an authorized or unauthorized freedom of eucharistic sharing, apart from serious intention to seek either organic union or full communion, and in an explicit or implicit disregard of doctrinal differences which exist or are widely believed to exist between the ecclesial bodies concerned. Those who advocate it normally hold that if the unity of all baptized believers in Christ is already something given—not a goal to be striven for by strenuous ecumenical negotiation between the separate institutional forms within which and under which the true invisible church of Christ lies hidden—then the eucharist is a divinely given means of making this already given unity more visible. This understanding of the theology of intercommunion presupposes that doctrinal differences between ecclesial bodies are not at the level of faith, but rather at that of school theological tradition, and can be disregarded. It also assumes that the quest for either organic or full communion by seeking to express e.g. common eucharistic faith, is misguided from the start and begins from mistaken premises.

5. The acceptance of very precise formulae concerning the eucharistic action is not a prerequisite for full communion or intercommunion, and thus far this position is non-controversial. But there are other respects in which the position described provokes vigorous dissent. It runs the minor risk of encouraging the celebration of the eucharist as primarily an expression of mutual good will; that is, as more a sign of the love that Christians ought to have among themselves one to another, than an explicit sacrament of our redemption in which those who rightly receive in faith truly partake of the body and blood of Christ.[3] It runs the major risk of implying that the Lord's intention for his church is to have a large number of diverse ecclesial bodies, all of which are equally valid or

invalid expressions of his will for his people, with the consequence that the painful realities of division and group rivalry are ignored or condoned. In other words, this theology of intercommunion, which begins with a powerful, well-based proposition that the church of Christ must be one, and goes on to offer an attractively short cut to the desired destination, can end by merely adding to the causes of divisiveness. For to many this theology presupposes a relativistic or sceptical doctrine that Christ's holy catholic church subsists in a multitude of churchly groups, all equally right or equally wrong, none of which mirrors or approximates to the intended form of the unique apostolic community. It is therefore asking Orthodox and Catholic minds to purge themselves of precisely the theme which the ecumenical movement most looks to them to affirm, namely, that unity is of the very esse of the church, and that the catholic ordering of ministry and sacraments is a providential instrument to this end. If this analysis is correct, we need look no further to find an explanation why some past proposals for intercommunion, without more ado or by a stated date, have turned out to offer a singularly ineffective road towards the establishment of communion and fellowship in the sacrament of our redemption.

6. The Anglican Communion has profoundly valued the visible continuity of the ministry, a continuity which receives classical affirmation in the preface to the Ordinal of 1661. Without passing negative judgement on non-episcopal ministries (whose spiritual reality and effectiveness may be positively affirmed as God's remedy for the shortcomings of the historic order), the Anglican tradition has consistently prized the preservation of the links in the historic chain which makes the episcopate the sign and instrument of unity and universality in the church. This ministry, with its apostolic commission, is seen as a divinely appointed organ which acts in relation to the whole body in Christ's name, and which represents the priestly service of the whole body in its common worship. To propose full communion with ecclesial bodies which do not wish to share this ministry, would therefore be felt to threaten a principle and a practice of some importance in Anglican history and theology. For the bishop is a focus of the unity of the church by virtue of his commission, and acute problems arise if the celebrant at the eucharist is not, and does not wish to be, a member of the body which, through the bishop, and through the celebration

of the eucharist, is expressing its visible unity in faith and life with the whole church. This point should not be represented as if episcopacy is the article of faith by which the church stands or falls, or as if it is the only possible instrument of unity; still less an infallible guarantee against the incidence of schism. The claim is not being made that the episcopate is of the being of the church in the sense that it is constitutive in the same way and on the same plane as the sacraments of baptism or eucharist or the true proclamation of God's Word. But unity and universality are of the church's very being. God intends pastoral care for his people in truth, unity, mission, and holiness. And the episcopal ministry in due succession and apostolic commission is the immemorial tradition of the catholic church, through which we accept as self-evident the authorized ministry of word and sacrament in the communion of faith, and therefore is also a providential instrument of the true marks of the church as a visible society in history.

7. If the whole church of Christ were one, communion would not need to be qualified by any adjective. We would not need to speak of communion as full or partial, perfect or imperfect, or inter- or any other qualification or prefix. The ancient churches enjoyed simple communion with one another in a single fellowship of faith, bound together by the churches of apostolic foundation, and those who passed outside this fellowship were held to be in schism from the unique orthodox catholic church with its ordered succession of ministry. At the present time this understanding of communion retains prominent advocates, especially among Orthodox theologians. With its roots in the conviction that the universal church is primarily a fellowship of local churches (i.e. the dioceses under their bishops) gathered in eucharistic communion with one another, this is an understanding of universal communion which is deeply congenial to the Anglican tradition, and there is a living heritage here from the early church which remains full of power. The eucharist has an eminent place among the constitutive elements of the church. It is natural to Anglicans to see the Eucharist (on the ground that it is the memorial in which the benefits of Christ's passion are made actual to believing communicants and for the whole church, and at the same time the true gift of the very presence of Christ on whom we feed in our hearts by faith) as the effective sign of the one body in Christ in the unity of the church, and there-

fore an anticipation of the ultimate triumph of the glory of God. To refuse or to withdraw from participation in the sacrament, through which the unity of the church is effected as a concrete reality, is an exquisitely painful denial of everything we understand to be the Lord's intention for his people.

8. Nevertheless Christendom is divided, and epithets and prefixes and qualifications to communion are found necessary. Roman Catholic theologians have found it necessary to distinguish between perfect and imperfect communion, the latter term being applied to the relations between Rome and Orthodoxy. Between Roman Catholicism and Orthodoxy, described as 'sister churches' in the Joint Declaration of Pope Paul VI and the Oecumenical Patriarch Athenagoras on 28 October 1967, there is at present no full communion established. These two great bodies recognize without reservation the enormous extent of their common beliefs, together with the validity of each other's ministry and sacraments. There is no questioning of the authentic succession or of the shared nature of the eucharistic faith of these churches. In certain limited circumstances, the Roman Catholic Church and the Orthodox Churches are able to exercise 'economy' and to allow the controlled admission to eucharistic communion of individuals of the other body when distant from their own priests. (Individual Anglicans have been similarly granted the sacraments by both bodies.) Yet a barrier is felt to hinder the practice which Anglicans are accustomed to call 'reciprocal intercommunion'; that is, the occasional and reciprocal sharing in the eucharist by members of churches which are seeking perfect or full communion with one another. For this is a corporate action by churches, going beyond the pastoral care of isolated individuals. And the reason for this sense of a barrier should merit respect: it is still felt on both sides that there is not as yet a genuine unity of understanding in regard to the status of the *Filioque*, which the West added to the Nicene-Constantinopolitan Creed, or of the Roman Catholic faith in the universal primatial jurisdiction of the Roman see as defined by Vatican I in 1870.

9. Between the Anglican Communion and the Orthodox churches the bonds are deep and powerful. Works of Orthodox spirituality are widely and gratefully studied by many Anglicans. Both bodies share the concept of the universal church as subsisting in the

eucharistic communion of the several local churches through their bishops. It is natural there should be a strong impulse towards the quest for full communion. The Orthodox churches have expressed vigorous regret at the decision of some Anglican provinces to admit women to the priesthood, and it is to be expected that, if a concordat of communion were to be achieved, Anglican women priests would certainly not be permitted to exercise liturgical functions in Orthodox churches (as of course they are already not allowed to do in some provinces of the Anglican Communion, this tolerance of diversity of custom being an effective condition required by the Lambeth Conference of 1978). Furthermore, the Orthodox churches would evidently wish to see the churches of the Anglican Communion proceeding more forcibly towards the omission of the offending *Filioque* from the creed. Its omission at the enthronement of Archbishop Runcie in March 1980 may be taken as programmatic. The doctrine contained in the *Filioque* is ancient tradition in the theology of the Latin West, found already in Hilary and Ambrose and therefore antedating the creed of the council of Constantinople of 381, at which the West was not actually represented, though it later acknowledged the council to have ecumenical status. To affirm that the Spirit proceeds from the Father and the Son was felt by Augustine to be necessary to protect the doctrine of the unity of the holy Trinity from Arian attack. In the doctrine of the *Filioque*, the Latin West had nothing it needs to apologize for. But it was a medieval mistake unilaterally to insert it into the ecumenical creed used at the eucharist.

Note should be taken of the fact that the Orthodox churches were at least in some degree surprised when the ARCIC Venice statement on authority appeared, in which responsible Anglican theologians expressed willingness to envisage a universal primacy in the see of Rome (autocracy set aside), nothing having been said of this by the Anglican theologians participating in the Anglican/ Orthodox conversations at the time of the Moscow declaration and statement. Orthodox antipathy to papal claims is usually deeper, and more eloquently expressed, than that of Anglicans of strongly Protestant sympathies.

10. Between the Anglican Communion and the Roman Catholic Church, steps towards full communion may be very difficult, but are at least much easier to consider than a move towards intercom-

munion, a term which Roman Catholics commonly understand to imply indifferentism. Inasmuch as full communion presupposes a continuing distinctness of identity and tradition within the ecclesial bodies concerned, the principle is not obviously alien to Roman Catholic thinking: it has an evident analogy to uniat status, under which ecclesial bodies may be united with the communion of the Church of St Peter and St Paul without being absorbed. The preservation of local and provincial autonomy, subject to the brotherly preservation of charity and mutual respect, is highly valued in the Anglican Communion. Central direction in matters of detail, that should be decided locally, would not be understood or welcomed. The formal decision of 1896 that Anglican Orders are null and void remains officially in force (with consequences recently renewed in vigour) and offers an insuperable barrier to corporate reconciliation, as at the time was avowedly intended by its principal promoters. Anglicans, who find themselves suspected on the Protestant side of being a diabolical conspiracy to undermine the sixteenth-century Reformation, find themselves regarded from the Roman Catholic side as a diabolical counterfeit for the real thing. Lying beyond the popular 'gut reaction' of non-rational instinctive hostility—largely confined to geographical areas where Roman Catholics and Anglicans work side by side sometimes (happily not always)[4] with the sense of being opposing camps with contrasting independent cultures, whose mutual coexistence is embittered by Roman Catholic rules concerning mixed marriages—there lies a substantial fear that, if Roman authority were to admit the validity of Anglican Orders, this might run the risk of strengthening a notion extremely unwelcome to Roman Catholics: namely, that the Anglican Communion is in will and deed an alternative and rival Catholicism which, because it has no central organ of control but works through a diffused authority and general consensus, is visibly less inhospitable to liberal humanist reinterpretations of divine revelation and to relativist ideas that in faith and morals nothing is too certain, and, in short, is open to compromise with modern paganism as authentic Catholicism is not. Anglicans will not be happy to recognize themselves under this description, but it is important for those negotiating with Roman Catholic authority to realize that this is how we can at times seem to appear. It may be predicted with reasonable confidence that Rome is unlikely to reconsider and to revoke the 1896 judgement on Anglican Orders if this single issue is to be considered as an item in isolation, even though the ARCIC Windsor and Canterbury statements on *Eucharist* and *Ministry*, with their subsequent *Elucidations*, are documents free of ambiguity, in which both Catholics and Anglicans recognize their faith and which therefore have, in passing, the unintended side-effect of destroying the central argument of *Apostolicae Curae* (1896), viz. that Roman Catholics and Anglicans are committed to essentially different beliefs about the eucharistic presence and sacrifice and consequently about the nature and office of ministerial priesthood. (*Apostolicae Curae* does not actually deny the preservation of the episcopal succession, Louis Duchesne's submission to the papal commission being decisively positive,[5] but treats this as an outward fact whose value is reduced to zero by a Protestant theology of ministry and sacraments.)

11. If the ground for reluctance to reopen the question of Anglican Orders is the fear of a rival Catholicism, the Anglican Communion through its central councils may well wish to explore ways of meeting this not unreasonable apprehension by asking Rome if, and on what terms, full communion may be made possible between the chair of St Peter and St Paul and the chair of St Augustine; or whether it is now scarcely realistic to hope and pray with Pope Paul VI (25 October 1970) that, without lessening the proper tradition of spirituality and piety characteristic of Anglican usage, the day may come when the Roman Catholic Church may be willing and able to embrace its 'beloved sister', the Anglican Communion, in the one authentic communion of the family of Christ. It should be possible to ascertain, informally, if and when and in what form the question could be acceptably and profitably put. But first, no doubt, it would be for the Anglican Communion, in the light of the reaction of its several provinces to the progress marked in the successive ARCIC statements,[6] to decide that it wants to explore this possibility. One thing seems certain: it will be misleading and lacking in integrity to hope for a recognition of Anglican Orders unless we also wish the Archbishop of Canterbury to be in full communion with the church where the apostles Peter and Paul taught and died.

8

Justification by Faith: a perspective

THE FOLLOWING paper was written at the command of the second
Anglican-RC Commission and is designed to try to trace a path
through a mass of material which can easily look like an impossible
jungle. Inevitably much has had to be left on one side, important
authors not mentioned, some issues relevant to the subject not considered. Nevertheless, I hope that by concentrating on the central
issues they may in some degree be clarified.

The structure of the paper, in numbered paragraphs, is as
follows:

1   Introduction: the issue at Trent in 1546
2-9   Luther
10   Luther's impact on Trent
11-12   Double Justice?
13-20   The final form of the decree of Trent on justification
21-31   Anglicanism
32-38   Concluding Reflections

1. When the Council of Trent began, on 21 June 1546, its six and a
half months of consideration of the doctrine of justification, the
second papal legate Marcello Cervini (a man of deep humanist
culture, later all too briefly Pope Marcellus II in memory of whom
Palestrina wrote a famous mass, and in the cool view of Paolo Sarpi
the only pope of the time to grasp that the Reformation was not a
revolt to overthrow Christianity) opened the debate by observing
the difficulty of the subject. It was not only intricate, but had not
previously been a matter of controversy. In dealing with the
authority and canon of scripture and with original sin, the fathers
of Trent had not had to think everything out from the beginning;
for there were precedents in rulings by earlier councils. But with
justification the Council was launched into open seas, drawing such
help as it could from the Catholic critics of Luther during the
previous twenty-five years. Cervini himself stated the question
before the Council to be 'how we may preserve the grace we received
in baptism and be justified before God' (Concilium Tridentinum
[= CT] V 257). He was followed by Cardinal Pole, the third legate,
also expressing apprehension of dangers ahead. A letter written by
Pole on 28 August (CT X 631) betrays his anxieties: the sense of

hostility and anger against the Lutherans, now in 1546 taking to arms against the Catholics in Germany, could produce a decree so unconciliatory to the Protestants that it might end by providing additional anti-Catholic ammunition for controversialists watching the Council for every slip. Pole feared that the drafters might wish to put so wide a distance between themselves and Luther that they would be unable even to admit language sanctioned by scripture because of a feeling that the Lutherans had appropriated it as their distinctive property. As for the fear of Luther, that was eloquently expressed on 17 June by an oration frankly identifying Luther with Lucifer as an angel of light and suggesting that Protestantism threatened the death of the Church of Europe in much the way that Islam had expelled it from Africa (CT V 249).

Luther

2. In seeing the issue of Justification as new and unprecedented, Cervini's judgment coincided with that of Luther himself. Luther's blinding vision of St Paul's meaning in Romans and Galatians convinced him that, with the partial exception of Augustine and sometimes Bernard, he was the first person to discern the authentic gospel.[1] This feeling may be partly explained by Luther's cool attitude to the schoolmen (to whom modern research has shown him to owe more than might easily appear), to the Nominalists, to the many commentators on the Sentences of Peter Lombard, to Thomas Aquinas. Bernard was at times congenial to Luther. But a great number of Luther's allusions to medieval predecessors show him both informed and unfriendly. He especially disliked Aquinas' discovery that Aristotle had said many things, particularly on ethics, which are either true or uncommonly plausible. Aquinas' acknowledgement of the independence of natural theology and the moral autonomy of man alarmed him even more than it had alarmed some of Aquinas' contemporaries. Among late medieval Augustinians like Bonaventure, a large debt to the writings of Aristotle is happily combined with expressions of caution. Some who felt that religion engages more than the logical faculty were ready to be critical. At the council of Florence the Greeks had complained that western theology was all Aristotle, not Peter, Paul, Basil, Gregory Nazianzen and Chrysostom (Syropoulos, p. 464 Laurent).

In his hostility to Aristotle Luther gives especially vehement form to an attitude that was not new with him. Luther's references to the schoolmen show that, while he did not think them invariably mistaken, he (more than Melanchthon) tended to begin with the assumption that medieval theologians were likely to be wrong, and if and when they had got it right, they must somehow have been conquered by the Holy Spirit against their will and natural instinct. Their grandest mistake Luther saw to be a failure to see that when scripture speaks of the justice of God, it does not mean distributive justice rewarding and condemning, 'giving each individual his due', but that righteousness of God 'by which he makes us just', *qua nos iustos facit*. This justifying act is by grace alone recognising no merit in what man does, and not even taking account of the moral qualities of a man's character. For all mankind is lost in original sin which, for Luther, is far from being abolished by baptism but remains a potent force within us and society until our dying day. Luther specially scorned the scholastic view, derived from Augustine's concessive clauses, that the sexual impulse in concupiscence is natural and, though all too liable to become a vehicle of sin, is not in itself sinful but implanted by the Creator. Talk of free will seemed to Luther unreal. In his tract 'On the Bondage of the Will' *(De servo arbitrio)* he takes over the many statements of Augustine which presuppose psychological determinism and sets aside the admittedly fewer qualifications in which Augustine protested, not always convincingly, that he had not abolished free will and moral responsibility. In 1525 in the controversy with Erasmus (for whose elegant liberal humanism he writes with crushing irony and contempt), Luther advances a full-blooded doctrine of the total incapacity of the human will to move itself in any degree towards the good, and therefore of man's absolute need for a sovereign and irresistible grace to which he can only surrender himself as clay in the hands of a potter. The human will is not perhaps a merely inanimate clod, but the best that can be said for man is that he is like a beast of burden: when God is riding it, it goes his way; when Satan is riding, it goes the other way; the two riders contend for the saddle. Admittedly, man has the illusion that in what he does he is acting freely; in reality our will is so mutable, never continuing in one stay, that any good is the product of the grace of the immutable will of God. Only this doctrine of the utter humiliation and abasement of man allows proper recognition of the all-powerful majesty of the Redeemer and Mediator. 'Those who assert free will simply deny Christ'. There is no such thing as a neutral mediating power in the soul called the freedom of the will. Salvation is therefore by a pre-cosmic divine decree of predestination, and, before the coming of healing and converting grace to the soul, man can only be purely passive and receptive. Therein lies the supernatural character of the gospel in casting down every human expectation and source of pride; for the natural man takes it for granted that he can and must do something. 'Human nature blinded by sin cannot conceive any justification except by works' (*Dispute on Justification*, 10 October 1536: WA 39/1, 82-126; transl. in *Works* 34, 1960). The surrender of faith issues in obedience and is accompanied by penitence or contrition; obedience, penitence, or contrition, are all 'necessary' but not in any causal sense something that brings salvation to us for they are human acts. To the awkward question, Is not faith a human act, a 'work', Luther replies that such language 'is tolerable but is not the usage of scripture. Good works are a necessary fruit of a tree that grace had made good, not necessary in the sense that they evoke grace or become a ground of eternal reward in heaven. Because sin continues in our nature till death, we are 'daily justified by un-merited forgiveness of sins and by the justification of God's mercy'.

3. Luther disowned responsibility for the abuses of this doctrine of grace at the hands of some of the more radical groups on the far left of the Reformation. But in the course of the sixteenth century a number of teachers appeared within the Lutheran camp whose doctrines sounded uncomfortably antinomian. It has always been easy for men imbued with the high excitement of feeling that they are participating in a new movement of the Spirit, to end in immorality: if the end is predetermined, why should the means be thought necessary? And why in the meanwhile should it matter if one lives in sin or in holiness, especially if the latter seems like the bondage of the law and a new dress for the monastic asceticism that Luther had mocked? The mature Luther came to feel some alarm before the dizzy consequences of speculation about the divine decree of predestination. It was bordering on *curiositas*, impertinently inquiring into matters God has not thought fit to reveal, and which he would no doubt have revealed had it been good for us to know. So Luther came to say we should not ask the reason why God gives irresistible grace to some, not to others, and be content to observe that scripture makes the fact certain. The fact belongs to revela-tion, the reasons lie hidden in the Deus Absconditus.

Luther's reason for reserve was pastoral. His stress on the all-important role of faith in receiving justification led him, and equally Melanchthon, to define justifying faith as trust, confident trust, *fiducia* and therefore to slide into the undoubtedly awkward position of saying (or at least seeming to most of his hearers to say) that one has justifying faith if one is utterly and unhesitatingly confident on the matter. The mark, indeed the very essence, of justifying faith is certitude, a confidence in the promises of God that his grace will bring one to heaven and a realisation that no 'work' on the part of man, whether external (fasting, alms, pilgrimage, etc.) or internal (hope or charity), can in any way be thought to be a condition or qualification for admission to eternal salvation. For salvation is the gift of sovereign grace on the ground of the merit of the redeeming work of Christ. Nevertheless, not all men receive this grace, and curious investigations of predestination tend not to enhance certitude but to undermine it. To tell the individual that lack of doubts is a sure sign of being one of the elect will sooner or later conflict with the common, perhaps virtually universal human experience of experiencing doubts and hesitations amplified by candid awareness of one's moral and spiritual inadequacies. God alone knows who the elect are; but the pastor has a problem on his hands if he has suggested that (at least so far as they themselves are concerned, if not others) the elect can somehow know too, and that if any do not feel sure on the point, that may indeed be a sign that they are not among the saved.

4. The shift to subjectivism was accelerated by Luther's ambivalent language about the sacraments as means of grace. One stream of language in Luther is emphatic about their 'necessity'; of the utter reality of the presence of Christ in, with and under the consecrated elements at the Eucharist (did he not write *Ein feste Burg* in 1527 as a battle-song against Satan's latest emissary in the form of Zwingli's eucharistic doctrine?); of their role as sign and witness in the divine purpose. But another stream is very hostile to the traditional scholastic doctrine, going back to the fathers, that the sacraments are efficacious means of grace to those who place no obstacle in God's way provided that what God commanded to be done in these covenant signs has in fact been done; that the sacraments have their validity, that is, *ex opere operato*, not because of the holiness or standing of the minister of the sacrament (which is Christ's sacra-

ment, not the minister's anyway). Both Luther and Melanchthon cordially dislike the notion of the *opus operatum*, which they have come to interpret to mean (a) that by its administration of the sacraments the Church interposes its own activities between the believer and his God, and (b) that there is no need for any act or response of faith on the part of the recipient (para. 30, below). In the case of infant baptism, Luther declared that in infants too there is a seed of faith, and that on this foundation there is a conditional gift of regeneration. Bellarmine thought this doctrine a major departure from Catholic tradition. Within the Lutheran tradition itself the doctrine did not pass without controversy and many divergent interpretations. The central problem in these controversies was whether the fruits of regeneration are shown by baptized persons, as they grow to maturity, in consequence of their exercise of free will, or whether in baptism God gives regeneration exclusively to the elect (Martin Bucer's opinion)—the call given to others being one they will not hear, and therefore becoming an additional ground for seeing unutterable justice in their rejection with the reprobate. The Calvinists felt that Luther and Melanchthon had sacrificed something of high importance when they spoke of the sacraments as signs and witnesses but not as instruments for the communication of grace. To Calvin, Luther's language was too inclined to the obsignatory view of sacramental action. At this point Calvin stood much closer than Luther to Trent.

5. Luther's exclusion of human works from the causes of justification found a biblical foundation in St Paul's language (a) that salvation is of grace, not of works, and (b) that, as in the case of Abraham (Romans 4 from Genesis), faith is 'reckoned' to be for righteousness. Luther interpreted these texts to mean that the sole ground of our salvation lies in the imputation to believers of the righteousness or merits of Christ and never in the good works that, on account of the merits of Christ and in union with him, the grace of God enables us to perform in this life. In his translation of Romans 3 : 28 Luther went so far as to interpolate the word 'only'. He strenuously and repeatedly denied that our eternal salvation is in any sense dependent on acts or intentions which result from the pouring of the Holy Spirit of divine love into the hearts of believers (so becoming one with their wills as to produce an imparted or

98

'inherent' righteousness by the formation of a habit, not merely by a jerky succession of unconnected acts of trust and aspiration).

6. A series of awkward questions was raised by this position, apart from the explosive, indeed volcanic force with which Luther proclaimed these things—in language of incomparable vigour charged with vehement paradox such as made even his sternest critics acknowledge the titanic and heroic power of this extraordinary man. Very sympathetic readers of Luther wished he had not spoken and written with so little consideration for the consequences.

7. The Lutheran definition of justifying faith as confident trust confuses faith with assurance which is one of its consequences, not the essence of faith itself. Moreover, assurance is an effect and consequence not only of faith but also of faith-and-love. It seems possible to speak with Luther of an absolute certitude as a trust in the immutable promises of God only if one has no awkward anxiety that human sinfulness, resistance to the divine grace, or even the Devil, may have the capacity to hinder in some way the full realisation of the divine purpose. As we have seen, Luther's language about predestination was soon discovered by its author to have a pastorally adverse effect, generating fearful scruples and even the sense of being in an endless whirlpool of agonising speculation about unknowable matters. Augustine believed perseverance to the end of life and at least final adherence to the Catholic Church to be among the essential signs of election (or at least a failure so to persevere to be one mark of being reprobate, a wolf in the sheep-fold). He did not believe that a baptized believer can be utterly certain of his salvation unless he is granted a special revelation (*City of God* 11, 12), an opinion given formal canonical status by Trent (VI canon 16). Augustine (*Ep.* 167, 15) had written to Jerome of the forgiveness we need for the imperfection of righteous works done by grace in this life. The Catholic tradition was against the stimulation of overscrupulous anxieties, and had long taught that a believer should think and act with the aid of grace and trust in the promises of God. 'On account of the uncertainty of the righteousness of our own deeds and the danger of vainglory, it is safer to rest our whole confidence exclusively upon the mercy and loving-kindness of God'. The sentence is not from Melanchthon but Bellarmine (*De Justif.* 5, 7). There was of course a rival Catholic

view, powerfully formulated by Vazquez (1549-1604), that such language might imply that good works are needless because, if no hope is to be placed in them, that will sooner or later end in antinomianism and loss to souls. Is it not certain on the authority of scripture that God will 'reward every man according to his works' (Romans 2 : 6, cf. 2 Corinthians 5 : 10)? To think that good works do not count defies both scriptural authority and all common reasoning about divine justice and fair dealing. Nevertheless in Stapleton, prince of Counter-reformation apologists, we find that no rightly instructed Catholic puts trust in his own merits: sins may supervene; none can be sure of his own justice; and he will seem to glory in himself rather than in the Lord. Stapleton is not explicit that a sinful element enters even into our righteous acts. That might seem close to Luther on man's incapacity to do good works under grace, with the inherent love poured in by the indwelling presence of the Holy Spirit, without discovering in himself some whimper of self-satisfaction—a pride which Luther abrasively dismisses as mortal sin! Even to admit an element of venial sin seemed to Trent worthy of anathema (VI canon 25). Luther made it impossible to speak of *good* works at all.

8. Further awkward questions arise from the *sola fide* formula. There is the difficulty that the epistle of St James 2 : 24 expressly denies that man is justified by faith alone, so that there is on the face of it a sharp tension between *sola fide* and recognition of the supreme authority of canonical scripture. But most adherents of *sola fide* have found ways round this obstacle, often by suggesting that Paul and James use 'faith' in different senses. The patristic tradition, especially in Augustine who is repetitious on the subject, understood justifying faith not to be bare assent, not a *fides informis* (defined by Peter Lombard, *Sent*. III 23, 5, as 'that unformed quality of faith by which a bad Christian believes everything a good one does') but a *fides caritate formata* in accordance with Galatians 5 : 6. In other words, justifying faith is not devoid of moral content, but merges, with no clear dividing lines, into hope and love and directs the soul towards righteousness. Moreover, the turning to God in faith is accompanied by a penitence which holds sin in odium, and such a penitence is also strong in ethical content. A faith into which both penitence and love enter is more than the total passivity of which some of Luther's utterances speak.

100

In St Paul the faith which is the (or an) instrumental cause of justification is contrasted not with love but with 'the works of the law'. There is a touch of defiance in Melanchthon's *Apology for the Augsburg Confession* when he determinedly classifies 'love' under the heading 'law', apparently without feeling that the paradoxical classification requires explanation and defence.

Between Protestant and Catholic there was no disagreement that works done before conversion, justification, and regeneration are indeed efficient causes (in the sense that through them the Holy Spirit *ab extra* prepares our hearts and minds), not meritorious causes (in the sense that the gift of justifying grace is made in reward of works done by pure free will without the assistance or illumination or pressure of divine grace). Everyone agreed on that. The disagreement began when Luther and the Protestants spoke of good works done *after* justification by divine grace, with the indwelling Spirit pouring love into the heart of the believer, as having no better standing before God than works done apart from grace *prior* to justification. The Protestants who spoke in this way were forced to interpret Philippians 3 : 7-9 as referring to works done subsequent to justification as well as prior to it, an interpretation which looked temerarious. It was deeply felt by the Protestants to be a basic principle that man, even justified man 'after faith' *(post fidem)*, can and should do nothing, no intention or act that might at any stage be thought to constitute a claim upon God for reward. The stress on the inwardness of faith in the mercy and grace of God as the sole acceptable motive for good works quickly produced a negative or at least a reserved attitude towards all external or visible religious exercises, such as fasting, alms-giving, or pilgrimage, or other ascetic acts of self-discipline. That was not new, for it was a commonplace of medieval Catholic moral theology that the ethical value of an action depends on its motive and circumstances. An apparently highly virtuous act when done for purposes of self-advertisement will not get one to heaven. And there can be extreme and very rare circumstances in which an act of which society normally and rightly disapproves can be done for motives so noble that the risk of scandal and obloquy actually add to the meritoriousness of the motives with which it is performed. In this stress on the inward roots of moral action within the soul the Protestants were not breaking with the Catholic tradition.

9. The Pauline term 'reckoned' or 'imputed' (Romans 4) led Luther to insist that the justified believer's good works, performed by inherent or imparted grace through the poured-in love of the Spirit in his heart, constitute no ground for eternal reward and form no condition of salvation. Salvation, he said, depends wholly and exclusively and necessarily upon the imputation to believers of the righteousness of Christ. This righteousness of Christ is 'outside' us, 'alien to us', and is therefore untainted by the self-satisfaction that haunts even our just works. In the course of the sixteenth century some Lutheran theologians went to extremes in stressing the purely forensic nature of the divine acquittal on the ground of Christ's merits, as a decree (like predestination) wholly independent of anything said, thought, or done by the incipient believer. The strongly impersonal language used by the advocates of the purely forensic view provoked reaction in the Protestants themselves, and the controversy was a contributory element in the sharp disputes among the different Lutheran schools in the second half of the sixteenth century.

It is not necessary to interpret 'imputed' in so drastic a sense, since the Greek word may mean in effect 'communicated' or 'attributed'. (Modern students of St Paul have perhaps learnt since Schweitzer that between the forensic language of justification and the language of participation equally prominent in Paul there is not, for the apostle, the dichotomy that older exegetes tended to find.) Moreover, it was already in the sixteenth century a major hurdle for the exclusively forensic interpretation on Romans and Galatians that there is a row of New Testament texts where 'justification' is used by the apostle in a sense implying renewal to new life, not merely a non-imputation of past sins. A substantial body of Protestant exegetes of good learning freely conceded that in scripture the verb 'justified' often means 'having the gift of righteousness communicated' to one. In other words, although the Protestants liked to schematise justification as distinct from sanctification, the apostle himself was less careful to observe the distinction (e.g. Romans 4 : 25 'raised for our justification'; 5 : 17 and 19; 8 : 30; 1 Corinthians 6 : 11; Titus 3 : 5-7). Curiously, it turned out to be easier for the Protestants to concede that in St Paul 'justification' often included what they wanted to distinguish as 'sanctification', than for Catholic controversalists to come to terms with the language of imputation. This contrast is not what one would expect.

Augustine (*de Pecc. Mer.* 1, 18) makes a sharp distinction: in sanctification believers imitate Christ, but the act whereby Christ justifies the ungodly is not for imitation. He alone can do this. Augustine also distinguishes the act of baptism giving remission of sins from the long daily process of renewal and growth under grace (e.g. *De Trin.* 14, 17, 23), in which the 'righteousness' of true saints is shown by their awareness of imperfection (*c.du.epp. Pelag.* 3, 19). But Augustine feared talk about 'imputation', at least after death (*c. Faustum* 33, 5). Might it make not only works but even faith itself less than necessary? In the seventeenth century Augustine's anxiety was shared by George Bull.

Luther's impact on Trent

10. One problem with the term 'imputation' for the Catholic theologians at Trent and afterwards was created by Protestant tendencies to interpret justification as wholly concerned with forgiveness, with the cancelling of the guilt and/or penalty of sin but not with the overthrow (or the creating of the possibility of the overthrow) of its present power. Trent had support in a number of texts from Augustine and Bernard to reinforce the doctrine that justification is more than the remission of sins but brings a gift of openness to the Spirit to make possible and indeed actual a life of righteousness and holiness. An Augustinian text (*City of God* 19, 27) concedes that 'in this life our righteousness consists more in the forgiveness of sins than in perfection of the virtues', a text that caused embarrassment to maintainers of the strong opinion that the justified believer's reward in heaven is given by a just Judge who rewards all goodness and justice in strict proportionality: i.e. from God we get exactly what we deserve, for good or ill.

But the Augustinian text cut no ice against the weaker and far more widely held view that the reward given by our just judge does not need to be utterly precise but can take a not ungenerous overall view and then give such reward as may seem reasonably fitting. Salvation, on the second view, is no matter of meticulous calculation of exact merit or determined credit in heaven, but allows an element of paternal love and mercy and (though Augustine was in two minds on this point if one were speaking of the Last Judgment) forgiveness for what is venial. To refuse hope of reward to a believer who had suffered much for the Gospel and served the Church in loyalty and self-sacrifice, even though he or she had made mistakes and perhaps stumbled gravely at times, would seem incongruous for God. Yet such a believer does not think to approach the Judgment with anything other than a cry for mercy; with an echo of the Canon of the Mass 'not weighing our merits but pardoning our offences'; with the psalmist's prayer 'Enter not into judgment with thy servant, O Lord, for in thy sight shall no man living be justified'. In short the strict doctrine of 'condign merit' (that is, the doctrine that divine justice is meted out in strict proportionality and without rough approximations) cannot make room for a doctrine that good believers, at the judgment at death or hereafter, should trust that they may be accepted on the ground of their Redeemer's merit: 'O Saviour of the world, who by thy cross and precious blood has redeemed us, save us and help us . . .' But the weaker doctrine of 'merit of congruity' (that is the doctrine that divine justice grants rewards which are not unfitting), is close to the idea that the baptized believer, who has faithfully served his Lord who 'is not unrighteous to forget his work and labour of love' (Heb 6 : 10) and has striven through bloody struggles to keep the right and good and his soul pure, nevertheless places no confidence in his works but rather in the purging love of the Redeemer and Mediator and the merit of his Saviour's Passion. So the wood, hay and stubble are burned away by the fire of the love of God.

Augustine himself anticipated the difficulty here, that a reliance on the imputed righteousness of Christ may be taken to weaken the believer's sense of resolve to fight the good but very tough fight of faith, and to make at least some Christians think 'it will all be right in the end' so that excessive strenuousness is not required. In Tridentine terms, the doctrine was at odds with the requirement of *satisfaction* of divine justice, as something required of the believer in his moral course and pilgrimage. The medieval penitential system spoke much of satisfactions (para. 14, below). 'Imputed justice' could be a threat to an entire way of thinking, and indeed Luther had drawn exactly that conclusion as he contemplated the way the penitential system operated. Moreover, the fathers at Trent had an additional source of worry. For the believer hereafter to trust wholly to God's mercy, not in any imaginable sense to the hope of heavenly reward for having preferred good to evil, also implied a question about *purgatory*.

In the later Middle Ages a rising volume of criticism of the doctrine of purgatory had been reaching the West from the

Orthodox East, to whom it sounded dangerously like Origenist universalism, and at the council of Florence (1438-45), as also earlier at Lyon (1274), there were exchanges on the subject. Admittedly the matter was not one on which the Latin West wished to say much beyond the statement that redeemed souls may be granted purification hereafter, and also that prayer for the departed, in accordance with very ancient Christian tradition (far more ancient than an accepted notion of purgatory), is not useless. Without denying the purification needed at death Luther was not persuaded that purgatory was evidently taught in 1 Corinthians 3 and his doubts about this exegesis (which Augustine shared, *City of God*, 21, 21, though well aware of the Platonic argument that divine punishment should be remedial in intention, 21, 13) came to be powerfully reinforced by his doctrine of justification through the imputed righteousness of Christ, and by his denial that the good works of the justified believer, though enacted by grace within and through him, have any bearing on his ultimate destiny. These considerations help to explain why the fathers in synod at Trent felt a certain paralysis on contemplating the notion of 'imputation'. To make any concession to the idea might make the Council an object of mockery (some felt): they would be accused of assembling to crush a heresy and of then accepting the heretics' cardinal thesis (CT V 535 and 542): 'Beware lest after the council the world groans to find itself Lutheran'.

Those at the Council who wanted the definition on justification to assist in bringing peace to Germany, as desired by the Council's prime mover, the emperor Charles V, were only a relatively small minority. Pole had to resign office as legate and leave Trent in the autumn of 1546 on the grounds of poor health, and his departure removed the most powerful figure to feel real sympathy with the Lutheran position on justification. The Spanish bishops and theologians manifested least sympathy for Luther. One bishop sharply observed that 'the Council should not be bland with heretics who have now vexed the Church for thirty years and have attacked Catholics with arms and war' (CT V 496, 10). In these circumstances the reader of the doctrine and canons on justification at the sixth session of the Council of Trent is likely to be astonished at the degree to which counsels of moderation prevailed.

Double justice?

11. At Trent, however, one possible route to convergence was not followed, despite its eloquent advocacy by the General of the Augustinians, Seripando. This convergence in justification was the doctrine of 'double justice'. That is to say: we may hope to get to heaven only if as baptized believers we strive for what is right and good, if we put ourselves in the way of attending to the means of grace, if we pray, study scripture, give alms, etc.: even the very best of our goodness is simply God's gift to us; for, as Augustine says (*Tr. in Joh.* 3, 10; *Sermo* 170, 10; *Ep.* 194, 19) 'when God crowns our merits he crowns his own gifts'. Moreover, because of human infirmity we have to confess that we have abused God's grace or failed to use it as we should; and therefore there is a large element of 'imperfection', to say the maximum in our favour. Before God's tribunal, therefore, we do not need only to bring the righteous works done by *inhering* grace poured in by the love of the Spirit, but also have to beg for mercy, for an *imputation* of the righteousness of Christ to supplement the incompleteness of that righteousness which is both Christ's and ours but which because it is also ours is less than his. In short, both inherent and imputed righteousness are required if we are to have a true hope of heaven.

12. This doctrine of 'double justice' is first attested in embryonic form in a sermon by Luther himself and printed in 1519, 'De duplici iustitia' (WA 2, 143-152), but the notion is only half-developed there. In a disputation of 1536 he makes another reference to the idea (WA 39, i, p. 93, 1-16), and is able to suggest that all 'iustitia operum' or works-righteousness will be imperfect, while perfect righteousness will be the 'perfecta imputativa iustitia' of Christ (WA 39, i, p. 241, 25 and 96, 6). The first theologian to see high possibilities in the idea was the Thomist canon of Cologne, Johann Gropper, who wrote in 1537 an *Enchiridion*, or handbook, to combat but also to conciliate moderate Lutherans. Possibly (it cannot be proved) he had read Luther's sermon of 1519. The notion was further taken up by another Catholic theologian Pighius, and soon succeeded in winning the advocacy of the influential Cardinal Contarini. Under Contarini at the colloquy between Catholic and Protestant theologians at Regensburg (Ratisbon) in 1541, the doctrine became the basis of an ecumenical agreed statement. An initial draft by Gropper, though rejected by Melanchthon,

constructed a notable article of Justification out of scripture and Augustine whose tract 'on the Spirit and the Letter' was known to be much admired by Luther. But the text was revised to meet the Protestants, incorporating a piece from Bucer's commentary on Romans and some excerpts from Melanchthon's 'Commonplaces'. Gropper's ecumenism greatly alarmed his militant colleague Eck. Though Bucer was willing to reach agreement, Melanchthon hung back, knowing that Luther distrusted the enterprise. Luther had already come to a confident judgment that the Papacy was Antichrist, and with the agents of such a personage one could hardly sup with too long a spoon. Eck's estimate of Luther was not much more cheerful. Luther characteristically expressed his apprehensions in the terse phrase that the negotiators were getting 'peace without God' (WA Br. 9, 350, 20). Contarini regarded the agreed article on justification as a triumph, though he soon found that the response of Catholic friends to whom he sent copies was less than enthusiastic. Above all, Pope Paul III and Luther were unanimous in thinking the agreement insufficient if the other side had not recanted their errors; so long as that was so, the agreement however acceptable as a set of affirmations must represent a false compromise. So even Contarini came to lose confidence that the agreement over which he had presided was any more than a clever compromise formula without real engagement of the heart and will to come together.

The collapse of the discussions followed quickly when it was realised that even if a path to convergence on justification had been found, the parties were far from agreement on eucharistic presence, on the priestliness of the Christian ministry, and on authority, matters to which much less attention had as yet been paid because justification by faith and the question of imputed righteousness had been assumed to be the crucial divisive issue, the root problem at the foundation of the entire Reformation debate. The Regensburg colloquy of 1541 is a classic illustration of a fearful truth for which Roman Catholic/Orthodox negotiations over a millennium provide plentiful examples, namely that an ecumenical agreement not only has to go deep in dogmatic matters but must also command the sustained heart and will of the parties to the conversation. If it does not do so, the parties end further apart, and rather angrier with each other, than they were before.

Two years after the Regensburg conversations of 1541, the personal friendship struck between Gropper and Bucer had cooled. When a second conference met at Regensburg in 1546, no progress at all was made towards prospects of reconciliation. The atmosphere of mutual regard and confidence had been dispelled. It was in this atmosphere in the same year 1546 that the fathers of Trent began their long debate on justification. The recent attempts at uncovering agreement had done little to encourage the council to think the road of 'double justice' might be viable. Seripando's indefatigable attempts to persuade the Council to write the doctrine into their formula met long speeches of opposition, especially from the Spanish Jesuit Laynez. Laynez contended that, though the life lived by the justified is imperfect, no guilt attaches to the imperfection because it is 'inevitable'. Any admission of imputed righteousness overthrows the notion of heavenly reward appropriate to the different levels of sanctity, making many mansions needless, and cannot be reconciled with purgatory. Seripando received clear-headed support from the Servite theologian Lorenzo Mazochi (CT V 581-90). But Mazochi was one of four theologians whose orthodoxy was already suspect because they advocated the view that in receiving grace the human will is passive: 'non videntur satis catholice locuti' was the tart comment (CT V 280, 13). The criticism presupposes that faith is an active, instrumental and efficient cause through which grace is made effective, not just the means by which it is accepted. By 26 November Seripando had abandoned any hope of persuading the Council to canonise a doctrine that he had come to hold dear, and in an impassioned and deeply religious speech (CT V 666-676) he begged the Council not to condemn it. It is one of the most moving and human documents of the entire conciliar record.

He had only a modicum of very ambiguous success in his plea. In chapter 16 of its doctrine, the Council affirmed that our salvation hangs on those good works wrought in the faithful in union with Christ himself through a grace which is antecedent, concomitant, and subsequent; that to the justified one must not believe that there is any deficiency or imperfection, since such good works constitute a satisfaction of God's law, inasmuch as they are done 'in God'. The inherent righteousness in us deserves heavenly reward, and therein the merits being rewarded are God's gifts, though it is his will that the merits be ours. This formula did not condemn Seripando's doctrine so much as cut away the presuppositions and considerations which led him to wish to hold it. Perhaps it went some little way towards him by insisting that there is no merit for the good work of the believer apart from the intimate union with Christ. The Council did not like Seripando's answer, but it had at least heard his question and seen that he had a point. Seripando's failure may be in part attributed to the comparative novelty of the idea he put forward, in part to his wish to get away from theology of the scholastic mould and to return through Augustine to the Bible—without its commentators. His hearers felt him to be talking an unfamiliar language, so antiquated as to sound strange. The fact that Seripando's doctrine did not suffer explicit rejection may have been assisted by his close relations with Cervini, whose interventions from the presidential chair were sympathetic to his questions.

13. **The final form of the Tridentine decree on justification**, 13 January 1547 (CT V 790; DS 1520-83; see H. Jedin's History of the Council, eng. tr. II 304 ff) begins with a doctrinal statement averting Pelagian exclusion of grace and Lutheran exclusion of man's co-operation as God's creation. By his own strength apart from grace, the sinner is incapable of saving himself. Through baptism (about election nothing is said) one must be regenerate in Christ, by faith in his blood and the merit of his passion transferred from being son of Adam to adoption as son of God. Justification is being made just. It is anticipated by prevenient grace through a process of preparation. The call of adults is not made in consequence of their merits, however. The will may reject or co-operate; were it not so, it could hardly be a will. God touches man's heart by the illumination of the Spirit, and man can respond, though unable without grace to bring himself to righteousness before God. Faith comes by hearing. As man is moved by the gospel to fear of divine justice and to consideration of God's mercy, he is moved to hate his sins and therefore to penitence. One who comes to baptism is asked if he repents, if he believes the Christian faith, and if he is resolved to lead a new life and to keep the divine commandments. Such dispositions show grace preparing one for the great grace of justification.

This consists not merely in remission of sins but also in renewal of the inner man by a voluntary acceptance of grace. In a scholastic manner (which Melanchthon could deploy just as much as Trent) the causes of justification are classified: *final*—the glory of God and Christ and eternal life; *efficient*—the mercy of God; *meritorious*—

Christ's passion; *instrumental*—baptism 'the sacrament of faith' (Augustine, *Ep*. 98, 9) without which justification never touched anyone; the *unique formal cause* is God's justice, being 'not that by which he is just but that by which he makes us just' (*De Trinit*. 14, 12, 15). So we are renewed in the spirit of our minds (Eph 4 : 23) and are not only reputed but are truly called just and are so, each individual according to the degree of his co-operation. Not that anyone can be just unless the merits of Christ's passion are communicated to him. The impious are justified as the love of God is poured into their hearts and inheres in them. Therefore in justification, together with the remission of sins, man receives faith, hope and charity as Christ's gifts. Unless it is joined to hope and charity, the assent of faith does not unite to Christ nor make one a living member of his body; hence 'faith without works is dead'. Without hope and love faith does not bring one to eternal life.

When St Paul says that a man is justified by faith and gratis, this is to be 'understood in the sense in which the perpetual consensus of the catholic Church has held and expressed it', viz. that faith is the beginning of human salvation, the foundation and the root of all justification, without which it is impossible to please God. This gift is gratis in the sense that none of the things that precede justification (either faith or works) merit the grace of justification. No sins are or ever have been remitted except gratis, by divine mercy for Christ's sake. Yet none may boast of his *fiducia* and certitude of the remission of sins; none may assert that sins are remitted only to the person who is calmly confident that this is the case. We should not say that the justified are exempt from all doubt as if diffidence were disbelief in God's promises. No-one who considers his weakness will think he can know with a certitude of faith not subject to the possibility of error that he has obtained the grace of God. But no pious person doubts God's mercy, Christ's merit, and the efficacy of the sacraments.

14. Moreover (Trent continues), no justified person is free from a duty to keep the commandments. None may say God's precepts are impossible (here citing Augustine, *De natura et gratia* 43, 50). His yoke is easy, his burden light. If holy persons fall into venial sins, they do not thereby cease to be just, but pray 'Forgive us our debts . . .' (a frequent theme in Augustine). 'God by his grace does not desert those once justified unless first he is deserted by them'

(*De natura et gratia* 26, 29 and elsewhere). Let no one flatter himself he will go to heaven by faith alone without troubling to suffer with Christ that he may be glorified with him; even Christ learnt obedience by suffering. In this life no-one can be sure of being in the number of the elect (as if the justified cannot further sin or can be confident of restoration if they do) except by special revelation (*De correptione et gratia* 15, 46; *City of God* 11, 12). Though all should place a firm hope in God, perseverance is a gift on which none should presume: let those who think they stand take heed lest they fall. If they fall, the power of the keys is there for restoration which we receive not merely by ceasing to sin or by contrition of heart but also by sacramental confession and absolution from the priest, by fasting, alms, prayers, offerings and other pious exercises. (An echo here of Augustine, *Ep.* 265, 8, I think.) Penance, like baptism, removes guilt and eternal penalty but unlike baptism, not the temporal penalty: satisfactions are required.

The word 'satisfactio' had vindictive associations; it could carry the suggestion of placating God. Unlike Cyprian who uses the word frequently, Augustine uses it very rarely (*Enchiridion* 65-66; 70; *Sermo* 351) for the act of reparation which is a sign to the Church that one's penitence has been authentic. Anselm uses the Platonic principle that where sin has brought about a breach of order, God cannot tolerate the disharmony and order must be restored. Through Christ man pays the debt he owes, not to placate an irate and jealous God but to put back the 'rectus ordo'. By late scholastic doctrine God's grace and justice forgive sins, and reparations (satisfactions) are not works by which we escape hell, but the acceptance of temporal penalties which signify a true making good. Not that our acts can be a simple equivalent or can meet the perfect requirement of divine justice; they are accepted by God in his loving-kindness, but he has already accepted the penitent back into fellowship through the keys entrusted to his Church.

15. Not only loss of faith but mortal sin robs one of the grace of being justified, but against the clever heretics, one must hold that even in mortal sin faith may survive leaving a way back by confession. On merit, Trent observes that the Bible is very clear that good works are rewarded. Our righteousness is not of ourselves, however, but of God, and that is why there is 'nothing lacking' to the justified. Good deeds done in God by inherent justice satisfy his

111

law in this life and, provided one departs this life in grace, merit eternal life. God forbid that a Christian should trust in himself and not in the Lord. So great is the goodness of God that he wishes the merits which are his gifts to belong to us men. (*Mereor* in Latin does not have the strong force of 'deserve' unless the context makes that certain. It should normally be translated 'obtain', 'receive'.)

16. The thirty-three canons with anathemas begin by a strong condemnation of Pelagianism but also of those who deny free will or reduce man to such passivity that he is indistinguishable from an inanimate object. Luther's declaration that after the fall 'free will is a mere name without the thing' is censured. None may say that all works done before justification are really sins, or that the more one tries to dispose oneself to grace, the worse one is sinning. Nor is it sin to turn to God out of fear of hell or in grief at one's sins. Justification by faith alone may not be taken to mean that no co-operation is required or that there are no preparatory dispositions of the will. Canon 10 condemns both those who say man can be justified without Christ's righteousness and those who say that through Christ's righteousness one is formally just. (The school term *formaliter* is unclear, an imprecision surprising in a conciliar anathema.)

Anathema is also put on the doctrine that we are justified by the sole imputation of Christ's righteousness or solely by the remission of sins when this means the exclusion of grace and love diffused in believers' hearts by the Spirit. Justifying faith is not mere confidence; nor to obtain remission is it necessary just to have no hesitation in believing that one's sins are forgiven. (This canon generated later controversy: did it mean that remission of sins is something one cannot be quite sure of?) Censure is pronounced on the view held by some radical Protestants (but opposed by many others) that the gospel of Christ has no precepts and that the Decalogue is a back number and does not apply to Christians. (Augustine, *De spiritu et littera*, 14, 23, and elsewhere, observes that except for the command to keep the sabbath, which Christians keep entirely spiritually, the Decalogue is binding on Christians. To the Anglican Bishop William Forbes (died 1634) it seemed self-evident that on divorce and remarriage Christ had spoken legislatively, as also to Lancelot Andrewes, Bishop of Winchester. Among the Lutherans some claimed that good works could not be called 'necessary': they were simply a spontaneous product of and sign of authentic faith, and the gospel contained no element of commandment. See the 'Solid Declaration' in the Formula of Concord, iv, 3. Augustine himself is not far from this in 'De Spiritu et littera', 12, 20. At Trent Seripando twice pleaded with the Council not to speak of Christ as 'legislator': CT V 486, 8 October 1546; 666, 26 November.)

17. The predestinarian language of Luther made him cold to the notion that predestination brings one under the sound of the gospel, to baptism and conversion, but thereafter it depends on our response to grace whether or not we get to heaven. Such a grace must seem altogether insufficient. Trent (VI canon 22) hates the doctrine that once a man is justified, he does not need to worry whether or not he will persevere to the end. Perseverance, in the teaching of the Council, is a special and distinct help of grace. The Lutherans departed from Augustine when they spoke of our justification as a lightning-flash act of God rather than as a process by which, after an embryonic growth which is also an operation of grace (Augustine, *Div. Qu. to Simplician*, i, 2, 2), faith comes to birth and, under God's further healing grace, our will is gradually conformed to his; in other words, in Augustinian theology our being made righteous is a matter of growth; in Lutheran theology justification is spoken of as a once-for-all act to which nothing can be added even by God himself. Trent (canon 24) does not pick up the point that the term 'justification' is being used in different senses, and places under anathema the view that through good works done by grace righteousness cannot be preserved and grow before God, or that good works are merely the fruit and sign of an already completed justification.

Behind this harsh exchange there lies more than a terminological disagreement. The central point is whether all our actions are determined by our character, or if there is also truth in saying that our character is, at least in part, the consequence of our actions, habits, and patterns of behaviour. Habit is second nature, but nature is first habit. Luther declared that a man is first declared just and then proceeds to act justly. Trent surely attributes much to the initial grace of God declared and communicated in baptism. But thereafter the baptized believer is granted grace to become more just by the very process of doing justly, and his actions themselves shape

113

his character, they are not merely a determinate expression of what either his genes and chromosomes or even irresistible grace may have programmed him to do. The Trent canon is therefore an expression of reserve before the implicit psychological determinism and hyper-Augustinianism in the doctrine of grace which it perceives in the Lutheran contention. This canon of Trent is directly attacked on the 'Solid Declaration' of the Lutheran Formula of Concord (iv, 35, transl. Tappert p. 557). It is difficult not to see these mutual condemnations as a dialogue of the deaf.

18. Trent's canon 32 repeats the Augustinian thesis that the good works of the justified person are God's gifts, but then places under anathema the Lutheran opinion that the justified person does not *truly merit* increase of grace by the good works which are done by the grace of God and the merit of Jesus Christ, whose living member the person is. 'Truly merit' could naturally suggest condignity more than congruity; but these terms are not mentioned, and either interpretation is left open. The mere word 'merit' was enough to confirm the worst anxieties of the Lutherans, not because they did not use the word themselves (it occurs in the Apology for the Augsburg Confession, the Württemberg Confession, and in a number of Lutheran writings of the age), but because the Lutherans heard Trent's language to be implying that the just have a *right* to salvation.

The Lutherans, such as Chemnitz (*Examen* X 4), were content to understand 'merit' to mean that God *rewards* good works, but felt deeply that to attribute anything to the action of man in winning salvation must 'take away from Christ the glory of propitiation for sins, of salvation and eternal life, which is owned to the obedience and merit of Christ'. Yet canon 32 of Trent insisted that it is by Christ's merits that the justified come to have merits. Sadly Chemnitz simply felt that this was an ingenious formula of whose good faith he took leave (grossly, as we would now judge) to doubt. The ultimate reason for this scepticism may no doubt be sought in the Protestant assumption that the Catholic Council was committed to the scholastic view, also to be found formulated by Julian of Eclanum in his polemic against Augustine, that in principle God's justice is a fair distribution to each individual of what is his due. Not a position readily reconciled with either grace or original sin. The final canon roundly rebuts the contention that the Council's doctrine derogates from the glory of God or the merits of Christ.

19. A retrospect on the doctrine and canons of the sixth session of Trent calls for the salute of admiration accorded by the liberal protestant historian of dogma, Adolf Harnack, who thought the Reformation could not have happened had this come earlier. It cannot be claimed that everything was left unambiguous, or that a large variety of interpretation was excluded. A remarkable silence appears in dealing with the Augustinian doctrine of predestination which provided the dynamo of Luther's main thesis. In the following year (1548) the Dominican Domingo Soto and the Franciscan Andreas Vega published explanations of the Council's doctrine of justification which were not at all points in agreement. Canon 13, condemning assurance in regard to the remission of sins, offered hostages to the critics, and twenty two years later received an elaborate defence running to 634 pages to show that the Council had not plunged everyone into a maze of doubt. This was by Martin Eisengrein (*De certitudine gratiae Tractatus Apologeticus pro vero ac germano intellectu canonis xiii sessionis VI S. Oecumenici Concilii Tridentini:* Cologne, 1569). The author himself realised that his exegesis reduced to minuscule proportions any difference between his Catholic understanding of the matter and that of moderate Protestants. (As this was not what all his fellow-Catholics wanted to be told, he generated friction. The book ended on the Index.)

To cut a long story short, the Council's decision on justification, as on most other matters, came to receive a wide diversity of exegesis from its defenders. Among modern scholars there has been lively disagreement about Seripando's doctrine. Did the Council actually reject it as uncatholic? Did it by studied ambiguity discourage his view without actually censuring it (the opinion to which the present writer would veer)? or did it avoid the issue directly, and endeavour to deal with the real question raised along quite different lines?

20. The record of the debate printed in CT volume V shows how most of the Council fathers felt they had two bogies to fear: imputed righteousness and unqualified assurance beyond possibility of error. The second was vastly less controversial than the first, since, although Luther had talked vehemently about faith being confident trust, a very substantial body of moderate Protestant opinion would have agreed with Trent that it was a mistake to confuse faith with

assurance, and that to speak about a total absence of hesitation without the remotest possibility of error was to make assurance indistinguishable from arrogant presumption on the grace of God. Among the Anglicans no sleep was lost on this matter.

Much more difficult was the question of imputed righteousness. In the discussion at Trent the point was tellingly made by Mazochi, against whom there was prejudice, that 'imputed righteousness happens to be the language of the Holy Spirit' (Romans 4 : 3 and 23 being cited). (CT V 584, 6). Seripando quotes one of his critics as having said that his view was indistinguishable from that of the Lutherans, and therefore deserved to be condemned with them (CT V 674). He replied that he did not wish to leave the Lutherans in triumphant possession of the apostle's language on this point. In the end, as we have seen, the canon (11) censures the view that 'justification' (which for Trent includes sanctification) is exclusively by the sole imputation of the righteousness of Christ, or consists only in the remission of sins to the exclusion of sanctifying grace and love. One must not deny that there is such a thing as inherent righteousness which is the work of the Holy Spirit within the believer. Luther and Melanchthon intended no such denial. But they could not really bring themselves to qualify their essential convictions that (though contrition is a sine qua non of justification) if ultimately salvation depends on what man does, then we are all lost, and if we are saved, it is by the mercy of God. The debates at Trent over the right understanding of 'imputed righteousness' show the Council fathers not so much interpreting this alien idea positively as saying 'Whatever it may mean, it cannot mean that no consent and co-operation in the moral struggles of the Christian life are required of the baptized, justified believer'. But then most Protestants were not saying it did mean that.

Anglicanism
21. The Anglicans of the sixteenth and seventeenth century offer a broad spectrum of views on the questions at issue in the preceding pages. It seems right to start with the Thirty Nine Articles since, although they no longer have formal authority, there remain Anglicans who hold them in respect today; and while the Articles have been far less influential on the formation of doctrine than the liturgy of the Book of Common Prayer (being known to and at one time required of the clergy but hardly known to the laity, even since

the early eighteenth century when they began to be bound up with the Prayer Book), nevertheless they have enjoyed a standing and a generally shaping influence on some aspects of Anglican theological tradition. Three articles deal with our problems:

Article 11, Of the Justification of Man

We are accounted righteous before God only for (*propter*) the merit of our Lord and Saviour Jesus Christ by (*per*) faith and not for our own works or deservings. Wherefore, that we are justified by faith only, is a most wholesome doctrine, and very full of comfort, as more largely is expressed in the Homily of Justification.

Article 12, Of Good Works

Albeit that good works which are the fruits of faith and follow after justification cannot put away our sins and endure the severity of God's judgment: yet are they pleasing and acceptable to God in Christ and do spring out necessarily of a true and lively faith, in so much that by them a lively faith may be as evidently known as a tree discerned by its fruit.

Article 13, Of Works before Justification

Works done before the grace of Christ and the inspiration of the Spirit are not pleasant to God, forasmuch as they spring not of faith in Jesus Christ, neither do they make men meet to receive grace, or (as the school authors say) deserve grace of congruity; yea, rather for that they are not done as God hath willed and commanded them to be done, we doubt not but they have the nature of sin.

22. Article 11 took its present form in the revision of 1563, at the time when the more Protestant party wanted the version of 1553 strengthened and when they suffered an alarming defeat over article 28, rewritten by Bishop Guest (as Lingard incisively discerned) to protect the real presence in the Eucharist in language that caused agony to the Zwinglians. John Hooper (d. 1555) had especially asked for Article 11 to deny justification by merit in set terms. The 1563 version borrowed language from the Lutheran confessions of Augsburg and Württemberg, but without taking over the thesis that one is justified if one believes one is justified. The article speaks of our being 'reputed' (*reputamur*) or reckoned just before God 'on the ground of Christ's merit through faith', not by the merits of our

works and deservings. So the meritorious cause of justification is the merit of Christ—a doctrine which does not differ from that of Trent. The instrumental cause is 'per fidem'. Faith is not defined, and there is no suggestion that it is other than the apostle's 'faith working by love', a trust in the promises of God which motivates the justified person to do what is good and right. Nor does the article seek to impose the view that salvation is solely by an imputation of Christ's righteousness to us *and of our sins to him* (a view that distressed Bishop William Forbes one generation later as an inherently problematic idea going substantially beyond scripture).

The 'Homily on Salvation' is found in the first book of Homilies (1542, issued in 1547) and expressly lays down 'Faith doth not shut out repentance, hope, love, dread, and the fear of God, to be joined with faith in every man that is justified; but it shutteth them out from the office of justifying . . . Nor that faith also doth not shut out the justice of our good works, necessarily to be done afterwards of duty towards God . . . but it excludeth them so that we may not do them to this intent, to be made good by doing of them. For all the good works that we can do be unperfect, and therefore not able to deserve our justification; but our justification doth come freely by the mere mercy of God . . . This sentence that we can be justified by faith only is not so meant of them (i.e. church fathers who use this language) that the said justifying faith is alone in man, without true repentance, hope, charity, dread, and fear of God . . . This saying that we be justified by faith only, freely, and without works, is spoken for to take away clearly all merit of our works, as being unable to deserve our justification at God's hands; and therefore to express most plainly the weakness of man and the goodness of God, the imperfectness of our own works, and the most abundant grace of our Saviour Christ; and thereby wholly for to ascribe the merit and deserving of our justification unto Christ only and his most precious blood-shedding'.

The homily goes on to explain that the faith which justifies is not our own and that it is not our faith which justifies us or deserves justification. (That is, the homily denies faith to be the formal cause of justification!) The doctrine means simply that we must renounce the merit of our virtues of faith, hope, charity and all other good deeds as things too weak and insufficient and imperfect to deserve remission of sins and justification. We must trust only in God's mercy and in that sacrifice which our high priest and Saviour Christ once offered for us upon the Cross, to obtain thereby God's grace and remission as well as our original sin in baptism as of all actual sin committed by us after our baptism if we truly repent.

23. The homily, the authorship of which was attributed to Cranmer by Bishop Stephen Gardiner, antedates the Tridentine decree by five years in the date of its composition, and it is evidently concerned to affirm *sola fide* but then to add crucial qualifications: e.g. that faith is not itself a work or ground of justification or merit, and that the necessity of using such language arises from the imperfection, on account of the persisting effects of original sin, of even our best virtues. *Article 12*, on the other hand, first appeared in the revised draft of the Articles proposed in 1563. Here good works are the fruits of living faith and manifest it; even those that 'follow after justification' have no claim sufficient to put away our sins before the severity of God's judgment. Yet despite their imperfections they are *pleasing and acceptable to God* in Christ ('Deo tamen grata sunt et accepta in Christo'). The last phrase is hardly distinguishable from what Trent intended to say by the use of the word 'merit', but among the Protestants 'merit' always tended to be heard as implying an independent act of man, by free will choosing to perform an external deed, such as almsgiving, which would constitute a ground for reward by a just Creator.

Article 13 begins with the non-controversial proposition that works done before the grace of Christ and the inspiration of the Spirit are not pleasing to God, since they do not spring from faith in Christ. Since the article is apparently speaking of works done before justification, it is also non-controversial that such works should constitute no ground of merit even in the weak, almost Pickwickian sense of 'merit by congruity' (as opposed to the strict proportionality of condign merit). The case of Cornelius (Acts 10) was often discussed in this context. His prayers and alms 'came up for a memorial before God'; was that what drew the grace of God to him? The Article regards congruous reward before justification (and possibly *post fidem* also, but that is far from certain) as ruled out: it would be Pelagian to suggest that man takes an initiative which grace then rewards with further help, valuable indeed, but not in principle totally necessary. More toughminded is the proposition that the virtues of the good person who acts by free will but without grace are no more than sins. Augustine had indeed come within an ace of saying this: for he taught that without grace the will is free to do evil but never to do anything really good (*contra II epp. Pelag.*, i, 7). The good pagan who does by nature the moral law is not among the number of Christ's justified, only among those whose actions we are right to praise, yet if his motive is not love to God it is questionable (*De Spiritu et Littera*, 48). The chastity of unbelievers has no merit before God (*De Nupt. et Concupisc.*, 4 f.).

It is remarkable that in a series of Articles so stamped with high Augustinianism, Article 16 (which caused pain to high Calvinists) declares that 'after we have received the Holy Spirit we may (possumus) depart from grace given and fall into sin.' The text is directed against Anabaptist perfectionism, but the Calvinist Puritans hated this clause and wanted the addition (after 'grace given'): 'yet neither totally nor finally'. In the Church of England their request was never granted. Moreover, Article 17 on Predestination contains nothing that would not seem evident to a Thomist; it is not sympathetic to the notion of a limited atonement. It is evidently possible to exaggerate the pervasiveness of Calvinist beliefs in the Elizabethan Church of England.

24. This discussion has treated the Articles as a historical witness to theological formulation in the Church of England at a highly controversial moment in its history.[2] The Articles were shaped during the decade when relations between Queen of England and Pope were rapidly deteriorating and tempers were rising fast on both sides. The Articles did not receive their final form and approval until after the Queen had been excommunicated and her subjects released from political allegiance to her (1570), and the 1571 version of the Articles contained problematic new matter such as article 29, which Bishop Guest could hardly bring himself to think consistent with his own article 28 and seemed much more angrily, aggressively Protestant than the moderate men wanted.

Within emergent Anglicanism three broad patterns of interpretation of the Articles can be discerned: the first inherited the Erasmian tradition that has profoundly stamped Anglican spirituality and piety, seeing the articles as compromise formulae necessary for the sake of peace in Church and commonwealth, but vastly less than a *regula fidei*, valued as a witness to truth against superstition and rationalism and therefore enshrining a liberal spirit. The second stream of interpreters tended to regret that the Articles gave an uncertain sound at various points where Calvinists would have liked tougher language; in principle they saw in them a charter of evangelical truth rooted in the supreme authority of Scripture—and the more emphatic one is about *sola scriptura*, the less authority must attach to a human confession of faith such as the Articles. The third stream has been the broadly 'catholic' stream, conscious how much catholic substance lies embedded in the protestant rhetoric and how relatively simple it is (as Sancta Clara, i.e. Christopher Davenport, was serenely to demonstrate in 1634) to reduce the dividing lines between the Articles and the decrees of Trent virtually to vanishing point.

25. Sancta Clara regarded the whole controversy about justification, as between Rome and Canterbury at least, as a mere war of words. He welcomed denial in the 1542 Homily (above, para. 22) that human faith is the formal cause of justification, and thought the difference only one of emphasis in speaking of faith, which the Roman Catholics spoke of as that faith given by Christ by which we believe the promises of God, while Protestants laid greater stress on the subjective act of confidence in the divine promises. He noted that in the articles there is no specific definition of what is meant by faith, and that the text of the Thirty Nine Articles contains nothing in itself with which a Roman Catholic needs to quarrel so far as justification is concerned. Sancta Clara's book assumes that the Thirty Nine Articles are possessed of some standing for the Church of England of his time. He writes as a man aware that all such documents require a hermeneutic; that is, their meaning is not always as obvious as it seems to the careless reader and may indeed be other than what such a reader assumes. He uses no force on the text, but is clearly aware that Anglican writers of the 1630s like Richard Montague (a confused writer) were understanding their position in a sense even more 'Tridentine' than he himself found it natural to be.

26. A broad survey of Anglican writing on Justification in the late sixteenth and seventeenth centuries can hardly be attempted within the space of this paper. The more Protestant-sounding accounts of the matter are given by Richard Hooker, who had been brought up as a Calvinist (though he superimposed on that foundation thick layers of Thomism and of Cyril of Alexandria), and by John

121

Davenant, bishop of Salisbury, writing in 1631. Hooker found himself suspected of being unsound on justification and preached a lengthy sermon to vindicate his position against more Protestant critics. His thesis is, briefly summarised, that merit has to be excluded because while the righteousness of sanctification is by inherent grace and is not merely imputed, it is never perfect in this world. Righteousness which is both perfect and inherent is granted to us only in the next world. But the righteousness of Christ in justification is not inherent, and is perfect. Thus far there is a mental distinction made between justification and sanctification. They are distinct *in re*, but in time not so. It is a mistake to talk as if we start by being justified and then at some later time first begin to receive the grace of sanctification. They are inseparable and contemporaneous. The faith of believers cannot be divorced from hope and love, and faith is a part of sanctification, not something left behind as we grow in grace. Faith is rightly spoken of as the 'foundation' (and so Trent had said). The high Augustinian comes out in Hooker as he proclaims that justifying faith is indefectible, for although man is unstable, God's promises are immutable, and none of the elect will ultimately be lost.

Hooker (like Luther in his commentary on Galatians) caused some consternation by proclaiming that the Roman Church has not abandoned the authentic foundation; its fault in his eyes is to have erected too large a superstructure, not all of the right sort. 'Our fathers were saved in that Church', and there is no question of denying the continuity of the Church Catholic in history.

Davenant is broadly similar in his thought to Hooker, stressing the perfection of imputed righteousness in justification, but refusing to separate the faith which is an instrumental cause of justification from hope and love. Davenant was happy to say good works are necessary for the justified, but feared to say they are a necessary cause of salvation; he would say they are a 'moving cause'.

27. The most learned and, in the proper sense, unprejudiced survey of justification to appear in the entire Reformation age came from the pen of Bishop *William Forbes* of Edinburgh who died in 1634; his work appeared posthumously in 1658. The book, translated into English (1850), remains an education to read. Forbes saw that it must be impossible to speak of justification as consisting exclusively in the non-imputation of past sins; it must carry forward into life in

the Spirit under grace. Scripture nowhere, either expressly or as a necessary consequence, attributes to faith alone the whole power of justifying, or, what is the same thing, asserts that faith is the only instrument or means of receiving and apprehending the grace of justification (p. 38). Penitence is a condition of forgiveness and 'in some sense has the nature of a cause'. (That was a position that Melanchthon had had to maintain against other Lutheran criticism.) So the forgiveness of sins is never conferred without internal sanctification of the soul (p. 216). To say that we are enabled by grace to receive both imputed and inherent righteousness does not produce two formal causes of justification since all is Christ's righteousness. Forbes smiles at the twists and turns of Suarez's exposition and defence of the Tridentine decree and its fear of speaking positively about imputed righteousness, and observes that even Suarez had to concede that in the justification of the sinner there coalesce together two converging effects of grace, the one positive and the other 'privative'. Forbes thought that was Anglican language (p. 204).

He felt as Gregory Nazianzen came to feel about the mixed blessings of Synods. The sixteenth century confessions of faith on either side all seemed to him inadequate, partial, and therefore unreliable guides. The continental Protestant assemblies which had harassed theologians wanting to unite justification and sanctification seemed to him deplorable and oppressive. 'Who that has eyes to see does not see that in most of the synods assembled by either party in this most deplorable age, scarcely anything else is attempted or done than to oppress and condemn the older and truer opinions . . . the majority of those who were present at these synods overcoming, as generally happens, the better part?' (p. 196).

Forbes's work is cast in the form of a critical commentary on Bellarmine's treatise on justification, his principal complaint against Bellarmine being that he treats all Protestants as antinomian libertines; otherwise on the positive side he thought Bellarmine merited much respect. Bellarmine had rejected condign merit (as had also Suarez—here against Vazquez). Forbes much liked the scholarly and impartial Catholic theologian Cassander (1513-66), a man whose writings had caused offence to partisan theologians on both sides by his observation that they were so often disagreed not about things but about words. Forbes found in Cassander the remark that 'merit' is not located in human acts but is a way of saying that there are works pleasing to God; all is derived from his grace and acceptation (Forbes p. 486).

28. Forbes' long Latin book first appeared twenty-four years after his death. Already the main body of Anglican theology was in reaction against Calvinism, and shared Forbes' regrets at Luther's extravagant love of hyperbole. Seventeenth-century Caroline divinity cordially disliked the indefensible disjunction of justification and sanctification. They were not afraid of the forensic or 'acquittal' sense of justification, and indeed it was no reluctant concession on their part to say that in St Paul the most obvious sense of 'justification' is not making righteous, but treating man and dealing with him as righteous. But they shuddered to a standstill before the notion that the act of God in justification (whether in mercy or in justice) is unconditional on the submission of man to the terms of the covenant of grace, and therefore that justification *sola fide* is another way of saying that the elect are predestinate by the operation of irresistible grace and do not need to concern themselves too much about moral lapses as they sit comfortably on the escalator carrying them securely to heaven. To Jeremy Taylor (1613-67); bishop of Down and Connor in Ireland, 1660) justification and sanctification are steps of progression along a single path; the distinction is notional, not actual. No one could read a lot of Jeremy Taylor without feeling that St Augustine would have written severe reviews of his works.

The most striking reassertion of Augustinianism came, among the Anglicans, in a very unexpected form in the *Harmonia Apostolica* (i.e. reconciliation of Paul and James) by *George Bull* (1634-1710), bishop of St David's in Wales. Bull's mind was remarkably independent. His defence of the Nicene Creed (1685) included a massive critique of the immensely learned Jesuit Denys Petau whose work had left a deep impression of the precariousness of orthodoxy among the early church fathers of ante-Nicene times; and the book earned him an accolade unique for Anglican clergymen: a formal vote of gratitude to him was voted by the French clergy in synod in 1700. On justification also Bull wrote as if he were considering everything ab initio from first principles. He was happy to affirm that righteousness is imputed to us for the merit and obedience of Christ, but not the simple and unscriptural formula that 'Christ's righteousness is imputed to us' unconditionally, irrespective of repentance and faith. His thesis was that *sola fide* must be checked by the text of 1 Corinthians 13 : 2: the apostle tells us that without love faith's value is zero. The apostle speaks of justification apart from works to show that we do not win merit by obedience; yet Bull thought, and was sure the apostle thought, that faith without obedience gets you nowhere.

Bull's thesis provoked vehement criticism from both Roman and Reformed: he was trying to discover a via media, but (as often in such enterprises) seemed to end by making a confused juxtaposition of incompatibles. Bull's critics urged that if the apostle really meant that we are saved by faith and obedience (though St Paul did not put it that way, in order to exclude merit), then the apostle was not actually excluding merit at all. Bull was saying that our justification, which for him merges into sanctification, is not achieved without the co-operation of our will. The Reformed critics quoted back at him Rom 3 : 24: 'Where is boasting? It is excluded'. In their view Bull understood St Paul not to have excluded it completely, even though one should not use the term merit.

Roman Catholic critics likewise asked why Bull had to feel such reserve towards the word merit, if he could grant that some kind of assent and co-operation on the part of the human will is a sine qua non of the righteousness formed in the soul by inherent grace and the love of the Holy Spirit. Bull wanted to regard the good works of the justified as an indispensable condition, not a meritorious cause. His critics felt that the former must pass into becoming the latter. So his Roman critics liked his essentially Augustinian and Tridentine thesis, but were mildly critical of the consistency of his terminology.

29. In the eighteenth century 'A summary view of the doctrine of Justification' came from the middle-of-the-road Anglican theologian, *Daniel Waterland* (1683-1740), Master of Magdalene College Cambridge. His essay (*Works*, ed. Van Mildert, vol. VI) affirms justification as God's act to be a judicial declaration by which man is offered discharge from the penalty but not the blame of his sins, and is a right and title to eternal life which is more than a bare acquittal; but Waterland did not want to follow Forbes in including the positive gift of the Spirit for the sanctification of the inner heart and soul, on the ground that the renewal of the inner man has no place in the baptism of infants. And justification (as Waterland emphatically asserts) is conveyed by baptism. The idea (once

advanced by Bucer) that the first justification of adults is antecedent to baptism, Waterland dismisses as a gross confusion of the grace of justification with the first preparatory renewings wrought by the Holy Spirit.

30. In the nineteenth century the most important book by an Anglican on Justification is that of *J. H. Newman* (1838). The book belongs to the era when he was seeking to restate the Middle Way between Rome and Protestantism as the true path of Anglicanism, and this led him to portray both Tridentine Catholicism and what he called 'Lutheranism' (about which one must admit him to be ill informed, though he had read Gerhard and Chemnitz) in ways that might not be easily recognised by adherents of these positions. The target that he treats with the greatest severity is the Protestant, high Calvinist Evangelical language in which he himself had been brought up—mainly as formed by the teaching of Romaine. Newman thought it absurd that the seventeenth century Protestant schoolmen had ransacked the resources of human vocabulary to discover language capable of expressing their conviction that in the human act of faith there is no sort of moral quality, lest man should make his own achievement an initiating ground for the help of grace, and yet that this act of believing must somehow be a 'living' faith, not mere assent of the mind; a repentance which turns to God and is not remorse or mere shame at the mess of one's life.

But above all, Newman sought to reaffirm baptism as the sacrament of justification and regeneration. The doctrine of the free, gratis character of divine grace, affirmed by Augustine and the Catholic tradition and supremely expressed in predestination, is given a quite radical slant if it is turned into a belief that grace somehow ceases to be 'free' when offered to the believer through the apostles' doctrine and fellowship, through the breaking of bread and the prayers, and through the sacraments of the gospel, assured to the faithful through a ministry of apostolic order in the visible communion of the historical Church. In fact (as Melanchthon's Apology for the Augsburg Confession protested) *sola fide* is not a denial of the communication of grace through the sacraments: 'We exclude merit, not the word or sacraments, as our adversaries slanderously say'.

But in the train of Luther there did come Protestants for whom *sola fide* should be understood with full-blooded subjectivity, and who did hold the position that Melanchthon disavowed. The Lutheran critique of 'ex opere operato' (condemned at Trent, VII *De sacramentis in genere*, canon 8; DS 1608, 3 March 1547) assumed the meaning to be that the sacraments work automatically without any movement in the recipient (*sine bono motu cordis*); an opinion startlingly akin to the view that Luther was attacked for holding, that in receiving grace man is utterly passive and cannot be said to 'do' anything. The Pietists inherited a mystical tradition of detachment from the visible institutions of the Church. Where the schoolmen had once granted that the grace of God is not tied to the sacraments, the Pietists tended to be surprised if they were found associated. They therefore made the Church a secondary consequence, an accidental gathering of believers who had as individuals been granted the experience of knowing themselves justified and regenerate. It was easy to move to the position that the normal order of the liturgical life of the Church, in the means of grace, ministry, word and sacrament, is to be set aside as a means of bargaining with God with the counter of human merit. Those who have thus experienced justifying faith and inward regeneration in their own souls by an unmediated experience of God's grace know themselves to be men and women of the Spirit and apart from the historic body, though they may find themselves able to use for edification some of the forms of that body.

Within this way of thinking a tension soon emerges. On the one hand, the faith which is the instrumental cause of justification is asserted to have nothing to do with the moral state of the individual will and even less to do with the intellectual assent his mind makes, and depends on God's decision. On the other hand such emphasis is laid on the liberating inward psychological experience that 'justification' comes to be used indifferently whether of God's decree or of the human act of trust which receives and rejoices at it. The crux of validity is found in the conversion experience of the believer. Add to this the heady wine of the doctrine of predestination in the maximal form of irresistible grace, and the individual believer will often be racked by anxiety whether his feelings (for he may trust neither intellectual assent nor moral will, and there is only feeling left) have really been a sign of regeneration or not. By contrast Newman affirms that the truth of justification is nowhere more apparent than in the sacrament of baptism. This justification does not leave the soul as it found it.

31. Any generalisation about classical Anglican treatments of the doctrine of justification is sure to have to carry some qualifying or exceptive clause. The seventeenth century Anglicans do not speak with a single voice. Hooker and Davenant at least sound more Protestant than Forbes, Herbert Thorndike, Hammond, Taylor, and Bull. But it is an illusion that the Anglicans are incoherent. Although the Thirty Nine Articles left them remarkably free, without prescribing on the subject in a manner that even the least Protestant of them would find it embarrassing to defend, there is a discernible shared point of view; namely that hyper-Augustinian doctrines of predestination and irresistible grace are not their natural air; that justifying faith ought not to be separated from hope and love; that one may speak of 'growth' in faith and indeed pray from the heart the Collect for Trinity XIV 'give unto us the increase of faith, hope, and charity . . .'; that (as in Hooker) sanctification is by inherent righteousness but in this life can only be imperfect; that baptism is the sacrament of justification and that, since no works prior to the grace of justification are meritorious, the grace conveyed in this sacrament is (most prominently) the non-imputation of sins on the ground of the merit of Christ, without excluding the moral ingredients of (a) contrition in adults (b) the resolve to follow good and avoid evil (c) the enabling gift of the seal of the Spirit. Imputed righteousness, however, is not only operative in baptism, but daily in the Christian life as we pray 'Forgive us our sins, as we forgive them . . .' And at the divine tribunal even the works of righteousness that God's grace has enabled us to do will remain flawed by imperfection because of the resistance to God's will that we daily experience within ourselves, because there remains that deep level of the personality not yet wholly surrendered to the love of God. Whether this imperfection is rightly spoken of as meeting its answer in the mercy of God imputed to us by Christ's perfect righteousness or by the purging fire of love; or if we may suppose that these two ways of talking are different ways of saying much about the same thing—these matters on which a reverential awe in debate seems appropriate. By 1 Cor 3 Scripture may seem to give more support to the latter way of talking.

Concluding reflections

32. It will be obvious to readers that much has been left out. In particular this paper has not included an account of the Roman

Catholic interpreters of the Trent decree, among whom some come very close to the position occupied by the seventeenth-century Anglicans of the Restoration period. Throughout this survey one common feature is recurrent, namely, the dream that one should be able to bring together Catholic and Protestant understandings of justification by admitting that we need Christ's righteousness for our salvation, both as inherent in the soul in sanctifying grace, and as imputed, whether in Baptism (because no preparatory dispositions and virtues can earn a reward of grace) or hereafter because of the imperfection of even the best co-operation of our wills with divine grace. Both the men of Trent and the moderate men of the Reformation (among whom the Anglicans tended to be easily the most moderate!) were convergent in wanting to affirm (1) that human moral achievements, even under grace, do not constitute an entitlement conferring a right to salvation (2) that if grace does not have its effects in the actual transformation of the moral life, it has been received in vain. In the sixteenth century the language used on both sides was cast in the mould formed by the schoolmen. The Protestants who had begun by handing out discourteous kicks at the medieval schoolmen acquired, with amazing rapidity, a scholasticism of their own with a series of fissiparous disputes.

33. The scholastic refinements in the debate about justification became so intricate that they contributed to generating a widespread feeling that the dispute was wearisome metaphysical subtlety, a mere game with words played by academic theologians providing the separated communions with a rationalisation for their separation. There is no doubt that Trent's stepfatherly treatment of the notion of 'imputation' aroused fear in Protestant hearts. Hooker was grieved to think Catholics supposed remission of sins to be applied, to those in venial sin, by holy water, an Ave Maria, a sign of the cross, etc., and to those in mortal sin by the sacrament of penance which not only cleanses the stain of guilt but can commute eternal punishment to temporal satisfaction in this life if time for amendment of life is granted; if it is not, then the hereafter must be terrifying unless lightened by requiems, fasts, pilgrimages, alms, and other acts of charity. But that was to say that his reservations were more concerned with devotional practice than with doctrine. On the actual nature of justification, on imputed and inherent righteousness, the gulf between Hooker and Trent is no sort of ravine.

34. Again, there is paradox in the embarrassment evident at Trent in the treatment of 'imputation', since at the very heart of Catholic piety lay, and lies, the mass and the doctrine of eucharistic sacrifice. That means to say that there can be no ground on which we may worthily stand before God except in Christ who has done on our behalf what we could not and cannot do for ourselves. The merits of his perfect self-offering the Church remembers and pleads before the very throne of grace, thereby entering into the movement of the Lord's heavenly intercession. In the mass there is both the supreme divine gift and the supreme human offering; but the heart of the matter is that all human offering is flawed and imperfect unless offered in union with Christ. Translated into other terms, such language is in essential principle a proclamation of imputed righteousness. Hence the appeal of men like Seripando that the notion is implicit in the prayer of the canon of the mass, 'not weighing our merits but pardoning our offences' (taken over without alteration into the liturgy of the Anglican Prayer Book). The Anglican eucharistic hymn ('And now O Father . . .'), has it:

Look Father, look on his anointed face
And only look on us as found in him . . .
For lo, between our sins and their reward
We set the Passion of thy Son our Lord.

35. On the Catholic side, by the seventeenth century it had come to look surprising to hear Protestant theologians of sense and judgment, not fanatics, freely conceding that although only faith justified, yet this faith is quite meaningless apart from its issue in good works done by grace and the indwelling of the Spirit. Had Protestants really the right to separate themselves from the Catholic Church on a distinction which required considerable academic and intellectual skill to state intelligibly and coherently and which then looked utterly tiny? Of all those who had been taken out of communion with Rome in the sixteenth century, the Anglicans often seemed to stand infuriatingly close. Their separation had been predominantly determined by Crown and Privy Council, by the political desire for national independence rather than by any instinctive uprising of lay protestant bible-reading piety, though the latter of course existed.

Anglican theologians became particularly prominent in using language that was uncommonly akin to the Trent decree on justification of January 1547, even if that decree included sentences and a few anathemas that men like Bishop Forbes thought an excess of definition and an importation of school-distinctions into articles of faith which he was sad to see. Forbes candidly felt that at times Trent disclosed a greater anxiety to condemn Luther than to proclaim catholic truth of the great tradition. But on most of the essential points he was of course in sympathy with what the fathers of Trent were trying to say by way of positive affirmation. In this situation it might seem that in the last decades of the twentieth century, where theologians have ceased to have much confidence in anyone's capacity to produce precise dogmatic formula free of any element of approximation or historical conditioning, it ought to be a relatively simple task to state the doctrine of justification in a way that reconciles. It will not be as easy as the survey thus far may suggest, for reasons I must now try briefly to set out.

36. The medieval schoolmen declared (e.g. Thomas Aquinas, ST 3 69, 4) that baptism is not merely an engagement of heart and will on the part of the recipient, but is a sacrament appointed by Christ for conferring grace. Here 'grace' means not merely the abstract capacity to do right, but actual goodness. Grace is a transforming power within the soul, conforming the disposition to the will of God. Thereby man is made pleasing to God (*gratia gratum faciens*); for his soul is shaped thereby into a beauty analogous to that of physical loveliness. By the action of grace Aquinas sees the root or foundation of virtue implanted in the soul to produce a 'habit', i.e. something permanent, not merely sudden and transient. The strength of this medieval doctrine lay in its doing full justice to the intimate link between baptism as sacrament of justification and regeneration. As soon as one is using the biblical language of regeneration, one must be speaking of new life and therefore of positive goodness. In the case of infant baptism what was, for the schoolmen, given was seminal rather than actual. There was therefore a difficulty in explaining how or why some baptized persons to whom these sublime gifts had been given wholly fail to grow up living lives of virtue or holiness.

The medieval answer was to say that while there was indeed an implanted 'habit' of virtue, the exercise of the free will was necessary on each successive occasion when one would be required to make a moral choice. In some people, the habit will lie dormant. In others

131

it is stirred to action in good works by the free choice of the will. We may leave on one side here the paradoxical use of the term 'habit' to describe patterns of behaviour which are acted out either not at all or in mere fits and starts. The doctrine of the continuance of concupiscence in the baptized was invoked to explain the frequent failure of human beings to act on the gifts given to them. But in principle medieval theology affirms there is a rock-bottom actual goodness in human nature as created by God and restored in baptism, with free choices and the interference of concupiscence to explain why things go wrong thereafter.

The scholastic tradition is echoed in the language of Trent that 'in justification, together with remission of sin, faith, hope and charity are infused into us.' That is not merely to say that real goodness is a necessary *condition* of justification (which we find in the Anglicans Bull and Thorndike) but that it is the very *content* of the gift of grace. In short, in Catholic theology, as also in the Pietist evangelicals of the eighteenth century, there is no distinction drawn between justification and regeneration. By the new birth man becomes actually good. If it does not always work out that way, one must seek the cause of the trouble in mistaken choices or the pressures of concupiscence.

37. Mainstream Anglican theology (Hooker, Thorndike et al.) regarded baptism as a covenant or pact. God on his part grants all grace necessary to eternal life, and yet he does not remove the freedom of the will and the individual can refuse to avail himself of what is thereby given to him. This position easily goes with an interpretation of the grace given in baptism as a potentiality rather than an actuality. The individual is brought to a status, and incorporation in the body of Christ, whereby he receives the possibility of attaining salvation. This mainstream Anglicanism was formulated in conscious reaction against high Calvinism. That is to say that there is an inherent and ineradicable conflict between the attribution of a role to free will and the full Augustinian doctrine.

Under Augustine's scheme, all men and women are originally born as part of the undifferentiated sinful mass of the posterity of Adam and Eve, and by birth have inherited moral impotence with the corruption of their nature, reinforced by the social environment. Antecedent, however, to the being of any of us, God had predetermined that some, indeed a substantial minority, shall be rescued from the punishment a rebellious sinful world most certainly deserves. By a similar antecedent decision of God, the reprobate are given no grace to rescue them; and none may complain, for nothing could be more absolutely just. Condign merit applies precisely here. The elect are endowed with grace which, because of the certainty that man will get it wrong if he has to do anything on his own, has to be irresistible, and will also ensure that the divine purpose in predestination is not frustrated, by giving the further gift of final perseverance. So the elect are not merely enabled to act rightly and to persevere to the end of their lives to die in grace; they are also caused so to do. To those not elect these gifts are simply not conferred. They have no capacity, therefore, to attain salvation. Some of them may indeed hear the call and offer themselves for baptism. But their baptism is, for Augustine, merely outward. The word does not speak within to their hearts, and does not come to transform their lives.

38. A vast proportion of the confusions of the sixteenth century debate may be attributed to the fact that the two systems of thinking, which lay side by side in the mind of Augustine in a glorious inconsistency, had in late medieval schools begun to drift apart, and in the Reformation separated out with a rending explosion. Luther's mind, well soaked in the anti-Pelagian writings of Augustine, reasserted the predestinarian side of Augustinian theology in the most vehement possible terms. Trent reacted by safeguarding free will and reaffirming the traditional pattern of medieval theology of baptismal justification. Within the Church of the Counter-Reformation even the decrees of Trent left many doors open; and hence the fiercely fought controversies first over Baius and Jansenius, then over Quesnel.[3] I shall not exhaust already weary readers with an account either of the Jansenist controversy or of the disputes among the Protestants between the Calvinists and the Arminians. In the Roman Catholic Church the authority of the Pope spoke for the preservation of the position of Trent, that is for the safeguarding of the freedom of the will and the co-operation of man with grace.[4] In the Anglican tradition the high Calvinist tradition, which since the days of the Elizabethan settlement had found the liturgy and articles of the Church of England a source of continual irritation, has always had isolated representatives but has never looked or sounded characteristically Anglican. There remain

in 1984 Evangelical Anglicans whose hearts beat faster with sympathy as they read Calvin's *Institutes*. On the other hand, there are many Evangelical Anglicans who fully share the opinion to which John Wesley was resoundingly converted, namely that high Calvinism cannot be proclaimed without risks of moral disaster;[5] that the preacher of the gospel is bound to place before his hearers the truth that in the gospel there is a real choice, and that the consequences of the choice affect one's eternal destiny.

An important discussion. Ct mellods. Also see Wesley as a mediator Love of My article in D. English (Ed) Salvation 1994.

9

Lima, ARCIC, and the Church of England

THE CHURCH OF ENGLAND'S General Synod in July 1983 had two documents before it on ecumenical questions: the ARCIC 'final' report coming from more than a decade of bilateral dialogue at an official level, and the Lima text from a wider body, the World Council's Faith and Order Commission, which seeks to focus issues arising in numerous bilaterial dialogues and also has a lively eye for contemporary social issues. Both documents reflect some continuing reaction during their production from the participating Churches; and by earlier comments the Church of England had a little finger in the pie and exercised some influence on their shape. At the same time, if the Church of England now indicates a wish to pursue the path these two documents invite participant Churches to follow, some changes will come about.

Though the two documents do not present complete or systematic treatises even in the areas they select, they presuppose a coherent and convergent approach in questions where Christians have disagreed and where the disagreements have either caused or justified the suspension of eucharistic communion. In Church history it is notoriously hard to find examples of schism originating exclusively in dogmatic disagreement. Conversely also, merely to map a route to theological convergence, strenuous as the work is, will not of itself be enough to make everyone want to travel along that way. Schisms are easily begun, seldom ended. They produce unpleasant symptoms, of which three are obvious. The two sides usually misrepresent each other's beliefs. They discourage mixed marriages. Normally on one side there is a denial of the validity of the orders and sacramental acts of the other side. In fourth century North Africa, the Donatists denied all validity to Catholic sacraments; the Catholics fully recognised all Donatist sacraments. In the sixth century the Chalcedonians recognised Monophysite orders; the Monophysites refused recognition to Chalcedonian orders. In both instances the party denying validity to the other was the one to react negatively, as if by a Pavlovian reflex, to ecumenical approaches. The psychological trap here is perhaps one on which history can uncomfortably repeat itself.

People often ask if ecumenical dialogue will ever change anything. The recent experiences of the Church of England have sufficiently underlined the universal truth that the road to unity is stony. One can sense the groans at the thought of yet more seas of ecumenical paper, blandly discussing highly charged emotional issues apparently impervious to rational examination. Many would rather talk about justification by social justice than justification by faith. But our European divisions have exported confusion to Asia and Africa and are, in a measure to which we have become insensitive, a cause of the alienation of modern men and women from the Church. So the stony road is one we have to travel.

Between the two documents being considered there is overlap with Eucharist and Ministry. Lima has a statement on Baptism. ARCIC had to attempt the high and icy ridges of Authority. On Baptism: Lima tries to build a bridge between those who accept infant baptism, in which St Augustine saw the most striking demonstration of prevenient grace, and those who require conscious repentance and faith, to which baptism is then the public sign and seal. Lima asks paedobaptists to avoid 'apparently indiscriminate' baptism, and begs those who regard believers' baptism as the norm to avoid repetition of the sacrament as a denial of fraternal charity. In Britain at least, it appears that relatively few Baptist ministers hold today that infant baptism must of its nature be inauthentic. On the Anglican side we have long had our own debates on the term 'indiscriminate', aware that no candidate comes with perfect repentance and full faith; we pray God to make up all that is deficient. The Lima text is both clearheaded and charitable. We should all consider our practice and act fraternally.

On the Eucharist the two documents have a different structure but converge at the focal points of the sacrament of our redemption. In this sacred, sacrificial meal we celebrate the memorial of Christ's sacrifice accomplished once for all on the Cross. We proclaim the Lord's death till he come. Therefore our action is a recalling of the past into the present in anticipation of the future meal of the Kingdom. The bread is broken and the wine poured out in representation of Christ's death, in which he is both the Offerer and that which is offered. We receive the very Bread of heaven and the Cup of Salvation, the Lord himself.

Lima and ARCIC stress in unison that in this memorial we are not only recalling the past. Our Anamnesis of his unrepeatable sacrifice is of the risen Lord who by the Holy Spirit is present in the here and now of the sacramental action. We are not lifting a chalice to honour a long dead hero who once gave a striking ethical example and happens to be the figure that, in the stream of time and chance, the Christian community has adopted as its leader and model. Our Anamnesis takes the form it does because that past event has universal significance and eternal validity. (Should there be hesitations about the theological weight the term Anamnesis is capable of bearing in eucharistic theology, those hesitations will be secondary to the substantive point that the Christian Eucharist is not merely drawing attention to a contingent event a long time ago.) Accordingly our remembering is more than a subjective act of the individual believer's imagination, but is an objective action of the whole Church in thankgsgiving, praise, prayer, and intercession to the Father.

Lima speaks more than once of the intercessory character of the Eucharist . That is, we ask the Father to accept our sacrifice and to grant that, by the merits of Jesus Christ and through faith in his blood, the entire Church may obtain remission of sins and all other benefits of his Passion. Neither ARCIC nor Lima suggests that our intercession and thanksgiving and offering of ourselves can be possible apart from union by faith and participation in Christ the Mediator. We are made one with our high priest who is not ashamed to call us brethren. That theme is expressed by ARCIC in the clause 'We entreat the benefits of his passion on behalf of the whole Church, participate in these benefits, and enter into the movement of his self-offering'. The text has already excluded repeating or adding to Christ's sacrifice. Therefore the question at issue in the discussion these words of ARCIC have generated, especially among Evangelicals, is not so much eucharistic as Christological. Is the Redeemer in solidarity with his people and does he bring them with him? Is his humanity a vicarious humanity and representative priesthood (as in the epistle to the Hebrews), in whom we may see 'the humanity of God'? Both ARCIC and Lima write with a fear that important critics of ARCIC evidently do not share, namely that some may think it possible for believers to offer an acceptable thanksgiving and intercession to the Father independent of the Mediator. The claim sometimes made that there is *no* movement at all from man to God is not easily voiced by those accustomed to say in their prayers 'And here we offer and present . . .' More important, one must ask if the critic presupposes elimination of free will and of participation in Christ which, in St Paul, is at least as central as justification.

Neither Lima nor ARCIC worked with a merely symbolist and anthropocentric view of the sacraments. Both texts presuppose an objectively given redemption, not one we create for ourselves by moral resolution or existential decision or ecstatic surrender to private or corporate feeling. Lima includes the sentence: 'While Christ's real presence in the Eucharist does not depend on the faith of the individual, all agree that to discern the body and blood of Christ, faith is required'. ARCIC similarly expressed the positive affirmations usually associated with 'receptionism', stressing the necessity of faith but averting the highly Pelagian dangers of saying that the individual's faith is creator of the presence of Christ.

The Roman Congregation for the Doctrine of the Faith (CDF), though giving no verdict but a contribution to the discussion, has expressed strong dissatisfaction with ARCIC's language about the Eucharist. The CDF suggests that it is a condition of that consensus in the faith which is at the basis and heart of unity, that all acknowledge the validity not only (with ARCIC) of the believing affirmation that the consecrated elements are what the New Testament says they are, but also of the old metaphysic of substance and accidents and of the proposition that 'the ontological substance' of the bread and wine ceases to be. The difficulty here will not be so much an assent or a denial as rather to know what in our time the proposition means. The debate within the Roman Communion about the CDF Observations is one into which Anglicans would be unwise and discourteous to enter. We wait to see whether Roman Catholic episcopal conferences generally will agree with the CDF in jettisoning the distinction, once fostered by Pope John XXIII, between dogmatic content and historically conditioned form. Until the CDF Observations, Anglicans had reason to suppose that today Roman Catholic theologians no longer occupy the ground against which Article 28 of the Thirty-Nine Articles directed its venerable cannon. There the principal complaint against the language of Transubstantiation is that it overthrows the nature of a sacrament: that is, the sign is wholly transformed without remainder into that which is signified, because its metaphysical substance is annihilated. The article's objection ceases to have effective polemical force if there is no such entity as a metaphysical substance capable of being annihilated; in other words, if the term Transubstantiation no longer explains *how* the Lord is present. On that understanding, there is no need in ecumenical charity to ask Roman Catholic brothers please to drop this word, to which they have a powerful emotional attachment anyway; it has been silently reinterpreted. That reinterpretation is apparently regretted by some staff members of the CDF. It is an intelligible nostalgia for a lost world.

Similarly Anglicans (and not only they) wait to see if the CDF view is endorsed that one precondition for restored communion is the unanimous acceptance of extra-liturgical devotion to the Blessed Sacrament, even where the form of devotion could obscure the (non-controversial) truth that there is a direct link between consecration, adoration, and communion.

On Ministry, Lima and ARCIC again move in close formation and use convergent language. The ordained ministry, commissioned by prayer and laying on of hands, is God's gift to his people continuing the work of apostles, prophets, and teachers of the New Testament. The Scriptures prescribe no single pattern or structure, but Lima commends the threefold ministry of the early second century as serving today for a sign and means of unity. Churches which have kept the threefold ministry are asked specially to consider how deacons can better represent the Church's calling as servant in the world. Lima also touches on three long debated matters. First, the priestliness given to bishops and presbyters because of their commission to care for word and sacrament and their responsibility for intercession, pastoral care, and discipline: Lima allows this to be distinguishable from the priestliness of the whole Church in union with Christ the great high priest. Secondly, the ordered transmission of the ordained ministry and the episcopal succession is a sign, though no guarantee, of continuity and unity. Churches which at present do not have this succession are, it is drily observed, more likely to value it if episcopal Churches recover their lost unity. Thirdly, the ordination of women: Lima fully recognises the head-on collision of views, and asks for fraternal study in the ecumenical fellowship of all Churches, lest we make things virtually impossible for one another.

For the problems of primatial leadership within an accepted episcopal order we have to turn from Lima to the two ARCIC statements. Anglicans think of authority as diffused through many media by which God guides the Church and protects his people

139

from error. A unique and supreme place is occupied in liturgy and theology by Holy Scripture, accessible to every one of the faithful, together with the creed or apostolic rule of faith for its interpretation. (Both the documents before us work from the Primacy of Scripture.)

We are further guided by the corporate mind of the faithful by which we may be delivered from mere individualism, from the egocentricity of supposing something true because we ourselves have said it, from imagining that our necessarily partial grasp of a problem is complete. Subject to consonance with Scripture, the Thirty-Nine Articles lay down that the Church has authority in controversies of faith. If we are asked what organs of decision-making we have, we usually answer by looking to conciliar consensus in obedience to the word of God. A council needs a president of accepted standing to make it work. The ancient Church looked not only to synods but also to churches of apostolic foundation, and among them, especially in the West, to the church where Peter and Paul taught and died.

The order of bishops does for us now something of what the apostles did for the first Christians. Within that order is there room for a primatial focus? that is, for a bishop who particularly symbolises the unity and universality that all bishops are there to embody? And if so, what special responsibilities should he have for keeping unity in the truth and ordering things in love? Freedom and authority, vitality and form, are mutually necessary to one another in the community of the people of God.

The ARCIC statements on authority spell out some of the small print which in such a discussion can be of cardinal importance. Among these one concerns the honour of our Lord's mother on whom Anglicanism has continued to occupy the ground of Trent.

On the Marian dogmas there may have been in the past too much talking and too little thinking. We can all affirm together that the mother of our Saviour was prepared by grace for the role she accepted, and that, whatever be the precise nature of her glory in the communion of saints, it is surely proportionate to the honour God gave her on earth. If one holds a strongly Augustinian doctrine of the deep corruption of human nature, it is natural to put the question whether the humanity of the woman, through whom the incarnate Lord took his humanity, was normal rather than the psychotic abnormality of our corrupt nature, and whether perhaps the grace which prepared her touched her life from the first moment of her being, as with the prophet Jeremiah. Trent preferred to make no ruling, on the ground of the lack of clear texts in Scripture or early tradition. It is obviously of some importance to safeguard the total solidarity of her humanity with ours. But the Marian dogmas are not an ecumenical 'no-go' area.

It would be idle to pretend that any large number of Anglicans admire the forms that Marian devotion has taken in some parts of the world. But we may recognise that what our Roman Catholic brothers have, as it were, on their statute book has no major place in their hierarchy of truths. While therefore the Marian dogmas may have been used in ways which obscure the one mediatorship of Jesus Christ, that is not inevitable or inherent in their nature. They are capable of being interpreted in an evangelical sense, and it is time that was frankly acknowledged.

It is perhaps among our Anglican characteristics that we dream dreams of universal eucharistic communion, but do not know how to bring them about. We do not easily believe that communion with one see, even so ancient and venerable a see, is a sufficient or indeed a necessary condition of authentic catholicity. But we instinctively warm to the unity and universality that belong to the very being of the Church and which the primacy of Peter's office represents. We do not readily believe that one man, limited in background and outlook as all men are, can in himself embody a sovereign teaching authority. But how delighted we are by the bold affirmation of faith before the indifferent secular world. When they come from the top, bold initiatives have great power.

The definition of Roman primacy at the first Vatican Council has received minimal, moderate, and maximal interpretations. For the maximalist, unity in the Church requires strong, absolutist authority, and where that authority has spoken, submission and obedience are the only appropriate response. For the moderate and the minimalist, the minority at the first Vatican council, who (it is claimed) prevented an absolutist form of the decree, are the truer vehicles of the authentic tradition. The moderate interpreters think complete reliability in teaching authority does not extend to everything, but is limited to very weighty matters. They do not claim universally binding authority even for the Marian definitions, on which the Orthodox churches were not consulted (and of which Orthodox theologians can be highly critical). They see reception by the Church, not as the source of authority, but as the ultimate sign of the truth of a definition. It is obvious that the moderate interpretation of 1870 is far from being incompatible with Anglican ways of thinking. The *Observations* of the Holy Office on ARCIC reject this Anglican view of reception, which is also characteristic of the Orthodox Churches, as well as of moderate Roman Catholic expositors of the first Vatican council. It is not for us Anglicans to tell our Roman brothers what they ought to say. Even if the maximalist view were to prevail, the dialogue must continue. But the maximalist position is not obviously in line with old Catholicism. It may need to vindicate its claim to represent the authentic voice.

Both texts, if taken seriously, are capable of bringing changes to us and others, and the present tendency everywhere is for negotiating Churches to stress their own identity and tradition. Ecumenism easily comes to appear like yet more shifting sand, and it is almost instinctive to feel that at least one's own tradition is reliable and knowable. To this something can be said: ecumenical conversation is not an exercise in diplomacy. (I do not mean by that that offensive abrasiveness is a requirement.) One is not bargaining or saying 'You can have this *if* we can have that'. Once we think of ecumenism as diplomacy, we think that if anything actually moves in the deadlock, that is because some poor fool has made a concession, has compromised with principles, has watered down the truth. This is a disastrous illusion. True ecumenism is listening and kneeling in the presence of God with brothers and sisters in Christ from whom the accidents of history have divided us, and asking how we may together learn the gospel way of authentic reconciliation.

An address to the General Synod of the Church of England at York on 13 July 1983.

10

Ecumenical stock-taking: Unfinished business

THE PROGRESS made by the Anglican-Roman Catholic International Commission was such that reunion of the two Communions within a generation was thought by some to be possible. That now looks a vain hope.

When Christian communities come to suspend communion with each other, they grow apart, and the longer the separation lasts, the harder reconciliation may become. They gradually develop a distinct ethos and express their faith in different terms. If their parting originated in bad temper, they normally frown on inter-confessional marriages, one side will normally refuse recognition to the orders of the other, and both parties hold distorted images of the belief and practice of the other side.

These unpleasantnesses occurred in ancient times between those who accepted the definition of the Council of Chalcedon and those who found its wording, in one preposition, objectionable. Between Chalcedonian and pre-Chalcedonian Churches relations are much improved, but have still some way to go to restored communion. Similarly, between the Orthodox Churches of the East (which now have an extensive diaspora in the West) and the Roman Catholic Church, a millennium of discussion has at some moments come remarkably close to peace and communion; but then the tide of success has receded, and the good will is easily replaced by mutual recrimination, each side holding the other at fault for the disillusionment and failure.

The Vatican's response of 1991 to the *Final Report* of the first Anglican-Roman Catholic International Commission (ARCIC-I) has, at least for a considerable number of students, appeared to be pouring tepid water on a dialogue which had been widely acknowledged, even by some in the Curia, to represent remarkable and genuine progress, going far beyond merely verbal similarity. When the *Final Report* appeared, initially anxious readers had been astonished and gratified to find that the agreed statements did not depend on foggy or subtle ambiguities, but incisively articulated the essence of the matter as shared doctrine. There is now perhaps a danger that, as with the ups and downs of conversation with the

Orthodox, disappointment may take over, each side thinking the other party's will at fault for the 'failure', if that is what it really is (a matter far from clear as yet), or even ready to charge the other party with failing to grasp the nature of real ecumenism.

The Vatican verdict nowhere says or implies that the ARCIC report is dissonant from official Roman Catholic teaching in such a sense that a bishop or priest using this text for catechetical purposes is being instructed to cease from doing anything so hazardous. What is being said is that the language is not identical with that familiar from the definitions of Trent or Vatican I, and that in consequence some few concepts associated by the Vatican with a generalised Protestantism (and not mentioned directly by ARCIC) have not been expressly excluded. For the Vatican, therefore, ARCIC's account of the articles of faith examined is not so much wrong as less than full.

The point about language is not a new one to surviving members of ARCIC-I; for the commission explicitly and consciously sought to avoid terms that carry a heavy polemical load of association.

ARCIC's programme was defined by Pope Paul VI and Archbishop Michael Ramsey in 1966; the ground principle should be to work together towards making united affirmations on the basis of 'the gospels and the ancient common traditions.' Members of ARCIC-I were themselves taken aback to discover how wide and profound was the resulting area of shared discourse. Question and answer, with no holds barred, elicited something that St Athanasius knew in the fourth century, namely that Christians using different terms (in Athanasius' time contradictory terms) could actually mean the same thing. The commission was heartened when in 1980 Pope John Paul was understood to approve the method of going behind habits of thought and expression born and nourished in enmity and controversy. ARCIC endeavoured with considerable, if not invariable, success, to avoid emotionally charged language. The commission, the Pope said, was writing for an age which no longer glories in strife but seeks to come together in listening to the quiet voice of the Spirit.

On the elements of eucharistic belief ARCIC felt it had reached 'substantial agreement', a phrase St Anselm of Canterbury used when dissenting from Cardinal Humbert's opinion that the Greek eucharist using leavened bread is invalid. The Congregation for the Doctrine of the Faith, in its observations of 1982, found ambiguity in the phrase. Though the analysis of the nature of the ambiguity was not very illuminating and even misrepresented ARCIC, it was perhaps a natural and defensible fear on the congregation's part that the unwary might think that matters not mentioned in ARCIC's eucharistic statement were unimportant. It was far from the mind of ARCIC, however, to suppose that eucharistic adoration, for example, is a matter of indifference, or that everything of significance had been said in the statement. The commission was going back to first principles in Scripture and sacred tradition and asking what is done in the eucharistic action. In that respect its agreement was far-reaching enough to provide a foundation on which remaining questions of disagreement, inherited from different community traditions, ought in time to find a fraternal resolution.

If so much could be said together, there seemed good hope that even more would be agreed as the two Communions learnt to trust each other better. The ARCIC members had quickly discovered how deeply their partners in dialogue loved God and his Church. If they shared so much at the deepest level of faith, could they avoid hoping that in due time, by God's grace, language would be given for expressing this sharing? For to love God and keep his commandments is intimately linked with love of God's children (1 Jn. 5 : 2).

That 'substantial agreement' is a phrase troubled by ambiguity is obviously correct. Whether one thinks that on eucharistic doctrine ARCIC achieved such agreement depends on the way in which one defines 'substantial'. For the Vatican it means everything of any importance, and in the terms defined by the teaching authority. An agreement on primary principles must fail to satisfy so tight a definition of substantial.

The Vatican verdict offers a series of points, not all equally momentous and load-bearing, but matters on which it feels unease with the ARCIC report—in some instances because of what is not said rather than because of what the report actually contains. The verdict's repetitions could suggest to a literary critic that the Roman text emerged from a conflation of independent drafts; but if so, the composers of those drafts were writing for an authority which they understood to feel distrust of ARCIC.

Not that the Vatican has in the least set out to rubbish the *Final Report* as incompatible with the Catholic faith—a judgement that would necessarily have been highly critical of, and humiliating for, the eminent and passionately loyal Catholic theologians responsible for much of the document's making. But one does not need to read much between the lines to see that there is a disturbing underlying assumption common to many of the points raised, namely: if nine reasonably literate Anglicans, standing in a tradition shaped mainly by Augustine and Hooker but above all by the Book of Common Prayer, could sign so deeply Catholic a document without one dissenting squeak, there must be some clever ambiguities or at the very least some discreet silences to make possible this surprising fact.

It is not as if the Anglican team was packed with Anglo-Catholics. The *Final Report* does not easily fit the Vatican's image of Anglicanism, nor that familiar Roman Catholic hope that the Anglicans will turn out to be ordinary common-or-garden Protestants in the end. There are moments in the Vatican verdict when what is under fire is not what ARCIC has set out but what some in the Curia think some Anglicans might be able to say if the *Final Report* alone were taken to be sufficient. Therefore there is a kind of search for unidentified submarines below the surface of apparently tranquil waters.

The principal issues now being raised by the Vatican verdict can perhaps be fairly summarised in terms of relatively few significant questions. Among these questions, two are of massive importance but are not thereby necessarily and inherently contentious between Canterbury and Rome.

In the first place, a recurrent theme in the verdict is that, for the Anglicans in ARCIC, the truth of an ecclesiastical definition primarily hangs on the content being consonant with Scripture and accepted sacred tradition, and therefore more on the content than on the organs of authority through which the definition has been proclaimed or is now proposed; whereas, for a Catholic of Roman obedience, the truth of a definition depends less on the *content* and more on the primate or the general council *by whom* the definition is given.

At the back of this contrast lies an old problem which, for Anglican theologians of the seventeenth and eighteenth centuries, turned on the question of 'fundamentals'. Are the fundamentals those defined by the Church, or is the true Church identified by the fundamentals (Word, dominical sacraments, Creed, visible continuity of ministry)? There will not be the easiest of conversations between those who think the essentials are constitutive of the

Church and those who think that the essentials are those proposed for acceptance by the Church through its organs of definition. Nevertheless the antithesis becomes uncomfortable to the point of misstatement when made too absolute. ARCIC sought to keep both aspects together: 'The Church's teaching is proclaimed because it is true: it is not true simply because it has been proclaimed.' (Authority II, 27.)

The ARCIC report unreservedly supported the idea that the Church needs organs of authority to guide the faithful and expressly recognised that 'a service of preserving the Church from error has been performed by the bishop of Rome as universal primate both within and outside the synodal process' (29), Leo I being an instance. But it goes without saying that ARCIC did not think the Church a body liable to limitless error and apostasy which can be held in the truth by no other organ than the see of Peter and vicar of Christ.

The Vatican feels distinctly uncomfortable, with repeated emphasis, when ARCIC notes an Anglican concern that dogmatic definitions be 'manifestly a legitimate interpretation of biblical faith and in line with orthodox tradition'. That looks like too qualified an acceptance of the primatial teaching office. However, not only Anglican readers will be disturbed or even alarmed at the implication, if it is indeed fairly deduced, that there is no conceivable limit on what the papal teaching office may think fit to define. The 1983 Code of Canon Law (749, 3) happily requires 'manifest demonstration' as a condition prerequisite for infallible definition, and that may encourage the hope of a gap less wide than is now being suggested.

It has been widely supposed by careful readers that in 'unpacking' papal infallibility the second of the two ARCIC documents on Authority made real progress—obviously far more than with universal papal jurisdiction, where ARCIC's language is considerably more diffident. Nevertheless, the Vatican verdict picks out the treatment of Mariology as if it were the crucial test of Roman teaching authority. And it is no doubt true that Anglicans, invited to justify a positive evaluation of Roman teaching authority, would be more likely to start from such highly significant actions as papal ratifications of general councils rather than from truths that look secondary in the sense of being dependent and derived.

The problem of relating theological content with the defining organ of definition easily comes to beset the discussion of the Marian dogmas of the Immaculate Conception and the Assumption. Here the Vatican verdict is spectacularly negative, acknowledging no reality to the degree of consensus which ARCIC's careful statement sought to articulate. Admittedly, the ARCIC paragraph includes a sentence that men of peace may well regret, to the effect that 'for many Anglicans, the teaching authority of the bishop of Rome, independent of a council, is not recommended by the fact that through it these Marian doctrines were proclaimed as dogmas binding on all the faithful'. That style of wording may have conveyed an impression of aversion or even scorn when what is being queried is definability *de fide*, with the platitude that high office may suffer diminution of respect if authority is invoked to impose what is not manifestly necessary for full saving faith.

That in devotion and practice the honour of Mary is unduly neglected by many Anglicans is not an issue in this debate. Nor are extravagances elsewhere. But it could have been a step forward rather than backward if the Vatican had felt able to acknowledge that in cold fact there is no real controversy between Rome and Canterbury that the mother of our Redeemer was prepared (like Jeremiah from the first moment of her being) for her divine calling of forming and shaping our Lord's humanity; moreover, that whatever the precise honour bestowed upon her in the communion of saints it is congruous with the honour bestowed on her on earth.

That I take to be close to the heart of the matter in the two Marian affirmations, and the fairly minuscule argument concerns the appropriateness and, some would add, the possibility of giving a very exact answer to the questions 'Did Mary feel the pull of human sinfulness?' and 'What precise form does her heavenly glory take?' The definitions of 1854 and 1950 provide answers to questions that had earlier been in controversy within the Catholic tradition. That of 1854 needs careful statement if one is not to prejudice the solidarity of Mary with the rest of humanity and to impinge on the theologically basic fact that she belongs to the creaturely order. The Vatican verdict is little concerned with these questions of content, and seems to place the truth of the doctrines less in what they say than in the papal right to define them.

Except between Franciscans and Dominicans, the Marian doctrines were not a cause of ecclesiastical division at the time of the Reformation. Of Mary's festivals, that on 8 December is firmly in the calendar of the Book of Common Prayer. The Vatican verdict cannot be faulted in thinking the matter merits further study. But Canterbury and Rome are not out of communion with one another because in dogma they disagree about Mary. Because they are separated, they talk as if dogma about Mary is causative of division, thereby obscuring the fact that the most potent reason for their division is that they are divided.

Unfinished business

This analysis of the Vatican verdict on the *Final Report* of the first Anglican-Roman Catholic International Commission suggests that Rome and Canterbury have more joint work to do. The ecumenical bridges have not been destroyed.

The second grand question now before us which, in the eyes of the authors of the Vatican text, separates Canterbury from Rome is the way of evaluating historical evidence at points where history impinges upon dogmatic affirmations. For instance, the Anglican-Roman Catholic International Commission (ARCIC) did not think it either necessary or correct to assert that the Petrine texts of the New Testament are in themselves a sufficient historical foundation for asserting that Jesus intended to found the papacy. That the role of St Peter in the apostolic age offers strong encouragement to the idea that the Church needs a Petrine office to be an effective bond of unity and universality is a far less controversial proposition, and while grounded in good historical evidence is more than a merely historical statement.

A related issue is whether we are bound to say, in direct and simple terms, that Jesus instituted the sacrament of ordination. There is good reason to believe that he commissioned the apostles whose title—'the sent'—presupposes just that; moreover, that they commissioned successors in local communities who, in time, would commission a further group of ministers with pastoral oversight. If that is what is meant, there is not too much to dispute about. The Vatican verdict, however, quotes the Second Vatican Council on the unbroken linear succession of ordinations as being constitutive of apostolic succession, and conveys the impression that, since the Council settled the matter, further consideration of history is happily irrelevant. Anglicans will not be the only theologians to be anxious at that impression.

149

There is, of course, no doubt about the continuity of the Christian communities in which the early pastors exercised over-sight—*episkope*—and the first epistle of Clement offers striking testimony to ministerial succession as a visible sign of continuity and authenticity (not to mention the accepted responsibilities of the Roman Church for other communities). It is, moreover, not an issue between Canterbury and Rome that history by itself has no method making possible the establishment of norms for the belief and life of the Church. The resurrection of Christ is affirmed on more than historical grounds, but is not deficient in a historical basis.

The question the Vatican has raised is entirely proper, only it is not one which presses on only one party to the discussion. Neither side (if side is the right term) can complacently feel thankful that, if there happens to be a leaky timber, at least it is up at the other end of the ship.

There is an appeal to history in the position that the Church's tradition offers insufficient authority for the ordination of women to the priesthood. ARCIC was concerned to state accurately the nature of the priestly office and of ordination. The question of who is eligible for ordination seemed to the commission a derived and secondary (not insignificant) matter in comparison with its primary task. The Vatican verdict is sure that belief in even the possibility of priesthood for women must presuppose a different and un-Catholic concept of the very nature of the sacrament of order. This position is supported by a reference to the correspondence exchanged between the Vatican and Archbishop Runcie. Any who, like the present writer, found both sides of that correspondence in some degree obscure may feel disappointment here. There would have been a good opportunity for a concise and lucid statement to clarify what the difference is.

Perhaps this is an area where again there is an antithesis between content and defining organ of authority. One can meet thoughtful Roman Catholics who think women could be priests if the pope were so to decide but not otherwise. Likewise there are Anglicans who think women could be priests, given an ecumenical consensus, or at least mutual respect for a liturgical and disciplinary diversity, like that in the case of clerical celibacy (or even the *Filioque* clause added to the Nicene Creed by the Latin Church?). In both Communions, others want to discern clear theological principle, decisive whether for or against. In this matter the organ of authority is easier to identify than the theological argument.

That is not to say that authority is not moved by reasons, or that no serious theological considerations contribute to hesitations about the priesting of women. Beyond all controversy, no one could want doubt to threaten the power of the sacraments to assure communicants of being thereby incorporate in Christ's mystical body. Among the theological themes that make for hesitation, first importance seems naturally to go not to the symbolic role of the presiding celebrant at the Eucharist, acting in Christ's name and person, but to the point that the Lord, who was surely not imprisoned in the social conventions of his time, did not commission women among the apostles, and that this has been a determinant of Catholic tradition through two millennia. The utilitarian argument that priesting women has awkward consequences for the internal harmony of the community and for ecumenical relations, especially with the Orthodox, depends on the practical effects of these other two considerations—2,000 years of tradition and the celebrant's symbolic role. Western theology unlike Eastern Orthodoxy likes tradition to be supported. Though the argument from unchanging practice through 2,000 years may have to be qualified by the reflection that tradition is not now felt to be so absolute by the present generation which has seen vast changes, the point still looks a lot stronger than consideration of symbolism inherent in the celebrant's maleness.

It will astonish a number of students to discover that the Vatican verdict directly links the maleness of the priestly office with the concept of 'character' in ordination: the argument used is that ordination assimilates the priest to the character of Christ, and therefore makes it necessary for the priest and Christ to be of the same sex. ARCIC wished its work to be reasonably clear to laity and therefore did not use the technical word 'character', preferring instead to express the idea of indelibility more accessibly with the phrase 'seal of the Spirit'. The bold and striking exposition of character in the Vatican's verdict goes much further than anything formally defined, but will be understood by those who know their way about the later medieval schoolmen.

ARCIC expresses the essential elements of what the Vatican verdict seems to be looking for in the proposition that 'the action of the presiding minister' in the Eucharist 'stands in a sacramental relation to what Christ himself did in offering his own sacrifice'. It will repay study to examine what is required by the Vatican verdict in addition to all this if due assurance is to be given. It may be proper to recall that ARCIC was not writing an exhaustive treatise on sacramental theory, but concentrating upon matters believed to be points of abrasion and disagreement. Character in ordination has not hitherto been one of these.

Anglicans, of the sixteenth century and since, have not followed the early Martin Luther who, confronted by priests failing in pastoral duty as he understood it, stressed that the true priest is defined by functions performed. Hooker (*Laws* 5, 77, 2) unreservedly affirmed indelible character in ordination. The historic norms of the Church of England lay down that the minister of God's word and sacrament acts in the name of Christ. Influential Anglican theologians have said that when a priest consecrates, blesses or absolves, he does so not on his own authority but, in the apostle's phrase (2 Cor. 2 : 10), 'in the person of Christ'.

Finally, the Vatican welcomes ARCIC's eucharistic statement, acknowledging that in this respect the commission achieved the most notable progress towards consensus. What ARCIC has said about both sacrifice and presence is congenial and indeed even a matter for 'rejoicing'. The joy turns out to be tinged with a touch of regret that the affirmation of the true presence of Christ and his sacrifice is not cast in language more familiar to Roman Catholics, which would be achieved by defining the mode of change with the adverb 'substantially'. This adverbial form can be found in seventeenth-century Anglican divinity wishing to affirm the reality of the change by consecration as independent of the feelings of the worshipper, but also wishing to avoid the precise philosophy of substance. Whether something significant is added to ARCIC's statement by the Vatican's preferred wording is a matter deserving of prolonged study. At the time ARCIC gave considerable thought to the matter and concluded that the term 'transubstantiation', which the commission evaluated positively, did not add to the essential meaning of the text.

The implication of these observations is no doubt that the Vatican's difficulties are not barbed-wire fences that present insuperable hurdles. The questions belong among those derived and dependent affirmations which ARCIC saw as consequential matters arising from the initial eucharistic agreement, needing to be explored together.

The Vatican verdict concludes with the important concession or proviso that its remarks are not intended to diminish appreciation for the work of ARCIC. It is among the first rules of ecumenical dialogue that the integrity of partners to the conversation will be respected, and such positive words should not be treated as soft soap. The request is for further clarification and in some areas for further study. If the analysis in this comment on the Vatican response is roughly correct, it will be evident that some issues raised are not only intricate but points where Rome and Canterbury do not stand on opposite sides of a high defensive wall; they are questions which today every theologian has to wrestle with, and that struggle may better be carried out together rather than in separation.

From this inevitably brief and preliminary examination of the Vatican text it seems a reasonable deduction that the Roman response is not as cool as it has been represented. It is an invitation to continue, not a closing of the door. No one wants a false irenicism which cries 'Peace, peace' when there is no peace. A cry of 'War, war' when there is no sufficient ground for war would be even more undesirable. The Vatican verdict deserves to be wholly supported in its evident conviction that good ecumenism is more than polite co-existence in a state of permanent eucharistic separation.

A long series of past episodes and exchanges leads people to expect failure and disillusion. It is not easy for the historian to think of many instances where a break in eucharistic communion has been healed. But there are some. Success is necessarily excluded only when it is axiomatic that what the other partner in the dialogue can accept must, for that reason, be inadequate.

11

Newman,
a man for our Time

IN THE early 1830s a young Fellow of Oriel, possessed of rare
literary powers but (as Routh the old President of Magdalen
remarked) evidently modest ambitions for success in his career,
became convinced that the liberalism of the eighteenth century
Enlightenment and the Evangelical Revival had combined to cause
much of the Church of England to forget its catholic inheritance
in Hooker, Andrewes, Laud, Cosin, and Thorndike. With a
heterogeneous group of allies among the Oriel dons, he set out to
recall this Church to the rock whence it was hewn. He met with
astonishing and lasting success, but also with fierce opposition and
even panic. Hooker had accepted that the Roman Catholic Church
was a true Church, though not flawless (the sixteenth-century term
for that was 'corrupt'). With a mounting crescendo Newman's
question came to be whether this entailed the conclusion that the
Anglican Church either must be, or could be empirically shown to
be, a Catholic sham. Finally he gave his allegiance to Rome for the
second half of his life. Apart from Manning, compiler of a catena
from the Church Fathers in Tract 78, he was the only Tract writer
to shift his allegiance.

'All I can say is', said Keble, 'that if the Roman Church is the
one true Church, I do not know it.' After Keble's death Newman
liked to quote his words as illustrating the principle of invincible
ignorance, and proving that the saintly Keble would get to heaven.[1]

Newman's exodus did not end, though it damaged, the
Tractarian revival. The changes that he more than any other man
brought about in Anglicanism were far greater than those which
he likewise tried to bring about in the Roman Catholic Church,
within which he came to reckon his life a miserable failure—while
never doubting that he was where he ought to be.[2] Some things he
said before 1845 sounded Romish to Anglicans. After 1845 he
incurred jealousy and distrust by sounding so Anglican and
English.[3] His influence within the Roman Catholic Church was
largely posthumous; during his lifetime he was suspected and
marginalized. Within the Anglican Communion his influence was
profound, and in virtually all his writings including those after 1845
(except for *Loss and Gain*, the autobiographical novel of 1848

154

where there is a touch of 'convertitis'), Anglican readers feel at home.

The subject given to me is Newman's significance for Anglicans, and to understand that it is necessary to begin with what was characteristic of faith and piety in the England of Newman's youth, the age of the industrial revolution and of Benthamite utilitarianism in which 'tradition' was a leaden word.

The fierce Protestantism of the Revolution of 1689 had associated Catholicism with much more than religion. It meant the power of Louis XIV, revocation of the Edict of Nantes, arbitrary autocracy, wretched conditions for the poor. The Revolution weakened the special relationship of Church and Crown (further damaged in 1714 with the accession of a German to whom the Prayer Book was incomprehensible). Above all, it was bad news not only for Roman Catholics but also for the high Anglicans prominent at the Restoration. Respect for ancient liturgies and a sacramental Church became a mark of Non-jurors, ejected from the Church by their conscientious inability to swear allegiance to William of Orange. Non-jurors became prominent in the rebuttal of the ferociously anticlerical Deists. Nevertheless, in the eighteenth century Church of England, two antithetical groups dominated the age: (1) the Latitudinarians or Liberals, men like Hoadly Bishop of Bangor for whom the Church was in effect the religious department of the government, an instrument for social control and ameliora- tion, putting a gentleman into each parish, but not the transmitter of a divine word of redemption; (2) the pietists or Evangelicals, who flourished especially in soil fertilized by Calvinism and then, with John Wesley, acquired the power to flourish almost equally well in a more liberal Arminian milieu, more congenial perhaps to an instinctive high Anglican like Wesley.

Both the Latitudinarians and the Evangelicals were in reaction against the religious conflicts and wars of the seventeenth century, and shared a dislike of theological intricacies: the liberals regarded dogmatic or revealed theology as narrow, the Evangelicals regarded it as spiritually desiccating. Justification by faith had been Luther's grand theme; but the amazing complexity of this matter brought fierce controversies within the Lutheran camp in Germany, culminating in that highly divisive declaration, the *Formula of Concord*. The eighteenth-century Evangelicals hated the intricate disputes, and wanted to believe that justification was 'the simple

*Wesley, who between
distinguishes justification [Part?] & the
[?] Spirit.*

TRADITION AND EXPLORATION

gospel'; that justifying faith is a purely inward feeling of trust; that the elect can know themselves to be elect by the feeling of assurance imparted to them by their trust in Christ. Because of the sympathy some of them felt for John Calvin, they also inherited a deep reserve towards the visible structures of the Church, towards any concept of mediation other than through the historic incarnation and through the Bible; in short there was no special mediation through the sacraments, which were moral aids to piety but not the only ordinary means to their respective graces.

Under the influence of an Evangelical schoolmaster at his school in Ealing, Newman experienced an adolescent conversion, and for a time was a moderate Calvinist (not of course of the extreme or Toplady school). The anniversary of this conversion was kept, even after his becoming a Roman Catholic.

Newman's engagement with popular Evangelicalism is at its most profound in his book on justification, published in 1838, originating as lectures in Adam de Brome's chapel at St Mary the Virgin. It is by general consent acknowledged to be his most remarkable theological book, though deliberately addressed to the general reader in largely untechnical language. He read widely and deeply in the controversial works of the sixteenth and seventeenth centuries and, though ignorant of German and even of the history of the Reformation in Germany,[4] found his way to writings by Luther and Melanchthon. He ended with the conviction that those who hold justification to be on the ground of the imputing of Christ's righteousness and those who hold that we are justified by the imparting of that righteousness are not as incompatible as they like to think. Believers are justified not by a Protestant 'faith alone', nor by the degree of inward renewal under grace, but by the indwelling Christ in the soul (the doctrine encapsulated in one verse of 'Praise to the holiest in the height', beginning 'And that a higher gift than grace, should flesh and blood refine . . .'). The formal cause of justification is God's grace and mercy, not a human act of faith. Evangelicals of the time commonly supposed that, by Reformation principles, justification 'by faith alone' necessarily excludes all means of grace through the God-given sacraments or divinely commissioned ministers (a proposition expressly denied in the Lutheran *Apology for the Augsburg Confession*, 1531). They suffered embarrassment in being unable to give a clear content to the term faith, and in being able only to say what it is not, such as intellectual assent or any kind of moral quality. But if faith is trust, it is paradoxical to assert that no element of love enters into it. Moreover, it is a mistake to set asunder forgiveness and inner renewal: they are simultaneous, not successive. Newman saw (was perhaps the first theologian to see) that Protestant language about the imputed merits of Christ being the believer's only hope is, in another idiom, saying what Catholics affirm in the doctrine of the sacrifice of the Mass: 'The Father looking on us sees not us but Christ in us.'[5]

The warm Evangelicalism of Newman's adolescence and undergraduate years left a permanent mark, but soon was succeeded by a more Liberal phase. His election to be a Fellow of Oriel brought him into the most brilliant intellectual circle in the Oxford of 1822. Tongue-tied and shy, he was fascinated by Richard Whately the logician, an uncouth person who upset his colleagues by spitting into the common room fire, but who stretched Newman's mind by sharp rationalism and antipathy to superstition, whether Catholic or Protestant.

To the end of his days, long after he had found inadequate the obsessive -isms of Evangelical Calvinism and its fascination with the interpretation of the Apocalypse, Newman would speak and write with respect and admiration for individual Evangelicals as men and women of great devotion, seriousness, and holiness. Through them God had 'touched his heart'. What they had not done was to touch his mind. Whately, he said in the *Apologia*,[6] taught him to think.

Whately wanted the Church of England to be more independent of Parliament and Crown. In the anonymously published *Letters on the Church* of 1826 (the authorship of which he never actually admitted but which Newman unhesitatingly ascribed to him),[7] Whately indicted Parliament as altogether incompetent to act as a house of laity for the Church. 'If anyone doubts the possibility of finding in eminent statesmen the grossest ignorance of the doctrines and institutions of the Church of England, let him read the speeches in parliament on the Catholic question.'[8] Protestant as he was, and the more so after he became Archbishop of Dublin in 1831, Whately saw what simplistic nonsense it was to say that where Protestants teach justification by faith, Rome teaches justification by works; or that it is any objection to transubstantiation that the senses perceive no change.[9] Whately urged that the untenability of Roman

Catholicism was shown rather by its too soft yielding to popular superstitions and by its too hard claims to infallibility. But such grounds were not easily maintained by a conservative Protestant Evangelical, whose beliefs about the Bible looked to a liberal strikingly marked by infallibilism and near-superstition.

For the young Newman, Whately's conversation was heady stuff. He became fascinated by Whately's insistence that much controversy is rooted in logical and verbal confusions. In a University Sermon of 6 January 1839 Newman declared: 'Half the controversies in the world are verbal ones; and could they be brought to a plain issue, they would be brought to a prompt termination . . . We need not dispute, we need not prove,—we need but define . . . When men understand each other's meaning, they see, for the most part, that controversy is either superfluous or hopeless.'[10] In these words we seem to hear Whately and Newman agreeing together, even after they had drifted apart.

But Whately was not the only influential figure in the Oriel common room. John Keble the poet, son of an old-style high churchman, supremely modest and self-effacing, was tenacious in adherence to the Anglican tradition of Hooker, Laud, Bramhall, and Jeremy Taylor (though a bit uncertain about Taylor), unsympathetic to Bentham, Mill, and progessivist voices.[11] When in 1864 Pope Pius IX appalled liberal society by producing the *Syllabus of Errors*, Newman remarked that the Syllabus was what John Keble had always thought.[12] A third don at Oriel brought Keble and Newman to understand one another, Hurrell Froude: provocative, blaming the state control of the Church brought in by the Reformation for the sad condition of things, but equally hostile both to the Reformers and to the anti-Reformation Council of Trent. His dislike of the English Reformers as characters was qualified only by his admiration for the matchless beauty of the Prayer Book.[13] Froude's conversation had a catalytic effect on Newman. Both men loved Walter Scott's novels with their rose-coloured picture of medieval times.[14]

Froude contended that Erastian subservience to government lay at the heart of the Church of England's ineffectiveness, and thought it made the Church of England preach to the English not the apostolic faith but what the English felt they wanted to believe. Their criterion of truth was what Englishmen found congenial. Froude's suspicion of Erastianism led him to a prolonged study of

Becket's resistance to Henry II (*Remains* IV). He studied ancient liturgies, confident that the indeed ancient Latin mass is a text first composed by St Peter himself (an opinion echoed by Newman later).[15] Froude longed for Canterbury and Rome to recover the spirit of the ancient Fathers, abandoned by Rome at Trent and by the Reformers when they treated the sacraments to rationalistic disparagement. Yet in the classical records of Anglican tradition Froude knew there was a powerful ingredient of faith and practice that can only be called Catholic. Cannot Anglicans once again speak, as did Hooker and Bishop Bull, of a power to make the body and blood of Christ being vested in the apostles' successors? Or with Hammond of the Church as an infallible transmitter and guardian of the faith? Or with William Law of the sacramentality of ordination? Froude admired Catholic ideals, not Roman actuality. But a note in his journal asks how we can know that Rome's changes from ancient practice are not a valid 'development of the apostolic ethos'.[16] He insisted on giving full value to the preface to the Thirty-Nine Articles enjoining that they are to be taken in their literal and grammatical sense, and saw that this did not mean that Cranmer's wobbly personal beliefs provided a rule for their interpretation. In short, the Articles of the Church of England are patient if not ambitious of a Catholic interpretation, a phrase from Froude which was like an arrow piercing Newman's mind.[17]

Hurrell Froude invited Newman to come on his Mediterranean trip during December 1832 and the early months of 1833. Never in good health, he died aged 33 on 28 February 1836, leaving a candid and intimate journal about his opinions and ascetic mortifications to quell temptation. Newman admired and loved Froude, but feared a plan to publish his journal and papers. Other Tractarian friends overrode his misgivings: publication would show a true saint, and his sharp sayings would make people think hard. Newman's misgivings were justified. The publication was disastrous for the Tractarian cause. Evangelicals, meeting at Islington in January 1837, were already denouncing Pusey as a heretic.[18] Now their worst suspicions were confirmed.

Froude's influence amplified an ascetic, almost monastic inclination latent in Newman's soul. A true Christian profession must be world-renouncing. Only God and the soul matter, not friends or relatives.[19] Already at the Evangelical adolescent stage of development Newman knew himself called to remain unmarried.

As Vicar of St Mary the Virgin his sermons summon his hearers to profound penitence. Public demand led him to print his parish sermons. Of the first volume Samuel Wilberforce wrote to complain that it induced fear and depression. Newman replied that in the present parlous state of the Church of England, sermons and services ought to be 'a continual Ash Wednesday'.[20] There is more pity than fear, but Newman was no doubt inclined to exaggerate how parlous things were. But his pastoral experience as Vicar of St Mary the Virgin convinced him that the Evangelicals' emotional creed could produce disaster. He knew of prayer meetings that had ended in fornication.[21]

Justification by faith alone was being interpreted to mean by feeling alone. Did Luther find humanity in bondage to good works and liberate them only to bring them into bondage to their feelings? At least the Evangelicals had implanted in his mind a conviction of the absoluteness of the Christian revelation, and therefore a reaction against the prevalent relativism which saw all religious positions as equally true to their adherents, equally untrue to others, so that the only criterion must be the sincerity with which the positions were held.

Keble's influence directed Newman to the rich mine of intelligence and spirituality in Hooker and the seventeenth-century Caroline divines. His Assize Sermon[22] taught him that the Church does not need the State to be itself, and should make its own decisions, for example about the appointment of bishops.

The student of St Augustine soon discovers that the man's heart is most transparently disclosed not in his great formal treatises, not in his polemical tracts against heretics and schismatics, against Donatists, Manichees, and Pelagians, but rather in the sermons he preached to his regular congregation of dockworkers and agricultural labourers, the sermons on the Psalms and on St John. So too with Newman. The heart of the Anglican Newman is not found in the writer of brilliant hard-hitting controversy, the author of the *Prophetical Office of the Church* with its vigorous attacks on both Rome and Protestantism. By 'Protestant', Newman meant something essentially negative, vague about positive beliefs, only incisive about what we doubt, deny, ridicule or resist.[23]

Newman never writes more brilliantly than when summarizing a position with which he disagrees. *The Prophetical Office* is a potent, even strident statement of the Via Media, the middle path between that excess of authority in Rome and the lack of it in the Reformation bodies. One does not have to read between the lines to see that Newman thinks authentic Anglicanism closer to Roman Catholicism than to popular Protestantism.[24] Yet with Rome there remains a divide: 'If we advance to Rome as a sister or mother Church, we shall find too late that we are in the arms of a pitiless and unnatural relative'.[25] The denial of the cup to the laity,[26] popular Marian devotions that encroach on the honour of Mary's Son,[27] an excess of dogmatic anathemas, seem to the Newman of the Via Media a barrier to the acceptance of Rome. But it is, he thinks, a foolish error to suppose that authority can lie in Scripture alone apart from the interpretation given by tradition in the witness of the community. And if as some Protestants long to hold, the sense of Scripture is clear, how is it that Protestantism has begotten so many sects with incompatible opinions?

The Prophetical Office of the Church was written at a time when some critics were beginning to express alarm that the Tractarian stress on the visible Church and sacraments would in the end lead them to Rome. Puritans had said that about seventeenth-century Caroline divinity in Laud and Bramhall and Taylor, and received from Bramhall the tart reply that, among Puritans, conversions to Rome much exceeded those among Prayer Book using Anglicans. The Tractarians were felt as a threat because for a century neither Liberal nor Evangelical had said anything about the universal Church. To proclaim that article of the Creed was sure to precipitate a row.

The Roman Catholic community in England had been steadily increasing. They grew from about 80,000 in the 1760s to three-quarters of a million by 1851.[28] Irish immigrants strengthened the working class churchgoers, largely absent from the Church of England. The Tractarians, then, were not hoping to strengthen the Roman Catholic Church. The Romeward movement had a quite independent existence. Newman after 1845, Manning after 1852, and other converts injected a high culture and intelligence into a community which needed more of these assets. Though figures like Lord Acton should warn against exaggeration, it is broadly true that the converts transformed the situation, and caused offence to old Catholic families by failing to conceal their pleasure in that fact. Newman's distinctive and personal contribution after 1845, perhaps, was to demonstrate that it was possible to be in communion with Rome and to be a hundred per cent English.

The Tractarians were misread by Evangelicals and Liberals when they were credited with a conspiratorial intention to get Canterbury to submit to Rome. They actually feared the Roman Catholic revival and were alarmed by the defencelessness of Anglicanism if its theology was either Liberal or Calvinist Evangelical. Their ideal was Catholicism without universal papal jurisdiction. But they were uncomfortable with some popular devotions admitted by Rome; and most of those in the Tractarian tradition, including Pusey and Keble, accepted the legitimacy of a married priesthood. A married priesthood was not, of course, any barrier to the acknowledgement of the validity of orders; witness Roman recognition of Orthodox orders. But conversion to Rome was a high barrier to a priest with a wife, unless he wished to find an escape from pastoral responsibility.

The group which conceived the plan of Tracts for the Times was miscellaneous with very diverse backgrounds, not at all tightly knit. There were significant differences among them. Newman was acutely conscious of his differences from Pusey, less so of those from Keble. They did not all share the same estimate of the Reformation, though it is safe to say that none of them sacralized the sixteenth century as the breaking out of light after fifteen centuries of Stygian darkness, surely the most improbable of all interpretations of church history.

The early Tracts achieved a success that astonished the group. They sold widely among parish clergy. But in Oxford itself, the grand draw lay not in the Tracts or editions of Anglican classics, but in the sermons of the Vicar of St Mary the Virgin, delivered on Sunday afternoons at 4.00 or 5.00. These discourses drew an ever increasing crowd from the more thoughtful and bookish stratum of the undergraduates.[29] (A letter to James Stephen, written in February 1835, mentions with surprise that his sermons were found attractive by women, 'who do not reason and only feel').[30] Contemporaries had become bored by the predictability of repetitive Evangelical preachers with their favoured themes of original sin, justification by faith, the atonement, the feeling of being assured of pardon and final perseverance. The Liberals like Hampden, the Regius Professor, had no real belief in the presence of Christ to his people in the sacramental life of the Church, no sense of mystery in divine revelation, and were much inclined to suggest or imply that Unitarians were just as good Christians as those who adhered to the incarnation and the Trinity, and indeed that all sects felt the same truth which they were expressing in different ways.

Newman's sermons are very unlike an Evangelical seeking to melt his hearers and move them to conversion. But they are strikingly biblical. More than one contemporary witness tells of the riveting way in which he used to read the lessons from Scripture. As a preacher he had no tricks of rhetoric. He kept his eyes buried in his carefully composed script. Yet his congregation was utterly held, and it was not comfortable stuff to hear. Apart from some satirical passages[31] there were no witticisms, few sharp epigrams or particularly striking utterances, but always a profound intensity on two central themes: that the good moral life is of the substance of worship, and that the Church and sacraments are not optional extras or marginal ceremonies that serious Christians can use or not use according to their fancy, but essential to the gospel: 'Forms are the food of faith'.[32]

Every sermon has a potent scriptural content. But Newman was clear that Scripture is not self-explanatory. It needs an authorized interpreter. If an inquirer asks the Archbishop of Canterbury what the Church of England believes on this or that major issue, and if the answer he receives is to the effect that for the Church of England the sole authority is the Bible which each believer is free to interpret as he feels led or inclined, the conclusion is almost irresistible that this Church does not know what it believes.[33]

Newman's hearers at the time felt that his sermons had little High Church theology, but were directed to moral issues. The reader of the printed text can quickly discern that they were learning much about the Church, about apostolic succession, about baptism and Holy Communion as mediating the very presence of the Lord and his sacrifice,[34] but these themes are integrated into the grand theme of the necessity of reality and the quest for authentic holiness. The sacramental ecclesiology is there because of the means of grace and sanctification. The Lord gave sacraments because we need them, and we need them because they bring to us the grace and help necessary for the path to a sober, righteous, and holy life.

A letter of 27 January 1846 to Henry Wilberforce recalls that Newman used to give private absolution according to the form in the Visitation of the Sick in the Prayer Book, and that at the early

Eucharist at St Mary's he 'had an absolute and overpowering sense of the Real Presence'. Newman did not first learn these things after becoming convinced that Rome has the Truth. They came to him out of the native Anglican tradition.

The St Mary's sermons are dominated by the quest for reality in religion. Strip away worldly compromises. Obey conscience, the very voice of God. In rational judgements second thoughts are often best, but not in matters of conscience where first thoughts are right.[35] There is no more exquisite pain in human life than that of a bad conscience, and murderers have preferred to die at the executioner's hand than to live with the memory of what they did. How many live lives haunted by the ghosts of the past, by sins brushed aside unconfessed and still unabsolved.[36] Newman's pastoral labours at St Mary's convinced him that there was danger or even catastrophe in telling people that a personal sense of assurance is the criterion of being one of God's elect,[37] and that there is no mortal sin other than lack of faith.[38]

To put such stress on feeling to the neglect of the ethical encourages superficiality. England, the richest country in the world,[39] is dominated by the appetite for wealth and power,[40] 'For the sake of gain, do we not put aside all considerations of principle as . . . absurd? . . . Is there any speculation in commerce which religion is allowed to interfere with? . . . Do we care what side of a quarrel, civil, political, or international, we take, so that we gain by it? . . . Do we not support religion for the sake of peace and good order . . . [and] only in so far as it procures them?'[41] People think the function of religion is simply to turn out good citizens and no more.[42] So the profession of the ordained ministry is regarded as comfortable.[43] In one sermon of March 1840 Newman allowed himself an express observation that, without questioning the legitimacy and propriety of marriage for the clergy, nevertheless there is a higher dedication possible to the celibate.[44] The domestic virtue of the parsonage family is admirable; but Newman regrets the rarity of the heroic in the Anglican ideal.[45]

To Latitudinarians and to many Evangelicals, sacraments were either merely symbolic reminders akin to visual aids or, if supposed to be more than that, perilously akin to superstition. In the 1820s it was still common for Holy Communion to be celebrated in a Church of England parish church only at Easter, Pentecost, and Christmas, the three being the minimum number specified by rubric in the Prayer Book for communicants.[46] Daily services were unusual. At St Mary's Newman established an early weekly celebration, Communion on saints' days, and daily mattins and evensong (here following the high Anglican tradition represented by Keble).[47] Newman was never interested in ceremonial or vestments, but by 1837 some of the Tractarian followers were beginning to look that way: in 1837 two Fellows at Magdalen took to wearing a stole.[48] Newman thought it a hindrance to Catholic recovery when followers 'become peculiar in externals' and practise 'ostentatious fasts'.[49] When people saw popery in bowing to the altar, Newman could reply that at Christ Church the Dean and Canons had long done so by immemorial tradition.[50]

The controversies that came to rage round Newman's head in 1841-2 left him sore. Any lie about him found ready credence. Yet why was he being censured for reasserting the beliefs of Laud or Bramhall, acknowledged pillars of Anglican ecclesiology and certainly no papists? The storm broke with Tract 90 in February 1841: the Thirty-Nine Articles, interpreted with hairsplitting exactitude in their literal and grammatical sense, were subordinate to and no rejection of Catholic tradition; only they are not wrong to question universal papal jurisdiction and to affirm the Real Presence without conceding transubstantiation. Tract 90 was more Anglican than it was represented to be; not much was said there which had not been quietly and less ingeniously said by Pusey in an open *Letter to the Bishop of Oxford* published two years earlier. Pusey disliked the manner of Tract 90. Newman's delight in exact logic made the argument sound clever, enjoyably so if you wanted to agree, evasively sophisticated if you did not. For example, people thought sophistry the observation that Article 22, which criticizes the invocation of saints, does not deny their intercession for us in that one communion and fellowship in which God has knit together his elect. They were nettled if told that the Benedicite ('O ye spirits and souls of the righteous') has an invocation. That there might be dangers Newman could readily concede.

Tract 90 was written to put a brake on over-enthusiastic followers urging that the claim of Rome was irresistible. Prominent among these was William George Ward, Mathematics Tutor at Balliol and logician; acute in conversation, confused and soggy as a writer, he proposed to cure the Church of England of its ills by radical Romanization, including both obligatory auricular confession and the Marian devotions of St Alfonso Liguori. Ward had in youth attended Roman Catholic services, and the fever was not implanted in him by Newman. But he claimed to be taking Newman's principles to their ultimate conclusion, asserting the right to interpret the Articles in a 'non-natural' sense, a view which Newman disowned.[51] Newman could reasonably point out that he remained opposed to removing the old Oxford requirement of assent to the Articles, and that if he was asking for latitude of interpretation here and there, his difficulties with the Articles were trivial compared with Evangelical embarrassment with the Prayer Book order for infant baptism or the absolution in the Visitation of the Sick or with the very uncalvinist Article 16. He had spoken of 'the stammering lips of ambiguous formularies'. Did not all admit that Article 17 on predestination was acceptable to both Calvinist and Arminian? Newman was asking for much less liberty than the Liberals. He felt sad to see how in the Church of England there is toleration for any beliefs except affirmations of Catholic truth[52] (a view which received astringent expression in *Loss and Gain*).

During 1841, with the major exception of the highly intelligent Bishop Thirlwall at St David's,[53] bishops fulminated against Tract 90. Even his own Bishop of Oxford, Richard Bagot, who endured hostility for giving support to the Tractarians, became intimidated into uttering words of mild regret. The immunological system of the Church of England was rejecting Newman as an alien intruder; Newman deduced that its self-understanding was to abjure a Catholic understanding of the Church and sacraments, which a Protestant Establishment must spontaneously vomit forth. Invite this Church to enjoy its Catholic inheritance, and instinctively it will scuttle for cover. The hammering charges of bishops (he called it a 'war dance') convinced the always touchy Newman that the Church of England did not now wish to be reminded of its Catholic heritage in Thorndike, Taylor or Sanderson. The anger and hurt felt by Newman, especially at insinuations that he lacked honesty and integrity, were so great that it took time for him to feel sure of his motives in wishing to become a Roman Catholic: he must not be converted merely because there are unreasonable people in the Anglican communion.[54] There was of course a positive pull to Rome in Newman's quest for mystery, awe, reverence, the reality of a religion where God comes to humanity through his own appointed sacramental signs. As he lost confidence, he came to think Anglican worship dreary.

At the same time Newman was drawn to Rome by his patristic studies, by idiosyncratic arguments from his readings in the ancient Fathers. Was the autocephaly of the Church of England analogous to the schismatic Donatists in fourth-century North Africa, or to the Egyptian Monophysites of the sixth?[55] In his retreat at Littlemore he translated Athanasius, and his notes to that translation show him torn between his admiration for Bishop Bull and his anxiety that emperor-toadying Arians like Eusebius of Caesarea were Erastian Anglicans before the latter. To Pusey and Keble such arguments seemed bizarre. Indeed, Newman himself knew that the Catholic denial of validity to Anglican sacraments was anticipated by the Donatist denial of validity to all Catholic sacraments; Bramhall had taught him that.

In 1841 Wiseman at Oscott nursed hopes that Tract 90 might facilitate a lowering of barriers to communion between Canterbury and Rome. Newman visited Wiseman high with optimism, but was cast down by the answer that it was not enough to show that the council of Trent and the Thirty-Nine Articles were compatible; the Church of England would need formally to accept the decrees of Trent as the principle for interpreting the Articles. Thereafter his hope that help might come from the Roman side faded. Nevertheless, Newman the Anglican Tractarian was not wrong to point out that the Anglican tradition, especially in the Ordinal and the Prayer Book when properly used as intended, was unintelligible apart from essentially Catholic elements. He was not wrong in holding that the Thirty-Nine Articles (so hostile to Baptists) are less Protestant than many in 1830 and later wished to believe, or in observing that the term 'Protestant' never occurs in Prayer Book or Articles. In both halves of his life Newman brought Anglican and Roman Catholic closer together, as he himself was to write in a letter of 15 October 1874.[56]

His treatment of the Thirty-Nine Articles in Tract 90 is logically much akin to his *Letter to the Duke of Norfolk* (1875) in which he proposed a 'legitimate minimizing' of the first Vatican Council on papal primacy, presented as an attack on Gladstone but, as everyone in the know realized, in fact attacking Manning. Anglicans believe that the Church has reliably transmitted the word and sacraments, since 'The Church has authority in matters of faith' (Art. 20). Then is it extravagant to hold that St Peter's successor has a privileged position in articulating the faith of the universal Church and in providing an organ of decision? Vatican I did not affirm popes to be inspired, only to be negatively protected on grave issues at critical times from leading the Church astray; and it is proper to ascribe such authority to the head of the episcopal college.

Although initially doubting the authority of a council so far from unanimity, and explicitly regretting that it made much harder the task of converting people to Catholicism, Newman was far more positive about Vatican I than Acton, for whom the decree affirming that the pope had supreme authority apart from the bishops was a problem which might be explained hereafter but was not now clear enough for internal assent.[57] But Newman explicitly anticipated the judgement of the majority at Vatican II that Vatican I was onesided and incomplete, needing a parallel statement about the episcopate. His *Letter to the Duke of Norfolk* caused almost as much *frisson* in Rome as Tract 90 had once done in Oxford.[58]

But my subject is not Newman and Rome but Newman and Canterbury. He put two weighty questions to the Anglican Communion which have not lost force. Although in the Church of England some have always held that an alteration in, say, the creed or sacraments or ministry would alter its being (not only what it has but what it is), others have held with Edmund Burke[59] that, like any other body corporate, the Church may change her laws without altering her identity, and this coheres with the right of reformation asserted in the sixteenth century without requiring the consent of others. So Newman restates Hurrell Froude's question: Does the ambition of the Church of England to be national lead it to feel so relatively indifferent to the claims of the universal as to have the unconscious consequence that Anglicans make their Church correspond to what the English wish to believe about themselves; that is, a wet and tolerant body, adhering to Christian tradition but remaining free in private judgement, not greatly interested in the notion of a visible Church that faithfully teaches a given revelation defined by Bible and sacred tradition? Anglicanism is periodically threatened by a Do-it-yourself spirit of consumer choice. And the ideal of a national Church can glide into making the Church a social instrument of government for secular ends. (Not that there are no analogies to that in Catholic tradition.)

Secondly, Newman's opaque musings about ancient Donatists and Monophysites veil a more substantial question. The Anglican Communion claims to be a branch of the one Catholica, but does not always know how to behave as such, does not easily recognize that the rights thus asserted imply duties. The Thirty-Nine Articles do not assert the pope to be Antichrist; in denying his universal jurisdiction they concede that he is at least lawful bishop of Rome. Yet all over the world Anglicanism is found to be in rivalry to the Catholica, offering, in Newman's cutting phrase, 'a mimicry of Catholicism'. Can it be the divine intention that branches of the Catholica be out of communion with each other?

The force of these two questions may be considerably mitigated if one notices how little thought Newman's concept of the Church gives to the ancient orthodox Churches of the east, who remain largely beyond his horizon and knowledge. They represent a living Catholic body, yet without papal jurisdiction. It caused them pain when Vatican II not only reasserted but even enhanced the supremacy of the pope over the episcopate generally.

Underlying this last question lies the central and most intricate problem of the contemporary ecumenical movement (so much misunderstood by those who think ecumenism a polite name for treachery), namely the question of the nature and being of the Church founded upon the apostles and prophets. 550 years ago at Florence a large-hearted pope was able briefly to restore communion between the Greek East and the Latin West on the basis that, within one Catholic Church recognizing Roman primacy, differing traditions can be legitimate. If Newman was not a typical Tractarian (as indeed he was not), that is because he did not think about these issues in the same way as Keble and Pusey; and his concept of the Church after 1845 could make room for neither Canterbury nor eastern patriarchs. But if, as Manning thought, he was an untypical, rather too Anglican type of Roman Catholic, that is essentially because he did not think it a necessary or authentic mark of Catholicism to be authoritarian, centralized, intolerant, and legalistically juridical. I take that to be the crucial sense in which Newman anticipated the convictions of the majority of bishops at the time of the Second Vatican Council.

12

Newman's doctrine of justification

NEWMAN'S *Lectures on (the Doctrine of) Justification*[1] is a book that deserves to be ranked at least on a par with any of his more widely read writings on theology. In the twentieth century perhaps the book is comparatively seldom read, certainly less than the *Apologia* or the *Grammar of Assent* or *The Idea of a University* or the letters and diaries. In Newman's time one cannot say that the topic was in the forefront of discussion. There was a widespread feeling that the debate belonged almost entirely to the past of the sixteenth century; that in a topic of amazing intricacy relatively few people really understood what anyone was saying; indeed perhaps it was a dispute merely about words and polemical slogans, not religious realities, and could be neglected by Christians seriously engaged in the battle of the mind against the rising tide of secularist thinking. The eighteenth-century Enlightenment had showed little interest in the problem, which was then regarded as an exhausted debate, productive of schisms and bloodshed in religious wars, and at all times likely to become enveloped in an arid scholasticism. The desiccated disputes of the Lutherans and then the Calvinists during the second half of the sixteenth century,[2] the fiercely negative language of, for example, the Westminster Confession of Faith, chapter 11, the divisiveness of the too charitably entitled Formula of Concord, helped to generate a quest either for cool-headed rationality or for warm-hearted pietism, both alternatives being free of dogmatic wrangles about revealed theology in areas where truth was hard to grasp.

Nevertheless, devout people in the eighteenth century had not entirely pushed the matter on to the shelf. The Evangelical revival, especially where it was rooted in a soil prepared by the fertilizer of Calvinism, stimulated a special interest in justification by faith alone, because for the Evangelicals this doctrine was understood to be making the inner feelings a matter of primary consequence. Religion for them was no affair of external rites like sacraments but exclusively of the individual heart; it was not located in respected charitable activities, not in attendance at church services, not in prayers whether private or corporate, but in the individual's continual consciousness of utter depravity before God and exclusive dependence on the imputing to the believer of Christ's righteousness, in which the believer in no sense shared. So at least Newman was brought to believe when, in consequence of his Evangelical conversion in adolescence, he came under the momentous influence of Calvinist Evangelical preachers and writers, such as Thomas Scott (1747-1821) or William Romaine (1714-95).

In the spring of 1837 Newman gave lectures on justification in Adam de Brome's chapel at St Mary's, Oxford. The impulse to propose this subject came from a controversial brush with the vehemently Protestant *Christian Observer*. Newman had been thinking about the subject, off and on, for a full decade past, and had done considerable reading in the principal Reformation divines on the subject. Cassander's Catholic *Consultatio*, written in 1564 (published 1577), was read and evidently found congenial. Newman had carefully studied Chemnitz, Chamier, Gerhard, and naturally the main Anglican writers—Hooker, Field, Davenant (a Calvinist in whom Newman found much to admire),[3] and Bull. The third book of Calvin's *Institutes* was also much pondered, and the cautious, conciliatory statements of Melanchthon. But in the delivered lectures and in the published book, with the exception of various appendices, Newman was anxious to make the central issues utterly clear to his hearers and readers. Accordingly, he avoided the elaborate technicalities with which the subject was commonly beset. Deliberately he adopted a style falling between lectures and sermons. In consequence, some parts of the text provide masterly and detached analysis, while other parts are like the parochial sermons in being in some degree rhetorical and homiletic. He wished to be understood by ordinary persons, clerical and lay alike. Although the book was not composed as a systematic or academic treatise, the work commanded the deep respect of weighty experts. The German historian J. J. Döllinger particularly admired it. Alfred Plummer's conversations with him report that he 'always spoke of Newman's *Justification* as the greatest masterpiece of theology that England had produced in a hundred years'.[4] As is commonly the case with Newman's writings, the prose is never so brilliant or the argument so acute as when he is stating the position of those with whom he makes no secret of disagreeing.

For Newman's *Justification* is a highly polemical work, and its main argument is directed against the beliefs which he himself had held as an Evangelical. At the age of thirty-six he had come to feel it essential to tackle the very citadel of the 'popular Protestantism,' the outworks of which he had already assaulted in the *Prophetical Office*. Without a treatment in some depth of the issue of justification, his statement of the *via media* must be gravely incomplete. The Evangelicals were legatees of the pietist convictions of Germans like P. J. Spener (1635-1705), inheritors of the tenaciously held opinion that the failure to grasp the doctrine of justification by faith alone lay at the heart of the Catholic distortion of the gospel of forgiveness and grace which was to them the very glory of the Reformation, thereby making the sixteenth Christian century age an age of sacredness as no century other than the first could be. Some of the less theologically minded Evangelicals liked to speak of the doctrine as 'the simple gospel'. The maze-like tortuousness and intricacy of the big books on the subject (including Spener's which is a fat and formidable work to read)[5] generally passed them by.

In the seventeenth century, Bishop George Bull had begun his *Harmonia Apostolica* (in which he set out to reconcile St Paul and St James, fitting Pauline doctrine into a framework taken from St James rather than the other way round), by making the sharp observation of the doctrine of justification that 'theology does not afford an article more hard to be understood'. It is, he remarked, an article of faith of the greatest consequence; yet sadly the subject is full of 'minute distinctions' and 'ingenious devices', wrapped in 'clouds and thick darkness'. Newman certainly owed more than a little to Bull's *Harmonia* and to his vindications of that book against critics. But, significantly perhaps, his references to Bull are not numerous; nor does he much invoke Jeremy Taylor. Such writers were explicitly unsympathetic to Calvinism. Bull once turns on one of his critics with the sharp words that he is 'greatly given to the theology of Geneva'. Bull looks back on a time when 'things had got to such a state that it was scarcely lawful to interpret either the decrees of our Church [i.e. of England] or even the Scriptures themselves otherwise than according to the standard of Calvin's Institutes'. He concludes that 'every age has its own flood of opinions to which if anyone oppose himself he is either carried along by it or overwhelmed'.[6] Although Bull and especially Taylor certainly anticipated parts of Newman's positions, quotations from anti-Calvinists could not have served Newman's pastoral purpose. He could win more support by appealing to Hooker or especially Davenant or Melanchthon. Taylor had been suspected of too much sympathy for Rome in his lifetime, and had had to produce his

Dissuasive to reassure; Calvinists disliked his recasting of the doctrine of original sin.

Accordingly, Newman's footnotes mainly refer to firmly Protestant authors, especially when he can find in them (as was not difficult) propositions that cohered with his main contention, namely that those who stand for imputed righteousness and those who stand for imparted righteousness are ultimately talking about one and the same thing.[7] Moreover (and here Newman's thesis became distinctive) believers are justified not by faith (Protestantism) nor by renewal (Catholicism), but by the indwelling Christ in the soul, 'God's presence and his very self and essence all divine'.

Newman wrote his book during 1837 and the first weeks of 1838, and found the subject one of extreme difficulty. The constant revision and rewriting were on such a scale that substantial sections were yet further reformulated at the proof stage.[8] 'Nothing I have done has given me such anxious thought and so much time and labour', he wrote to Mrs Thomas Mozley on 9 January 1838.[9] The main body of the lectures was already in proof before he even began to compose the necessarily technical (but crucial and to the theologian absorbing) appendix on 'the formal cause' of justification. So he wrote to Mrs John Mozley on 29 January.[10] Newman found himself taken by surprise at the difficulty. The subject had been in his thoughts 'years and years before a scientific treatment of either Church Authority or the Arian Question could be'.[11] 'What has taken me so much time is first the adjustment of the ideas into a system, next their adjustment in the Lectures, and thirdly and not the least the avoiding all technicalities and all but the simplest and broadest reasonings.' Because of the sheer difficulty of the subject, Newman feared that his book could be found 'hard and laboured to read'.[12]

The last proof was finally returned to the printer on 21 March 1838, and by the first week of April the book was in the shops. A few days after the last proofs were returned to press, Newman first acquired a copy, in French translation (for the German was beyond his powers), of Möhler's momentous *Symbolik*, the most eloquent and well-formulated restatement of Catholic doctrine published in the first half of the nineteenth century.[13] It is a surprising fact that his *Justification* owed nothing to Möhler, for they shared many things in common, despite the fact that in 1837-8 Newman's heart and mind were resolutely Anglican.

As copies became available to him, Newman particularly despatched complimentary copies of the book to at least two significantly interested parties. One was the rector of Winwick in south Lancashire, J. J. Hornby, who in 1834 had edited the *Remains* of the Irish Anglican layman Alexander Knox. One chapter in the first volume printed an essay by Knox on justification, which caused some stir. Knox interpreted Article XI of the Thirty-Nine Articles in a way strikingly akin to that of Bishop Bull. In Knox's understanding that Article certainly excluded individual merit from being a cause of personal justification and also certainly asserted 'imputation'; what it did not affirm was that such a 'reputative' justification is wholly independent of a prior root of righteousness implanted in the soul by God. Justification, in short, is not purely forensic without moral content.

The second principal recipient of an author's copy was George Stanley Faber (1773-1854), Master of Sherburn hospital, Durham, and at one time, as a young man (1795-1803), a fellow of Lincoln College, Oxford.[14] Faber was typical of his times in being an Evangelical clergyman fascinated by the discovery of the inner chambers of the Pyramids. He published work in which he searched the prophecies of the Apocalypse for the secret signs of Antichrist. He believed that Negro people have black skin because of the transmitted penalty of the sixth plague of Egypt in Exodus. He had written a widely used study of predestination, liked by Calvinistic Evangelicals, from whom he dissented by his contemptuous rejection of unrestricted private judgement. He felt confident that the sense of the Scriptures is perspicuous, and the individual must submit, not make up his own mind about the meaning. Faber was provoked by Hornby's publication of Knox's essays and letters, and shortly before Newman lectured wrote an attempted rebuttal of the dangerously papistical doctrines propagated by Bishop Bull and Alexander Knox. He was attacking two Anglican authors with whose writing on the subject Newman felt the deepest affinity. Newman accordingly sent him an early copy of his lectures, with a courteous letter. Faber's reply was also courteous, but reserved his position; he was reading the book amid the hubbub of London and needed to retreat to the quiet of the countryside to digest Newman's argument as it deserved.[15]

In the second edition of his book of 1839 G. S. Faber inserted a sharply hostile appendix about Newman's book. He complained both that he found Newman 'painfully difficult, if not absolutely impossible, of comprehension', and that the book's ingenuity of mystification would seduce incautious admirers into all the grossness of Tridentism'. For Newman 'mixes up together wholesome food and rank poison, the sound doctrine of the Church of England and the pernicious dogmas of the Church of Rome'.[16] After Newman had become a Roman Catholic in 1845, Faber put into print that he believed Newman to have been a secret Romanist for a full decade before being finally received. Faber's nephew F. A. Faber, an Anglican clergyman, thought the charge unfortunate, and sought to mediate between Newman and his uncle. Newman included his letter to the nephew of 6 December 1849 in his *Apologia*, chapter 4.[17] Stanley Faber at first withdrew the accusation that Newman was for ten years saying what he did not actually think, but in 1851 renewed it with a peculiarly hurtful letter to Newman, advising him to bear with resignation the consequences of being a Roman Catholic priest who, as it was understood, would 'always lie for the good of his Church'.[18] Newman sent the letter straight back to him.

Newman's *Justification* set out to distinguish his middle way in Anglicanism from popular Protestantism of the time (to which he gave the blanket title 'Lutheranism') and from the Roman Catholic doctrine defined at Trent in 1546-7. Newman cannot honestly be said to have known very much about Martin Luther or the history of the German Reformation.[19] He did not read German, and showed no sign of sharing Bishop Bull's remarkable enthusiasm for the Augsburg and Württemberg Confessions.[20] He had evidently given some study and thought to Luther's tract 'On the Liberty of a Christian'. His quotations from Luther also show that he knew the 1533 commentary on Galatians, of which a bowdlerized version in English had been produced by Elizabethan Puritans (omitting the more Catholic bits, and especially the acknowledgement that the Church of Rome retained the fundamentals of the faith). He drew more from Gerhard's seventeenth-century systematization of Lutheranism in the age after the Formula of Concord.[21] Newman was familiar with Calvinism, both by virtue of his early education and through his reading of the *Institutes* and commentaries.

The reader of *Justification* quickly receives the deep impression that the middle way for Newman is nearer to Rome than to Wittenberg or Geneva. The popular Protestant conception of justification is treated as morally dangerous, ecclesially sectarian, and selective in its use of a handful of scriptural texts. The Catholic view, by contrast, is never dangerous, though indeed incomplete and defective. Moreover, it is grounded, as Newman demonstrates at length, upon far wider biblical foundations, was endorsed by Augustine's transformist doctrine of grace and the main line of tradition, and had the merit of simplicity in treating right conduct as being in God's sight a matter of the most profound import for salvation.

The Protestants, Newman bluntly declared, were in this question like the Arians who settled everything to their own satisfaction by appealing to a few texts, which were then erected into an all-embracing principle for interpreting everything else. Newman distanced himself from the then widely held view among Evangelicals (a view which Philip Melanchthon expressly disowned in his *Apology for the Augsburg Confession*)[22] that to speak of justification 'by faith alone' necessarily excludes any means of communicating grace through the dominical sacraments or apostolic ministers. His most penetrating critique, however, lies in his pinpointing of a central difficulty of embarrassing proportions for the Protestant Evangelicals, namely that, while asserting faith alone to be the sole instrument of justification, they find it impossible to offer any but the foggiest definition of what they mean by faith: they can say something only of what it is not, namely not a mere assent to belief in God, or to the gospel history, or even submission to due authority. They are anxious to assert that it is to be radically distinguished from any moral quality: repentance or love may be accidents, but love is a by-product, not of faith's essence. From Gerhard, Newman cites the phrase that faith is a 'fiduciary apprehension', a feeling of trust and total dependence on the Redeemer for mercy. Into that trust no element of love may be intruding. Nevertheless, the Protestants very rightly say that justifying faith must be a lively faith, not a mere mental assent. Newman wants to bring them to acknowledge that if faith is to possess the vitality they attribute to it, it will not be evacuated of repentance, love, and openness to renewal under God's grace. Trust necessarily includes elements of hope and love.

If the point is conceded that a saving and justifying faith is not to be divorced from repentance, obedience, and renewal, another great Evangelical divorce collapses also, namely their grand dichotomy between deliverance from guilt and deliverance from sin. Because they have made so absolute a separation between justification and sanctification, they have set asunder forgiveness and renewal. In time and experience, to be forgiven by God is not utterly distinct from being renewed in inner character by the grace of Christ and the indwelling of the Holy Spirit.

Newman was in no doubt that the term justification is a judicial term, and that in theology it speaks of the divine declaration which is also in its essence both forgiveness and renewal. He found in Calvin's critique of the Tridentine Decree on Justification (January 1547)[23] the remarkable concession that justification and renewal are not temporally successive, but simultaneous. Was the question, then, whether renewal belongs to the substance of justification, or whether renewal is not more than an inseparable accident? The very question implies the answer that renewal belongs to the essence of justification. Therefore the act of justification is not merely a declaration about a past event or testimony of a present fact or an announcement of what will be at some future time (such as the Last Judgement), but a causative act which does not leave the recipient a believer as he was before. It is no great step from granting that justification and renewal are conjoined in time to saying that they are conjoined *in re*, and Calvin's critique of Trent is found to say that forgiveness and regeneration are two ways of speaking about the same thing. The Evangelical Protestants are not mistaken to speak of justification as 'external'; but it is not more external than a sacrament. The external word has as its content the inward grace. When we speak of justification as God's act, we may say that he 'imputes' Christ's righteousness to believers; when we consider our own condition in being accepted and made heirs of eternal life, we should say that we are thereby being made righteous. One ought not to say that when God justifies a believer, the only difference is not in the believer but in the way God thinks about him; that would set aside the truth that the justified are so from eternity in the predestinate purpose of God.

As we have seen, Newman's language about Luther at times looks superficial. He holds Luther immediately responsible for most of the excesses of Evangelical pietism. Luther

found Christians in bondage to their works and observances; he released them by his doctrine of faith; and he left them in bondage to their feelings. He weaned them from seeking assurance of salvation in standing ordinances, at the cost of teaching them that a personal consciousness of it was promised to every one who believed. For outward signs of grace he substituted inward; for references towards the Church contemplation of self. And thus, whereas he himself held the proper efficacy of the Sacraments, he has led others to disbelieve it; whereas he preached against reliance on self, he introduced it in a more subtle shape; whereas he professed to make the written word all in all, he sacrificed it in its length and breadth to the doctrine which he had wrested from a few texts. (*Jfc.*, p. 340)

Newman's view of Luther particularly enraged Julius Charles Hare, archdeacon of Lewes (1795-1855) who was moved to write a *Vindication of Luther*, and to publish a charge to the clergy of the diocese of Chichester in which he launched a frontal attack on Tractarianism as leading irresistibly to Rome (an opinion of the movement which Newman the convert came to adopt early in the 1850s).[24] Perhaps Newman chose Luther for his target because relatively few English people knew much of his writings, whereas they knew Calvin much better. Calvin and Calvinist writers are almost always cited by Newman as witnesses, even if at times reluctant or even unconscious witnesses, to the truth for which he is contending. The radical Protestant tradition in England had never really felt comfortable with Luther. Admittedly, when they sang *Ein feste Burg* (if they did), they were unaware that its author had written the hymn as a battle-song against Satan's latest emissary in the form of Zwingli's Eucharistic doctrine in the year 1527. In his *Actes and Monuments* John Foxe had expressed deep admiration for Luther's stand against the Papacy and insight on the centrality of the doctrine of justification; but Foxe found Luther's intransigence for the real presence embarrassing, and explicable only on the hypothesis that this great hero had not fully realized the extent to which the rags of popery have to be discarded.[25] At the opposite end of the ecclesiastical spectrum, Bull and before him William Forbes, first bishop of Edinburgh in the 1630s, had regarded Luther as a great but distinctly over-excitable person, who had grossly exaggerated, and embarrassed his own sympathizers.[26] So in Anglican writing about the age of the Reformation neither low churchmen nor high churchmen had found very kind language to use about Luther. That may have made it easier for Newman to pick on him as the fount of the excesses to which he now deeply objected in the Church of England's hospitality to the Evangelicals.

Historically it is undeniable that antinomianism appeared within the Lutheran camp in the sixteenth century. Luther used language which was one-sided and which was taken to mean that our salvation depends so wholly on the imputed righteousness of Christ that we need not trouble to have, by grace working within us, any righteousness in our conduct and character. He was taken to mean that by the divine decree of election the end is wholly determined in advance, and some people drew the inference that we do not need to bother too much about the means. Moreover, Luther and Melanchthon had defined justifying faith as confident trust, *fiducia*. That was heard to mean that one is justified if one is unhesitatingly sure about it, and the subjective certitude is a criterion of being in a state of grace before God. Conservative critics soon observed that this doctrine of faith as assurance was confusing faith with one of its consequences. The problem was to draw the line between confidence resting on the mercy and promises of God and mere human presumption. The thirteenth canon of the Council of Trent on justification (session VI) attempted a *via media* on the subject, but was then widely understood to have censured the notion that the believer was entitled to have any kind of confidence at all.

The debates at Trent in 1546[27] show that the bishops and theologians present were haunted by the two difficulties of assurance and imputation. Several voices spoke for the doctrine that, while believers are indeed made just by 'inherent' or imparted righteousness in the gradual process of sanctification as the Holy Spirit pours the love of God into their hearts, nevertheless 'on account of the uncertainty of the righteousness of our own deeds and the danger of vainglory, it is safer to rest our whole confidence exclusively upon the mercy and loving-kindness of God'.[28] At Trent the most eloquent advocate of this position was Seripando, the General of the Augustinians, and perhaps one of the relatively small group of theologians at Trent not bewildered by the complexity of the problems raised by the issue of justification.[29] In the event Seripando was not able to persuade the Council to endorse his understanding of the matter. On 8 November 1546 Seripando sent an agonized note to the legate Cervini, regretting the failure in understanding manifested by the third draft of the decree, produced by someone so terrified of falling into the Lutheran heresy that he fell into error at the opposite extreme.[30] Seripando wished the council to acknowledge the validity of 'imputed' righteousness; the term had been used by St Paul, and should not be left in the triumphant possession of the Lutherans. The failing on the Lutheran side was primarily in their insufficient or even non-existent stress on inherent or imparted righteousness. Imperfect it must be if it is ours, even though the good works are done in God by the indwelling power of the Spirit. But Seripando could not accept, as Newman could not, the notion that justification can mean a declaring of something to be the case when it is certainly not so and is not in the future going to be so.

Seripando's view of imputed and inherent righteousness coincided precisely with that of Richard Hooker who wrote: 'We participate Christ partly by imputation, as when those things which he did and suffered for us are imputed unto us for righteousness; partly by habitual and real infusion, as when grace is inwardly bestowed while we are on earth, and afterwards more fully both our souls and bodies made like unto his in glory'.[31] In the *Discourse of Justification*, in which Hooker sought to ward off anxieties that he was not a sound Protestant, Hooker similarly insisted that because of the imperfection of inherent righteousness (in so far as that is truly ours, by God's grace), we need to rely on Christ's righteousness imputed to us by the divine act of justification. Hooker saw that it must be a mistake to make the divine act of justification to consist exclusively in remission and divorced from the renewal which that makes possible. Hooker's friend Richard Field's treatise of 1606 *Of the Church*[32] agreed with him. Newman found support for the doctrine in the pages of John Davenant (1631). Such language offered an easy bridge to the terminology of the Council of Trent, which affirmed the ground of salvation to be the death and merits of Christ, and handled with great caution the merits which by grace God confers on the justified man. One should not say that the moral value of a righteous life is in no sense the believer's because the gift of grace is seen in it. Nor may one say that the justified person, whose good works are done by the grace of God and the merit of Christ, does not merit increase of grace.[33] But nothing is said about merit of condignity or entitlement. What is clear from Trent's statements on justification is the rejection of the notion that inherent or imparted righteousness has nothing to do with salvation.

The Protestant reaction to Trent on justification was (sadly) largely one of distrust. Writing to Cranmer in 1548 Melanchthon voiced the belief that the decree of Trent was crafty and ambiguous.[34] Chemnitz similarly expressed the view that canon 32, with its explicit declaration that by Christ's merits the justified come to have merits, was disingenuous.[35] In the nineteenth century the austere Calvinist James Buchanan[36] dismisses Trent on justification as quite unrepresentative of authentic Catholicism, 'vague and general', altogether 'less explicit and offensive' than the reality, too moderate and indeed remarkably close to Luther except for the muddle confounding justification and sanctification. It was irritating to find it so good.

The strict Calvinist doctrine is found in a classical formulation in the Westminster Confession of 1644, chapter 11, with a wealth of detailed precision and anti-Catholic sharpness strikingly absent from the Thirty-Nine Articles, whose inadequacies (or 'mingling of the Gospel with Popery') the far more Protestant Confession was intended to remedy and rectify. It is characteristic that where the Articles simply repeat the medieval canonists' claim that England has the privilege of being outside papal jurisdiction, the confession requires one to say that the pope is ex officio Antichrist. In the doctrine of justification, the crux of the Calvinist position lies in the denial that the divine act of acquittal takes into account any moral consequences in causing renewal in the penitent sinner's heart and mind. In the strongest possible sense of the word it is 'unconditional'. To this interpretation of justification it is cardinal that, because of the total destruction of God's image in fallen humanity, there is no spark or seed or latent capacity for righteousness in the sinner, whose sins have robbed him of free choice and even impaired his powers of clear rational judgement. There is no potentiality that can have significance for the divine acquittal.

The principle was from time to time stated by Augustine of Hippo (it was part of the Platonic philosophical tradition) that no sin ever goes unpunished even if forgiven. To the Calvinists the punishment for sin is to be seen in the death suffered by Christ. That was for them a satisfaction of divine justice which demanded the appropriate penalty. Newman encountered a rigidly juridical statement of this doctrine of Atonement in the pages of Thomas Erskine (1780-1870), where the theme was fitted into a theology marked by liberal rationalism; Newman thought he eliminated mystery and turned the Atonement into a lawyer's Opinion.

There was of course a grave problem for the Calvinists in combining so strictly juridical a theory of Atonement with a doctrine of the inscrutable sovereignty of grace, infinitely transcending our finite notions of law and justice. We may reckon it no justice to punish the innocent and to acquit the guilty, which would be a mark of a corrupt judge. But God's justice is other than ours. Because he is the source of law, his grace is free to acquit.

Nothing, therefore, within the believer, past, present, or future, even if entirely the work of the Holy Spirit's indwelling presence, can be deemed relevant to the divine acceptance of the sinner. Even after faith and baptism, our best achievements are flawed by pride and egotism. Only a perfect righteousness, one therefore which is Christ's and external to the believer's inward state, can satisfy the requirements of divine holiness. On this view, the question presses how Christ's goodness, righteousness, and holiness, being wholly external, can come to the believer's heart and mind to be appropriated.

At this point the term imputation takes on a special significance, a metaphor from financial accounting being brought in to help with a difficulty in the juridical framework. 'Imputation' is not easy to pin down with precision. In Scripture the verb 'to impute' is applied in cases where a just and good person is reckoned as such, or where a wicked person is reckoned as such. It is not used of a transference of reward from the wicked to the just or from the just to the wicked. The theological doctrine of imputed righteousness, when complemented by the idea that human sinfulness is imputed to the Redeemer, seems to be responsible for the linguistic usage of English that impute is usually a synonym for accuse, and often for 'falsely accuse', or 'attribute faults or crimes unjustly'.

Scripture does not provide a text to say that 'Christ's righteousness is imputed to us'.

A further question needing elucidation is the nature and role of faith in justification. In Catholic theology the faith that responds to divine love in Christ is not divorced from the sacraments and is essentially bound up with repentance, obedience, and renewal. Such a faith includes but is evidently more than the assent of the mind, whether to the core of the gospel history or to belief in God and his providence. It is a submitting of the rebellious individual will to the judgement and love of God and to the forming, nurturing authority of the holy community in the Church, where the gospel is proclaimed in word and sacrament and is lived out in life.

For Augustine of Hippo the term justification signifies the entire act and process of change in the sinner at and consequent upon conversion. He distinguishes between the way of sanctification, in which believers are called to imitate the Lord, and the act whereby Christ justifies the ungodly, an act which only he could do and which is not for our imitation.[37] He contrasts the decisive moment of baptism giving remission of sins and the long daily process of renewal and growth under grace.[38] Believers live all their lives 'under pardon',[39] and 'in this life our righteousness consists more in the forgiveness of sins than in perfection of the virtues'.[40] The righteousness of saints is manifested by their awareness of their imperfection.[41] Augustine, however, does not happily use the term imputation. In one text[42] he expresses fear at the open door to laxity or antinomianism in the notion that after death the soul may rely on the imputing of Christ's righteousness to make up for any shortcomings. On the other extreme, he regarded it as Pelagian to confine the initial grace of justification exclusively to the remission of sins.

All parties to the sixteenth-century debate agreed that faith is an indispensable means, an instrument or condition through which the Atonement is applied to the baptized believer so that justification is declared. Is justification by faith *alone*? St James said it is not so. St Paul does not say 'alone', but does affirm that justification is by faith and not by the merit of works. All parties therefore concurred in saying that justifying faith is a 'lively' faith, not any kind of faith such as bare mental assent in which will and feeling are irrelevant. The Protestants were in great difficulty in answering the question, What ingredient is it in faith which imparts liveliness or vitality to it? The apostle has a text in Galatians 5.6 on faith working by love, or formed by love. Luther's commentary on Galatians feared that on the exegesis of medieval schoolmen this text could be taken to mean that a man is justified by good works of love, or that there is unformed faith, as if a chaos prior to being given form by love. He denied that the passage had anything to do with justifying faith, except that it is the test of true faith that works of charity result from it, and that is its life; that is, it is not feigned. Newman asks whence faith can derive the indispensable vitality if there is no constituent element of repentance, love, and openness to renewal. And if justifying, saving faith must be allowed to include repentance and obedience, the grand dichotomy between deliverance from guilt and deliverance from sin ceases to look as if it might be faithful to one or two places in scripture. Moreover, to be forgiven by God is not in time or experience wholly distinct from being renewed by grace in the Holy Spirit. Calvary and Pentecost are not to be radically divorced. Justifying faith is no transitory or momentary act but the entry to a permanent state or 'habit' of the soul affecting the character.

Once it has been conceded that justification, as a declaration of acquittal, spills over into acceptance and renewal of the inner heart and mind, the disagreement between Catholic and Protestant about the effect of justification is reduced to minuscule proportions. Because on the Catholic view justification is the name for the total act and process, much more consequence is given to justification than on the Protestant interpretation. Nevertheless the Protestants read the Catholic position in a way of their own, as implying that one can never be certain of being forgiven; that while mortal sins after baptism can be absolved with the result that eternal punishment is averted, yet satisfaction to God and the Church has to be made in time both here and by purification hereafter; that it is because the Catholic must continually go in fear that the Eucharist must be more than a memorial sacrifice or feast but a 'repetition' or re-enactment of the one propitiatory sacrifice of Calvary, thereby restoring hope to the worshippers present. Lack of assurance lies at the root.

Newman sensitively interpreted the eucharistic sacrifice more correctly. He was aware that for Trent there is but one unrepeatable sacrifice on Calvary, yet that the offering of the Church is a true sacrifice. So 'the Father looking on us sees not us but Christ in us' (*Jfc.*, p. 161). The sentence quoted illustrates the way in which Newman coalesces what Christ does for his people with that which he does in them. If one asks how Newman came to hold the indwelling presence of Christ in the soul to belong to the essence of authentic justification, the answer cannot be simply that he found congenial language in Bull and Alexander Knox. In broad terms he agreed with Knox, though characteristically he commented that Knox could usefully have taken pains to use language in more direct conformity with the Anglican formularies, the Prayer Book,

Articles, and Ordinal.[43] Newman himself is most careful to underpin his argument with citations from these historical documents of his Church. From his Evangelical years, he could not but be aware that while Calvinist Evangelicals liked to speak as if their position were supported by the Articles and the English liturgy, numerous Evangelicals were in fact embarrassed by the many strongly Catholic features of the Book of Common Prayer, such as the absolution prescribed in the Visitation of the Sick (pointedly contrasted by Newman with a deathbed scene in *The Dairyman's Daughter, Jfc.*, p. 330) or the traditional elements in the Eucharistic rite, such as the prayer that by this thanksgiving 'all thy whole Church' may be granted remission of sins and the benefits of the passion. Evangelicals at times hinted that they would welcome a liturgy and confession of faith which were 'more scriptural' and might suggest that it would be well if Roman Catholics could come to say the same. That the Book of Common Prayer embodied the apostolic tradition was not the judgement of 'far gone Evangelicals, as they are called'.[44]

It would have been difficult for such far-gone Evangelicals to understand that the force which really drove Newman to his interpretation of justification was his Bible study. Father Stephen Dessain rightly stressed this point in the chapter which he contributed to *The Rediscovery of Newman*.[45] He printed a pencilled note found in Newman's personal copy of the *Lectures on the Doctrine of Justification*. It is worth repeating here:

The object of my book is this—to show that Lutheranism is either a truism or a paradox; a truism if with Melanchthon it is made rational, a paradox if with Luther it is made substantive; Melanchthon differs scarcely more than in terms from the Catholic; Luther scarcely in sense from the Antinomian. My book then is of the nature of an Irenicon in the doctrine of which it treats.

The acknowledgement that Scripture was the primary influence that led Newman to recast the doctrine of justification in a way that distanced him from the 'popular Protestantism' of contemporary Evangelicalism does not mean that Newman had no other debts. Bull had, of course, done something for him on the rational and intellectual side. But if Bull's discussion of justification has a weakness, that lies in the relative absence of very deep religious feeling in his writing on the subject. Like Paley, for whom Newman felt no rapport at all, Bull saw things in a cool clear light and had thought deeply about the subject. But one does not rise up from his book, as one might from Newman's, moved by the passion of the intense quest for scriptural and religious truth here and now. In that respect Alexander Knox probably did more for Newman than did Bull.

But there is one Anglican theologian of the seventeenth century, little cited except in the appendix on the 'formal cause' of justification, whose affinities with Newman's position are evident and whose passionate religious feeling went hand in hand with a rare lucidity of mind and expression, namely Jeremy Taylor. His discourse on justification brings justification and sanctification into the closest connexion. They are allowed to be distinct to the detached reflecting mind, but not in religious experience where they are two ways of speaking about one and the same thing. Newman clearly felt an answering chord within himself when he read Taylor's observation that a fully detailed understanding of every intricate point in the doctrine of justification can be highly perilous to the soul. The subject is so complex and so fascinating that the theologian runs the risk of losing his own soul in mastering the labyrinthine arguments. Above all, for Taylor the heart of Christian faith and life lay where it did for Newman, namely in the indwelling Christ in whom the believer participates through the sacraments.[46] Hence Newman's statement in the book of 1838, later corrected in a footnote as a departure from Roman Catholic understanding, that not only baptism but the eucharist must be understood as sacraments of justification, and indeed constitute the primary means of this great grace (*Jfc.*, pp. 152, 184, 187, 226).

Newman was aware that Protestant critics would dismissively say he had failed to distinguish justification from sanctification. That is what they soon were saying as if that settled all questions. He was bound to feel that they had not considered the matter deeply enough. The distinction for religious experience is largely academic. He also expected criticism from another quarter, in those who would decry his interpretation as a piece of 'mysticism', a pejorative term in the 1830s (*Jfc.*, p. 145). He was sensitive to the unsacramental mind-set of liberal Protestants who would think that a stress on sacraments, which belong to the world of sense as well as of mind, could encourage superstition, or would introduce 'a pantheistic spirit' into the gospel. Nothing could be less like pantheism than Newman's theology. He wished to rest on the apostle's noble words: 'I live, yet not I but Christ lives in me.'

Newman's Protestant critics came to read his book as consciously preparing the ground for the conversion of 1845, reconciling the Thirty-Nine Articles with Trent (which on justification is not very difficult to do), attempting a 'concordism' that might open the way for an ecumenical reconciliation between Canterbury and Rome. If there was any element of that in Newman's mind in 1838, it lay in his subconscious. He dedicated the published lectures to Richard Bagot, the Bishop of Oxford, an act which could be understood not merely as aspiring to gain his support in any coming controversy but also as a declaration of Anglican allegiance. In the ensuing storms Bishop Bagot was coolly neutral, and was sadly felt by Newman to have done nothing to support him when critics were telling him to get out and go to Rome. The book of 1838 is wholly Anglican in content and temper. It is instructive, nevertheless, that when as a Roman Catholic he came to reissue this volume, together with his other Anglican works, he found relatively few places where he needed to alter the text or to add a warning footnote that he would not put it that way thirty-six years later. Like much else in Newman, the book is among the major muniments of the modern ecumenical movement.

Anglicans Never seem t Suspect that Wesley like 64 — w B Pope Germane Line later, perhaps unconsciously! Toweds Wesley How te was Nearer Han te was Italian of my article "Catholic Salvation" D. English 1994.

13

Newman's Sacramental Faith

READING John Henry Newman is both a captivating and a disturbing experience, whatever the reader's point of view. A sorcerer with our English language, a master of satire when describing opinions he thinks ridiculous or impossible, he also has an altogether remarkable power to clarify complex problems. And there is a consistency of mind and heart equally apparent in both halves of his life (taking 9 October 1845 as the point of division). Even in the anti-Anglican polemic of some of the dialogue in *Loss and Gain* (1848) or parts of *The Present Position of Catholics* (1851), Newman says next to nothing he had not been saying as an Anglican to whom, at that stage, Rome seemed an opponent or at least less than an ally.

It is notorious that after 1845 he mountingly failed, for more than three decades, to gain the confidence of the communion he had joined. The tensions with Archbishop Cullen in Dublin, with Faber and the London Oratory, finally with Cardinal Manning, were painful to a degree. In a society where Anglican and English were so nearly synonymous, Newman's continuing and immutable Englishness had the effect of making other converts (or Irish Catholics) feel that he was not more than half converted.

As an Anglican Newman had enjoyed success. His books and tracts commanded serious attention. He was the acknowledged leader of a movement with influence and power. He and his Tractarian allies were determined to bring the Church of England to recover its independence of the State, governed by a Parliament made altogether secular by the constitutional reforms of 1828-32. That was a programme for the whole Church, not for a party. But the fear of a thesis which necessarily desacralised the English Reformation became so vehement in expression that Newman's longing to catholicise (not to romanise) the Church of England met frustration and negativity. The success of his Anglican career became blighted by the gnawing rats of doubt. Liberals and Evangelicals were little Englanders at heart. The concept of a

Catholic Church was almost unreal to them; at least the only actual embodiment of the doctrine known to them looked unattractive and alarming.

So Newman left Canterbury for Rome, and never had any doubt that this decision had been correct. Yet just as he had longed for the Church of England to recover its Catholic heritage, so after 1845 he longed for Rome to be less authoritarian, centralised, legalistic, and intolerant. 'Cruel' was his word for the excommunication of Döllinger so quickly after the first Vatican Council. In short, he met frustration in the Church he joined in 1845 because he wanted to make it more like his ideal for (not of course the actuality of) the Church of England. He combined an anti-Gallican Ultramontane ecclesiology with a powerfully minimising interpretation of papal teaching office and universal jurisdiction.

Foot-faulted

Moreover, the concept of teaching office in the Church which took him over the line in October 1845 was not congenial to the Roman Curia. He held to the infallibility of the Church before 1845, and saw how, within an Anglican and conciliar ecclesiology, it was natural to regard the see of Peter as the organ and voice of decision in matters of critical controversy. But he also believed that the meaning and interpretation of an *ex cathedra* utterance is a matter for long study by the 'school of theologians' and depends ultimately on the sense in which it is understood and received by the faithful. It seemed ironic when, in defending his essay 'On Consulting the Faithful in Matters of Doctrine', Newman was foot-faulted for pointing out, entirely correctly, that the faithful had been consulted before the promulgation of the Immaculate Conception in 1854. He might have added that before the decree on papal infallibility in 1870 massive efforts were made to gain lay signatures on fly-sheets in support of the proposal. Newman never imagined that the *schola theologorum* was not integral to the *magisterium*.

In a letter of 15 October 1874 Newman wrote: 'All my life I have been lessening the differences between the Catholic faith and the Anglican opinions.' The sentence expresses a paradox. From 1842 to the beginning of October 1845 Newman had wrestled at Littlemore with the question where his true allegiance ought to lie. He was acutely conscious that exasperation with the Church, especially at being badly treated, is never any sort of reason for

189

leaving. The hammering attacks of many (not all) Anglican bishops upon the central thesis of Tract 90 that the Thirty-nine Articles, very exactly interpreted in their most literal sense (as they ought to be), are patient if not ambitious of a Catholic interpretation, deeply hurt a thin-skinned and sensitive soul. Newman never sought to contend, as others (Ward or Oakeley, for instance), that the Anglican Articles are in complete accord with the canons of Trent. That was a view from which he actually dissociated himself, before and after 1845. Tract 90 said little that had not been put quietly into print by Pusey two or three years earlier in an open *Letter to the Bishop of Oxford*. But Pusey made the argument look dull, while Newman scintillated with logical acuteness, delighting allies and spreading panic among fearful adversaries. The main Tractarian platform for the renewal of the Church demanded recognition from the Church of England that the Articles be interpreted in the light of the Prayer Book rather than the other way round. That was immediately to bring Canterbury closer to Rome.

Thereby Newman made the decision for conversion more difficult for himself. Those who heard his sermons in St Mary the Virgin in the 1830s appear to have come away with the memory of an impassioned moralist rather than of a preacher proclaiming High Church sacramental doctrines. The reader of the Parochial Sermons, however, quickly discovers that the congregation had not always grasped what was being said to them. To hold that ordination is rightly bestowed through the ordained by prayer and laying on of hands, not merely by a vote of the congregation or an investiture by the magistrate, is to assent to a doctrine of ministerial succession, transmitting an apostolic commission and making visible the continuity of the Church. And this ministry exists to serve the sacraments of the Lord's appointment and to proclaim his word through his representatives as pastors and priests. The congregation were being told to receive communion frequently, not merely once or three times a year. They were not being left in doubt that they needed the Lord's sacraments to receive his own self in the Eucharist and thereby to be transformed to be more like their Master. And the language in which Newman spoke was shot through with an awe and fear that in English pulpits had become seldom heard; for the sacrament is mystery.

We approach and, in spite of the darkness, our hands or our head or our brow, or our lips become, as it were, sensible of the contact of something more than earthly. We know not where we are, but we have been bathing in water, and a voice tells us that it is blood. Or we have a mark signed upon our foreheads, and it spake of Calvary. Or we recollect a hand laid upon our heads, and surely it had the print of nails in it, and resembled his who with a touch gave sight to the blind and raised the dead. Or we have been eating and drinking; and it was not a dream surely, that One fed us from his wounded side, and renewed our nature by the heavenly meat he gave.

Newman preached thus in Advent 1838. As Vicar of St Mary's he felt the most intense sense of the presence of Christ when celebrating the Eucharist. In absolving penitents he freely used the Prayer Book form in the Visitation of the Sick, and knew that seventeenth-century predecessors had done the same. One of the St Mary's sermons is clear that the Lord's mother was without stain of sin. Virtually no one complained about the sermons. They drew large congregations of riveted listeners, among whom, to Newman's surprise, there were many women as well as thoughtful male under-graduates. (Newman was never a man for supposing that reflective theology was a feminine accomplishment; he would later cause a *frisson* at Dublin by beginning lectures to a mixed audience 'Gentlemen . . .'.)

The Vicar of St Mary the Virgin found himself drawing large numbers of grateful adherents by his sermons, and selling the *Tracts for the Times* to numerous parish clergy far beyond Oxford. He could reasonably conclude that the Tractarian campaign to assert the Church's independence of the secular power, and her Catholic title deeds, was a success—like a steadily rising flood (he felt), if not a forest fire. Yet the row over Tract 90 opened Pandora's box—the Englishman's residual religion, when all else has gone, a fear and even hatred of Catholicism with its 'popery', clerical celibacy, gross concessions to peasant superstitions, persecution of Protestants, wretched conditions for the poor, and an arbitrary ecclesiastical autocracy, with which no one could hope to reason. By March 1842 Newman was writing to a friend: 'If all the world agrees in telling a man he has no business in our Church, he will at length begin to think he has none.'

The long wait at Littlemore was not tactical. He could never think it justified to hop from one branch of the Catholic Church to another merely because the company seemed more congenial. He had to become inwardly convinced that in the Church of England, since 1689 largely dominated by latitudinous Liberals and Calvinist

Evangelicals, there was now no feeling for a Catholic sacramental faith. It had become a state or parliamentary Protestantism. Invite this Church to enjoy the recovery of her Catholic inheritance in Hooker, Laud or Thorndike, and everything would be said and done to label such doctrines 'popery'.

Classical problems

Nevertheless, there remained two classical Anglican problems to circumvent: the first was the conciliar claim that the ancient Church was organised territorially, without a centralised bureaucracy in Rome, and the looser more conciliar Anglican structure was nearer to the Church with the later medieval papal monarchy. The second was the contention that while the Real Presence in the Eucharist is to be affirmed, and therefore a real change in the consecrated species, yet it is not necessary to deny that the bread and wine after consecration will satisfy hunger and thirst and are what bread and wine have power to be and do. In a word, there is risk that the late (post-Lanfranc) language of transubstantiation may make the consecrated elements all reality and no sign, whereas the sign is the medium through which the reality is given. To meet these two propositions Newman wrote a very un-Roman book, the *Essay on the Development of Doctrine* (1845).

The book caused some consternation at Rome. But it was not long before Newman was receiving grateful letters from correspondents to whom the dogma of the Immaculate Conception would have seemed difficult had it not been for Newman's concept of a dogmatic development under the watchful control of the Roman see. Newman excused the book with the observation that it was written before his conversion, yet perhaps no book of Newman's would have so profound a reception.

Lady Blennerhasset was utterly fascinated by the hairsplitting exactitude with which the first Vatican Council was interpreted in Newman's *Letter to the Duke of Norfolk* (1875). It seemed to her to leave the Vatican the option between public censure and making Newman a cardinal. Happily the second course was followed. The *Letter* shows Newman fully aware that there were analogies with Tract 90. And the *Letter* contains some of the most positive passages about high Anglican ecclesiology that Newman wrote after 1845. He used to recall with gratitude John Keble's habit of saying: 'All I can say is that if the Roman Church is the one true

Church, I do not know it.' It proved that the saintly and invincibly ignorant Keble, so closely resembling in character St Philip Neri, would get to heaven.

14

Paul VI and Vatican II

Le Deuxième Concile du Vatican (1959-1965). Actes du Colloque organisé par l'École Française de Rome en collaboration avec l'Université de Lille III, l'Istituto per le Scienze Religiose de Bologne et le Dipartimento di Studi Storici del Medioevo e dell'Età Contemporanea de l'Università di Roma-La Sapienza (Rome 28-30 mai 1986). (Collection de l'École Française de Rome, 113.) Pp. xx + 867. Rome: École Française de Rome Palais Farnèse, 1989. 2 7283 0188 3; 0223 5099.

Paolo VI e i problemi ecclesiologici al Concilio. Colloquio Internazionale di Studio, Brescia, 19-20-21 settembre 1986 (Publ. dell'Istituto Paolo VI, 7.) Pp. xv + 719. Brescia: Istituto Paolo VI/Rome: Edizioni Studium, 1989. L. 90,000. 88 382 3590 2

THESE TWO fat volumes, one mainly French, the other mainly Italian, present the papers read at two major colloquia in 1986, having some overlap among the contributors, notably the names of Levillain, Poupard and Conzemius. The papers offer important historical matter on the making of certain major texts of Vatican II and so give the reader a glimpse into the very workshop where the finer points came to be decided. The two collections assist with the current process of re-evaluating the council, a process precipitated in part by Lefebvre's rejection of both council and pope, in part by the evident anxiety of supreme authority at the Vatican to recover the monolithic pre-conciliar Church by using Vatican I to interpret Vatican II rather than the other way round. Since certain pieces of Vatican II do not merely restate but enhance papal supremacy, the latter undertaking has a good chance of success, but at the price of pushing to one side themes self-evidently present and prominent both in the constitution on the Church, *Lumen Gentium*, and in the decree on ecumenism, *Unitatis Redintegratio*.

At the council's dark hour or 'black week' late in 1964 both these documents came under critical fire, with the risk of rejection by Paul VI. Their ultimate approval and promulgation hung upon changes which, at the urging of the minority, the pope imposed by his own authority, admittedly to the gloom and pain of the majority anxious to see collegiality in real operation. Nevertheless, the fact that the immediate (not, we may believe, long-term) aftermath of

Vatican II has been no new spring but a traumatic experience of decline in vocations and exodus of priests has seemed somehow to vindicate the enraged minority at the council who held that, without massive haemorrhage and near loss of identity, the Roman Catholic Church cannot cease to be authoritarian, centralised and juridical in thought and manner of proceeding.

From two such rich collections, it begins to become invidious to select particular authors, and several of the papers have fresh information. If, on the whole, the papers in Italian and French are those of the greatest weight, many English readers will find much that is new and wisely expressed by American and English contributors, notably Canon Howard Root's essay (in the Italian collection) on 'Montini and the Anglicans, 1955-1966'. His story begins with Bishop George Bell's visit to Montini at Milan in 1955, and continues with the astonishingly positive consequences which flowed from the encounter of those two great men. The essential story that seems to emerge from the material which the two symposia have gathered is perhaps fairly summarised as now follows.

With its huge number of bishops and not always welcome attention from the Western press, Vatican II was no easy assembly to organise. The overworked curia found itself inevitably responsible for preparing the agenda, the procedure and the schemata of a council for which it felt little or no enthusiasm. John XXIII called the council under a sense of personal inspiration, and in general terms *aggiornamento* was a magical word to describe his programme. But in detail how was that vision to be achieved, and what items were to be placed on the agenda? Bishops were asked for suggestions. Several urged that one step forward could be yet another Marian dogma, declaring Mary to be, for example, mediatrix of all graces or mother of the Church or some other title of honour. Or there might be a solemn recommitment of the Latin Church to priestly celibacy, to try to silence the perennial unrest on this issue. Some of the suggestions sent in to the Vatican reveal a determination to combat the besieging modern world with high walls and boiling oil. But Pope John wanted a council that would be listened to by a wistful world, which could invite separated ecclesial communions to come to the warmth of St Peter's hearth, certainly not a council to multiply the already substantial corpus of anathemas on the statute book designed to keep at a safe distance over-friendly Protestants and over-liberal Catholics. For the council and perestroika which arrived the curia was not geared; rigid and too scholastic draft schemata received a rough handling, and the officers were hardly prepared for journalists instinctively regarding all secrecy as a hypocritical attempt to conceal matters that their readers had a right to know. Leaks of the most innocuous information were treated as frightful indiscretions. If the Vatican's own press officer was allowed into the assembly, he was given nowhere to sit.

The Italian volume includes a lengthy appendix containing twelve summaries of the reporting of the council in the European and American press; all are of interest, but perhaps there is special attraction in reading the account of public opinion in Belgium and the Netherlands, since that is compiled by J. Grootaers, to whose editorial labours we owe a gripping volume of 1986, publishing diaries and memoranda from the papers of Mgr Gérard Philips at Louvain. The study of that volume is at several points an illuminating and necessary supplement to the fresh information in these two collections.

Naturally enough the press could not help being fascinated by the divergence between the majority and the minority, but most of the journalists discerned less of the inner conflict of authority and ideology. Vatican II was the first assembly to operate on the basis of *Pastor Aeternus*; had not Vatican I made all future councils superfluous or at best advisory? 'Ex sese, non autem ex consensu ecclesiae': are the words asserting a purely juridical position, that in the pope is the final court of appeal? Or are they of general application? Tension was present not merely in the relation between permanent curia and impermanent council, but in that between the concept of the pope as transcendent over all bishops and the pope's position as standing within the episcopate.

Ottaviani became spokesman for the conservative curialists, while Alfrink and Frings (with Josef Ratzinger as his personal theologian of remarkably independent sympathies) were prominent for a conciliar and open Church, in which bishops could hope to be consulted about more than unimportant matters and feel themselves to be as much *cum* as *sub Petro*. The latter standpoint turned out to enjoy a substantial majority among council fathers; but this created a potentially delicate relationship to the supreme authority, the pope. Not that the majority wished to diminish or dethrone papal leadership or powers of initiative, but rather that they were unable to digest or defend the concept which set the 'Petrine office' (O. Karrer's term) quite above and apart from the episcopate in general. No account of papal primacy makes sense which does not begin from the fact that the pope is a bishop. Granted that St Peter was leader among the apostles, and was thereby able to speak for his brethren, was he so distinct from the other eleven as to be able to make decisions without necessarily consulting with any of them? So also, has the pope a power to command the Church without undertaking consultations and without feeling bound by Scripture and sacred tradition?

The majority wanted a more pastoral concept of authority in the Church, a recognition that not all authority in the Church flows down from the summit of a pyramid, and that there is a 'dispersed' authority in the universal eucharistic *koinonia* of the local churches under their diocesan bishops. The majority did not aim to re-introduce Gallicanism, but rather to balance the one-sided ultramontane triumph of 1870 with an altogether more Cyprianic doctrine of authority vested in the collective or 'collegial' episcopate as a whole—a wish to which Newman gave expression at the time of Vatican I. Perhaps the bishops in 1963 were hardly aware that the bishops had similarly come to the Council of Trent with the ambition to recover powers of which the medieval papal monarchy had deprived them and had been disappointed of their hope. To the minority the doctrine of collegiality in chapter iii of *Lumen Gentium* was dangerous modernism and incompatible with Vatican I. Hence the elaborate care taken by the principal drafter, Mgr Gérard Philips of Louvain, to restate and even to underscore the doctrine of Vatican I that the infallibility of the Church may be exercised, on particular themes and in certain conditions, by the pope apart from the bishops but not by the bishops apart from the pope, whose irreformable decisions need no confirmation by others to have juridical validity (*LG* 25).

Amendments to *Lumen Gentium* iii requested by the minority were not accepted by the doctrinal commission, but were conveyed to Paul VI. Philips was pressed to take account of the misgivings of the minority, and hence the *Nota praevia*, usually printed at the end of *Lumen Gentium*; it originated as an answer to the *modi* requested by the minority in their comments on chapter iii. As Philips correctly pointed out, the *Nota praevia* did no more than make explicit in scholastic form what was already present or implied in the text of

197

the constitution itself. Therefore it cost nothing to accept it, as Paul VI wanted. Nevertheless, the *Nota praevia* informed the ecumenical observers, trumpet-tongued, that Vatican II was to mark no receding from the peak of the papal authority asserted at Vatican I, and it was no doubt good that they should be under no optimistic illusions on this point. For Paul VI the *Nota praevia* brought the political advantage that its very un-Gallican language won over the adhesion of most of the minority, and therefore made it possible for the constitution to be a consensus document of the council. The *Nota praevia* stands printed in the *Acta*, but evidently as less than a fully conciliar act. Whether admired or not, it is a model of clarity.

Nevertheless, *Lumen Gentium* and the decree on ecumenism retained clauses that displeased the minority. The council found itself voting *placet* to declarations that the responsibilities of the magisterium include that of safeguarding legitimate diversity; that while, of course, no one truth is in logic truer than any other truth, nevertheless in Christian faith there is a hierarchy of truths (and this concept, not exactly smiled on in *Mortalium Animos* of 6 January 1928, DS 3683, is crucial in ecumenical dialogue); that the local bishop in his diocese is no mere deputy for the Holy Father; and above all that the authentic Church of Jesus Christ 'subsists in' that body which is in communion with Rome but is perhaps not necessarily and exclusively located in that body; accordingly, that the Roman Catholic Church is not condemned to being wholly negative to other ecclesial communions in which numerous Catholic elements of both faith and order may evidently be seen. The interpretation of 'subsistit in' (which replaced an original 'est') remains a matter of high debate today, since it is capable of being understood in the sense of either the majority or the minority at the council. The majority welcomed the phrase: they did not wish to say that, because the Roman Catholic Church is where the true Church is found, other ecclesial bodies are necessarily false and, to the degree that they approximate to Catholic faith and order, a diabolical counterfeit. As for collegiality, that has remained largely a dormant idea. The *Nota praevia* is evidently correct in warning against the imprecision of the term 'collegium', which naturally means a society of equals. All bishops are equal in sacramental power, and the bishop of Rome has no greater power in that respect than a rural bishop in the upper Andes. But in canonical jurisdiction differences appear. *Lumen Gentium*, nevertheless, did not encourage the notion (much debated at Trent) that bishops receive all jurisdiction by delegation from the successor of St Peter, and granted that the authority of a pastor, which must include the right to call a halt to a scandal, is inherent in the commission at consecration. The distinction between *potestas ordinis* and *potestas jurisdictionis* is not very ancient.

Paul VI took quiet steps to ensure that the majority's enthusiasm for pastoral language did not eliminate the juridical element. In the French volume J. B. d'Onorio even goes so far as to identify respect for juridicism as a distinctive mark of Catholicism over against Protestantism (p. 683). Canon law is that which gives the pastor the power to act to protect the salvation of souls. Paul VI liked the word communion to be qualified by the epithet 'hierarchical', presumably meaning that the reality of communion needs to be expressed through the bishop in catholic unity; but the sense is not perfectly clear. In *LG* X the application of the epithet 'hierarchical' to the priesthood, in addition to 'ministerial', is more obscure, though it evidently suggests the distinction of nature, not degree, between the universal priesthood of the whole Church and the intercessory and sacramental priesthood of presbyters and bishops; perhaps it is a way of saying 'pertaining to the clergy', but it is hard to be sure exactly what is intended.

Paul VI found congenial reading in Fr Yves Congar who, after Jean Daniélou's withdrawal from the drafting of *Lumen Gentium*, supported Gérard Philips and the Louvain group. Surprisingly for a master of the problems of ecumenism, Congar had little contact with the observers, and his influence on conciliar texts was normally very indirect. In the French volume Étienne Fouilloux describes his role, making use of his papers at Le Saulchoir. It may be necessary to remember that some people use private diaries as a safety valve for their disappointments and frustrations, not necessarily as a balanced and considered statement of their real judgement.

In the Italian volume Professor Tresfontaines gives a blow-by-blow account of the crisis over *Lumen Gentium* and the *Nota praevia*, with its disillusioning effect on the majority in making clear that collegiality was not going to be allowed to work in the way they had hoped for. An exciting paper is contributed by Fr (now Bishop) Duprey, describing how the draft decree on ecumenism, after receiving much preliminary support, was similarly subjected to amendments asked for by the minority, rejected by the Secretariat for Unity under Cardinal Bea, but then given to the council on 19 November as 'formulated authoritatively' or, in other words, required by Paul VI as a condition of his consent. Two days previously Paul VI had told the council moderators that he could not promulgate the decree. Bea and Willebrands saw this as a catastrophe impending for Roman Catholic ecumenism. The amendments required by the pope were in part only stylistic, but included at least two which disturbed ecumenical observers by amending clauses which allowed that non-Roman Catholics actually find, and do not merely search for, God's word in the Bible, and have some, if less than the full, reality of the eucharistic mystery. Mgr Willebrands saw that the decree as a whole must not be sacrificed for matters of only relatively minor importance, even though of real substance, and that the Secretariat for Unity should compromise for the sake of the much greater whole. The final text did not deny to Protestants all reality whether in word or in sacrament.

In the French volume Fr A. Wenger's chapter on Mgr Villot shows how the disappointment frankly expressed by the observers at the *Nota praevia* and at the imposition of changes in the decree on ecumenism so irritated Felici, the council secretary, that he persuaded Paul VI to dispense with their too influential presence at the fourth and last session; but the decision to disinvite was reversed after cogent representations from Willebrands, who clearly saw what destructive and, in public relations, disastrous consequences would follow.

In the Italian collection a remarkable French paper by R. Laurentin relates how, on 21 November 1964, Paul VI solemnly proclaimed Mary to be Mother of the Church; many council fathers rose to give prolonged applause, but not all. Cardinal Bea had expressly asked for this title not to be used; there was no doctrinal issue at stake, but not all Protestants would immediately realise that, and the psychological effect could be to heighten the fences. The title itself, though not ancient, had been used by Montini at Milan, and it had been included in a schema circulated to the bishops on 22 April 1963 in the time of John XXIII. The title, born no doubt of reflection on John xix 27, was thought eminently defensible by Newman in his reply to Pusey's *Eirenicon* (in which Newman could happily surrender as indefensible a number of manifestations of popular devotion): see *Difficulties of Anglicans* ii

200

84 and 100. It expressed love and affection, but no fundamental doctrine. The Polish bishops had asked for the title Mediatrix to be proclaimed, a proposal also opposed, on stronger grounds, by Bea; and it was not favoured by French and German bishops. But fervent devotion to Mary was too strong for Bea. Gérard Philips, no doubt trying to avert purely papal, non-conciliar pronouncements on the subject, included in *Lumen Gentium* the Mediatrix title (but, at Laurentin's suggestion, in a list of other titles, thereby relativising its importance) and also the sentence at the end of *LG* liii that 'the Church honours her with filial affection as a dearly loved mother'. Paul VI's proclamation pleased a nettled minority who had felt that to make the statements on Mary a sub-section of the constitution on the Church was a discourtesy to her. It was by implication a statement that the pope can make such proclamations on his own supreme authority, whether the council likes it or not; and the fact that it was a title, not a doctrine, would exclude it from being an exercise of infallibility. The title Mother of the Church therefore gratified bishops who wished to foster a Mariology independent of Christology, yet without in fact making a strictly theological statement at all.

A more striking independence of the council was shown by Paul VI's refusal to allow the fathers to discuss the dangerous topic of priestly celibacy, on which the council's views might turn out to favour change, though the council was allowed to say that, subject to a papal decision about timing, there should be no objection to married deacons. In August 1968 came *Humanae Vitae*, an act of great courage but in practice having awkward consequences in weakening respectful obedience to the magisterium by a high proportion of the laity and so the wish to observe the duty of private confession. More 'collegiality' could have discouraged Paul VI from making too lonely a decision and from leaving many bishops qualifying their support. The steady crescendo in papal claims to speak and act without regard to the episcopate provokes the disturbing reflection that authority ends by being weakened if it does not truly reflect the consensus of the faithful, among whom the bishops worldwide occupy a special place, and, therefore, that recent attempts to bring *Humanae Vitae* under the umbrella of those rare statements classified as 'infallible' may prove counter-productive.

Not only within the Roman Catholic Church but far beyond its frontiers the pope bears an office and function which Christendom needs, witnessing to Catholic unity even while being felt by some to be among the barriers to it, acting as a breakwater, if not an always persuasive bulwark, against the floodwaters of scepticism and relativism corroding the Church even while many benevolent supporters long for more far-reaching reconstruction. It is not in the least in the interest of the ecumenical movement that the authority of the pope should be weakened in consequence of a wedge appearing between pope and the general mind of the episcopate.

15

Why Music in Church?

THE Church Music Society, born 75 years ago, has reason to look back with a sense of proper pride in its achievements, especially in improving the repertory and the standard of performance. It must be a source of profound gratification to it to contemplate the way in which the Royal School of Church Music, born of this Society's impetus in 1927, has steadily flourished under its successive Directors. Dr Watkins Shaw's fascinating history in the current Annual Report of the Church Music Society shows how since then the Society has more than found an independent role, both in publishing works ancient and modern, and in encouraging the application of thought to church music generally. The Society began on the initiative of people who were neither clergy nor professional musicians. Your committee is now in the main a powerful body of musicians, academics, composers, makers of noble sound, and I count it a very high honour to offer you some general reflections on a subject that is peculiarly your own.

Your learned and distinguished chairman Dr Shaw suggested to me that I try to investigate the question, 'Why have music in Church at all?' To ask such a question is not a reflection, I think, of a deep malaise, such as is often reflected in those unhappy people who ask 'Why are we here at all?' (usually expressing pain rather than wanting to know). Our question is about the role that music ought properly to have in the life and worship of the Christian community. Is it intrusive? Is it merely icing on the cake, or has it some genuinely load-bearing function to carry out? Can it be in itself the vehicle of worship that could not be offered effectively in any other way? Insofar as music is an independent art, does it threaten a take-over, displacing the functions of the religion it was initially invited to support?

Students of moral theology tell an anecdote about a Dominican and a Jesuit who fell out in an argument whether or not one could pray and smoke simultaneously. The Dominican denied it, the Jesuit affirmed it. Both agreed to consult their superiors and in each case they received answers exactly confirming their position. And both answers were indeed correct. For the Dominican asked his superiors, 'Can I smoke while I am praying?' The Jesuit asked, 'Can I pray while I am smoking?' (The story is evidently of Dominican origin.)

*Can one pray and
listen to
music?*

There are respects in which the relation of music and worship seems a parallel case. Some people work well, or so they assure us, when the radio or record player is providing them with audible wallpaper. Sometimes the background sound sweetens an otherwise unattractive task. Yet even they can be seen to switch off when the most intense concentration is required, and when they need no drug or analgesic to dull the pain of hard work. Moreover, great music makes imperious demands on the ear: 'Such sweet compulsion doth in music lie', writes Milton. It has a way of forcing you to listen to it, even if you may have a duty or a pleasure to be doing something else. An element in great music that makes it great is precisely that it asks to be listened to not as audible wallpaper but for its own sake; it requires the listener to apply his attention even to familiar music as if he were hearing it for the first time and were continually wondering where the music will go next. Certainly if the music is familiar, one's mind can wander away for a time on an innocuous ramble and then return without having completely lost track of things. But even the very familiar can be played, and can be listened to, as if it were being done for the first time. If you happen to be a performer, then you know that the concentration needed to play or sing *well* something as simple as a hymn-tune is far from zero. Among the arts how absorbing music is of the mind and energy! It may be listened to as audible wallpaper, but it can hardly be played with the same degree of inattention in the performer as in the listener, unless one's part is that, say, of the pizzicato double bass or percussion in a dance-band performing a highly repetitive routine that must become a Pavlovian reflex.

In short, great music asks everything of a performer, and if it receives everything from the performer, it will ask the same of the listener too.

And yet it is easy to show that even then the music leaves room for the mind to be directed to other things, through itself as a medium. For the greatest of all musical instruments is no doubt the human voice, and it is normal for a human voice to sing words whose content is far from unimportant. An ancient pupil of Aristotle asks why it is that a solo singer gives more pleasure when accompanied, whereas a voice singing wordlessly is less attractive than a pipe playing exactly the same notes (*Problemata* 19). There is no necessary conflict of interest between the music and the spoken word. Richard Strauss's opera *Capriccio* has a libretto that turns on the conflict between the two, left happily unresolved at the end, because everyone knows that the conflict is 'powder-and-lace' artificiality. We can all think of instances where words of rare power are perfectly matched with music, and stay for ever to haunt the memory. *Erlkönig* was a tragic and moving poem when Goethe first wrote it. With Schubert's miraculous setting, it strikes home with an added dimension of terror, power, and beauty. But would even Schubert's music be memorable if sung wordlessly to la-la-la or whatever? It is the marriage of music and words that makes it great.

I shall seem to some to labour the obvious. But even if obvious, the point is pretty fundamental to our problem, namely that music can be married to words without taking away from their force; indeed, it has the capacity to increase their force, their power to stay with the mind and to haunt the memory, in a way that they would hardly do without any music to be associated with them.

Marriage is not too strong a word to describe the relationship. Church musicians are familiar with the discomfort caused when a hymn-tune with indissoluble associations with one set of famous words is used by a less than sensitive organist for an entirely different set of words which may also happen to be in the appropriate metre.

In Christian worship there has never been a time when music has not played a role. In the letters of St Paul we have two explicit instructions that the Christian brothers and sisters are to teach and admonish one another in psalms, hymns, and spiritual odes. They are to have a song in their hearts: a certain hilarity is a proper mark of the Christian profession because a sense of detachment from the world's getting and spending, or from the political power-struggles, goes very naturally with an awareness of possessing a heavenly citizenship. (I suppose another element in that detachment, which is productive of the dispelling of excessive gloom, is also a religious confidence in providence which does not expect that providential care to mean material prosperity for everybody all the time, and which is also aware of the extremely limited human capacity for foresight.) 'Teaching and admonition' does not sound cheerful until one penetrates a little further into the way in which the early Christians thought about the nature of their task as a community. St Augustine observes that a congregation will 'enjoy' a sermon even more if it leads them to weep with tears of penitence and to determine their obedience to the biblical text. Not that the object of the service is to please. Its first object is to worship God, and then by word and action to instruct the minds and move the wills of the people. The pleasure of an enjoyed service is like a by-product. But Augustine does not think the people come to church services to forgo all pleasure absolutely; nor does he suppose that there is anything tainted or wicked about this enjoyment, provided there is no danger of a religious hedonism—that is, of God being sought for his consolations rather than for what he is in himself.

The earliest Christians probably followed synagogue custom in their chanting, at least for the cantillation of the psalms, giving the custom of putting several syllables to a single note. Perhaps their hymns were sung syllabically, that is to say, with a distinct syllable for each note. If the apostle's spiritual odes are regarded by him as distinct from the psalms and hymns, we may be tempted to wonder if this may be a reference to the Alleluia. It became the custom for the Alleluia to be chanted by a cantor who would dwell on the last syllable at a length which might be considerable, giving it a melisma which was ornamented and rich. In Augustine's time in North Africa the Alleluia chant was not short, as we know from two pieces of evidence. When the Vandals invaded the country from Spain, they arrived at one city where the people were in church. Archers came into the back of the basilica during the liturgy and at first listened without disrupting the service until the cantor mounted the ambo and began to chant the Alleluia. The length of the performance was more than one Vandal could bear, and the congregation was suddenly horrified to see the cantor fall dead with a Vandal arrow in his Adam's apple. The other evidence is less tragic. Augustine was faced by critics of the Christian conception of the world to come who asked how in heaven, without sex, food, or above all the fun of bargaining in the market, they would escape falling asleep with boredom. Augustine charmingly replies that in heaven the melisma of the Alleluia will be of such length and beauty that they will never be bored (*Sermo* 362, 28). The reply, incidentally, implies that our song on earth is a foretaste of that in heaven.

No doubt the Alleluia chants of the Church continued a practice of the Jewish synagogue within which the first Christians were nurtured. The Old Testament has plenty of exuberant language about singing and dancing before the Lord. We do not really know what music the ancient Hebrews sang for the psalter. But perhaps those obscure headings in the titles of the Psalms printed in English in the Authorised Version carried technical indications for the musicians: much as if we now had a rather tattered hymnbook from which all the actual tunes had been lost and we had to reconstruct *Hymns Ancient & Modern* from a collection of headings like 'Riley 7676D. Crotchet = 100'. On the whole, religious customs tend to the conservative, and it is therefore reasonable to suppose that early psalm-chanting did not greatly differ from that which we find in the Byzantine liturgical use, where the cantor and the people alternate in antiphonal exchange, almost certainly keeping to a single note with a rising start and a falling cadence so that the effect would be like intoning. In any event, the effect would be to give the maximum of audibility to the words in a large place of assembly like a basilica.

In a famous passage of the *Confessions* (x, 33, 49-50) Augustine recalls how when he first arrived in Milan as municipal professor of rhetoric, not as a Christian, he used to go to the cathedral to hear Ambrose preach, merely because he recognised a fellow-professional in the arts of eloquence. But his feelings were soon engaged by the psalm-chants and other music of the Church, his mind unexpectedly gripped by the content of what this highly intelligent bishop had to say; and soon his steps were on the way to picking up his codex of the apostle Paul and being stung to the point of moral decision to offer himself for baptism. In the retrospect of the *Confessions* he says that at one time of his life the sound of music was of intense importance to him. It is probably of himself that he writes when he says (*de Libero arbitrio* ii, 13, 35), surely with a touch of distance and irony, that there are 'many for whom happiness consists in the music of voices and strings, and who count themselves miserable when music is lacking to their lives.' The six books 'on Music' were written soon after his baptism at Milan in 387, but are notoriously devoted in the main to rhythm and metre and then, in the very Neoplatonic final book, to a thesis that the study of musical theory accustoms the mind to grasp immaterial reality. At the back of this is no doubt the almost universal prejudice of ancient men that the theory of music is a proper subject for a gentleman, but its practice ought to be left to the lower classes. Gentlemen, says Aristotle in the *Politics* (1339a-1341b), play instruments only when drunk or for a joke. Eight centuries after his time Boethius will write his immensely influential work on music, sadly mutilated at the end, explaining musical theory on identical assumptions—except that he makes a few concessions to the judgment of the ear and does not give everything to purely mathematical theory. But the Platonic tradition, in which both Augustine and Boethius stand, discerned principles of mathematical proportion as built into the structure of the cosmos itself, and therefore regarded musical theory not so much as a route to the better appreciation of the latest composition in the Lydian mode but rather to the mathematical design and order pervading the universe. The theory of music is akin to metaphysics, and the fact that it has something to do with sound is, for the ancient theorists, almost an embarrassment.

The mature Augustine is more sympathetic to the Platonic or metaphysical view than to the practical. It is almost with a sense of apology that in the *Confessions*, written about 13 years after his conversion and baptism and about four years after he had become bishop of Hippo, he admits that he still finds some degree of pleasure in hearing hymns well sung by trained voices: 'But my enjoyment is not so intense that I cannot tear myself away.' One must remember that Augustine's conversion has not merely been to Christianity but to a highly ascetic renunciation of marriage and a secular career. He never loses the fear that the pleasures of his five senses, of which he writes as no other ancient writer had done, may end by trapping him in this world when his eyes wish to be upon the next. And so, in this passage of the tenth book of the *Confessions*, we find Augustine in effect asking our question, 'Why have music in Church at all?' The essence of his position may be summed up in the formula, 'Indispensable but dangerous'. It is indispensable because when the sacred words are sung, the heart is stirred to deeper fervour and devotion than when they are said; or again because (as Plato had long ago taught) certain modes are suitable for the expression of particular mental moods. Plato had said that some modes are associated with love songs rather than moral gravity, and thought the austere Dorian mode more suitable for nationalist Greeks than seductive foreign imports from Lydia and Phrygia. (All nations talk as if seductive arts are a foreign infiltration.) So, too, Augustine is well aware that music is far from being incapable of solemnity and seriousness. He even grants that there is a 'hidden kinship' between music and the soul, a doctrine which is again Platonic (from the *Timaeus*). Augustine explicitly formulates the proposition that 'all the emotions of our spirit' are capable of musical expression in voice and song in an appropriate mode. But . . . the senses are so demanding; they refuse to take second place and remain in a subsidiary role. Augustine is left with a sense of guilt when the music is more important to him than the meaning of the words. The moral power of the words may be obscured and made less direct, and so singing will become more important than what is sung. One of Augustine's letters (to Januarius, 55, 34) explains more of the background of this passage of the *Confessions* by disclosing the presence in the North African Church of Augustine's time of a puritan movement which is adopting a reserved attitude towards music in Church. On the other hand, he faced also a very numerous schismatic sect, the Donatists, who were well known for their robust congregational hymns and who regarded the psalm chanting of Augustine's *ecclesia catholica* as altogether too sober and dull. Augustine did not wish the Berber population of Numidia (that is roughly Algeria today) to be led into schism by exciting charismatic hymn books. It therefore seemed pastorally necessary to allow a due place of honour to music within the life of the Church. The people wanted it and enjoyed it. Moreover, Augustine could remember the lump in his own throat and the tears in his own eyes induced by the Milan chanters when he first went to hear Ambrose, months before he had decided to become a Christian. In other words, music could be a bridge. He did not want to burn it.

Augustine writes as a man who has been led to God not merely by a vast crisis of moral decision but also by the contemplation of beauty. No writer of the ancient world has so powerful and articulate a sense of the beauty of nature or of art. The loveliness of a landscape or of an artistic achievement can raise the question of the source of the sense of beauty, and Augustine finds that source in the *summa pulchritudo* which is God. Not that God has colour or form. He is that to which form fails to attain. All earthly beauty is mediated through our senses in one form or other; but for Augustine there is also a beauty in mathematical proportion which is a more purely intellectual beauty, and that can set him on the upward road. Music has a privileged position among the arts because of the degree to which it depends on the one sense of hearing, to the exclusion of the other four senses. But its foundations lie in order and proportionality, in the ratio of 2 : 1 that makes the octave, 3 : 2 the fifth, 4 : 3 the fourth, and 9 : 8 the whole tone, defined by the difference between the fourth and the fifth.

We owe to Plato not only the notion that musical proportion is a clue to the structure of order in the world but also the puritan fear that the wrong kinds of mode may be used, with enervating effects on the moral character. Modes suitable for austere or funerary or noble occasions are not those suitable for drinking or love songs. These sentiments are not much echoed by the early Christian writers on the subject. But they lie behind the medieval and modern demands that church music and indeed all sacred art ought to have a distinctive ecclesiastical style. As we all know, these demands have been much more frequently voiced than met. It is incomparably easier and more plausible to say that this or that style in art is something we are accustomed to in churches than to say that there is a highly specific kind of art which is sacred. If one thinks that medieval Gothic is the ideal style for a church building, one is offended by the vast gold cherubs and other rather bulbous creatures that now adorn the sanctuary of, say, that noble cathedral of St James at Compostela. But for the generation which erected these uninhibited figures this type of decoration was an offering to God's service of the finest art of their own time; and since the sixteenth century and even before, that great movement of the spirit we call the Renaissance was seeking forms of expression in the arts which were autonomous, independent of the Church, or at least not limited by the specific service of the liturgy. The free development of both vocal and instrumental music has been made possible by the sixteenth century transfer of wealth and patronage from bishops and monasteries into the hands of lay patrons; for one does not need to be a Marxist to observe that music needs somebody with leisure if it is to be written, performed, and listened to. And in experimental or new music, the publisher alone is unlikely to be long the principal bearer of the high capital cost of investment in the publication. Mozart may have resented the Archbishop of Salzburg, but he would not have got far without him, and in any event it was not in the power of Mozart to be on easy relations with any employer of his extraordinary genius. But the characteristics of the last four centuries have been the emancipation of music from its religious nursery, and the continual pressure from the musical side to reduce to zero the difference in style between the secular and the sacred. This has been countered from the ecclesiastical side by fairly frequent admonitions to keep church music religious, to resist the temptation to have mass for the sake of the music instead of the other way round (or, in Protestant terms, to choose a hymn because of its noble tune rather than for the content of its words).

Both the Council of Trent and the sixteenth century Reformers speak with a single voice on their fear of music in Church which is either so elaborate as wholly to obscure the meaning of the liturgy or so secular that it is associated with the amorous songs of the theatre. Martin Luther is here, as in much else, the occupant of a rather individual position, in that Luther loved extrovert and cheerful music, and had no inhibitions about taking over popular lovesongs and transforming them into chorales. The Swiss Reformed churches, on the other hand, followed Zwingli in regarding music in church services as inherently dangerous. Not until almost the end of the 16th century did music begin to re-enter Swiss Reformed worship because the people saw no good reason to be without it. Popular demand was too strong to be resisted.

We see at once that the sixteenth century marks no real change in the terms of the discussion going back through Augustine to Plato. On the one hand, music is a sacred art with a unique affinity to religion, having an inexplicable but certainly experienced capacity to express human feelings through their entire gamut. On the other hand, the danger of lascivious association is expressly formulated by Plato, and passes into the stream of Christian thinking. And the Christians, aware that a concrete message about God and Christ and salvation is entrusted to the Church and has to be communicated, add to Plato the fear that the music may obscure the words. This obscuring may be achieved in two ways. First the simple sense that the number of notes to any one syllable becomes so great that all distinctness of meaning is surrendered. But there is also the second and profounder sense that the sound in itself makes so tremendous an impact on the mind that the music altogether takes over, and makes the liturgical action (or the sense of the hymn) a wholly accidental and secondary feature of the performance.

It is hardly possible to exaggerate the difficulty of achieving a right judgment in all things at this point. As all my audience knows better than I, Bach, Handel, Mozart and Haydn and other lesser men freely reused music from their operas and other secular works for supplying church music; and vice-versa. The slow movement of Mozart's Divertimento for thirteen wind instruments makes a moving anthem for Trinity Sunday, *'Quis te comprehendat?'* I confess I find the music even more moving for wind instruments than when sung by a choir with organ accompaniment, and cannot quite listen to the anthem without an awareness that the same music has an even more exquisite setting outside ecclesiastical usage. But no one could plausibly urge that its employment as an anthem is inherently unsuitable, for the opposite is clearly the case. The music expresses a sense of awe and quietness with exquisite adoration. Verdi may not have been a very religious man, but he could write some very fitting church music. From a Christian point of view, there has never been good reason to require that all composers should have convictions as strong as J. S. Bach's; or, for that matter, Joseph Haydn's.

In the Catholic tradition Gregorian Chant has been accorded pride of place as an ideal form of church music. This is explicitly set out in the *Motu proprio* of Pius X (22 November 1903), and is then reaffirmed (with an adverbial qualification) in the Constitution on the Liturgy of the second Vatican Council. We are evidently not intended to think the absence of barlines a kind of foretaste of eternity. Gregorian chant reduces the personal prominence of the individual participant, and obviously subordinates music to words. It is not too difficult to be learnt by comparatively inexpert musicians, and therefore makes the chant accessible to a considerable number, allowing for something approximating to congregational participation, in the kind of way that Anglican congregations have long sung Marbeck, even though it is very doubtful that Marbeck ever intended his 'Book of Common Prayer Noted' to be used by other than clerks in the choir. Nevertheless, the special appropriateness of Gregorian chant is felt not least because of a long psychological association for Catholic worshippers. There is really no music which can be said to be liturgical in any absolutely specific sense. Pius X's ruling of 1903 recommending Gregorian as the supreme model for Catholic musicians does not represent any very ancient and unbroken tradition; and the second Vatican Council gives it pride of place with the qualification 'only if other things are equal,' *caeteris paribus*—a clause with a somewhat oracular effect, which reads like a courteous genuflexion towards Pius X before preparing to abandon him. Presumably it means that operatic types of music, such as had long been current in Italian churches, should be avoided. (The great Dr Burney gives us much evidence of what it was like in the 18th century.) There is evidently a requirement that the music in church should as far as possible be of a kind accessible to the largest possible number of people. Those who listen must feel themselves to be participants in the action as much as those who are trained to sing.

The truth is, I suppose, that clergy have always wanted Christians to enjoy themselves in church services, and we have seen that in a true and proper sense enjoyment is the right word, even if the lessons or sermons or the liturgical action may move one to profound penitence. For the experience is then a katharsis. But the clergy have also perennially feared that the sensuous side of that enjoyment might take control of everything else; and the reason for that apprehension is evident, namely that among the arts music possesses this extraordinary power, a power utterly to absorb, for the very good reason that it cannot be performed well unless it does utterly absorb the performers and will not be understood by the listeners unless they allow it to become a controlling medium through which their souls aspire to the divine beauty.

We have already seen that among the arts music most obviously depends on mathematical order. Even people quite innumerate are found to possess a strong sense of rhythm and pulse, and are discovered to be counting without realising that that is what they are doing. But among the arts music is also that which is most widely detached from concrete objects which we apprehend by our five senses. For because the sound is ordered in the way it is, we are not merely hearing noise. Our minds, especially after a little acclimatisation and training, learn to hear the ordering of the intervals of the various parts in the way that the composer himself designed them. The hearer participates in the order of the sound.

The music that human beings can make their own is normally an expression of feeling: triumph, love, joy, lamenting, anger, hatred, anxiety, nihilistic melancholy. Music has the power to give such feelings intense expression. Like words, music is transient, and in this is unlike a picture or a piece of architecture or a beautifully designed object. But at the time it is happening, it is all-consuming.

And we speak of music as something we *play*; as if this passionately serious occupation were a game for the human race, among whose most distinctive capacities is that of designing and playing games. Games have strictly ordered rules, and to flout the rules is to ruin the game. Except for those professionally involved, they are not in one sense necessary, though most human beings need them. For they take us out of the bewildering muddle and mess of our everyday humdrum lives, and give us a chance to achieve perfection within a very confined and limited frame of reference.

Music also has this in common with a game: that if it is played according to the rules, and not in an inappropriate way and at an inappropriate time, it is capable of an ennobling effect on both performer and listener (with something of the same sense of exhilaration as some get from playing in or watching a brilliantly played football match). It has some mysterious therapeutic capacities, as those who use it for explicit music therapy with the maladjusted can tell us. These capacities were known to the ancients, as we see from the first book of Samuel where Saul's mental disorder and depression are open to healing from David's skill on the harp; or from the early legends of Pythagoras sobering up a dangerously excited young man at Taormina by singing him a song in the Phrygian mode (Augustine, *contra Julianum* v, 5, 23). A commentator on Aristotle of the sixth century, that is of the age of Justinian, named Elias, declares that music alone among the mathematical sciences has curative powers for both body and soul.

And yet music in itself is morally neutral. The gifted musician may be wise or foolish, a prince of virtue or a demonic colleague of impossible egotism. But the music itself cannot be any of these things; and the technical mastery of its secrets, though requiring an absolute dedication of the would-be composer or performer, as great as that required of any other artist, need not necessarily have a therapeutic effect on the musician himself.

These last observations have some bearing on a question I tried to formulate near the beginning of this lecture, namely, to what degree music has come to displace religion in the modern western world? That for many of our contemporaries this has come to be the case has long been evident, I think. It was true already at the beginning of the 19th century, with the virtual deification of Beethoven during his lifetime and certainly for a long time thereafter. The belief that Beethoven's music transcended all the truths of existing religion and philosophy was actually one which, according to Bettina Brentano (von Arnim) in conversation with Goethe in 1810, Beethoven held himself:

Music is a higher revelation than all wisdom and philosophy. It is the wine which rouses to new creations, and I am the Bacchus who presses this glorious wine for men and makes them spiritually drunk: when they are sober again they will have fished up much which they can keep on dry land.

(Bettina von Arnim (Brentano), *Goethes Briefwechsel mit einem Kinde*, ed. G. Konrad, 1960, p. 246, cited by H. G. Koenigsberger, 'Music and Religion in modern European History', in *The Diversity of History*, ed. J. H. Elliott and H. G. Koenigsberger, 1970, p. 63.)

The quotation may tell us more about the romanticism of Bettina Brentano than about Beethoven. She at least simply equates music and the divine; and Wagner, though doubting the absolute veracity of her report of Beethoven's remarks, entirely shared her view of what music is. And of course it is true enough the last quartets of Beethoven, or the *'Et vitam venturi'* fugue of the *Missa Solennis*, constitute a kind of religious exploration in awe and wonder at the indomitable and eternal spirit of man. It is no doubt also true that for a large number of our contemporaries music is not so much the partner of religion as a substitute for it—and there is the added attraction that the moral element, the uncomfortable proclamation of judgment, is not something that it is music's genius to convey apart from the words—though paradoxically there is no melody more frequently making its way in unexpected places than that of the *Dies Irae*.

The take-over phenomenon is intimately linked with the shift to the subjective which is one of the defining characteristics of the Romantic movement generally. This shift is still a potent force among us, as any study of existentialism or of modern student idealism would suffice to demonstrate. The Romantic view of religion has made for depth and width in our understanding of what religion means for humanity. But at the same time it has become less clear in what sense the affirmations of, say, the Creed, are affirming something to be the case independently of the affirming mind, or whether religious language is either imaginative poetry or a declaration of moral policy expressed in picture terms.

And behind that lies a doubt whether our aesthetic and moral values are something into which we seek to enter, affirming because they are appropriate to our experience of the world; or whether they are imposed by our creative minds upon an indifferent and neutral jungle. Many voices in our time tell us to believe that the source of beauty and the grounds of moral judgment lie solely in the constructive, creative, decision making powers of the human mind; and on this view we shall take a highly positive view of religion as man's principal form of protest against the apparent meaningless of existence, in which the things we most care about hang by the thinnest thread, and in which we impose a pattern of value on the chaos of life which is, in a free translation of the book of Ecclesiastes, 'one damn thing after another'.

A religious person will not be cool towards the way in which great music can lift and inspire. 'He who is not against us is on our side'. What moral qualities may be brought out by the sheer determination and ascetic dedication required of anybody who is going to succeed as a musician! And how good that men and women should be turned away from the immediate, from the material, from getting and spending, and contemplate a unique world of order which music gives the entrance to. And yet there is a word more to say: we cannot bear to live in a world of projections and desires that bear no relation to what is not ourselves, and to be told that the values we most prize are not in principle other than teddy bears we have failed to leave behind in the playpen is unconvincing. As for the permanent force to be found in religious faith: if we do not think that the deepest needs of humanity can all be exhaustively supplied by political action, by the achievement of agreement among the economists and social engineers (not colleagues among whom agreement is usually striking), or by further spectacular advances in technology, then religion has not been declared redundant at all.

My last remarks will seem to some a digression from my main theme. I do not think they are. To sum up what I have tried to say in this lecture: Music is an independent art, which since the Renaissance has moved out of the ecclesiastical nursery but has never parted company with its *alma nutrix*. The developments of the modern world have not essentially changed the terms of the question in which Augustine formulated our problem in A.D. 400. We need music in Church; it does something for us which is integral and indispensable; we fear it when it takes over, not merely because it may obliterate the distinctively Christian, but because it may end by the mere glorification of man himself. And man being held in honour is uncommonly akin to the beasts that perish.

A Lecture to mark the 75th year of the Church Music Society, delivered in the Great Room of the Royal Society of Arts, London, on 1 October 1981, Sir David Willcocks, CBE, MC, in the Chair.

16

Romanticism and Religion

THE TITLE of the discourse that I have the honour to submit to you joins together two rather woolly and imprecise terms. Religion is not, without much further definition, a clear word for a readily identifiable subject. It is obscure, first, whether it refers to a particular religion, and, if so, which; secondly, whether there is a latent implication that underlying all particular religions, or even quite independent of them, there is a universal Religion (with a capital R, so to speak), and whether this last is more than a vague religiosity. On the other hand the word has the merit of being a great deal more precise than Romanticism. I propose to discuss not men and women being romantic, but the movement of thought, literature, and art that is commonly so described. Yet the movement is an amorphous entity. Many who have lectured or written books about it have found themselves wondering what it is which makes the label in any sense useful or illuminating as a blanket description of so many diverse characters and contradictory attitudes. After reading several large books about or indeed by the Romantics, one is met by so many contradictions and incompatibilities that one may easily begin to doubt whether there was such a 'movement' at all. Had this much acclaimed movement in the history of western culture of the nineteenth century any real existence in space and time? Or was it like, say, the collapse of the western Roman empire in the year A.D. 476—a non-event imperceptible to anyone living at the time and created by the retrospective judgement of people living much later (in this case at the time of the Renaissance)? After reading other writers we begin to think the opposite, namely that at the end of the eighteenth century there was a *nouvelle vague* in literature, philosophy, and theology which made much noise of rejecting generally established fashions, but was in reality far less differentiated from the immediately preceding age than it was asserting to be the case. The Romantics claimed to reject the Enlightenment, but in actual fact they only produced a few semi-quaver variations on the old themes.

Faced by this situation, it is no surprise that many judicious historians of ideas, including the high authority, Arthur Lovejoy, patron of all *Ideengeschichte*, have roundly condemned all attempts to define Romanticism, regarding them as merely fatuous.[1] The term Romantic, we may agree, is useless and vacuous to an analytical philosopher. But it does not follow that it ought therefore to be abandoned by all conscientious historians of literature and thought. The end of the eighteenth century certainly saw a shift in the interests and presuppositions of writers, philosophers, and some theologians; and for this shift it is convenient to have a shorthand label.

There is something to be learnt from the history of the word. This has been slightly different in the various European languages, but broadly it may be said that the term 'romantic' passes from being applied to a novel of gallantry to being a description of enthusiasm, mysticism, and those non-rational aspects of human experience which most thinkers of the eighteenth-century Enlightenment found uncongenial. The word which rationalists used in a pejorative sense for attitudes they regarded as embarrassing, their successors used in a positive sense. But, except in Germany, the writers and artists we have come to label Romantic seldom described themselves under this title. It would be absurdly pedantic to insist that this in some way diminishes the right of historians to describe men like Wordsworth, Coleridge, Byron, Whitman, or Victor Hugo, as romantics. Let me borrow an analogy from quite another field. The Neoplatonists of late antiquity had not the least notion that they were teaching a Platonism to which the prefix neo- would be appropriate; but the historian of philosophy is entitled to think that the label has its uses. Similarly the epithet Anglican makes a comparatively late appearance as a description of a certain type of theology and church polity, but sensible men would think it insufferable pedantry to deny the term to Hooker, Donne, George Herbert, Joseph Butler, and George Berkeley, none of whom would naturally have used the word of themselves.

The reflections that follow are in no sense intended to cover the field, but rather to introduce discussion by concentrating on one or two striking aspects of this vast subject. In particular I shall omit (but not because the theme is unimportant) Wordsworth and the Romantic attitude to nature.

The Romantic movement can be initially described, if not defined, in the familiar terms of what it reacted against in the mind of the eighteenth century. The reaction against classical forms and rationalist ideals produced a vehement emphasis on strong sentiment and uninhibited natural feelings. To this was soon added the stimulus given by fear of the French Revolution, the seismic effect of which was felt all over Europe to endanger the social values of the *ancien régime* in every country. The desire to recall a lost, irrecoverable past has become one of the notions that we easily associate with the Romantic ideal. In Coleridge it becomes an escape into a dream world of opium-assisted fantasy. It is worth stressing that the past which seemed so desirable and inaccessible was often not classical antiquity but the medieval world of Christian chivalry and Catholic ceremonial. The Oxford Movement and Walter Scott's novels stand as obvious examples. But the retrospective look was not incompatible with a progressivist dream of an ideal future, to be realized by the release of humanity from the constricting shackles of formalism and dryness.

With such assumptions it was easy and natural for many to look nostalgically towards Christianity, especially (but not necessarily) in its more catholic forms. They were in search of mystery. In the age of the Enlightenment this search could lead to freemasonry, though this form of semi-cultic mystery left men like Lessing disenchanted and dissatisfied by what they found. Among the Protestants, the pietists had developed strong interests in the writings of the great mystics. The evangelicals, who taught that regenerate believers experience an unmediated presence of the Spirit of God, found highly congenial reading in writers whose concentration on the inward experience of the soul often went with an indifference to, or at least some variation from, orthodox dogmatic tradition. The works of Eckhart, Tauler, Guyon, above all Jacob Boehme, were widely read among devout pietists. In Württemberg, the eminent prelate F. C. Oetinger (1702-82) was combining the tenure of high ecclesiastical office with a universalist theology, with deep study of Boehme, and with private investigations into the mysteries of alchemy and Paracelsus. Schelling, who was led by Oetinger to the study of Boehme, is only the most notable among a number who turned towards the mystical tradition at this time. On this subject, however, it is unnecessary to dwell, as we now have the useful survey of this topic by Professor Ernst Benz published earlier this year.[2]

More commonly, it is true, the Romantics found what they needed in cooler and less obscure pages, particularly in Spinoza and Rousseau. In regard to the study of Spinoza, Lessing acted as a catalyst for the Germans. On the literary side Lessing's polemic against the artificial perfections of Corneille and Racine and his advocacy of the full-blooded naturalism of Shakespeare, set up the ideal of free expression of natural feelings. On the religious side the theological tracts of his last decade show a clear move away from any conception of divine transcendence and freedom and towards belief in an immanent destiny with a deterministic doctrine of human nature. In both respects Lessing, himself a simple child of the Enlightenment, must be reckoned one of the major influences making Romanticism possible.[3]

What changes did this mean for the interpretation of religion?

If you had asked St Augustine in the fifth century or St Thomas in the thirteenth from what sources he derived his religious principles and doctrines, he would have replied without hesitation or hedging: from the authority of divine revelation and from reason which is a divinely given aid. In holy scripture God had granted a special disclosure of truth. Reason could interpret the documents and could make clear deductions. Reason could also think and talk about God without any appeal to the special revelation in scripture. Inferences could be drawn from the nature of the world, from its order and beauty on the one hand, from its impermanence and transitoriness on the other. By both routes one could arrive at the rational proposition that beyond the visible, tangible world there lay an immaterial world of divine truth, goodness, and beauty. This beauty was not merely in the eye of the beholder. The truth and the goodness were not values that depended on human exertion for their actualization. They were there to be believed and discerned independently of the believing and discerning mind.

It would be a long, though no doubt for a theologian fascinating, history to trace the transfer of interest from ontology to psychology. Two obvious milestones are Zwingli's eucharistic doctrine, startlingly modern in its insistence on the fundamental importance of the psychological question, and John Locke's discussion of miracles where he insists strenuously that they are not mere prodigies but events that evoke faith, the faith being essential to the evaluation of the event as miraculous.[4] But this investigation would take us far afield. Spinoza and Rousseau, very different as they were, agreed on one crucial point. Neither of them believed in a free, transcendent divine Being, disclosing revealed truths *ab extra*. Rousseau's Vicaire savoyard rises to his greatest eloquence when he comes to speak of conscience,[5] explicitly defined as feelings not as judgements of the reason; for to make ethics a matter for the reason is to make it a subject for intellectuals and experts in such inquiries.

In Rousseau, as in Joseph Butler and Kant, the mainspring of religious belief lies in ethics, and the supreme organ is the conscience. But whereas for Butler and Kant the activity of the conscience is a rational judgement applied to moral issues, for Rousseau it is an innate feeling, a divine instinct, a following of the laws of nature prior to any encrusting prejudice that upbringing may superimpose. Although conscience cannot develop without reason, it is in principle independent of it, and is operative before the age of reason is attained.

Such language puts us on the road towards a fundamental, uncriticized presupposition of a growing number of thinkers of the Romantic age, namely, that the value of any given affirmation about man and the meaning of his existence lies in subjective sincerity, in the inward conviction with which it is held. Whereas Augustine and Aquinas would have held that the truth of a theological affirmation could be tested (by appealing to revelation or reason), such language had come to look rationalistic in the sense that it assumed confidence in reason to reach some measure of the truth. The traditional affirmations were held because men believed that they stated what is the case. The Romantic view of religious and moral affirmations was to change that profoundly. They were on the way to being personal moral judgements, statements of moral policy, or aesthetic appreciations.

This view was undoubtedly hastened by Kant's strong dichotomy between the realm of nature and the realm of ends, the sphere in which man asks how and the sphere in which he asks why and wherefore. I do not know, and have found it extremely hard to discover any precise and direct evidence to show, how far loss of confidence in the objectivity of moral judgements and religious affirmations may have been encouraged by Kant's epistemological doctrine that we know objects not as they are in themselves, but as they appear to us, and that, while empirical knowledge offers us many particular impressions, our own minds by spontaneous action give organization and shape to what we perceive. Be that as it may, from Kant onwards there is an ever-widening gulf between the neutral, objective statements of impirical natural science and a

221

world of moral value to which the epithets 'neutral' and 'objective' come to seem mountingly inappropriate. Rousseau had seen the moral conscience as that which elevates man above the beasts. The more attractive became the hypothesis of biological evolution, the more likely it was that men would wish to read human history in the manner of Apollo in Keats' *Hyperion*:

> Knowledge enormous makes a god of me.

Values are not inherently there in the realm of nature which is value-free and the object of detached scientific study. They are created by the mind of man imposing shape and structure on the objects before him.

In one form or another an interest in the subjective act of believing rather than in the nature of the object of faith comes to dominate almost all the principal religious thinkers of nineteenth-century Europe. It is equally apparent whether in Kierkegaard, arch-enemy of liberalizing apologetic, or in the liberal Coleridge's famous plea—'*Evidences* of Christianity! I am weary of the word. Make a man feel the *want* of it; rouse him if you can, to the self-knowledge of his *need* of it . . .' Schleiermacher, founding father of modern Protestant theology and (through his influence on J. A. Möhler) of some liberal catholic theology also, saw all dogmas as attempts to express the experience of dependence, awe, reverence, and redemption, in a rational and verbal form. The classical statements of past ages, the decrees of general councils, he treated as historical documents which had the status of signposts rather than adequate, binding formulae with an authority almost beyond criticism for all loyal Christians. The task of the Christian theologian therefore becomes that of interpreting the present consciousness of the living community. There is in a man a basic religious instinct, a latent consciousness of the need for God, an intuition of the divine Presence prior to all images and all intellectualized statements. The inner consciousness is the arbiter of both the meaningfulness and the historical evolutionary development of all dogmas. Therefore the medieval distinction of Natural and Supernatural ceases to be of any importance. The supernatural is not something wholly discontinuous with the natural. The person of Christ is best understood under the category of the religious genius, the incarnation of the divine Ideal. His significance is seen in what he releases and makes possible for his followers, drawn to him by the beauty of his life and teaching. Likewise, inspiration is not for the communication of revealed propositional truths. It is like poetic inspiration, an elevated excitement which heightens the natural capacities and gives the impulse to express faith and insight in writing.

In speaking of the root of religion as the feeling of absolute dependence, awe, and reverence, Schleiermacher did not intend to disparage the value of the reasoning process. Nor did he intend to deny or doubt that the experience of awe is occasioned by reality and trust. He removed any possible conflict between the scientific method and religious affirmations about, for example, creation, miracle, and the last things, by treating the latter as expressions of a human attitude of awe or as declarations of moral policy— principally the former. When looking at a valley, there is no conflict between saying that its curve is beautiful and saying that its shape is the result of glaciation. An aesthetic account and a scientific description can both be wholly true without the least clash between them.

The Romantics, therefore, tended to classify religious language with that of aesthetic experience. This has had far-reaching consequences, and it may be claimed as perhaps the most valuable, certainly the most influential, element in the philosophy and theology of the Romantic era. For no psychologist would find it easy to draw a line between the one and the other. For most normal adults the aesthetic and the religious are often continuous, so that (unless you have just been studying Kierkegaard's *Either-Or*) you cannot say where the one ends and the other begins. But that is not to say either that all religion in whatever form has an artistic value, or that all aesthetic appreciation of beauty is a form of religion. The later Romantics of the second half of the nineteenth century are much inclined to use religious vocabulary for describing an aesthetic attitude. The point emerges with great clarity from Professor Graham Hough's delightful study of Ruskin, D. G. Rossetti, Walter Pater, the pre-Raphaelites, and W. B. Yeats.[6] But there is always the danger that cloudy language about art being worship may obscure real distinctions. A religion of good taste is not very good religion if that is all it is (at least, religious people would not think so). Above all, in aesthetic experience it is the act of experiencing which is supremely valuable. The criterion of value of a work of art lies in the effect it is capable of having upon the beholder or the listener. Religious experience is far more concerned about the independence of the object which evokes it, and, except in those evangelical circles in which we have already seen some of the essential roots of the Romantic movement, mystical theology has normally taught that feelings of deep exaltation and emotion are to be distrusted in the spiritual life.

The same point can be put another way. Religious language has an obvious affinity with the language of poetry. The great American theologian Horace Bushnell (1802-76),[7] who was very far from being a fool, explicitly defended the view that all good theology is poetry, tales (if you so wish) of mystery and imagination of a special sort. Now it is very evident that, in its attempt to point to a reality transcending not only sense-experience but all human capacity for adequate verbal description, theology is bound to work with symbols, the language of myth, and poetic vision. But theology cannot be defined as poetry in a reductionist sense, without its nature being transformed. For its *raison d'être* is to try to speak, however haltingly, of a reality that exists independently of our minds, which transcends and enfolds them, and which is experienced by Christians as an invasive power to which the name 'grace' is given.

Three other consequences of the Romantic approach to religion deserve to be mentioned briefly. The first is the impetus which the movement gave to the notion of the community. The rise of the secular national state was no doubt principally responsible for the parallel reactions in European Christendom which we can see in the work of Lamennais in France; in the Tractarians in England; in Chalmers and the Scottish Disruption; in the Mercersburg group in America.[8] Nevertheless the discovery of the notion of the divine right and mission of the Christian community, apart from any right of voluntary association conferred by the civil power, was not merely the reaction of men huddling together to keep warm on an icy, wind-swept mountain-side. With the noteworthy exceptions of Kierkegaard, who wrote off institutional Christianity as a hopeless compromise, and the Ritschlian liberal protestants, who preferred an individualistic Kantian moralism, most of the leading religious thinkers of nineteenth-century Europe and America attached intense value to the community ideal.

Secondly, Romantic theology profoundly stimulated the study of the psychology of religion. The phrase 'religious experience' must for ever be associated with that compulsively readable classic, William James's Gifford Lectures. James himself regarded religious truth as verifiable in practical action which required venture and risk. That is to say that the truth of religion is created as this risk is accepted. It is dependent for its realization on human moral intentions.

The move away from the notion that formal logic is a guide and arbiter to the truth of religious propositions finds powerful expression in John Henry Newman, but of course in a very different form. Newman's two most original books, the *Oxford University Sermons* and the *Essay in Aid of a Grammar of Assent*, were written at very different periods of his life; the one when he was an Anglican, the other when he was a Roman Catholic. Yet each complements and fills out the argument of the other. Newman was mainly interested in those kinds of assent where our certitude is not dependent on the inferences of formal logic. He treats logic as a set of artificial rules created by the necessary conventions of human communication, sharing with pure mathematics the danger of being exposed to corruption as soon as they are applied inappropriately to actual experience of life. The conclusions you reach on merely logical grounds are not in general of existential importance to you. Your emotions are rarely involved. You do not fear their refutation. Deep personal convictions are not indeed tenable in defiance of logical considerations, but are discovered on the far side of a gulf which is crossed by what Newman calls 'the illative sense'. This illative sense is a capacity of the mind to discern truth in an accumulation of probabilities, akin to intuition, but differentiated from it. In religion this illative sense is important precisely because faith is a matter engaging more than the logical faculty.

Newman's *Grammar of Assent* illustrates simultaneously the power and the vulnerability of the Romantic view of religion. On the debit side it is never perfectly clear how the subjective illative sense differs from a blind guess or a spontaneous intuition which, as an individual and personal thing, will no doubt differ in each man. On the credit side, the doctrine of assent is immeasurably deeper and stronger than that found, for example, in William Paley. Paley at the end of the eighteenth century applied a highly gifted mathematical and logical mind to the problems of Christian evidences. It is some measure of the quality and clarity of his writing that, despite the essentially eighteenth-century character of his work, one of his books remained a prescribed text in the University of Cambridge until 1920(!). Yet Paley wrote with little apparent sense of personal engagement. He might almost have been writing about beetles. If we think Newman a better theologian than Paley, that is not because he had a better mind (though I think he had), but because we ourselves cannot help agreeing with Newman, as with the entire Romantic tradition, that the meaning of religion is not entered into merely by syllogisms or by arguments about problems of ancient history. The subjectivity of Newman seems to us so vastly more illuminating than the cool objectivity of Paley.

Yet subjectivity had its problems, which may be illustrated by an anecdote. On the night before he was ordained in 1846, Frederick Temple (1821-1902), Fellow of Balliol, later to be Archbishop of Canterbury (1896-1902), wrote out a list of aphorisms as guide-lines for his life, which he invariably kept in his purse. One of them read: 'Never preach anything that you have not yourself experienced.'[9] Here is the romantic view of religion in a nutshell. It sounds splendid advice. But reflection makes one wonder. If a man is entrusted with a message to deliver, it may not be so good. He may too easily end by making his narrow experience and comprehension the yardstick of truth; in short, replacing 'I believe' by 'One does feel'.

The third topic to which the Romantics gave a powerful impulse was the comparative study of religions. By concentrating on the primacy of experience over all dogmas and intellectualized formulae, they opened the way, first, to thinking of faith as an essentially human act apart from any divine revelation to evoke it, and secondly, to the proposition that underlying all the different modes and expressions of the various religions there is a single common experience which is uniform and identical. This consequence is paradoxical, for here if anywhere we have a simple restatement, with hardly a variation, of one of the basic axioms of the Enlightenment. In his *Reden* of 1799, Schleiermacher poured scorn on the rationalistic view that all particular religions are conventional accretions superimposed upon a primordial, pure, 'natural' religion. Yet by concentrating attention on the innermost feelings of the religious consciousness, apart from ethical action and rational propositions, he made it difficult to provide clear criteria for adjudicating not merely among the deviations within the Christian tradition but also among the different religions. To

226

say that experience is primary, and that dogmatic definitions have only a relative significance and value, could lead straight back to the Enlightenment's view that theological controversy and denominational differences are anachronistic survivals, caused by failure to appreciate the revised estimate of the nature of doctrinal affirmations. Schleiermacher realized of course that beginning from religious experience raised entirely new questions about the status of different religions, and that it would no longer be possible to talk as if one religion were true and all the rest false. It is one of the minor legacies of his position that the comparative study of religions has had some difficulties in classifying itself as an intellectual discipline. It has not been clear whether it belongs to the philosophy of religion in general, or whether it has to be an enormous empirical investigation into the phenomenology of all the particular branches of the subject.

I beg to conclude with some general reflections on the subject. The thesis of this paper has been that the shift to the subjective is one of the defining characteristics of the Romantic movement, and that this shift is at bottom a reaction to the religious crisis of the Enlightenment. The consequences of this shift remain with us to the present time, as any study of existentialism would suffice to illustrate. There has been great gain from this shift, but also some loss. The Romantic view of religion has made for greater depth and width in our understanding of the meaning of religious experience for humanity. At the same time it has become hard to be sure in what sense the affirmations of theology affirm, or are intended to affirm, something to be the case independently of the affirming mind, or whether we may legitimately take the obvious and easy way of regarding religious language either as imaginative poetry or as a declaration of moral policy expressed in pictorial terms of a story (cf. Matthew Arnold).

This hesitancy is in part a reflection of a doubt whether our aesthetic and moral values are something into which we have to seek to enter, and which are affirmed because they are appropriate to our experience of the world and illuminate the facts; or whether they are arbitrarily imposed by our creative minds upon an indifferent and neutral jungle. Strong reasoners in our own time tell us to believe that the source of beauty and the grounds of moral judgement lie in the constructive, creative, decision-making powers of the human mind. Religion in this view makes excellent sense as man's principal form of protest against the apparent meaninglessness of existence, imposing a pattern of value on the chaos of existence. The difficulty to the acceptance of this view, which is no doubt the ultimate logic of the Romantic position, is that we cannot bear to live in a world of projections and desires that bear no relation to what is not ourselves. Yeats' happy shepherd advised us not

> To hunger fiercely after truth,
> Lest all thy toiling only breeds
> New dreams, new dreams; there is no truth
> Saving in thine own heart.

This antithesis is the basic legacy of the Romantic movement. It is an antithesis with which I do not think it possible for humanity to remain permanently satisfied.

y J. Hobbinton
on the Evangelical
Movement
esp section — Romanticism —
of the way in which Henry Jett
sought to see Wesley as a precursor of
Schleiermacher.

17

Royal ecclesiastical supremacy

IN THE draft bull excommunicating King Henry VIII, of the year 1535, three themes are linked together as providing overwhelming grounds for the condemnation: the divorce of Catherine of Aragon, the claim to be supreme head of the Church of England, and the judicial murder of John Fisher.[1] The saintly and renowned humanist Fisher, the man Henry VIII himself had been heard by Pole to describe as the most learned man he knew, is a symbolic figure by his unyielding opposition to the divorce and to the king's consequent expulsion of papal authority from his realm in response to the humiliation of Pope Clement's rejection. None of the three acts was well regarded in Europe at large, and together they looked like the tyranny of a Night of the Long Knives. Reginald Pole's *Defence of the Unity of the Church* must have been telling Henry what the king already knew when the writer observed that Henry's actions had brought political danger—whether from Charles V or from the French—a severing of a branch from the root of God's tree by rejecting the universality and unity embodied by Peter's see, and a threat of civil insurrection and future conflict about the succession to the throne once Mary had been declared illegitimate. That seemed a lot of trouble to buy. As for the title 'head of the Church', Pole acidly remarked that this head was chiefly noted for plundering the Church. It seemed absurd that one claiming such a title could not minister the sacraments, and yet could constitute himself as the judge of controversies in matters of faith. Flatterers might tell him that royal supremacy over the Church was enjoined by the Bible, in St Peter's exhortation to 'honour the king', and try to set scripture up against tradition and Catholic consensus; but Pole mercilessly demolished such flimsy arguments. Everyone knew that the title of supreme head of the Church had been conceded most reluctantly after intimidation. It was an act of power lacking moral authority. As for the loot Henry had taken from the Church, Pole tersely reminded him that tyrants usually fall for lack of friends, not for lack of money. The whole story of the moral disintegration of a man who had once been enthusiastically acclaimed as a paragon among English kings is seen by Pole as almost an instance of *ate*, an insanity depriving the king of his wits and impelling him into storms for which he had no one but himself to blame.

229

My purpose in this essay is to try to set Fisher's protest and martyrdom in a broader context than the particularities of Henry VIII and his quarrel with the papacy, broader even than the now commonplace observation that well before 1534 there was growing tension between canon and common lawyers in England. It was not new for conciliar minds to seek some limitation and restriction upon the apparently total autocracy claimed for the papal monarchy by recalling that the authority of emperors and kings was also, according to scripture, God-given. Therefore, in insisting that the Church's canons should not be enforced where they passed into realms governed by the statutes of the king in parliament, they were not necessarily setting aside the law of God. Moreover, canonists such as Gascoigne were aware that even the pope can make no enactment or dispensation contrary to God's word, or indeed to natural law. *Plenitudo potestatis* was not unlimited in practice, and there was to be some bias in the protestant contention that the pope claimed to 'add, alter, and diminish, nay also to dispense with the words that Christ himself spake, as well as the writing of the Apostles'. At least, that opinion was taking sides in a canonists' dispute, and the 'Protestant' barb (which I have cited from Archbishop Matthew Parker)[2] would have had plenty of critics among some medieval canonists of repute. The general opinion was that the pope could interpret, but not dispense from, the word of God.

Accordingly, whatever might be the precise extent of authority contained in the power of the keys entrusted to Peter (Matthew 16 : 18-19), these powers had to be balanced by the truth that the powers controlling the secular order were also no less ordained by God. Could one not affirm both the king's supremacy and the pope's, recognising them to have different spheres of responsibility? In his second book Reginald Pole insists, 'I shall not diminish the authority of the king if I preserve his authority and Peter's side by side.'[3] Indeed, as the English Reformation advanced under Henry's son, Edward VI, it became alarmingly clear that the religious and social upheaval of the age could put the monarchy itself at risk. Many pages of the fiercely protestant John Hooper[4] are devoted to the assertion of royal supremacy not against the claims of the papacy, though Hooper did not forget that theme, but against the sedition of Anabaptists. He wanted the clergy in his diocese of Gloucester to read Romans 13 to the people every Saturday and Sunday: to have shown the pope the door did not mean that there could be room for corrupt Englishmen with minds full of 'contempt, hatred, grudge, and malice against their king, magistrates, laws, orders, and policies'.[5] The king's determination to be master in his own realm (as none of his predecessors had been) did not mean that all Englishmen admired his break with the catholicity represented by Rome. Evidently some Englishmen were just as hostile to royal absolutism as to papal. To remove papal authority could entail moral and social collapse.

Contemplation of the relations between the Church and civil government through the long course of Christian history suggests that Romans 13 has usually been more influential than the Apocalypse of John.[6] By one of the more paradoxical twists of exegesis, the Apocalypse's warnings against the Babylonian harlot of the Roman government have been ingeniously readdressed in the post office to apply to the bishops of Rome, the list of whom has its fair share of martyrs. The more tough-minded English reformers regarded it as self-evident, something every schoolboy knew, that as long as there are seven hills beside the Tiber, it is certain that the pope is the very whore of Babylon and Antichrist.[7] Admittedly this opinion was to be much dented by Grotius's exposition of the Book of Daniel,[8] and in the middle of the seventeenth century Archbishop John Bramhall associated the antipapal exegesis with 'Protestants out of their wits'.[9] But a century earlier this exegesis of the Apocalypse was general, and had had notable medieval exponents from the Waldensians to Frederick II (Hohenstaufen). Cranmer himself followed Wycliffe in holding that in accordance with Revelation 20: 2 Satan had been released from his prison after precisely a thousand years.[10] There might be disagreements about the exact date on which his millennium of imprisonment had started, and therefore some hesitation about the point at which evidence of his release should be located; but at least by the sixteenth century one could be confident that Satan was well and truly released and active in subtle infiltration of the Church.[11] Surely he had taken possession of the Roman see, sitting where he ought not in the very sanctuary of the Lord, the 'man of sin'? So Romans 13 and the Apocalypse were harmonised, idealising the prince and rubbishing the pope. Admittedly, some medieval popes, and especially at the beginning of the sixteenth century, had discredited themselves and damaged the office.

The persisting strength of English Lollardy is shown by the enthusiasm with which leading reformers took up the Antichrist theme. Moreover, Wycliffe had proclaimed that the civil power's duty was to reform the Church, with a moral right to remove and redistribute its endowments.[12] In *Piers Plowman* even Langland (who, with Chaucer, could easily be regarded as a fellow traveller by Lollards) had a famous prophecy of the coming king who was to cleanse God's temple of impurities.[13] Both Langland and Wycliffe took a low view of the Donation of Constantine. It must be a source of surprise that the dissident Lollards allowed their hostility to the Church, to priests both as a caste and as a male preserve, to tithes, to all sacramental actions for which laity are dependent on clergy, to take them so far as to lead them to put trust in princes. Was not that to trust in the arm of the flesh indeed? Moreover, Lollards (as their Conclusions of 1395 declared)[14] were pacifists who rejected killing whether in war or justice, and soon found that the secular authorities were as unsympathetic as the ecclesiastical. But confronted by a body as powerful as the medieval clergy, with financial resources in land topped up by fees for requiems which Lollards especially abominated,[15] they could turn to no source of power other than the king and the nobles. There was plenty to make Henry VIII's revolution look like the fulfilment of a dream among humble farmers and 'white-collar workers' in Kent, Sussex and East Anglia, where Wycliffite translations, especially of the Apocalypse and of the epistle of James (with its denunciations of opulent Christians), were studied at clandestine meetings in barns. Admittedly Lollards suffered under Henry; but some of his programme was in line with much they had been saying. For example, Wycliffe and his followers objected to the quantity of money exported from the country either to the papacy or to international religious orders. (Cranmer himself felt that the papal fee for his consecration and pallium was excessive.)[16] Lay power was to be the instrument and weapon to liberate Englishmen in soul and body from the burdens imposed by an opulent and essentially foreign hierarchy, an alien multinational corporation. One cannot say that all Englishmen of the sixteenth century manifested xenophobia, since a number of documents speak of their hospitable welcome to foreigners. But Wycliffe anticipated some of the nationalist feeling apparent in the declaration, astonishingly found in the gentle, rational, and learned Matthew Parker, that 'Almighty God is so much English'.[17]

When one reads in John Hooper that bishops have no duty other than to preach God's word whereas it is the duty of the prince to judge whether or not their preaching and teaching are correct,[18] it is difficult not to feel that the Reformation let loose some strange notions about Church and state. Yet the doctrine of the theological responsibility of the prince had a long history going back far beyond Wycliffe, and beyond the medieval struggles about investiture. Educated men of the sixteenth century read Justinian. Lectures on the civil law were part of the standard syllabus at Oxford and Cambridge.[19] In Justinian's *Code*, and in the *Novels* supplementing it, it is axiomatic that the emperor's authority extends beyond matters merely temporal and secular. He has a duty to protect orthodoxy and to harass heresy. So Justinian legislated to safeguard and enforce the true faith against heresies such as the Monophysite alternative to Chalcedon. He legislated to ensure the clergy did their duty. He issued formal edicts regulating the number of clergy on the establishment at Hagia Sophia. He provided controls for orphanages and hospitals which were ecclesiastical foundations. His enactments were intended to ensure that endowments were used as intended by the pious benefactors, and not bent to profane purposes or private gain.

As in the sixteenth century, so also in the sixth, the imperial responsibility to legislate against heresy was no private matter; the unity of the Church in truth profoundly affected the social and political cohesion of the empire. Dogmatic disputes shared with excessive interest rates the largest responsibility for causing urban riots. Justinian's subjects were deeply divided on the issue of Christology, above all whether one should say *in* (two natures) or *of*. But he could not be neutral. He could not gain political control of Italy and the West unless he made Chalcedonian orthodoxy, and the preposition *in*, a foundation for his ecclesiastical policy, so that his personal convictions were reinforced by political necessity. The great emperor Anastasius, his predecessor but one, creator of the conditions necessary for the greatness of his own *imperium*, had run into endless trouble with Italy and the West because he was not sound on Chalcedon. He upheld the reunion formula or 'Henoticon' of Zeno with its very cool reference censuring heresies 'even if held by bishops at Chalcedon or elsewhere'. In 518-19 papal pressure to gain recognition for Chalcedon was to entail riots with large loss of life in some Eastern cities. Justinian's Monophysite subjects in Syria and the Nile valley, with a few advance outposts in the monasteries of Constantinople itself, looked for support to his wife

Theodora. In her highly unregenerate youth she had once been spiritually assisted by an anti-Chalcedonian priest in Alexandria, and never forgot her debt. She hid numerous Monophysite bishops in her large palace, and even provided for them the noble church of St Sergius and St Bacchus, still standing today, to give them a place of liturgical assembly.

The Monophysites deeply objected to Theodore of Mopsuestia, Ibas of Edessa, and Theodoret of Kyrrhos—all long dead, but masterful expositors of 'two-nature' Christology and stern critics of the doctrine of one nature. In 543 Justinian issued a decree condemning their doctrines as expressed in selected excerpts or 'chapters', and included in his censure speculations ascribed to Origen by monks of the New Lavra in Palestine. But the imperial edict was not the end of dissension. Did it not need an ecumenical council to ratify the emperor's condemnations? Was the emperor, even if possessed of immense theological learning, the judge of fidelity to the word of God? An ecumenical council naturally had an aura about it, and for Justinian it could have the attraction that he would be seen to be doing for the Church in his time what the great Constantine had once done at Nicaea. But an ecumenical council needed Roman concurrence, and indeed that of all the patriarchs and a great body of the metropolitans, unless it could be satisfactorily shown that a patriarch himself had lapsed into grave heresy. The West suspected, with some reason, that a condemnation of the 'Three Chapters' was intended to swamp the Scotch of the Chalcedonian definition with a flood of Monophysite soda. In Italy Pope Vigilius might be safe from interference. His predecessors before 518 (when communion between Rome and Byzantium was restored after more than three decades of schism) had enjoyed freedom from imperial interference. Paradoxically, the Byzantine decision to give the popes everything they asked for meant that the kiss of peace in 518 was to turn into a lethal squeeze, once Justinian had reabsorbed Italy into his empire and again made the pope his subject. Vigilius could not decline the summons to travel to Constantinople. Justinian's general council of 553 was an assembly with papal consent for its assembling.

Predictably, the Council ratified the emperor's censures on Origen and on the Three Chapters. But could Vigilius be brought to agree? Though residing in or close to the city and the Council, he had declined to attend the conciliar debates, wishing to preserve his independence of decision on the question of ratification. In his estimate the Council had only an advisory role, giving a demonstration of the general opinion, after which he would announce the final verdict. The Greek bishops gathered in Council regarded this as extraordinary arrogance. They threatened Vigilius with excommunication, and used the remarkable formula, later to enjoy Gallican echoes, that even if they withdrew their communion from Vigilius, they maintained it with the *sedes*; only not with the *sedens*.[20] To the ancient Church, authority resides in the throne rather than in the person who may happen to be sitting on it. After several changes of mind and rough treatment at the hands of Justinian's minions, Vigilius finally surrendered to the emperor's will and assented. It was a manifestation of imperial supremacy, and everyone knew it. Yet the outward form of ecumenical conciliarity was preserved, and subsequent tradition knew how to deal with awkwardnesses in some of the language used at the council by means of the rigorous critical process of 'Reception'.

In the Greek Orthodox tradition this process of Reception went so far that, because of one or two moments of embarrassment for readers (especially when Vigilius strenuously asserted the rights of his see and indiscreetly spoke of one *operatio* or *energeia* in Christ),[21] the Acts were left uncopied. The Greek Church remembered the canons and formal decrees, but not the actual Acts, which survive as a whole only through the Latin tradition.

Justinian's imperial supremacy did not shut out the pope. It subjected him to torture and splendid banquets as alternating methods of extracting agreement. In the emperor's political theory there was no element of secular nationalism. Nevertheless it is possible to find in antiquity at least a regional patriotism as joining forces with antipapal feeling. Dissident bodies snubbed by the emperor, such as the North African Donatists, spoke of the empire as an agent of Antichrist with whom the Catholic Church was on altogether too cosy terms. Even Donatists were not above appealing to the magistrate whenever it seemed in their interest to do so.[22] But they had a highly independent estimate of Church authority, with a clericalised ecclesiology defined by rigorously preserved apostolic succession and a high sacramental doctrine of episcopal power.[23] Their doctrine of legitimacy did not include either the *cathedra Petri* or the emperor. 'What has the emperor to do with the Church?' asked Donatus.[24] Donatus would much have liked the

Roman see to recognise his party; as it had not done so, it had *ipso facto* discredited itself. By associating with the wrong group, it had acquired the pollution of communion with apostates.

In reply, Augustine's anti-Donatist writings do not work with a strong dualism of Church and state. More than once he criticises the Donatists for being out of communion, not merely with the *Catholica* represented by Rome or Jerusalem or 'the apostolic sees' (usually, not always, plural), but also with the communion acknowledged by the emperor.[25]

In one passage of the third book of his *Contra Rufinum* (III, 18) Jerome confidently avers that an imperial rescript can legitimately overthrow a synodical decision. Western Christians imagine such ideas to be rather more at home in Byzantium than in the West. Yet it is in Greek canon law, not Latin, that one finds the first prohibition on bishops appealing to the court for review of a synodical censure: in the twelfth canon of the Council of Antioch, *c.* 330.[26]

Distance between the emperor and the Church was naturally desirable from the point of view of the imperial government. Successive emperors, from Constantine the Great onwards, found that a close involvement brought them down into the sandy arena of gladiatorial combat between the different factions of party strife with which Christian history has been plagued. The ruler was faced with the great problem that to enjoy the wholly loyal support of his Christian subjects, he had to be orthodox in their eyes. In the conflicts between Chalcedonian and Monophysite there were no doubt some who regarded the christological intricacies as quite beyond their powers of discernment, and who were therefore content to say that what was good enough for the emperor and the patriarch was good enough for them.[27] But to a Monophysite in the Nile valley, his own patriarch at Alexandria was the man who counted, and anything emanating from Constantinople was suspect from the start. Once Pope Leo I had decisively sided with Chalcedon's two-nature christology, the authority of Rome counted for nothing too. For Copts, Ethiopians, Syrian 'Jacobites', and Armenians, the papacy was thereby involved in irremediable heresy and its authority reduced to zero. The same held good for the Byzantine emperors.

The close involvement of the secular ruler in the party strife had a further disadvantage, namely that dissent from the position supported by the emperor was more than a religious disagreement: it amounted to disaffection in political terms, and was on the way to becoming treason. In the seventh century the Egyptian and Palestinian opponents of Chalcedon did not invite the Arabs to invade. But, once the Arabs had conquered, they found themselves able to enjoy far greater religious freedom (qualified as that might be) than they had done under the Byzantine emperors. During the bitter iconoclastic controversy, John of Damascus could compose fulminous denunciations of the heresies of the iconoclast emperors and enjoy serene impunity because he was an Arab living outside the territories where the emperor's writ still ran.

The authority and power of the Roman see in the Western Churches evolved in large measure because in situations of sharp controversy a final court of appeal was required. Popes found themselves being appealed to for decisions substantially before anyone thought of developing a theory or an exegesis of Petrine texts to provide a ground for this exercise of jurisdiction. Appeals to Rome over the head of local regional authority, however, could be feared and unpopular in both Church and state. English kings of the medieval period disliked such appeals as much as the North African bishops of St Augustine's time. Disputes were frequent about episcopal appointments. The Germanic races had an instinctive sense that rights over people go with ownership of land, and that the lord of the land has special rights in relation to the priests appointed to serve the churches which the landlord has himself built.[28] The lord was the *patronus* of the *beneficium*.[29] Accordingly, kings expected to exercise rights of patronage. On the other hand, the *ecclesia catholica* was not a national body; and the cathedral chapters expected to nominate as well as to elect. When kings nominated one candidate and chapters nominated another, the dispute might be taken to Rome, and the popes could produce a third.[30]

Norman kings of England were self-willed men who wanted their own way with the Church. William Rufus declared that Anselm of Canterbury had no business to vow obedience in homage both to the king and to the apostolic see: two allegiances were mutually incompatible, and, if the archbishop recognised Urban as his lord *in spiritualibus*, that was disloyalty to the crown. When Anselm wished to go to Rome for his pallium, the king would not allow the act, as an acknowledgement of foreign authority. Eadmer says that sycophantic bishops told the king that, if Anselm in any way acknowledged the pope's jurisdiction, he was breaking the faith he owed to the king.[31] Anselm eventually defied the king and was received at Rome by Urban's successor Paschal. William then forbade Anselm to return to England unless he renounced obedience to the pope, and he insisted on his own right of investiture. Eventually Anselm was readmitted by Henry I. In August 1107 the king held a council in London to decide on nominations to the numerous vacant sees, and granted Anselm the decisive voice in the choice of candidates and the right of investiture by the giving of the pastoral staff. But the king insisted on homage by bishops and abbots after their election and before the archbishop went forward with the consecration. After all, the Church had owed its place in society to the patronage of kings and nobles in the barbarian kingdoms; one tenth-century pope could rebuke the archbishop of Cologne (in a row over a nomination to Liège in 921) for ignoring the custom that only the king could confer the episcopate.[32] After Gregory VII such language was unimaginable.

Papal power was enforced through 'provisions' or nominations to bishoprics and benefices and through the power of dispensation. In the letters of St Augustine it is taken for granted that, when appeals go up to Rome, the pope's prime duty is to see that conciliar canon law is observed. He is the principal executive officer to enforce the rules of procedure laid down by Church councils. Nevertheless, situations may arise where the strict adherence to canon law will produce riots in the city or other disadvantages. In such cases Augustine assumes that the bishop of Rome in conference with the local primate of Carthage has the power to dispense from strict canonical procedure.[33] Dispensing power later became of the greatest practical importance because of the Church rules about forbidden degrees of affinity in matrimonial cases. Questions of marriage and divorce were of special concern if people were to remain in good standing in the eyes of the Church. Papal power to dispense from rigid rules became a major source of authority. Unfortunately the system involved the Roman curia in all the costs and pettifoggery attaching to complex litigation. To Henry VIII and his lawyers it was a source of offence as well as of much lay irritation when matrimonial and other cases had to be taken to a foreign court for decision. But Henry was not a total innovator in demanding that the appointment of bishops and matrimonial causes depend on his royal authority. What was new and revolutionary in Henry was his shattering of the universal assumption that the English Church was without question part of a universal Church, or at least a Western Church,[34] of which the bishop of Rome was the executive head. Not even Wycliffe could have entertained a notion as radical as that. Marsilius and Ockham could write incendiary pages attacking papal power as currently operating, but could hardly have envisaged Christendom as a congeries of independent national churches established on the principle *cuius regio eius religio*. Nevertheless, once one set aside the ecclesiology of the Isidorian decretals, it was an easy move to thinking of the Church as organised territorially, with the metropolitan of the province exercising real jurisdiction in relation to his suffragans, with the life of the Church of the province ruled by scripture, by the canons of Church councils received by the universal Church and especially in the province in question, but not by the personal decisions of the bishop of Rome. There was truth in the contention that the primarily territorial structure was predominant in the ancient and early-medieval Church.

Henry VIII's apologists could defend his actions on the ground that it was his 'private' Church of England of which he claimed to be the head.[35] The defence presumably assumed the old Germanic notion of the landownership entailing religious control. But Henry's ideas of supremacy were certainly fuelled by his reading in Justinian. His address to the Convocation of York in 1533 makes an express appeal to Justinian's ecclesiastical legislation to prove that he is not claiming new powers.[36] There indeed was a great emperor, a master of the civil law, legislating with unquestioned sovereignty on matters which, in the medieval West, were ordered by canon in a pyramid of authority with the pope at the top, everything flowing down from the power of the keys entrusted to Peter. Protestant defenders of the thesis that the prince is judge of doctrine found Justinian an uncertain aid, because of the proposition in Justinian's Code (I.i.l) that the bishop of Rome is the acknowledged guardian of orthodox belief—a point which Philpot had to concede at his trial in October 1555.[37] But Jewel recalled hearing Peter Martyr lecturing at Strasbourg on Justinian's removal of two popes from office, Silverius and Vigilius, and felt encouraged enough to include the point in *The Defence of the Apology of the Church of England* (1570).[38] At least it was clear that Justinian did not derive *imperium* from the pope. His sovereignty as emperor was quite independent.

Awareness of the overlap and potential conflict between canon law and civil law first appears, to the best of my knowledge, in the fearful disputes about the legitimacy of Pope Symmachus at the time of the Laurentian schism at Rome at the beginning of the sixth century.[39] In England the issue arose sharply in Magna Carta (1215). English kings long before Henry had imposed penalties on clerics who appealed to Rome against the king, and had enacted such statutes as Praemunire, and the statutes of Provisors. With Henry VIII, what had been only brave words for Edward III was now being acted on.

In Henry's Inns of Court there were hard-headed anticlerical lawyers like Christopher St German (1460-1541) insisting that, where there is conflict between canon and statute law, canon law yields.[40] St German appears as a supporter of the king's unilateral 'reform' of the Church, and an opponent of canons and legatine constitutions encroaching on the proper rights of the temporal power. For him it is axiomatic that an opinion enforced with the threat of penalty for heresy must be supported by sufficient and unambiguous authority: can the bishops be said to have utterly clear authority for all that they enforce under the *ex officio* procedure? St German also thought that a secular ruler has the right to lay down judgements on history where that is done to provide a ground for political actions in the present. He was anxious to vindicate the thesis that Henry's Act of Supremacy of 1534 in no sense added new powers; the Act could not be understood to grant Henry the *potestas ordinis*. So St German justifies the assertion of the Act in Restraint of Appeals that this realm of England is shown from sundry ancient chronicles to be an empire. An 'Empire' here, as Walter Ullmann showed,[41] meant a sovereignty of jurisdiction in which the ruler was the source of all authority whatsoever, like Justinian an unquestioned master in his own house, and (to St German) because of his responsibility to defend truth in the Church, possessing the right to decide disputed points of biblical exegesis. The Act's historical assertion was of momentous consequence for the juridical conceptions underlying Henry's claims to ecclesiastical supremacy.

Did Henry need to do it? European monarchs and emperors had long used their powers to ensure that important sees were held by the men they wanted. Bishops were often well educated, frequently of aristocratic or even royal blood, and formed the nucleus of the king's council. (They are the oldest element in the English House of Lords.) Henry VIII was not the first, as also not the last, to use his powers to nominate figures politically congenial to him. That is not to say that political considerations were all-important even for him. Cranmer may have been timid and vacillating, but he was certainly learned; Cuthbert Tunstall was gentle and saintly; Stephen Gardiner a first-rate canonist as well as a fluent linguist in French and German and probably having some Italian. Even Henry wanted his bishops to be acknowledged for their godliness and good learning, not merely to have the right prejudices about his divorce and the iniquities of the pope. Moreover, Henry was far from being the only European monarch to expect to have a decisive voice in the choice of his principal bishops. The pope, Clement VII, did not object to the nomination of Cranmer to succeed Warham. Over episcopal appointments, then, Henry had not crossed swords with the Vatican. The Act of 1533, however, on the appointment of bishops—still on the English statute book today even if in practice other arrangements now prevail (as in the case of the Concordat with France in regard to episcopal appointments in Alsace and Lorraine)—is militant. It eliminates from the nomination process both the pope and any independence of mind on the part of cathedral chapters (though allowing them a nominal elective role). Yet did the Act make assertions about royal powers such as no one had heard in Europe before this time? Frankish kings of Merovingian and Carolingian times had exercised wide powers, which were in most cases taken for granted. Hincmar of Reims felt it necessary to admonish Louis III not to demand, please, that a candidate nominated by the crown be elected; he should keep the customary procedure by which the crown granted the neighbouring bishops leave to proceed to an election, authorised the entrusting of the temporalities to the new bishop, and permitted the metropolitan and provincial bishops to go ahead with the ordination. At the same time Hincmar carefully dissociated himself from the view (evidently held by some) that kings ought to confine themselves to temporal matters and to think Church affairs none of their concern.[42] The investiture struggle showed the Church trying to fend off established lay control, whereby the priest was no more than the landowner's chaplain and servant. Henry VIII's actions are evidently more than yet another act in the investiture controversy, but are nevertheless intelligible as a reassertion of lay power over the Church—and not only *de facto* but *de jure Angliae*. He claimed that he was not innovating but recovering ancient liberties—and that was the language of Gallicans, if not from the time of Philip the Fair, at least since the Council of Constance.[43]

Pope Paul III cannily suggested a Gallican liberty as a way of retaining England within Catholic unity.[44] Why could not Henry take the French line, holding communion with the rest of the Western Church and Rome, yet strenuously keeping papal jurisdiction at a distance? Henry's father-in-law, Ferdinand the Catholic, ruled not only southern Spain but Sicily. He continued the secular independence of the Norman kings of Sicily, who had called councils on their own say-so, had forbidden appeals to the Curia, had refused entry to papal legates trying to visit the island, and had wholly controlled the nomination of bishops. The *Capitula* of the kingdom of Sicily include the text of a proclamation by Ferdinand dated 22 January 1514, which declares his devotion to the Roman Church, and then adds the proviso that in Sicily the king remains responsible for both spiritual and temporal affairs. The Curia is not to intrude.[45]

One wonders if Henry VIII might have followed his father-in-law's example, asserting both his royal supremacy and his devotion to Catholic doctrine, including the see of Peter if not the incumbent sitting on it. Henry's defenders liked to point to the deplorable corruption in holders of the Petrine office like Alexander VI—an argument to which Pole responded with the observation that the juridical rights of the English Crown were surely independent of the moral qualities of the kings wearing it. One could assert the honour of the office without having too much regard for the holder.

By an ironic paradox Henry's daughter Mary could restore papal supremacy over the Church of England only by invoking her royal prerogative, in face of the reluctance of many in parliament to see the Church restored to communion with Rome for fear that the pope and Pole would expect and require the restitution of confiscated Church lands, held by those whom even the strongly protestant John Foxe frankly described as 'cormorants'.[46] Pole suffered the humiliation of long delays before being allowed into the country with legatine authority. And in practice the example of Mary in voluntarily forgoing the confiscated Church properties was not followed by many.

Henry VIII's Act of Supremacy was not really thunder out of a clear sky. Philip the Fair of France had treated Boniface VIII in an analogous manner. In the pre-Reformation age the English people seem to have entertained mixed feelings towards the chair of Peter. Some certainly looked to it as a source of truth as well as a fount of canonical authority. But there were others who did not feel this way about it—who resented the manner in which Innocent III had dealt with King John. From the chronicle of Matthew Paris (1199-1259) one might easily gain the impression that English prosperity had been disastrously hindered by bribery and corruption at the Roman Curia.[47] Grosseteste thought the papal practice of stuffing foreigners into English bishoprics and benefices so disastrous that everyone ought to be stirred to resistance and protest. When Pope Innocent IV conferred a canonry at Lincoln on his own nephew, Grosseteste declared his simultaneous obedience to papal jurisdiction and his conviction that such an act could come only from Antichrist, on which ground he flatly declined to accept it: papal authority should be used for edification, not, as in this case, for destruction. Grosseteste wanted the spiritual and the temporal kept apart in distinct spheres, the secular arm concentrating on the defence of the realm, just administration of law, and upholding good conduct by example; the spiritual arm to minister the word and sacraments with holiness of life, vigils, fasts, and assiduous prayers. He wanted to keep the secular arm in England from intruding its power into the Church by patronage rights, and wished to maintain the independence of the Church courts. He expressed apprehension lest the coronation unction might give the monarch the illusion that he had received some sacerdotal powers together with this biblical sign of the seven gifts of the Spirit.[48]

Grosseteste was no doubt not the antipapal hero the Lollards made him out to be. Their feelings about the papacy were fairly unqualified. Wycliffe denied that the pope had any greater power of the keys than any other priests. He told King Richard II that royal sovereignty in England ought to have no rival, that the king was entitled to stop money flowing to Rome, and that the papacy as an institution was Antichrist. The temporal power had a moral right to take endowments from unworthy clergy. The canon law of the Decretalists should be set aside,[49] and the Church ordered in accordance with the Bible and the ancient Fathers.

The persisting influence of Lollardy into the England of Henry's age no doubt helps to explain why the influence of Luther on the English Reformation, while certainly substantial, was not always dominant. As early as the 1530s there were contacts with Bullinger and the Zwinglian polity of Zürich. Granted that many of the Thirty-Nine Articles owed much to the Augsburg and Württemberg confessions of 1530 and 1552, both striking for their conservative moderation and conciliatory tone; granted that in 1562-3 Bishop Edmund Guest, known for his Lutheran sympathies in Eucharistic theology, had drafted Article 28 of the Thirty-Nine Articles in terms which simultaneously denied Transubstantiation as eliminating the sign from the sacrament and (as Lingard saw) sought to protect the Presence of Christ—to the consternation of the Zwinglian faction; granted that the Thirty-Nine Articles actually recognised the bishop of Rome to be Catholic bishop of that city and denied only his jurisdiction in England and (what none could assert?) the permanent gift or habit of inerrancy in incumbents of that see: nevertheless, the puritan dissatisfaction with Cranmer's Prayer Book and Ordinal and Articles is naturally seen as a continuation of the underground dissidence of Lollardy. The agonies of the vestiarian controversy reflect Zwinglian influences, which regarded Luther and Brenz (and Bucer) as dangerous compromisers encouraging the English reformers to produce 'a mingled estate', 'a mixture of the gospel and popery'.[50]

One writer influenced more by Luther than by Lollardy provided a virtual blueprint for Henry VIII's revolution. In 1528 William Tyndale published *The Obedience of a Christian Man*, telling Henry that his duty was to reform the Church. The pope and bishops had gathered to themselves too much of the wealth of England. 'Monks devour the land.' Whatever goes into their treasury ceases to circulate; land bequeathed to them falls under the dead hand, mortmain. Clergy claim to owe no obedience to princes; their prime love is power; and they use auricular confession to extract personal and political secrets. Tyndale was one of the many who have imagined that because the pope has a priest in every parish, he must be wonderfully well informed. He was much offended when the clergy handed heretics over to the secular arm for 'just punishment mitigated by due mercy', a formula which everyone knew to mean burning. The bishops had made the king into the pope's hangman. Let Henry rid the land of the pope's usurped power. He should abolish Church courts through which bishops harass laymen, sometimes (as Foxe later complained) putting questions that simple artisans and yeoman farmers could hardly grasp. The king should subordinate to his own statute law the canon law by which laity are oppressed and to which they have given no consent. He should redeploy the resources of idle monks for educational purposes and the better instruction of a sadly ignorant clergy.

Tyndale's book was apparently put into Henry's hands by Anne Boleyn, whose family had at least anticlerical and perhaps protestant sympathies, and whose house was a place where imported Lutheran books might be found. But Tyndale's next book would not have been accepted there. He expressed vehement disapproval of the divorce, agreeing with Martin Luther, who declared that for Henry to divorce Catherine and marry Anne would be adultery, a considerable time before the vacillating pope came to give a verdict. Tyndale's condemnation was fatal to him. Living at Antwerp (where, despite the emperor's control over the port, it seems that protestant merchants and travellers could pass remarkably freely), he was eventually betrayed. As the flames rose round him he prayed, 'Lord open the king of England's eyes'.[51] In fact his book of 1528 may have done that already: for Tyndale there taught that kings, not popes are God's deputies on earth. Their subjects owe them an undivided allegiance. The king is answerable not to them but to God alone, and 'none may question whether his acts are right or wrong'. This was heady and intoxicating reading for a self-willed, egocentric monarch with the mind of a spoilt child.

Yet Henry's determination to be master in his own house went back to the very start of his reign. In his *Defence of the Unity of the Church* Pole tried to remind Henry of his coronation oath to uphold the liberties of the Church. He evidently did not know that at the time in 1509 Henry had attempted to add the qualifying proviso 'if not prejudicial to his jurisdiction and royal dignity'. As early as 1515 he had been claiming, 'We are by the sufferance of God king of England; and in times past the kings of England never had any superior but God; we will maintain the rights of the Crown like our progenitors.'[52]

The title 'supreme head, under God, of the Church of England and Ireland' cannot have looked anything but ridiculous and offensive to most of Henry's contemporaries. Tunstall's well-known remonstrance on the subject expressed what was surely a common feeling both to conservatives and to 'gospellers'.[53] 'Caput ecclesie' was a title protestants found no less irksome than Catholics. Both Luther and Calvin referred to the assertion, implying Henry to be pope in his own kingdom, with astonishment and scorn.[54] It is especially instructive to notice that at his trial in 1556 Cranmer was accused of having been personally responsible for seducing Henry into claiming the title, and that Cranmer, with eminent reasonableness, justly replied that the responsibility lay with his Catholic predecessor Warham, supported by the considered judgement of the universities of Oxford and Cambridge.[55] Royal supremacy was no protestant doctrine in the form in which Henry was to assert it, even though the German Reformation was to depend very much upon the decision of the princes.

A sensitivity to protestant feelings, more than any desire to placate her restive Catholic subjects, moved Elizabeth in 1559 to accept Lever's suggestion that she change 'head' to 'governor' (below p. 253).[56] It must be clear (though Henry himself had conceded the point) that the control of Church policy implied no claim to the *sacerdotium*. Even that and the explicit disavowal in Article 37 of the Thirty-Nine Articles were to be unacceptable to Cartwright and the puritans. During the 1560s the widening split between the Marian exiles entrusted with episcopal office and those who had not been so favoured reinforced the latter's conviction that a royal supremacy must be set aside. It was the queen's resolve which maintained the episcopal succession, a 'popish pontifical' called the Ordinal, crucifixes, wafer bread, saints' days and surplices; and to puritans the authority which upheld such things was *ipso facto* discredited. Already in the 1570s Whitgift could foresee that an overthrow of the episcopal order could entail the destruction of the monarchy.[57] I suspect that John Foxe's surprising support for the queen and the episcopal order, despite his strong affinity with the puritan stance, explains why, when Cartwright accused Whitgift of gross insincerity in his laudatory words about Foxe, Whitgift was able to assert his cordial gratitude to the martyrologist.[58]

Professor Scarisbrick has given a brilliant elucidation of the gradualness of the evolution of Henry's notions of royal supremacy.[59] As late as 1530 the king could grant that in matters of heresy the pope ought to judge;[60] his jurisdiction was the point in dispute. But after the Act of Supremacy of 1534, Henry, with the undergirding of Cromwell, began to think himself responsible for laying down norms of authentic doctrine in his private Church of England. Had not the Supremacy Act simply transferred to the king all the powers, ranging from dispensation up to dogmatic definition, ordinarily exercised by St Peter's successors? Could he not issue injunctions for his Church *motu proprio*, without the least consultation with Convocation?[61] There was a more sensible, if in practice weaker, answer, namely that the dispensing powers had now passed to the archbishop of Canterbury, and that the responsibility for determining the doctrinal platform of the English Church fell to the college of bishops. The Ten Articles of 1536 bore only the king's name and title as their authority, but explicitly claimed to have had mature consideration by Convocation. Nothing is revealed of their extensive affinity with the Articles agreed at Wittenberg between an English delegation and the leading Lutheran divines;[62] but the 'protestantism' of the Ten Articles is of the most 'milk and water' kind apart from the emphasis on the non-fundamental character of images, saints' days, invocation of saints, holy water and candles and other ceremonies, and on the distinction between the accepted propriety of prayers for the departed and the abuses associated with purgatory. The statement on justification 'by contrition and faith joined with charity' anticipates Trent. Foxe thought the Ten Articles contained 'many and great imperfections and untruths not to be permitted in any true reformed Church'.[63]

The following year saw the appearance of the 'Bishops' Book', which for protestants was hardly more consoling;[64] and the revision of this in 1543 to produce the King's Book went so far in an unprotestant direction as to make everyone take for granted that Stephen Gardiner's hand was ubiquitous in it.[65] The King's Book includes a striking passage on the refusal of the Orientals and Grecians to accept the Council of Florence on Roman primacy, demonstrating lack of Catholic consent. The right of national churches to follow their own order is also asserted, with a duty to honour, after Christ the only head of the universal Church, 'Christian kings and princes which be the head governors under him in the particular churches'.[66]

To ensure royal control, Thomas Cromwell was nominated as the king's vicegerent to govern the bishops' proceedings, taking his seat in Convocation above the archbishops. A church historian might ask if he or Henry could have been aware of the presidency exercised at the fourth ecumenical council of Chalcedon in 451 by the long row of high-ranking lay officers of state nominated by Marcian and Pulcheria. The presidency of these lay officers of state could be deduced even from the jejune information, apart from a

Latin translation of the Definition of Faith and the twenty-seven canons, provided in Merlin's *princeps* of the collected *Concilia*.[67] In 1536 and in 1538 Cromwell issued sets of ecclesiastical injunctions in the king's name, with a preamble making it explicit that they are grounded in the king's 'supreme authority ecclesiastical'. But this supremacy was enlarged by Cromwell to be held and exercised not by the king alone, but by the king in parliament. Henry's acts in relation to the Church were made parliamentary statutes, and it was only parliament which could make the denial of royal supremacy a crime. So the supremacy of the crown merged into parliamentary control.[68] The lawyers were insistent that the Act of Supremacy was no innovation. A contemporary, George Wyatt, wrote that it was 'not done to give the king any new title or office, but to declare how that authority was always justly and rightfully due to the crown of the Realm, and that no foreign prince or potentate had anything to do in the same, as the bishops of Rome called Popes pretended and of long time usurped'.[69] To the common lawyers it was axiomatic that papal power had never been exercised in England except by the king's permission, and what the king could permit he could also disallow. Cromwell tied the autocratic omnipotence of the crown to that of parliament, and thereby began the long debate on what limitations there might be to the royal ecclesiastical supremacy.[70]

The flexibility of interpretation attaching to royal supremacy and the way in which it could be used by parliament to resist both king and bishops were brought out in a conversation between Bishop Stephen Gardiner and Lord Audley, Thomas More's successor as lord chancellor (1533-44). The conversation was reported by Gardiner in 1547 in a letter to the protector Somerset, in which Gardiner submitted to Somerset his difficulties about accepting Edward VI's injunctions for the Church.[71] Gardiner argued with some subtlety that these injunctions laid down prescriptions which were not authorised by Act of parliament. Could the royal prerogative override parliament in this way? He recalled how Wolsey had been caught, together with all the clergy of the Church of England, under the statute of Praemunire. Although it was at Henry VIII's express request to the pope that Wolsey was appointed as papal legate in England, nevertheless the lawyers held that his authority was contrary to parliamentary enactment even if he had been carrying out the king's wishes. The judges had appealed for precedent to the case of Lord Tiptoft, earl of Worcester, who fell from power in

1470 and was unable to avert execution by the defence that his savage cruelties on Edward IV's behalf had been carried out in the cause of his sovereign, and had been in accordance with the law he had learnt at Padua even if not with the enactments of parliament. Moreover, it was held against Wolsey that, in defiance of Magna Carta, he had issued injunctions which were against the common law. In 1545 Gardiner had been sent as ambassador to the emperor, in the course of which he had assured the emperor that the king of England was not above the order of the laws enacted in parliament. Only a year previously, under Henry, he had been concerned with members of the privy council about the dangers to the king in contravening an Act of parliament. His earlier conversation with Lord Audley had ended with Audley warning him off so delicate a subject. Audley observed that the Act of Supremacy confined the king to spiritual jurisdiction, and that another Act provided that no ecclesiastical law could stand against common law or parliamentary enactment. By this last proviso the laity were protected against king and bishops clubbing together to oppress them through canon law. Audley saw the uncertainties of interpretation of Praemunire as the principal source for lay liberty from ecclesiastical tyranny.

In his reply to Gardiner, Somerset seems not to have taken up the legal points raised, but rather to have confined himself to pressing Gardiner to accept the 1547 Book of Homilies. The royal injunctions for Winchester cathedral pointedly forbid anyone to call the doctrines of the Homilies heretical, or new, or any other such opprobrious epithet.[72] Gardiner's conscience was troubled by the possible antinomianism of Cranmer's homily on salvation, sufficiently at least to make him prefer to stay in prison.

Audley's interpretation of royal supremacy to mean lay power over the Church and even the crown prefigured the view that it was a basic 'principle of the Reformation' to deny to the Church any 'divine right', anything other than the right of a useful, merely human society within the sovereign state. Those who asserted that a bishop had jurisdiction inherent in the commission bestowed in ordination came increasingly to be regarded as Catholicising. In April 1628 the archdeacon of Durham, John Cosin, was accused of denying the king's power to excommunicate and the title 'head of the Church', and persuasively observed that, while the practical exercise of pastoral jurisdiction was made possible by the king, there was no sense in which the king could be said to be the source of episcopal authority. The source of that was clear from the rite of the Ordinal.[73] Nevertheless, the protestant thesis that divine authority lies exclusively in scripture implied a desacralisation of the Church and its ministers, which made it easier to interpret royal supremacy simply as expressing the view that authority in this Church lies with the secular power. It is deeply significant that the first sentence of Article 20 of the Thirty-Nine Articles ('The Church hath . . . authority in controversies of faith', echoing the Württemberg Confession, 1552) was so disliked by puritans that some printed editions of the Articles omitted it. Even King James I once imprudently suggested (in his *Apology for the Oath of Allegiance*, 1607) that the Bible being the sole source of divine truth, it was for each believer to judge of the dogmas of the faith—a proposition which removed all possible basis for the king's policy of coercion towards recusants and dissenters.

Even during Henry VIII's reign the doctrine of royal supremacy carried very different meanings to different people. During 1543 Stephen Gardiner was engaged in controversy with William Turner, alias Wraghton, author of *The Hunting and Finding out of the Romish Fox*.[74] Turner asked if the king's assertion of supremacy was a denial of the pope's name, or purse, or doctrine. To the majority it was hardly a denial of Catholic doctrine. For a short time Henry could look for friends among the Lutheran princes of Germany, and send divines to Wittenberg to reach agreed statements with the Lutherans which Luther and Melanchthon were to think insufficiently protestant except as a provisional measure. But in England the Latin mass remained intact, and the Six Articles Act strongly enforced transubstantiation and the necessity of priestly absolution in case of mortal sin. The bloody executions of 1540, especially that of Barnes, and the discarding of Anne of Cleves, were well understood to signify that the king was not by this time thinking of moving in a Lutheran direction.[75] Nevertheless, as the French ambassador shrewdly told Francis I in a letter of 6 August 1540,[76] it was no easy matter for Henry to keep a people in revolt against the Holy See and the authority of the Church, and yet free from the infection of heresy; nor on the other hand was it easy to keep those tenaciously attached to orthodoxy from looking with affection towards the papacy—an attachment which would increase as men like Cranmer showed mounting sympathy for Luther and then (from 1550) for Zwingli and Bullinger. Royal supremacy was tolerable on a temporary basis for the Erasmian Henrician bishops so long as they were not asked to accept heresy.

On the other side, the same was found to be true by the protestants. The extent of protestant disillusionment with Henry's policies for the Church of England is dramatically and bitterly set out in the well-known letter of Richard Hilles to Henry Bullinger, written from London in 1541. Hilles portrayed an arbitrary bloody tyranny by a king who had exchanged Romanising for womanising, and was now actively engaged in the persecution of godly men and women. The martyred Barnes (to whom no reason for his execution was given) had already told Luther that Henry's Church policy was wholly determined by political considerations, not in the least by religious conviction or the word of God.[77] The impression among both conservatives and radical reformers was that the royal supremacy was merely an act of naked power with no visible moral basis. William Turner initially refused to grant Henry the title of supreme head of the Church of England and Ireland, but dedicated his book of 1543 to Henry as 'supreme governor under God', explaining that this was to give him as much honour 'as is lawful to give unto any earthly man by the word of God'.[78] It had the further advantage of answering 'certain wanton persons where as I have been, call the king's highness pope of England'. Under pressure Turner was willing to concede that the king is 'supreme head of the Church of England and Ireland', with the proviso 'if ye understand by this word Church an outward gathering together of men and women in a politic order', and not the Church of which the New Testament speaks (!). 'Every vicious king is a member of the devil', and therefore not a member of that Church, still less head of it. On the other hand, Turner was firm that royal supremacy was grounded in scripture, not in Acts of parliament or the pope's canon law. To maintain all the pope's doctrines and ceremonies and to expel his authority seemed to Turner absurd nonsense. His book with its scathing attacks on the Henrician bishops strikingly anticipated the puritans of the 1560s and 1570s, for whom Elizabeth's claim to royal supremacy was intolerable when it meant the refusal to reshape the Church of England after the pattern of the best reformed churches such as that in Scotland. As Beza sharply put it, papal power had not been abolished, but merely transferred in its entirety to the queen.[79]

On the Catholic side, Stephen Gardiner, Bonner and Tunstall conceded the royal supremacy because the alternative was to follow

More and Fisher to the scaffold,[80] because except for the authority of the pope no changes of any significance had been made in Catholic doctrine and little in ceremonies, and because to abandon their posts must be to hand the Church over to the wolves. William Turner lambasted them for imposing penalties on folk found eating meat on Fridays while keeping a thunderous silence about the king's sexual mores and 'four lords of England that put away their wives not for fornication but because they liked whores better', and likewise about the disgraceful plunder of the abbeys for which 'all the whole realm smarteth unto this day'.[81] But with Henry threatening to surrender to protestantism as a whip to bring them to heel, perhaps the bishops had less choice than Turner wanted to see. Who could tell how long the king would live? Protestantism might be quite strong in London and among Cambridge dons (Foxe sadly noted more than once Oxford's strong preference for the old religion),[82] but the main population of the land, especially in the North, was in no deep sense protestant in sympathy. Were they not a heartbeat away from restoring the status quo? It was not the last time that Catholic bishops would find themselves compromising with a hostile government for the sake of survival in hope of better days in future. But even Gardiner could not stand by his earlier defence of the royal supremacy when Edward VI was using it to introduce Swiss protestantism. Restored under Mary and elevated to be chancellor, Gardiner could pungently comment at long last that among the disadvantages of Henry VIII's assertion of his headship of the Church was the consideration that, if he had thereby taken the English Church out of communion with Catholic Christendom, he had no Church to be head of.[83] At his trial in 1556 Cranmer found himself in the bizarre position of being instructed by his sovereign, whose supremacy he asserted, to recognise that of the pope, which he felt bound to deny as incompatible with loyalty to the crown.[84]

Under Elizabeth the royal supremacy enforced the *via media* of 'golden mediocrity' as no other factor could do. In March 1560 Matthew Parker was writing to Nicholas Heath and the other deprived bishops regretting their request that the Church of England should again acknowledge the primacy of the Roman see. Like the ancient British Church before Gregory the Great, the Church of England was independent of Rome and of the papal claim to a universal jurisdiction; moreover to acknowledge the pope was treason.[85] But within a short time Parker was defending the royal supremacy against the puritans. Parker, admittedly, did not himself believe that the queen had powers as absolute as those claimed for the pope. When in 1566 he found her reluctant to give royal sanction to the Thirty-Nine Articles of 1563, he solemnly warned her that 'as governor and nurse of this Church' she would have to give account at the Last Judgement for her stewardship in this regard.[86] Certainly her prerogative was more than a papist would grant, but it was (he said) less than Burghley supposed.[87] Elizabeth found that Grindal preferred to resign rather than to acknowledge that the queen could exercise her supremacy so as to abolish prophesyings: 'Remember, Madam, that you are a mortal creature.'[88] Parker and Grindal both found that the queen and parliament were slow to grant that matters such as the Thirty-Nine Articles or 'prophesyings' were to be referred to the bishops and divines of the realm and unsuitable for lay decision.

Nevertheless, the royal supremacy prevented the Church of England from becoming presbyterian, and became increasingly hated by the puritans. The *Zurich Letters* printed an account of 'The State of the Church of England' by the vehement puritan Perceval Wiburn, bitterly complaining of the way in which very large numbers of clergy once ordained under the Latin pontifical were continuing in charge of parishes without any reordination as reformed ministers. (Not that he would have thought the English Ordinal anything but utterly popish.) Wiburn thought the royal supremacy the one and only doctrine one could be reasonably sure of being held by all the clergy of the Church of England. Hooker was explicit that royal supremacy could not mean unrestrained autocracy. The crown was limited by parliament, and parliament itself had acknowledged that the definition of orthodox doctrine must rest on scripture and 'the first four general councils or some other general council', and that if some future parliament were to declare something to be heresy it could only be 'with the assent of the clergy in the convocation'. Even parliament, therefore, allowed that dominion was limited. On the other hand, Hooker defended the right of the prince to nominate bishops and to maintain the order of the Church. He was able to reply to Counter-Reformation critics with the observation that Philip II of Spain had published the decrees of Trent in the Netherlands with an express proviso that

253

there was no prejudice or diminution to his customary rights in nominating to benefices.[89]

At the Hampton Court conference of 1604 the puritan Reynolds hoped to ingratiate himself and the puritan cause with James I by a panegyric on the royal supremacy. James remembered that John Knox had similarly flattered Elizabeth by telling her to use her supreme power to suppress popish prelates. After the prelates had been suppressed, Knox and his friends had carried through a reformation of the Church of Scotland which in effect set aside the royal supremacy. Puritans, said the king, praise the royal supremacy to annoy the bishops. Once the bishops are out of the way and they have taken over the Church, the monarchy will fall also: 'No bishop, no king'. 'I notice', he added, 'that puritan preachers do not in the bidding prayer acknowledge me to be supreme governor in all causes.'[90]

To Henry VIII royal supremacy was the mark of breaking with Roman jurisdiction (not doctrine). Paradoxically, it became the bastion for maintaining Catholic episcopal order in England. But the Stuarts were to learn the hard way that, by defending the Anglican 'mingling of the gospel and popery', the monarchy itself would be brought down. Independents hated the contention that any ministerial structure in the Church belongs (as Whitgift was to claim for episcopacy) to an 'order placed by the Holy Spirit in the Church'.[91] When the Westminster assembly of divines wished to use the language of 'divine law' to suggest that the Church had some right to make its own decisions independent of the House of Commons, they were sharply instructed to think again and to revise their confession of faith.[92] A Victorian parliament and laity was disquieted when similar language began to come from the Tractarians.

Cardinal Allen in 1584 observed with a not unjustified bitterness that the royal supremacy over the Church, for refusal of which Catholic recusants were being brought to execution on the charge of treason (not heresy), was not actually believed by the protestants themselves; moreover, the doctrine of the supremacy treated national churches as if they were totally free to make all their own decisions in utter disregard of the Church universal, a proposition needing only to be stated for its inconveniences, not to say absurdity, to become evident.[93] Already by the reign of James I the fire of well-directed criticism was reducing the area defensible by loyal advocates.[94] None claimed that the monarch could minister the word and sacraments to the people of God, could absolve or excommunicate, and the only question at issue was whether it belonged to the king to call and preside at synods, sanction canons, hear ecclesiastical appeals, grant benefices, appoint and depose bishops. Moreover, the defenders of the supremacy had to assert that it was a moral right, not an act of mere power. They had to avoid shooting themselves in the foot by the argument that the powers claimed for the pope were so monstrous as to prove the papacy to be Antichrist whereas the same powers could be claimed by the secular ruler, as 'God's Vicar' in his own kingdom, without laying himself open to the same charge. The best defence lay in the godly prince of the Old Testament; but it was not evident that this commanded the consent of all sensible and educated men, or that the supremacy could be safely grounded either in natural law or canon law, and the brutal truth was that the New Testament offered no help at all. (One recalls Cranmer's bizarre observation in 1540 that the apostles did their best in appointing clergy because, *faute de mieux*, they had no Christian princes to whom to turn.)[95]

In 1988 belief among members of the Church of England in the reality and moral rightness of royal supremacy (very different from loyalty to the sovereign which can never have been stronger) must be described as tenuous to the vanishing point, and in actuality to mean no more than that the sovereign is the first lay person of a Church particularly characterised by the voice and honour traditionally accorded to the laity in its government. The notion that someone could die for refusing either to affirm it as did John Fisher, or to deny it as did Thomas Cranmer, has become incomprehensible except by a strong effort of historical imagination. It is a classic instance of how an idea intensely important and divisive in the sixteenth century has now faded into virtual insignificance. At the same time there remains a residual, perhaps atavistic anticlericalism which can think of parliament as the means of voicing dislike of anything done by clergy or bishops or synods, and can appeal to the unquestioned power of the sovereign in parliament to order things as they will. There certainly continues an ill-defined feeling that the mystery of the monarchy is supported by the national character of the Church of England, so that to disestablish the Church could lead to an overthrow of the monarchy. Within the Church of England there is a sometimes sharp division between those who regard the Church as the English at prayer, with the freedom to do whatever the English wish, regardless of 'foreigners', and those who have never ceased to think of the Church of England as a parenthetically and sadly separated branch of the *Catholica*, which is not free to act on its own in handling fundamentals like creed or ministry.

A full history of the evolution which has led to this position would be a long and different story from that of the present essay. It would entail a study of the consequences of the suspension of Convocation early in the eighteenth century and of the constitutional revolution by the parliamentary reforms of 1828-32; a study of Wake, Gibson's *Codex*, Warburton's *Alliance*, Pusey's qualified and very Gallican defence of the supremacy at the crisis of the Gorham controversy, and an examination of the twentieth-century calls, first from high Anglicans but more recently and more vocally from Evangelical Anglicans, for disestablishment and the separation of Church and state. The contemporary attacks on the representativeness of the membership of the general synod of the Church of England mark a counter-move in the opposite direction. At least, by an informal concordat, the crown now, since 1977, nominates bishops by selecting one of two names, both being understood to be sufficient for the task of episcopacy, submitted by the ecclesiastical 'Crown Commission'; and this procedure is obviously a major and beneficial modification of Henry VIII's arrangements. Today most of the actuality of royal supremacy is the proposition that canon law may have no force in conflict with common law or statute law—a proposition which belongs to the pre-Reformation debate and has nothing specifically protestant to it. In an age when the royal supremacy is in effect reduced to about the dimensions of the Cheshire Cat's grin, it is difficult to comprehend that Thomas More and John Fisher suffered judicial murder rather than tolerate it. As the Scots showed James I, royal supremacy could be operated in such a way as to leave the Church independent in all essentials. And medieval Catholic kings could maintain sovereignty in their domains without taking their Church out of Catholic communion. In the sixteenth century, royal supremacy first took the Church of England out of communion with the *cathedra Petri* and then stopped (for a time) puritan forces from removing the episcopal succession and other Catholic elements in the Prayer Book and the Ordinal.

That was to require a redefinition of Catholicity closely akin to that of Gallicanism. The Greek refusal at the level of ordinary priests and laity to come to terms with the admission of Roman primacy by their representatives, except for Mark Eugenicus, at the Council of Florence made a deep impression in England, and especially on Henry VIII. As early as the King's Book of 1543, the authorship of which was generally attributed (despite his denials) to Stephen Gardiner, the root question is seen to be one of ecclesiology, defining Catholicity not in terms of Roman jurisdiction but in terms of the profession of the true faith in unity with other Catholic churches.

Such an ecumenical ecclesiology will have room for a focus of unity and universality in Roman primacy and need not exclude a salute of honour for royal supremacy, provided that such a secular assertion of power over the Church is (as the apostle said of apostolic authority) deployed for edification rather than destruction, for the support of the Church in its work in the world rather than as a formula for ensuring the permanence of Christian division.

18

The status of Ecumenical Councils in Anglican thought

1. The Theory of Councils and the early history

After the council of Jerusalem in Acts 15 a long time passed before another council was held. The next councils of which we have any information were called to decide on a common policy towards the Montanists, to agree on the date of Easter, and to discuss the canon of the New Testament. Tertullian says that in the Greek churches synods were held to examine difficult and profound questions, and that these synods were held in awe by the faithful as a *repraesentatio totius nominis Christiani*.[1] In the person of the bishop the entire church entrusted to him is reckoned to be present.[2] And the presence of the Lord himself is assured by his promise, Matt. 18, 20. Councils were especially necessary if a common course of action was to be reached on matters where scripture was found to be either unclear or quotable on both sides of a controversial question such as the readmission of the lapsed. That scripture was the supreme authority was a self-evident proposition, and where it spoke clearly the task of a council was straightforward. But where it spoke less clearly, conference was necessary and a search was made for agreement on the widest possible basis. Cyprian's African bishops sent their decisions to Rome and other churches 'lest our numbers should not seem enough'.[3] The text of Matt. 18, 20 was understood to imply that if the Lord is present when only two or three gather in his name, a fortiori he is there when many more are gathered.[4] The larger the council, the wider the representation of the universal church (representation being understood in a sense stronger than the notion of a parliamentary deputy). It followed that if the decisions of a council were to be reviewed, the body which reviewed them would be either larger in number or wider in its territorial representation, and, if possible, both.

So in 325 the emperor Constantine called at Nicaea a synod of about 220 bishops, almost all from the Greek East, but with important Western delegates. Nicaea was the largest synod hitherto called. Because of the importance of its decisions for orthodoxy in the subsequent conflict with Arianism, its defenders came to invest it with a unique aura, first magnifying its numbers even further to

300, to 'more than 300', next to the sacred number of 318;[5] then giving it the epithet of 'world council', 'ecumenical,'[6] in contrast to the local, provincial synods that had met previously; finally insisting on its universal reception by orthodoxy, its ratification either by the emperor or by Rome.[7] Those who used these last arguments were convinced that the Nicene homousios expressed the true sense of scripture, but they had to persuade those who were hesitant on the point. The retrospective ratification of subsequent assent by the faithful was effectively the decisive factor, and this found strong expression in the Councils of Constantinople of 381 and of Ephesus in 431. The council of Constantinople (381) made its way only slowly to 'ecumenical' rank. It first received the nimbus of special authority at the council of Chalcedon in 451,[8] which reaffirmed its decree (objectionable to Alexandria and Rome) about the privileges of Constantinople as second see after old Rome and which cited its creed partly to justify the production of the Chalcedonian definition as yet another supplementary interpretation of the Nicaenum. The second council was not numbered among the general councils by Rome until 519; previously Rome accepted only Nicaea, Ephesus (431), and Chalcedon.[9]

The gradualness of the process of reception to ecumenical status is a common feature apparent in the history of the majority of general councils, and must be taken into account in any theological statement about their authority. Not all councils that, at the time, were accorded the title of 'ecumenical' council were later recognized as possessing this high authority. The council of Ariminum (359) which rejected the Nicaenum in favour of an inclusive, vague formula with room for Arianism, is an obvious example. From the middle of the fifth century Eastern Christendom became divided (and remains so divided) between those who accepted the ecumenical authority of Ephesus 449 and those who accepted Chalcedon 451. The council of Ephesus 449 had all the apparatus of a general council, but its dogmatic decisions were not acceptable to strict Chalcedonians, and they looked back on the Second Council of Ephesus as an example of a general council that had erred and therefore forfeited proper claim to the dignity of the ecumenical title.

The process of recognition was also slow for the fifth general council of 553 which condemned Origenism and the 'Three Chapters'. After many changes of mind Pope Vigilius had finally assented to the decisions of the council, but Western hostility to the condemnation of the Three Chapters (as being a compromise to placate the Monophysites) remained powerful and produced temporary schisms in the Western church. When it was accepted, the fifth council did not rank in Western eyes as possessing quite the same majesty as the first four councils. In the period before the fifth council was accepted it was common to assert (against Monophysite critics of Chalcedon) that the number of general councils accepted by the orthodox catholic church was the sacrosanct number four, corresponding to the four canonical gospels.[10]

This language, with its implication of exclusiveness (neither less nor more than four, as Irenaeus had written of the gospels),[11] continued to be used even after the fifth council was received. Gregory the Great writes that he accepts the four councils as the four gospels, and then adds as an afterthought that he also accepts the fifth council.[12] There was, therefore, a natural tendency to regard the first four councils as possessing a specially privileged position among ecumenical councils; but those who spoke in this way did not mean to imply that no council after Chalcedon could ever be received as possessing an ecumenical standing. The sixth ecumenical council of 680-1 was concerned with a cause nearer Rome's heart—the condemnation of monotheletism (even at the price of being forced into conceding the error of Pope Honorius in admitting the heretical doctrine)—and this council encountered greater difficulties in the East than in the West. Even after its general reception, however, it continued to be customary to regard the fifth and sixth councils as contributing supplementary, qualifying footnotes to the decisions of Chalcedon. All six councils had ecumenical rank, but this did not mean that they were all of equal importance.

A similar 'supplementary' status was accorded in the Greek East to the Quinisext council of 692 (or Second Council *in Trullo*), which claimed to be ecumenical and was recognized as such in the East. Its 102 canons include a number of anti-Western points: canon 36 reaffirms the so-called 28th canon of Chalcedon on the privileges of Constantinople; canon 13 reproves the rule of celibacy for simple priests; canons 28, 55, 57, and 82 censure Roman liturgical customs. Although the Roman legates at the council signed the canons, their signature was evidently disowned at Rome ('they signed because they were deceived', says the Liber Pontificalis).[13]

It was with the object of circumventing this refusal of Roman recognition that the patriarchs of Constantinople began to treat the Quinisext canons as being supplementary to and therefore bearing the authority of the earlier ecumenical councils, especially the Sixth Council of 680. It became common for its canons to be cited simply as 'of the sixth council';[14] and this passed to Gratian,[15] despite the warnings on this subject given by the ninth century papal librarian Anastasius.[16]

Accordingly, the council of 692 retains ecumenical authority for the Greek East. But in the West better information about its history than was available to Gratian has prevented the same recognition.

The Seventh council (Second Council of Nicaea, 787) was received at Rome. Its iconophile decisions accorded with the position of Pope Hadrian I. Nevertheless it did not achieve recognition in the Frankish empire, where it was vehemently attacked in the *Libri Carolini*, and the consequent uncertainties left a mark upon later Western language about this council. Hincmar rudely described the Seventh Council as *pseudosynodus Graecorum*.[17] This view was strongly opposed by the papal librarian Anastasius (d. 897) who provided a Latin translation of the Acts of both Seventh and Eighth Councils. The hesitancy may be detected in the compilation of Gratian in the 12th century where the following propositions lie side by side: (a) the first four general councils are the principal ones;[18] (b) newly elected popes in their profession of faith at consecration confirm eight councils;[19] (c) the number of councils listed with dates extends only to the first six—the decrees of the Quinisext of 692 being cited as decrees of the sixth council;[20] (d) decrees of the Nicene council of 787 are cited by Gratian in his work from time to time, as an accepted part of the corpus of canon law;[21] (e) no general council may be called except by the Pope (a proposition from the pseudo-Isidorian decretals).[22] When Thomas Aquinas is discussing images in the Summa Theologica there is no appeal to the decisions of the Seventh Council.[23] The silence does not, of course, imply any rejection, but simply that the medieval West never thought in the Greek way of a sacred canon of seven general councils in which the seventh was on just the same self-evident standing as the first four or six. Moreover, for the West the series of general councils was continuing, in the eighth council that condemned Photius, and then in the successive Lateran councils

(I, 1129, Investiture; II, 1130, Arnold of Brescia; III, 1179, papal elections; IV, 1215, Waldenses, Joachim, etc.), though, at the same time, the West was conscious of the limited character of the Western general councils. Even Innocent III knew that the Roman church was not actually the universal church. Here again, therefore, the Western theologians were allowing some distinctions in degrees of authority among the general councils that they accepted.

After Photius and the end of the intense, heroic struggle against Iconoclasm, which had been fought with the toughness of the German *Kirchenkampf* of modern times, the decrees of the seventh council were valued in a way that put them on no subordinate level, as if the presence of the icons were a mere matter of optional devotional practice. The establishment of the Feast of Orthodoxy on the first Sunday in Lent (probably from 867 onwards) commemorated the triumph of the Iconophiles, and was an annual reminder, unparalleled in the West, of the East's debt to its iconophile martyrs.

The definition of the Seventh Council rejects the iconoclast argument that the icon should be replaced by the cross, and affirms that, by the divinely inspired authority of the Fathers and the traditions of the Catholic Church, holy pictures in mosaic and painting, as well as the cross, may properly be placed in churches and may adorn vestments and vessels. The pictures may rightly portray Christ, the Theotokos, the angels, and the saints. They serve to lift men's minds to those whom they represent. They should be reverenced, but not worshipped with that worship that befits God alone. (I. e. *proskynesis* is appropriate, but not *latreia*).

The historian of the first seven general councils is bound to notice that there is a certain shift in the ground of authority to which they appeal. At the first general council at Nicaea in 325 the orthodox had great difficulty in justifying the council's use of the non-scriptural word homousios in their creed. At the second council at Constantinople in 381 the affirmation of the Godhead of the Spirit was principally based upon liturgical tradition in (a) the baptismal formula, (b) the *Gloria Patri*; but since the former was also there in scripture the argument did not materially modify the appeal to the authority of apostolic tradition in scripture. Even so, the discussions preceding the Council of Constantinople (381) paid much attention to the tradition of orthodox fathers, and the first patristic florilegium occurs in St Basil, *On the Holy Spirit*.[24] The appeal to florilegia with extracts from orthodox fathers became important in the third and fourth general councils of Ephesus and Chalcedon; likewise for the fifth and sixth. Thereby the presuppositions were provided by which the Seventh Council could defend the icons by appealing not to scripture except in fairly general terms but principally to the traditions of the Fathers. The definition of the Seventh Council includes a verbatim quotation of St Basil: 'The honour paid to the image passes on to the prototype.'[25]

2. The Anglican evaluation of general councils[26]
(a) Article XXI (1563 and 1571, derived from the 42 Articles of 1552/3)

'General councils may not (*non possunt*) be gathered together without the commandment and will of princes. And when they be gathered together (forasmuch as they be an assembly of men, where of all be not governed with the Spirit and the Word of God) they may err, and sometimes have erred, even in things pertaining unto God. Wherefore things ordained by them as necessary to salvation have neither strength nor authority, unless it may be declared that they be taken out of Holy Scripture.'

A commentary on this, from the circle in which Article XXI was first compiled, is provided by cap. 14 of the *Reformatio Legum Ecclesiasticarum* (1551-53, first printed 1571). I translate the Latin.

(b) Reformatio Legum Ecclesiasticarum, cap. 14 (ed. Cardwell, p. 6)

'Although to councils, especially general councils, we gladly accord enormous honour, yet we judge that they ought to be put far below the dignity of the canonical scripture. Moreover, we make a considerable distinction among the councils themselves. For some of them, such as the preeminent four, Nicaea, Constantinople I, Ephesus, and Chalcedon, we embrace and accept with great reverence. The same judgement indeed we hold concerning many other councils that were held later, in which we see and acknowledge that the most holy Fathers promulgated many definitions, with great weight and entire holiness, concerning the blessed and supreme Trinity, concerning Jesus Christ our Lord and Saviour, and the Redemption of man procured through him, in accord with the divine scriptures.

We do not, however, think that our faith is bound by councils except so far as they can be confirmed out of the holy scriptures. For it is manifest that some councils erred sometimes, and that their definitions contradict each other, partly in matters of (canon) law, partly even in faith. Therefore councils will be studied with honour and Christian reverence, but will be subject to the test of the pious, certain, and upright rule of the scriptures.'[27]

Cap. 15 lays down a similar criterion for the Fathers. They are on no account to be despised (*minime contemnendum*), but Scripture is of greater authority.

(c)   The Homilies of 1571 (commended in Article XXXV) contain in homily 2 a vigorous attack 'on the peril of idolatry' attaching to the Roman doctrine of images, and paints a horrific picture of the corruption surrounding the Byzantine personalities principally concerned in the Second Council of Nicaea of 787. The *Libri Carolini* had lately been printed for the first time (1549) and provided fuel for Protestant iconoclasm. The Homily, on the other hand, speaks in unreserved language about the first six general councils.

(d)   Article XXII rejects as res futilis, inaniter conficta, the doctrina Romanensium . . . de veneratione et adoratione tum imaginum tum reliquiarum.

The background of the Article is the profound distrust of the superstitions of popular religion, which, it should be said, is also apparent in the decree of Trent (sess. 25 can. 14, of 4 Dec., 1563, Denzinger 984-988), though Trent of course adopts a much more positive view towards the invocation of saints, the veneration of relics, and the cultus of the saints through statues and pictures, citing the decree of the Seventh Council in vindication of its view.

No Anglican document of the 16th century can be said formally to state an iconoclast theology in the sense that this is true of the Iconoclast councils of 754 and 815 which carefully formulated a sophisticated argument about the nature of the true religious image. Whenever an Anglican writer of the first Reformation period expresses reserve or indeed hostility towards images of saints the discernible motive is fear of sentimental religion divorced from the gospel or at least not visibly expressing its characteristic faith. The question is regarded, that is to say, as a matter of devotional practice.

(e)   Although not an ecclesiastical document, the Act of Parliament 1 Eliz. c. 1, 36, 1559, deserves mention. It decreed 'that judges
ecclesiastical appointed under the king's commission shall not
adjudge for heresy any thing but that which heretofore hath been
so adjudged by the authority of the canonical scriptures or by the
first four general councils or by some other general council wherein
the same hath been declared heresy by the express words of the said
canonical scriptures, or such as hereafter shall be termed heresy by
the high court of parliament of this realm with the assent of the
clergy in convocation.'

This is cited by Richard Hooker, EP VIII, 2, 17.

Two questions are raised by the Anglican documents of the
first Reformation period, viz. the authority of any general council,
whether Nicaea, or Chalcedon, or any other, and the authority of
the Seventh Council of 787 in particular.

In the first period the question of the authority of general
councils was dominated by Trent, and the ground occupied by the
Elizabethan Anglicans was that general councils were very important, but their dogmatic decisions were binding when they were seen
to be supported from scripture. Hooker speaks of general councils
as God's gift to the church, a way of reaching harmony on points
of disagreement, which had apostolic precedent and remained
highly esteemed in the ancient church until pride, ambition, and
tyranny made them scenes of faction. Even so, abuse does not do
away with the use. And Hooker remains persuaded that a true
council, in which faction was set aside, would be the ideal way of
resolving the disputes of the Reformation age. (EP i, 10, 14). Likewise he discusses the doctrines of the Trinity and the Person of
Christ with a reference to the decisive definitions of the 'four most
famous general councils' (EP v, 54, 10). Hooker does not discuss
images, but vigorously defends the observance of saints' days, the
use of the sign of the cross, etc. He does not otherwise give any
major analysis of our problem, which did not seriously arise in his
conflict with the Puritans.

Richard Field, on the other hand, gives several pages to the
question (*Of the Church*, 1606, V, 48-52), holding that, while not
absolutely necessary to the church, general councils are the best
practical way of defining orthodoxy against heresy, remedying
abuses in the church, and ending schisms. Field gives to the clergy
(primarily, but not exclusively the bishops) the responsibility for

defining doctrine, but thinks that the laity have a proper and considerable part to play in the discussion. He insists that the members of the council must be entirely free to express their mind if the council is to have real authority, denies that they may only be held by leave of the Pope, and declares (with Melchior Cano) that the authority of general councils is not on the same level as scripture. In the Catholic tradition, both Thomas Netter Waldensis (the hammer of the Wycliffites) and Cardinal Nicolas of Cusa allow that general councils may err, e.g. Ariminum and Ephesus 449. Field's list of the councils received with deep respect by the Church of England begins with I-VI, as concerned with matters of faith. 'The Seventh . . . was not called about any question of faith, but of manners.' Field welcomes the Seventh Council's condemning of latreia of pictures; it seems 'to allow no other use of them but that which is historical'. Yet even the Roman Catholics concede that there are risks of abuse, opening the way to gross idolatry.

Field in short has no objection in principle to the decree of the Seventh Council as theology, but he regrets some of the practical consequences.

A similar position is in effect occupied by Laud in the *Conference with Fisher* (33, 13), though he does not discuss the particular problem of the Seventh Council. His principal target is Bellarmine's proposition that a general council may err if it is not confirmed by the Pope, but is infallible if so confirmed. His instances of confirmed general councils that have erred include the Lateran council of 1215 on Transubstantiation; Constance on communion in one kind; and Trent on the invocation of saints and the adoration of images. For the ancient church commemorated with honour but did not invoke the saints; it prayed by the merits of Christ, but not by the merits of the saints. Even Trent admitted that to believe there is any divinity in images is idolatry. Yet the religion of Spanish peasants is precisely this.

Herbert Thorndike (*Epilogue to the Tragedy of the Church of England*, III, 1659, ch. 31) deals with the question at much greater length and detail. The first six councils he regards as binding on the consciences of Christians, but observes that the canons of the Quinisext of 692 were not recognized by the West. The Seventh Council he simply denies to have truly ecumenical status on the ground that, although there were papal legates there and though its decisions were accepted by Pope Hadrian, the Council wholly ignored Christendom north of the Alps and was rejected by the church in the Frankish empire. Thorndike concedes that the *Libri Carolini* were wrong in attributing to the Seventh Council the doctrine that images may be adored: 'That honour of images which the decree maintaineth is no idolatry. But he that says it is no idolatry which they enjoin does not therefore justify or commend them for enjoining it.' The practical dangers of debased popular religion are in fact visible and too great to be tolerable. Yet certainly the church may have images—for ornament of church buildings, for the instruction of those who cannot read, for the stirring up of devotion. Thorndike thinks it a fault in the 'Homily on the peril of idolatry' that it fails to recognize this point. But, he adds, 'all these reasons are utterly impertinent to the worshipping of images'. 'Whatsoever is appointed by the Church for the circumstance, furniture, solemnity, or ceremony of God's service, . . . is thereby to be accounted holy and so used and respected. The memories of God's saints and martyrs are fit occasions to determine the time and place and other circumstances of it . . . . If, instead of circumstances and instruments, the saints of God, or images, or any creature of God whatsoever, become the object of that worship for which churches were built and for which Christians assemble; by that means there may be room to let in that idolatry at the back door, which Christianity shutteth out at the great gate.'

The situation of the sixteenth century Anglicans, confronted by the decrees of Trent at which (they felt) the Pope was acting as judge in his own cause, led them to a natural prickliness about general councils, especially when they read in Stapleton that general councils needed no evident or even probable support in scripture for their decrees.[28] The insistence that general councils cannot be held without the will of princes looks odd today until one remembers that modern travel and currency regulations have the effect of enforcing the same point. The proposition was basically an appeal to history against the papal claim (still standing in CIC) that the Pope possesses the exclusive right to summon ecumenical councils—a claim falsifiable by the simple fact that all the ancient ecumenical councils were called by emperors, not by popes.[29] That is to say, it implied a refusal to acknowledge the 'general' or universal status of those councils which were merely Western and Roman in their ambit, from the Lateran councils onwards. On the other hand, the insistence that general councils remain subordinate to scripture brought out the importance of *reception* in the acknowledgement of their authority, and led to considerable interest in the historical process by which these councils came to be regarded as having special status.[30] It led, moreover, to stress being laid on distinctions between councils (e.g. the preeminence of the first four). That even Chalcedon did not possess *absolute* authority even for the Western church was proved by the refusal of Leo the Great and his successors to accept the (so-called) '28th canon' on the privileges of Constantinople. So not all decisions of general councils possessed equally binding authority. The legal form of papal (or imperial) ratification could not be regarded as tantamount to a 'Causa finita est', for the Pope might be a Honorius infected with heresy; and even if he were always orthodox a papal pronouncement could not add to the truth of a council's definition. In the last analysis the acceptance of a council as General rests with the universal church whence, in the first place, a council derives its authority and credibility. And the universal church judges by the apostolic tradition stemming from scripture.[31]

This Anglican attitude to general councils expresses profound respect. At the same time the decisions of the great councils do not relieve the modern theologian of the need to think. Just as the fathers of Nicaea and Chalcedon found that they could not safeguard the apostolic tradition by merely repeating the words of scripture, so also the contemporary theologian cannot defend the truth in the 20th century by merely repeating the definitions of the fifth.

Anglican/Orthodox discussion has in the past betrayed some anxiety on the question whether the Anglican church accepts (a) the infallibility of general councils, (b) the seventh council. For the churches in the Orthodox tradition these are natural questions to ask. They have a strong tradition of deep reverence for the Seven councils, expressed in diptychs, icons and inscriptions decorating churches, in the long profession of faith made by an Orthodox bishop at his consecration when he promises to uphold their definitions without deviation, or in the textbooks used by candidates for holy orders in Orthodox seminaries. Moreover, all the first seven general councils took place in the Greek East and had relatively small Western representation (one, Constantinople 381, having none at all). Furthermore, Anglican theology has absorbed much of the attitude of Augustine towards councils,[32] viz. that (1) while they are important, their definitions never quite possess a final and absolute authority in such a sense that they may not need supplementation or even correction by later councils with wiser, second thoughts; (2) their decisions do not make it superfluous to study scripture and to use one's reason. Another, probably more influential factor making for a difference of attitude arises no doubt from the accidents of our Anglo-Saxon university syllabuses, in which the study of early Christian doctrine often stops with Chalcedon and Dr Kelly.[33]

Sometimes it is asserted that Anglicans accept the first four councils *and no more*—the canon is exclusive. It would be hard to find documentary proof of this point except perhaps (as in an important paper by Yves Congar, *Le Concile et les Conciles*, 1960, 98) by means of selective quotation, and the assertion seems to be a misconstruction. Certainly the first four councils are accorded pre-eminence because of the gravity of their matter and their accord with scripture. But the principle of accord with scripture is extended (as in the *Reformatio Legum*) to later councils as well. The fifth and sixth councils are accepted in substance by representative Anglican divines of the classical period, and their reservations about the seventh council concern not the theology of the definition but the consequences of a popular, sentimental religion in which the crucial qualifications and distinctions drawn by the seventh council are not observed. Moreover, in estimating the later councils of the western patriarchate which the Roman Catholic church numbers among the 21 general councils that it receives, Anglicans are far from rejecting them out of hand. While regretting the limited and onesided character of some of the decisions of Trent, numerous Anglicans, precisely on the principle of accord with the apostolic tradition, would receive many of the council's decrees with respect. The same is more obviously true of Vatican II.

19

Making and Remaking in the Ministry of the Church

RECENT DISCUSSIONS of the ordination of women to the priesthood and/or the episcopate in some provinces of the Anglican communion have raised in particularly sharp form much wider issues of authority. In a body which understands itself to be part of the orthodox catholic tradition, and not to embody any breach of continuity with the Church built upon the foundation of the apostles and prophets, is it possible for unilateral decisions to be taken in indifference to other communions which, in Anglican eyes, unambiguously represent the same continuity of visible communion? Unilateral action has consequences not only for the internal coherence and interchangeability of ministry within the provinces of the Anglican communion but also for the progress of ecumenical dialogue and *rapprochement* between Canterbury and Rome or Constantinople and Moscow. The problem has a bearing, though in a different way, on conversations between Canterbury and Wittenberg.

In the present paper the intention is to try to disentangle some of the complexities by looking at the contemporary situation in the light of some pieces of the past record. Such a retrospect need not and does not imply that the Church is and needs to be imprisoned in the past. For some theologians, among whom Maurice Wiles has been prominent, an expert knowledge of Christian antiquity is the ground for a liberation from its legacies. Here let it suffice to say that an imprisonment in the past must be for the Church a betrayal of what is given in trust.

Nevertheless, all theology which is plausibly to claim the name of Christian is necessarily going to keep an eye on the past, since it must presuppose that in Jesus of Nazareth humanity is granted a self-disclosure of the Creator and the revelation of what God intends humankind to be. The apostle was unsympathetic to those who thought they had another gospel to offer. At the same time he was sharp to a local Church where some believed themselves to have so privileged an access to the word of God that they were under no obligation to consider fraternal relations with other Churches (Gal. I: 8; I Cor. 14: 36). In so crucial a matter as the memorial of our redemption, the apostle thought the Corinthians would be wise to adhere to the *paradosis* (I Cor. II: 23). Relations with other Churches could be affected if they did not do so.

It is today non-controversial among theologians that 'tradition' is not some second source beside the deposit in scripture, out of which truths of a quite different nature and kind can be produced. To speak of Tradition (the typographical compliment of a capital letter implying that it is regarded with a measure of considerable respect) is to recognize that the prophetic and apostolic witness of the past record can become revelation now because of the experience of grace in the community of the Spirit through the Church living out its life in history. In the life of the Church we are anchored to the past as members, by faith and baptism, of a community of discipleship which has a continuing history. We join a community linked to Peter and Paul, to Mary mother of Jesus, to Bethlehem and Golgotha, to the mission to the Gentile world (which Paul at least did not understand to be shutting the door on Jews), to the community's accepted norms and title-deeds in scripture, in the baptismal confession of faith, in the ministry with apostolic commission which so soon became a visible and concrete manifestation of continuity.

Thereby the community is aware of possessing both a sacred trust or deposit to be faithfully handed on, and also a living authority in the universal fellowship of the Church guided by ministerial organs of decision-making and by the 'reception' or critical appropriation of these decisions by the whole people of God. Even though the process may take time (as in the fourth century with the creed of Nicaea), what is felt to be rightly defined under the protection of the Holy Spirit is also received under the same guidance and protection. In Church history a century is never very long.

The ordained ministry, with apostolic commission to be pastoral in relation to the community, does not exist merely to mediate and transmit faithfully what has been received from a sacrosanct past. It is also called to proclaim, to utter prophecy in the Spirit addressed to the contemporary situation, to teach (a term which must imply far more than a repetition of the formulas of long ago, shaped in utterly different circumstances and with metaphysical presuppositions no longer shared), and to serve the needs of the community in circumstances that are changing fast.

271

To say so much is obvious enough. But perhaps it needs to be stated, platitudinous as it may seem, because it is the parameter which sets the context for our problem. The polarity of prophecy and tradition is inherent in the very being of the Church. We owe to Irenaeus, in reaction to the crisis precipitated by the Montanists, the contention that the spectacular immediacy of prophetic inspiration is not more supernatural than the transmitted catechesis and sacramental life of the community, assured by a succession of ministry continuous through time and space. The anchor to the past, to the incarnate Lord and to the apostles, to the deposit of faith providentially preserved in written form in scripture, might suggest that we have a duty to be ultratraditionalists, resistant to all changes. But the experience of the Holy Spirit here and now constantly calls us to confront changing situations requiring fresh approaches. What is it to be *semper eadem*? What is open to development, which is after all but a four-syllable word for change?

Reflection on the doctrine of the Paraclete in St John's gospel would suggest that the Spirit leads the Church into richer and deeper understanding of the will and mind of the Lord, but never into any break or discontinuity with that will and mind.

Coherent with this principle, we seek to interpret scripture by the closest attention to scholarly historical exegesis; but those who believe that the Bible is the book of the living God, interpreted in each successive generation, will think twice before committing themselves to the opinion that an exclusive application of critical historical method is all we need. Hence the concept of tradition combines both transmission and development, both the testing by the deposit of apostolic faith and order and the readiness to follow the Spirit guiding the Church in the confrontation of new problems. Tradition and prophecy are two antithetical poles which Christians have to learn to see as complementary, if only because it is being rooted in the past, in scripture and authentic interpretation of Scripture, that offers a rock on which to stand for the facing of the present and future. A doctrine of the Church has to be grounded both in Christology (or the historical continuity with the apostolic commission from Jesus) and in the freedom of the Spirit bestowed at Pentecost and ever granting renewal and correction and adaptation.

I must turn from tradition and prophecy to another issue. What must we share in common to be able to worship together at the Lord's table? Obviously diversity has at all times been a phenomenon in the life of the Church. In the generation following the death of the last of the twelve apostles, that diversity may have looked uncommonly like anarchy, whether in faith or in ministerial order or in moral practice. At a very early stage as the apostles passed from the scene, the Church found it necessary to lay down certain markers or frontiers. In the order of their appearing they are a familiar trio: a ministry in continuity with the apostolic community and with apostolic commission; a baptismal confession of faith structured round the affirmation of belief in God the Father, maker of heaven and earth; in Jesus the Christ his unique Son, who was so truly human that he was born and crucified, yet experienced both in such a way that the birth and crucifixion were divine wonders; and in the Holy Spirit in the Church; lastly in chronological order, but in no way inferior in weight, the biblical canon.

It seems a truism to say that there is sharp friction in Church history when someone wants to dig up and modify or even discard any one of these three elements. Perhaps in some superlunary realm the Church could get along happily without such bonds. But in this sublunary sphere the Church needs to affirm its faith, needs to acknowledge the witness of the prophetic and apostolic writings, needs to admit to its body by baptism and, in obedience to the Lord, to renew itself continually by the eucharistic memorial. Moreover, it needs for its own coherence a ministry generally accepted as possessing a commission, given by Christ in his Church, to serve and safeguard the Word and sacraments. In these areas of Bible, creed, sacraments, and ministry, the Church has believed it has divine gifts (cf. Ephesians 4), *dona data*, touching the deepest roots of Christian existence and therefore to be handled with the utmost sensitivity.

If these items fall in the category of basic and foundational things, that does not mean, or at any rate did not mean for the ancient Church of the patristic age, that there may not be considerable diversity, notably in liturgical custom. The notion that precise liturgical uniformity is essentially desirable has pastoral roots; but its actual imposition has owed more to Charlemagne than to medieval popes, or in England much more to successive Acts of Parliament wishing to restrain Anabaptist sedition and non-vernacular rites in Latin, using the engine of Acts of Uniformity, than to any ecclesiastical body. In fact, liturgical diversities have rarely been a cause of schism, though frequently a cause of mutual vituperation. On 27 July 1628 Canon Peter Smart preached in Durham cathedral to denounce his fellow canon John Cosin for 'ducking to the altar', standing at the altar in a cope, singing instead of saying the Nicene Creed, 'wearing strange Babylonish garments, with trippings and turnings and crossings and crouchings'. In Cranmer's first English prayer book of 1549, kneeling, crossing, and other gestures 'may be used or left, as every man's devotion serveth, without blame'. In St Augustine's time there were different customs in Africa, Rome, and Milan. His mother Monica arrived at Milan and began to observe customs not at home in Milan. When in Rome, advised Ambrose, do as Rome does. He meant, you are not in Rome now, and therefore should not be doing it here. And in one letter Augustine complains of the bewilderment caused to congregations when the clergy introduce liturgical usages they have seen abroad.

There are some liturgical differences which express a difference in theology, a deliberate difference, which may be the expression of separation and schism.

We have become accustomed today to a greater degree of plurality: Roman Catholics have four prayers of consecration from which to choose, the second of them sharing perhaps with Rite B in the American Anglican book (1978) the distinction of being among the finest canons in our English language. The Church of England's Alternative Service Book of 1980 is a bit more inhibited and bottled up, but certainly remains sure that in the eucharistic action there is a powerful work of the Holy Spirit through which believers are joined with the entire people of God and all the company of heaven, the spirits of righteous souls who have been made perfect, until we are granted to stand before the Father and Jesus the mediator of the new covenant as we make the memorial of his blood shed for our redemption. It is instructive that a recent pamphlet by an Evangelical writer has pleaded for an urgent revision of the eucharistic rites of the Alternative Service Book to eliminate not only the evident presupposition that consecration signifies a change but also the specifically Christian theme of redemption. Would not a simple thanksgiving suffice, as in the Jewish Passover ceremonies?

Unilateral declarations of independence are not something that the inheritors of Henry VIII's Act of Supremacy can easily deny ever to be appropriate in any circumstances. Admittedly his Act was not thunder out of a clear sky: English kings had long been agitated by the weight of papal taxation on English churches and by the invasion of rights of patronage and appointment. But we need not doubt that the unilateral act would not have occurred when it did, and in the form it took, had Henry not wished to divorce Catherine of Aragon. As Martin Luther tartly remarked, Henry had not so much abolished papal jurisdiction as transferred all its powers to himself. And if thereby, asked Bishop Stephen Gardiner of Winchester in 1555, he had taken his Church out of the *ecclesia catholica*, had he a Church to be head of? Henry's answer was given in the King's Book of 1543 (for which Gardiner disowned all responsibility): the Greek East refused to acknowledge papal universal jurisdiction after the union at the Council of Florence in 1439; therefore such jurisdiction lacked catholic consent, and there was no departure from the catholic tradition if organization were to return to being territorial.

The element of nationalism undeniable in the German and English Reformations had been asserting itself long before 1517 or 1534. The famous declaration of Bishop Aylmer of London in the 1570s that 'God is English' echoes the jingoism of the Hundred Years War. The battle of Agincourt in 1415 provoked vehement expressions of mutual hostility and national pride among the English and French delegations to the Council of Constance, gravely hindering Sigismond's work of reconciliation, peace, and reform. No one can read the enormously influential Protestant history of John Foxe, the *Acts and Monuments*, without discerning a powerful streak of English nationalism, a pleasure at the thought that Catholicism in England is happily discredited by Mary's loss of Calais and defeat in France, while Protestantism is divinely vindicated by the political successes of Elizabeth, 'our new Deborah'.

Perhaps there is still a residual element of nationalism latent in the English wish to make their own independent and sovereign decisions, whether about a common European currency or about the polity of the Church. Anglicans today, however, may find it hard to think as unilaterally as the men of the sixteenth century did, and the gradually strengthening consciousness of shared interests with other partners in the European community may have side-effects in ecclesiastical matters.

Henry VIII looked across to Byzantium and the Eastern Churches for precedent and justification of his assertions of independence. Himself a remarkably learned man, he was glad to see in Justinian's ecclesiastical supremacy an anticipation of his own claims. Was not this realm of England shown by sundry ancient chronicles to be an empire? And to be an empire was to have an emperor sovereign over matters both secular and ecclesiastical.

It has been the dilemma of the Roman see that, against national Churches, it has embodied the ideal of a universal community transcending nationalisms, and yet has to make claims for itself which make it particular and less than universal.

Conciliar writers such as Gerson had been anxious to set the authority of the Roman see in service to, and so in subordination to, a universal Church which was extended far beyond those churches and bishops in full communion with the Roman see. At a succession of fifteenth-century councils—Pisa, Constance, Basle, culminating in Florence—the agenda included reconciliation with the Orthodox churches, though only at Florence was there real conversation directed to that specific end. And at Florence Pope Eugenius IV badly needed restored communion with the Orthodox of Constantinople and Kiev to bolster his own weak position in the West. He adopted a wide programme of reconciliation with other separated bodies—Armenians, Copts, and others—and provided the Armenians (as he had not done for the Greeks) with a detailed Thomist catechism of instruction in the theology of the sacraments. For Eugenius IV the supreme authority of the Roman see was the prime and indispensable element in the re-establishing of unity. Gerson could hardly have denied that communion with the *cathedra Petri* was a sign of universal communion, but did not think of communion with the pope as an absolute *sine qua non* of catholicity, as if everything flowed from this one source. At a time when there were three popes to choose from, it was hard to think that way.

The Acts of the Council of Constance provide rich illustration of the difficulty experienced by those present in thinking of the papacy as the sign and instrument of something transcending national frontiers. After the Council had obtained the resignation of two out of the three rival popes and the withdrawal of obedience from the Spanish pope, Benedict XIII, who intransigently avoided resignation, the Italians wanted an Italian pope, the French a Frenchman who would live at Avignon, the Germans desired a German, and the little English delegation blew their trumpet with ear-splitting tones in the hope that someone would take them seriously. Each nation at Constance had its own ambitions, and got its own independent concordat from Martin V.

The national character of the Eastern churches is still strongly felt, e.g. in Romania or Russia, and is particularly in evidence in the case of the pre-Chalcedonian churches: Armenians, Copts, Ethiopians, Syrian Orthodox or 'Jacobites'. The Persian Nestorians survived in their old home until the terrible massacres in South-East Turkey in 1917 (and now have to make do in San Francisco where the American Presbyterians transported them in 1934). The Orthodox (Chalcedonian) churches are also a family of ethnic churches: Greek, Russian, Finnish, Bulgarian, Romanian, Serbian, Polish, and so on. Bonded in fraternal togetherness, each has its own patriarch, giving honour but little jurisdiction to the ecumenical patriarch at the Phanar. Independent of one another, they are not so independent of civil government, which may legislate for their constitution, control episcopal elections, veto synodical decisions, confiscate church property, and occasionally stand back to watch the Church fall apart in faction and strife because it lacks any central authority apart from the State. Moreover, ethnic churches (with a few exceptions) tend not to be strongly missionary. In England the fortuitous coincidence of the emergence of the trading corporation called the British Empire and the Evangelical Revival, followed by the Oxford Movement with its ideal of heroic priestly self-sacrifice, had the result of commerce and Christianity marching together up the Niger and the Zambezi with the Bible, *Hymns Ancient & Modern*, and perhaps (on the Zambezi) an English Missal. The Anglican Communion has resulted from the extraordinary discovery that the way of worship expressed in the old English Prayer Book in Tudor prose possessed amazing powers of being found deeply evocative for peoples whose native tongue was not English, or at least not English English.

Nevertheless, the claim of Henry VIII to govern a territorially independent part of the Church has bequeathed a legacy of 'provincial autonomy', which turns the Anglican communion into a fairly loose federation of kindred spirits, often grateful for mutual fellowship but with each province reserving the right to make its own decisions. This concept of provincial autonomy does not prevent one province from putting pressure on other provinces to follow its example. Tension can arise when that pressure becomes imperative and demanding. A province which has vigorously asserted the right to make its own independent decisions may then press other provinces not only to acknowledge the 'catholicity' of what has been decided but also to take the same decisions.

Provincial autonomy may encourage regional diversities. Yet the pressure which one progressive province may place upon others is a reflection of an instinct to reduce diversity, to give expression to the universality of the Church by diminishing differences.

Differences in liturgical usage have always existed, and between East and West have occasionally been sources of friction. Cardinal Humbert deduced the invalidity of the Eastern celebration of the eucharist from the fact that Orthodox custom was to bury in the ground the consecrated remains, at a time when Western custom was either reverently to consume the remains or to commit them to the flames. The presence of the Filioque in the Creed was defended by Anselm at the Council of Bari (1098). Argument that it was a liturgical difference between East and West which was paralleled in other similar diversities is among those deployed in his later work 'On the Procession of the Holy Spirit', where (ch. 13 end) he even claimed that it is the kind of variation which the Church in one kingdom is entitled to make without departing from orthodoxy, and which is therefore the more justified when all the Latin-speaking kingdoms follow this usage. In the ninth century Ratramnus of Corbey had implicitly defended the Western Filioque by listing the variations of usage and custom in the Churches from the earliest times (*Contra Graecorum opposita* IV, *PL* 121, 303-11). Any Greek criticism of Western customs, such as sacerdotal celibacy, was in any event met by Ratramnus' assertions of the supremacy of the Roman see (IV, 8), a jurisdiction which made all argument superfluous.

But the arguments about the Filioque were a source of difficulty and embarrassment because there were always some in the West who thought the Greek Churches at fault in not having adopted it; a solid and overwhelming majority in the Greek Churches thought the Western addition, about which they had never been consulted, an act of gross irreverence to a creed agreed by an ecumenical council. On both sides there were those who wanted to put pressure on the other half of the Church, and found it hard to consent to the view that, in a matter so central, dogma could be regional and not of universal obligation. The sharp antagonism of Humbert has been more characteristic of the Latin West than the quiet plea of Anselm of Canterbury that both traditions be as freely tolerated as other liturgical differences. Admittedly even Anselm thought the Greek usage of leavened bread in the eucharist was a departure from that of Jesus and the apostles, and a mistake; but it remained the case that the Greeks used bread. Therefore, he said, there was agreement *substantialiter*. Anselm is, I believe, the earliest person to think of 'substantial agreement' as a way of asserting a common faith in essentials while allowing for diversity in inessentials.

Nevertheless, in matters of religious faith and practice, to be in agreement on 98 per cent has the consequence that the remaining 2 per cent comes to be of intense importance. Between Anglicans and Lutherans the differences seem remarkably small. The Lutheran confessional documents allow no doubt on the proposition that Melanchthon would have wished the Reformation churches to have been able to retain the episcopal order. But today there are Lutheran divines for whom a fatal obstacle to full *communio in sacris* consists in the Anglican conviction that a person ordained to the episcopate is ordained for life to that order of ministry. By contrast, there are Lutheran theologians who regard the ordained ministry as a function rather than an order, and deduce that a retired bishop has ceased to be a bishop. An Anglican will observe that Melanchthon himself affirms the classic distinction between the power of order and the power of jurisdiction: that is, a retired bishop may act episcopally subject to the jurisdiction of the diocesan in post, but not otherwise. So the power of order is retained, and the retired bishop may do what a bishop does if he has the permission of the diocesan, with whom lies the power of jurisdiction.

These reflections come close to the old distinction, found in Augustine and much exploited by Anglican theologians of the seventeenth century, between fundamental and non-fundamental doctrines. The distinction has some affinity with, but also some differences from, the more commonly Catholic concept of a hierarchy of truths which allows for the evident fact that, while the doctrine of the Trinity and the dogma of the Assumption of the Virgin may appear of equal importance to a canonist, inasmuch as for him both rest for their truth on the defining authority, they are not of equal significance or even value for a theologian. Any Mariological statement is sure to be dependent on and secondary to a prior Christological affirmation.

In this area of theological discourse, there is an obvious danger of blandly assuming disagreement to be a sign of unimportance.

One cannot satisfy the sceptical or the questioning with the contention that what Christians disagree about must, for that reason, be deemed secondary, or even a matter of indifference. The impassioned debates of sixteenth-century Lutherans may suffice to demonstrate that people can take radically opposed views concerning the definition and identification of what is to be deemed 'indifferent'. For Acontius the area covered by the term *adiaphora* was the greater part of traditional theological understanding. So radical a reductionism solves the problem of remaking Christian doctrine by making most of it optional, with any actual assertion positively discouraged.

It is unnecessary to observe that behind the debate about the rightness and the consequences of unilateral action by part of the Church there lies a question about the concept of divine authority and revelation. What is non-negotiable because it is given *iure divino*?

For conservative minds, whether Catholic or Protestant, revelation is doctrine formulated as far as possible in clear-cut propositional statement grounded either in an inerrantly inspired Bible, inerrantly interpreted by men of the Spirit who show themselves to be so by their assertion of biblical inerrancy, or in an unfailing organ of teaching authority, a magisterium (as in modern times it has come to be called—the term is not ancient in this sense) whose rulings through the centuries can be conveniently gathered in a canonist's handbook, and whose verdicts are really all one needs to know.

A less hard concept of revelation would speak of scripture and the consensus of the faithful, expressed through the formative councils such as Nicaea and Chalcedon, the definitions of which 'witness' to a divine self-disclosure in Christ for the redemption of humanity. In the Church of England the current form of the Declaration of Assent speaks this language of 'witness'. It remains a presupposition that a criterion of truth in the Church is consonance with scripture and ancient tradition or at least an absence of evident dissonance.

An altogether softer evaluation of revelation would see it as a divinely inspired, immanent enhancement of the natural consciousness of the Christian community, enabling it to cut free from the shackles of the past and from the habits of religious convention. Thereby the Church is an agency of creative independence, whether by charismatic renewal or by jettisoning the ways of the past. The criterion of fidelity to the historical foundations of the faith, and to the formative decisions of the age when Christianity was, so to speak, deciding to be Christianity in the ordinarily recognizable form, becomes hardly more than marginal. For the basic criterion is that what Christians are now doing and believing should not appear locked into obsolete linguistic habits, such as 'exclusive language', or social presuppositions no longer shared. The crucial test is that Christians should not be ludicrously at loggerheads with the self-evident assumptions of their secular contemporaries who, after all, are also God's creation living in God's world and are likely to have things to teach those who allow their faith to shut them into a cultural ghetto.

This last, soft view of revelation may be accompanied by a fairly drastic rationalism towards the community of the Church, with the idea that if one is to understand the Church *qua* institution or the role of the sacraments, one will do best to study magic or textbooks on primitive Melanesian tribesmen rather than Küng, Rahner, or their Protestant counterparts like Pannenberg. To the historian it is familiar that the Protestant affirmation of *scriptura sola* may be so stated as to desacralize the dominical sacraments and the ordained ministers who have to serve and dispense them. There is always the latent suspicion that appeals to externally given and guaranteed revelation are forms of hidden coercion used to suppress dissent. The wish to repress dissent, however, is apparent as much in the 'liberal' camp as in the 'conservative'.

No Christian has a link with Jesus the Christ which does not in some degree depend on the medium of tradition, or a lifeline transmitted horizontally through the space-time continuum, a sacred tradition which, for all the earthiness of its transmitting vessels, mediates the gospel of God's love and judgement. Of the continuity of the present community with its roots and title-deeds, the scriptures, sacraments, and historic ministry constitute the primary and visible signs, and there is no escape from the disturbing consequences of changes in the way these are understood. A feeling of detachment from the legacy of the past, however beneficent that legacy is taken to be, encourages a relativizing of the degree of authority to be associated with scripture and with inherited custom. This relativizing process can make unilateral decisions by part of the Church easier, because the divisions of Christendom may come to seem less evil too.

The Latin patriarchate in Rome has in the past made unilateral decisions which have caused unsolved difficulties in relation to the Orthodox Churches. The Orthodox were complaining in the time of Anselm of Canterbury that they had not been consulted about the addition of the Filioque to the Creed in the eucharist. The Orthodox have no difficulty in agreeing with Rome that our Lord's mother was prepared by divine grace for the role which she had to fulfil in the mystery of our redemption, but have considerable qualms about the correctness of the definition of the Immaculate Conception in 1854, affirming Mary to be untouched by original sin. But then the Orthodox do not have in their bloodstream the Augustinian doctrine of original sin as an inherited psychotic cancer of the soul, common to humanity apart from Christ. The assertion of the pope's universal ordinary and immediate jurisdiction at the first Vatican Council in 1870 looks unilateral to the Orthodox, who have no difficulty about Roman primacy defined in terms of dignity, honour, and leadership. Pius IX's wish to defy the rationalism and liberalism of the secular world was expressed in an assertion of papal authority apart from the universal mind of the Church in the Catholic episcopate, and this was not the way in which the Orthodox have thought about conciliar authority.

The historian can do nothing to make unilateral actions appear constructive in their consequences for the *ecclesia catholica*. They are both a cause and a symptom of division. At the same time the difficulties they cause are also a reflection of the perennial tendency to merge unity and uniformity, and to demand that the 'others' should organize themselves and talk in the same way. That there is mutual confidence of shared faith and common possession of Bible, sacraments, and ministry seems a prerequisite condition for coherence and *koinonia*. But how far diversity can go without threatening separation is, like 'validity', a less objective matter than is often supposed.

A factor that has no doubt operated in unilateral decisions, whether in the Roman Catholic communion or among the Anglicans, is a latent feeling that the separated communions are not serious about the dismantling of barriers between them, and therefore that they do not need to take account of each other or of the judgement of other ecclesial bodies. While there are some fundamental dogmas which have to be universal, there is a legitimate diversity which is regional in origin. The argument for the ordination of women to the priesthood and/or episcopate seems, at least in some statements, to presuppose that in an American or European cultural context it is socially necessary because refusal is felt to be an injustice; such statements can allow for such ordinations not to be required in parts of Africa or Asia where the customs of society would be against them. To think along this line is to suggest perhaps that doctrines and practices binding upon Roman Catholics are not of universal authority, and that there are Anglican usages which Anglicans do not and should not expect others to appropriate, however splendid (like Anglican Chant for the Psalms) the others may think them to be. Within their own community the usages and doctrinal expressions are valid, but that validity is assumed not to be of general extension. We do not expect the customs of Birmingham to obtain in Bokhara.

The problem confronting the remaking of ministry to meet feminist criticism of the tradition is that there is no unanimity on the degree of relativism with which the matter can properly be handled. Unhappily the observation commonly met with that all will be reasonably well as long as diversity is not allowed within a given ecclesial body necessarily presupposes a total indifference to the dismantling of existing barriers between separated ecclesial communions.

In a Western liberal democracy we are acclimatized and conditioned to think that our values should be and are liberal by intuition, and that they are inherent in the culture which is our particularity. A secular liberal democracy does not naturally look for some external source to impart validity and authority to its values and judgements. Moreover, the various versions of liberal democracy in different Western countries are in some degree distinctive, perhaps even 'local'. We do what 'we' do. And the 'we' is coterminous with the society where we find ourselves. Nevertheless, most thoughtful people in the Western democracies would be hesitant before the propositions that the validity of certain customs and values is wholly dependent on what our particular and local society finds congenial or important, and that we do not need to bother our heads whether what we do and believe might need to be related to something universal, or even transcendental.

Unilateral decisions in the Church presuppose that the local and regional should be prior to the universal. That proposition is one to which we citizens of modern liberal democracies in the West are naturally inclined to warm. Nevertheless, there remains a question-mark as soon as the society which is 'we' extends beyond our local and regional frontiers to embrace an ideal universally extended in time and space. What is particular is often entirely compatible with what is 'catholic', both in the sense of universal extension and in the sense of unquestioned sacramental authenticity. But the Church in history has had and still has insoluble or at least hitherto unsolved problems arising from particularities which are felt to conflict with the universal and the unquestionable.

Notes *pp. 12-20*

Chapter 2: Ministry and Tradition

1. For a clear account of the controversy see Timothy Ware, *Eustratios Argenti* (Oxford University Press, 1964) chapter 3. A brief summary in F. Kattenbusch, *Lehrbuch der vergleichenden Confessionskunde* I (1892), 405.

   Rejection of Roman (Catholic) or 'Latin' baptism is sharply formulated in 1054 by the patriarch Michael Cerullarius: see Anton Michel, *Humbert und Kerullarios*, Paderborn, 1930, II 144-151, text at 277, and in C. Will, *Acta et Scripta* (1861), 182.

2. Social instability comes when a ruler reigns over a multiplicity of kingdoms or ethnic regions, as in Britain or in the Iberian peninsula, mainly because the most powerful partner often forgets the weaker partners in making decisions. If (as in 17th century Britain, where England is Anglican, Scotland Presbyterian, and Ireland Roman Catholic—but Wales not yet Baptist) religion is added to this multiplicity, serious civil war can follow.

Chapter 3: The Vindication of Christianity in Westcott's thought

1. A. C. Benson, *The Leaves of the Tree* (1911), pp. 45-6. A. V. Baillie (Dean of Windsor, 1917-45), who had been one of Lightfoot's Auckland Brotherhood, was invited in 1891 to become one of Westcott's chaplains, but refused for reasons which bear out Benson's comment: 'Great as was my admiration for Westcott, I never felt quite happy with him. He seemed so detached and aloof from life. While my whole nature had been warmed by the knowledge that Lightfoot loved me as an individual, I had always a feeling that Westcott's interest in a man was as a specimen of the human race' (Baillie, *My First Eighty Years* (1951), p. 86).

2. Benson, *op. cit.* p. 44.

3. G. W. E. Russell, *Dr Liddon* (1905), p. 174.

4. H. S. Holland, *Personal Studies* (1905), p. 164. Personal contact did something to diminish Liddon's suspicions of Cambridge divines. As colleague of Lightfoot in the chapter at St Paul's he learnt so to respect him that, in spite of unallayed anxieties about his opinions concerning the early history of the episcopate, he could name Lightfoot as one of the orthodox authorities to whom he begged Gore to submit his offensive essay on inspiration before publishing it in *Lux Mundi* (J. O. Johnston, *Life of H. P. Liddon*, p. 366). He had been much touched by the dedication of the second edition of Lightfoot's *Apostolic Fathers*. Scott Holland claimed that Liddon's distrust of Westcott was mitigated by Westcott's courtesy to him, contrasting with Tait's sharpness, when he gave evidence before the Commission on Ecclesiastical Courts (1882). Preaching a university sermon at Cambridge in 1888 he went out of his way to pay a compliment to Westcott and Lightfoot with the declaration that in the defence of the New Testament against the Tübingen critics 'Cambridge has contributed more than her share' (*Sermons on Special Occasions* (1897), pp. 339-40).

5. Samuel Rolles Driver, Fellow of New College from 1870, was Regius Professor of Hebrew in succession to Pusey from 1883 to 1914. William Sanday, Ireland Professor of Exegesis from 1882 and Fellow of Exeter from 1883, was Lady Margaret Professor from 1895 to 1919 and died in 1920.

6. *Selected Letters of William Bright*, ed. Kidd and Medd (1903), pp. 347-8.
7. *Lessons from Work* (1901), p. 63.
8. *The Gospel of Life* (1892), p. xvii.
9. *Op. cit.* p. xviii.
10. *Lessons from Work*, p. 79.
11. *Memoir of Henry Sidgwick* (1906), pp. 393-4.
12. C. K. Barrett, *Westcott as Commentator* (Cambridge, 1959).
13. In a letter to Lightfoot of 24 October 1866 Westcott remarks ironically: 'All the questionable doctrines I have ever maintained are in it' (*Life and Letters*, I, 290).
14. For this and further material to the same effect see Lightfoot, *Essays on the Work entitled Supernatural Religion, reprinted from the Contemporary Review* (1889), p. 24.
15. *Fortnightly Review*, XVI (1874), 504 ff.
16. In a letter to Gladstone of 1895 Lord Acton writes an estimate of Seeley which takes it for granted that he is the author of *Supernatural Religion*, remarking that he 'suffered damage at Lightfoot's hands in his character as a divine' (Figgis and Lawrence, *Lord Acton's Correspondence*, I (1917), 172). The anonymous essay on Lightfoot, attributed to H. W. Watkins, in the *Quarterly Review* (January 1893), reprinted with a preface by Westcott in 1894, similarly refers to 'a writer whose name has never been authoritatively disclosed but is widely known'.
17. In 1889 Lightfoot yielded to pressure from friends and republished the essays as a book, which provoked Cassels to an immediate *Reply to Dr Lightfoot's Essays*. His apologia comes down to saying (a) that while Lightfoot has admittedly corrected some mistakes they are not more than trivialities and his substantial case is unaffected; (b) that while several of his secondary authorities do not support the opinion in the text, he has only prefaced his references by 'cf.', which is not more than an invitation to his readers to look at the opinion of the scholars cited for the sake of comparison and does not imply that they hold the view expressed by Cassels himself; (c) that he has not argued that the Gospels were first written in the second half of the second century, but only that it could not be *certainly* demonstrated that they were written at an earlier date; (d) that since miracles are antecedently incredible, the attempt to vindicate them by claiming the Gospels as eye-witness accounts is foredoomed.

Cassels's last shot was a book on *The Gospel according to Peter* (1894), again published anonymously, arguing that the newly discovered fragment was primitive, independent of the Synoptists, and probably used by Justin Martyr.
18. *Theologische Literaturzeitung* (1890), col. 298.
19. Hort's *Life and Letters*, II, 410.

Chapter 4: 'Ego Berengarius'
1. The old editions of Berengar's Reply to Lanfranc (Vischer, 1834, and Beekenkamp, 1941) are now wholly superseded by the distinguished edition by R. B. C. Huygens, Corpus Christianorum, continuatio medievalis 84 (Turnhout, Brepols, 1988): *Beringerius Turonensis, Rescriptum contra Lanfrannum*. For Lanfranc's attack one must still use the editions of J. A. Giles (Oxford, 1844) and Migne, *PL* 150, 407-42; but important notes on manuscript variants are given by J. de Montclos, *Lanfranc et Bérenger* (Louvain, 1971), pp. 540-5, showing Migne 411 B1-C14 to be

interpolated. On the ideas there are essential guides in M. Gibson, *Lanfranc of Bec* (Oxford, 1978); Gary Macy, *The Theologies of the Eucharist in the early scholastic period* (Oxford, 1984) with his article 'The Theological Fate of Berengar's oath of 1079; interpreting a blunder become tradition', in Jane Kopas (ed.), *Interpreting Tradition*, Annual of the College Theology Society 29 (Chico, Scholars Press, 1983); O. Capitani, *Studi su Berengario di Tours* (Lecce, 1969).

2. Bishop John Fisher's formidable polemic against the Zwinglian Oecolampadius in the 1520s sees Zwingli as reviving the heresy of Berengar and Wyclif (*contra Oecolampadium* II 22 and preface to III; *Opera Omnia*, Würzburg, 1597). Fisher portrays Berengar as at first a Zwinglian who, before Nicholas II in 1059, changed to the Lutheran view that while Christ's true body is present after consecration, the bread and wine remain.

As in some Anglicans (e.g. William Forbes), the Lutheran position did not reject transubstantiation but the defining as an article of necessary faith a school doctrine which Duns Scotus had observed to depend on Church authority rather than on scripture—a view also held at Trent by Melchior Cano whom none could suspect of Protestant sympathy. Perhaps out of respect for Cano's view, the Council of Trent commended *transubstantiatio* as a 'very apt' term for safeguarding the real presence and imposed anathema on its denial, which is perhaps less than requiring its necessary affirmation. The anathema touched not the Lutherans but the Calvinists for whom transubstantiation was appalling heresy. The catechism of Trent presents Berengar as the wicked fool who presumed to deny real presence and so anticipated Protestant heresies. Sixteenth-century debate (especially on the questions whether transubstantiation had been formally defined under anathema at the Fourth Lateran Council of 1215, and what degree of authority that council possessed) fostered the illusion that in 1215 the term transubstantiation was principally used to condemn the long dead Berengar.

Fisher's picture of Berengar as moving from Zwinglianism to Lutheranism is also found in Thomas More, *Confutation of Tyndale's Answer* (Yale edn., VIII 661). John Foxe, however, who had read Bullinger on Berengar, knew that Berengar was no Zwinglian (*Acts and Monuments*, ed. Pratt v 291, vi 330).

3. The *Ego Berengarius* of 1059 is quoted in full by Lanfranc, *de corpore et sanguine domini* 2, *PL* 150, 410D, 411A, whence it passed to the canon collections of Ivo of Chartres, 30 or 40 years later, and so to the massive collection of Gratian where it was inserted in the extra section *De consecratione* on Eucharist, baptism, and confirmation. (D. ii c. 42). Cf. J. H. van Engen, 'Observations on "De consecratione"', *Monumenta Iuris Canonici* C, Subsidia 7, Proc. sixth intern. congr. Medieval Canon Law ed. Stephan Kuttner and K. Pennington (Vatican City, 1985, 309-20).

4. Lanfranc 414D was horrified by Berengar's discovery that Humbert's formula was internally self-contradictory, and declared his principal object in writing to be to show that no such *contrarietas* exists, 415B.

5. Most strikingly in A. J. Macdonald, *Berengar and the Reform of sacramental doctrine* (London

1930), on the historical side a work retaining value, less discerning in theology. For Jean de Montclos (above, n. 1) Berengar is a mere symbolist, a Zwinglian before the time. Although this is oversimplification, Montclos' book is of course indispensable to the study of this subject. It is impossible to write on Berengar without consulting it at every point.

6. Wyclif's cheerful adherence to *Ego Berengarius* is a repeated theme in his *De Eucharistia* and *De Apostasia*; occasionally also elsewhere. (It antedated Satan's release from a millennium in prison, first apparent in Innocent III.) Luther's most strident insistence on its correctness is found in his impassioned anti-Zwinglian tract, *Vom Abendmahl Christi*, 1526 (WA 26, 261-509 at 442 f.); Luther also dissociated himself from Wyclif whose opponents commonly represented him as restating the heresy Berengar's confession denied, and he regretted the comment in the glossa ordinaria on *Ego Berengarius* (below, p. 30). A modern Lutheran treatment very sympathetic to Humbert is K. H. Kandler's *Die Abendmachlslehre des Kardinals Humbert und ihre Bedeutung für das gegenwärtige Abendmahlsgespräch* (Berlin and Hamburg, 1971). Dom B. Neunheuser, *Eucharistie in Mittelalter und Neuzeit*, Handbuch der Dogmengeschichte IV 4b (Herder, 1963), p. 20 is more distant about the formula's 'imperfections' which made it so easy a target for Berengar.

7. Syropoulos' diary of the council of Florence, p. 464 Laurent (Concilium Florentinum 9, 1971). Wyclif, *De apostasia* 4, pp. 55-6, mordantly declares 'I never expected to see the day when an article of faith would need to be

explained by Aristotle and Porphyry', and asserts that, if the Pope is not ultimately subject to scripture in his decrees and dogmas, he might declare the language of substance and accidents divinely inspired. Thomas Netter, *Doctrinale Fidei, Euch.* lxxvi (ii. 461 ed. Blanciotti; Venice, 1757) dismisses Wyclif's remark as a vulgar insult to Innocent III.

8. Hans Jorissen, *Die Entfaltung der Transubstantiationslehre bis zum Beginn der Hochscholastik*, Münsterische Beiträge zur Theologie 28, 1 (Münster, 1965).

9. The classic discussions remain Josef Geiselmann's *Die Eucharistielehre der Vorscholastik* (Paderborn, 1926), and his *Die Abendmahlslehre an der Wende der christlichen Spätantike zum Frühmittelalter* (Munich, 1933).

10. Hincmar of Reims, *De praedestinatione*, ii. 31 (*PL* 125, 296) associated John the Scot with the view that 'sacramenta altaris non verum corpus et verus sanguis sit Domini sed tantum memoria veri corporis et sanguinis eius'. Ivo, *Decretum*, iv. 104 (*PL* 161, 289D) included a warning letter from Pope Nicholas I that John the Scot is suspected of doctrinal deviation.

11. Augustine's texts are best collected by Karl Adam, *Die Eucharistielehre des hl. Augustin* (Paderborn 1908), but few would accept his view that Augustine began with a merely symbolist interpretation and shifted to a more realist understanding. Augustine regarded the Eucharist as both symbol and reality, *sacramentum* and *res* together. See C. Boyer in *Augustinus*, xii (1967), 125-38; M. F. Berrouard in *Bibliothèque Augustinienne* lxxii, 817-19; A. Sage in *Revue des études augustiniennes* xv (1969), 209-40.

12. Lanfranc, *de corpore* 9 (419C) to which Berengar replies, *Rescriptum* II (p. 101 Huygens). Many pages in *Rescriptum* II were devoted to Berengar's exegesis of Ambrose, above all his *De sacramentis*. Berengar's letter 86 (ed. Erdmann) proposes a disputation on the *De sacramentis* with the Dean of Angers Cathedral who was a supporter of Lanfranc.

13. Ambrose, *De sacramentis*, iv. 4, 15-16 (the effect of Christ's words is that 'they are what they were and are changed into something else'). Lanfranc, whose codex of the work survives in Caen library (Le Mans 15), recorded a different reading of the text more favourable to his own theology: *De corpore* 9 (420D). Berengar's reading is supported by the vast majority of manuscripts but in Lanfranc's defence it should be said that his reading is attested by St Gallen 188 (late seventh century).

14. Pellican first expressed doubt (1509) which became conviction by 1525 (letter to Erasmus, ep. 1635, vi, 215 ed. Allen). Zwingli (ed. Corpus Reformatorum) ii, 567, iii, 247, was soon followed by Oecolampadius (1525), and then Bullinger (1535). Melanchthon drew up a patristic florilegium for Philip of Hesse at the Marburg colloquy in October 1529 (Luther, WA Brief v. 1478 p. 158) complaining that Zwingli's rejection of authenticity was motivated by dislike of the work's theology, and judiciously adding that even if the work is not by Ambrose, it is very ancient. Oecolampadius composed a counter florilegium in 1530 (*Quid de eucharistia veteres tum Graeci tum Latini senserint Dialogus*). I have not seen Gottfried Hoffmann, *Sententiae Patrum: das patristische Argument in der Abendmahlskontro-* verse zwischen Oekolampad, Zwingli, Luther und Melanchthon (Diss. Heidelberg 1971). The main reports on the Marburg colloquy are conveniently gathered by Gerhard May, *Das Marburger Religionsgespräch 1529* (Gütersloh, Mohn, 1970); Osiander (p. 55) mentions debate on patristic texts including Ambrose.

O. Faller's critical edition of *De Sacramentis* is in *CSEL* 73 (1955) with bibliography of the debate since (not before) 1690; R. H. Connolly, *The De Sacramentis a work of St Ambrose* (1942) presents decisive arguments for authenticity, to which no reply has been made.

15. *Rescriptum contra Lanfrannum*, iii. 751 ff. (pp. 210-11 Huygens). Guitmund of Aversa, *De veritate corporis ete sanguinis*, i (*PL* 149, 1438C) is driven to appeal to the fallibility of the senses which, for example, see an oar in the water as crooked. Berengar's problem was still worrying Duns Scotus two centuries after his time.

16. Lanfranc 420D 'commutari secundum interiorem essentiam'; 430BC 'credimus igitur terrenas substantias . . . converti in essentiam dominici corporis'. He understands Berengar to believe that the bread and wine remain 'quantum ad substantiam' (440B).

17. Ambrose, *De sacramentis*, iv, 3, 10; a favourite passage of Berengar.

18. *De sacr*. iv, 6, 27 (in the Milan canon missae); *Rescriptum*, ii, 2661 ff.

19. *Rescriptum*, ii. 523 'inefficax erat panis natura ante consecrationem ad vitam aeternam, post consecrationem efficax'. In his account of the Roman synod of 1079 he says 'efficacia ad salutem animae' (line 229, ed. Huygens, *Sacris Erudiri*, 16, (1965), 399).

20. ii. 460. 912. Berengar affirms 'conversio intelligibilis' (1503), a concept akin to 'transubstantiatio' as later expounded.
21. ii. 1790 ff.
22. ii. 1827 ff.
23. Giles's text omits *nisi* after *sensualiter*; *nisi* is attested by part of the ms. tradition, and by Ivo.
24. *Rescriptum* i. 911. 1116-17. Berengar thought the formula of 1059 eliminated the religiously vital idea of *mysterium*: iii. 617 ff. (p. 207 Huygens).
25. The early correspondence between Berengar and Lanfranc had brought Lanfranc under as much suspicion as Berengar (413A). In writing *De corpore*, therefore, Lanfranc was in some degree silencing whispers that at heart he too had reservations about Humbert's formula.
26. Lanfranc (5, 415B) ascribes to Berengar a denial of *material* change. Berengar, *Rescr*. i. 1057, 1130, denies that he would use such language: he denied only such change as annihilates the subject or substance. The consecrated species are 'not common bread and wine but sacrosanct' (ii. 2582).
27. Cited by Lanfranc 421A; confirmed by *Rescr*. iii. 633. Cf. Aug. *Tract. in Joh*. 50. 12-13. On the ground that Christ's glorified body is at the Father's right hand, Lollards did not bow at the elevation but gazed up to heaven (Netter, *de Euch*. 56, 341 Blanciotti).
28. William of St Thierry (*PL* 180, 360C) ascribes to Augustine the formula 'et ipsum est corpus et non ipsum'.
29. Huygen's new edition of Berengar's *Rescriptum contra Lanfrannum* is twinned with a facsimile volume (Corpus Christianorum, Continuatio mediaevalis 84A, 1988) with an introduction by Wolfgang Milde on the manuscript itself. This has clarified much that was previously unclear. The work contains no reference to Lanfranc's promotion to the see of Canterbury and is therefore probably before 1070.

30. Donatus: *Rescr*. iii 80 ff. Elsewhere Berengar specially delights in grammatical points. Boethius: i. 1161-5, citing *contra Eutychen,* praef. 31-3, as also in the account of the Roman synod of 1079 (lines 56-60, ed. Huygens in *Sacris Eruditi* 16 (1965), 392). Another reminiscence of Boethius' Opuscula Sacra occurs at *Rescr*. i. 1070 f., echoing *De Hebdomadibus*, Opusc. Sacra iii. 41 ff. ed. Rand.

On grammar and dialectic in the dispute see Sir Richard Southern, 'Lanfranc of Bec and Berengar of Tours', *Studies in medieval history presented to F. M. Powicke* (Oxford 1948, repr. 1969), 27-48.
31. Similarly, Boethius, *In Isagogen Porphyrii*, I. 2, p. 6, 5 ff. Brandt (CSEL 48) '. . . ut neque accidens sine substantia neque sine accidenti substantia esse posset' (cf. p. 16, 1 also).
32. Printed among Alcuin's works in Migne, *PL* 100. 1077BC. The source is John Chrysostom, *Hom. in ep. ad Hebr*. 17, 3, *PG* 63, 131; Mutianus' Latin translation at p. 348.
33. See the canon 'ex concilio Turonico cap. 4' in Ivo of Chartres, *Decretum*, ii. 19 (*PL* 161, 165B) The Epistle of Clement to James (ibid. 24) directed that the remains at the Eucharist be reverently consumed. In the eleventh century it was customary in the West to consume the remains by fire (e.g. Guitmund, *PL* 149, 1450A). The Jerusalem custom, brought westwards by pilgrims, was to reserve the remains in a pyx and distribute

to the people at the next communion; Humbert accused Michael Cerularius of carelessness, burying remaining species in the earth (C. Will, *Acta et Scripta* (1861), pp. 109 and 146). Cf. 'Fragmentum disputationis contra Graecos' in Martène-Durand, *Thesaurus Anecd.* v (1717), 851C 'You bury Christ's body in the earth and compel him to see corruption'. That the location of the pyx was not publicly marked is evident from Caesarius of Heisterbach, *Mirac.* ix. 35.

34. *Rescr.* i. 1791. 1800 citing Augustine, *De ordine*, ii. 13. 38.

35. Ratramnus is critically edited by J. Bakhuizen van den Brink; Paschasius by B. Paulus (Corpus Christianorum, Continuatio mediaevalis 16 (1969)). Heriger's piece is printed in *PL* 139, 179-88 under Gerbert's name; on the authorship see C. R. Shrader in *Medieval Studies*, 35 (1973), 178-204.

36. Lanfranc 427B. 435C. At chap. 10, 421C Lanfranc cites the *Passio S. Andreae* 6 (ed. M. Bonnet, Acta Apostolorum Apocrypha ii. 13). The Acts of Andrew were condemned in the *Decretum Gelasianum*, which Ivo incorporated in his *Decretum*, iv, 65 (*PL* 161, 280C).

37. See the *Gesta Romanae ecclesiae contra Hildebrandum*, by Benno and other anti-Gregorian cardinals, printed in Monumenta Germ. Hist., *Libelli de lite* ii p. 370. The charge of being 'an old disciple of Berengar' appeared at the Synod of Brixen (June 1080) where the bishops supporting the emperor Henry IV declared Gregory deposed. Gregory's protection of Berengar is explicit in two spurious but contemporary letters in the pope's name; printed in H. E. J. Cowdrey, *The Epistolae Vagantes of Pope Gregory VII* (Oxford, 1972), pp. 156-7.

38. It is noteworthy that the consecration is both by prayer and by the words of the Lord. 'Per mysterium sacrae orationis' comes from Ambrose, *De fide* iv. 10, 124 (*CSEL* 78, 201) via Durandus of Troarn, *PL* 149. 1403C.

39. The protocol of the Roman synod of 11 Feb. 1079 is preserved in Gregory VII's Register in the Vatican archive, printed in E. Caspar's edition, ii. 425-7. From the Register it passed into a few canon collections, especially in English manuscripts. Berengar's new confession is recorded in the chronicle of Hugh of Flavigny (*PL* 154, 316 = *MGH SS*, viii. 443) and in the Life of Gregory in the *Liber Pontificalis*, ii 285-86 Duchesne. Nevertheless, the new *Ego Berengarius* never became widely diffused or discussed. (I have to thank Dr Martin Brett for help on this point.)

40. Apart from its place in the protocol of the synod (Reg. vi, 17a), Berengar's new confession was also inscribed on a blank sheet at iii, 17a (fo. 109) as a subsequent addition. In regard to ignorance of Gregory VII's formula, Bellarmine, who had read Thomas Netter and knew of the council, could note with surprise that Duns Scotus evidently knew nothing of it: *De eucharistia*, iii, 23. I know of no reference in Aquinas.

41. Thomas Netter Waldensis, *Doctrinale fidei*, De eucharistia 42-3 (ii. 265-9 ed. Blanciotti).

42. Adelmann's letter to Berengar is edited by Huygens in *Studi Medievali* viii (1967), 476-89. Berengar's letter to Adelmann, which survives only in some fragments, is edited by J. de Montclos, *Lanfranc et Bérenger* (1971), 531-9; corrections by H. Silvestre in *Recherches de*

Théologie ancienne et mediévale, xxxix (1972), 127-30. On Berengar's debt to Fulbert see F. Behrends, 'Berengar of Tours, Fulbert of Chartres, and Fulbertus exiguus', *Revue Bénédictine* 85 (1975), 333-47.

43. See J. H. van Engen, *Rupert of Deutz* (Los Angeles, 1983); M. L. Arduini, *Neue Studien über Rupert von Deutz*, Siegburger Studien 17 (Siegburg, 1985). Rupert's works are edited by H. Haacke in Corpus Christianorum, where the column numbers in Migne are noted in the margins.

44. There are judicious pages on Alger in Cardinal Henri de Lubac, *Corpus Mysticum: L'eucharistie et l'Eglise au moyen âge* (2nd edn. Paris, 1949), 166-7, 173 f: Alger's juxtapositions and even concordisms anticipate Abelard's *Sic et Non* 117 (*PL* 178. 1518-37).

45. J. Geiselmann, *Die Abendmahlslehre an der Wende der christliche Spätantike zum Frühmittelalter* (Munich, 1933), 60-4 demonstrates Alger's method in detail.

46. Florus, *adversus Amalarium* 9 (*PL* 119, 78A) appeals to the prayer 'Quod ore sumpsumus domine, mente capiamus' in the old Latin sacramentaries; for example, the Gregorian Sacramentary, 302, p. 165, Deshusses. From this Florus makes the deduction 'Therefore this food is of the mind, not of the stomach.' (Florus echoes Augustine, *Sermo*, 57, 7; cf. *Tract. in Joh.* 25, 12.) Berengar has a similar argument (*Rescr.* iii. 477 = 704) from the prayer in the Gregorian Sacramentary, 234, p. 148 'ut quae ore contingimus, pura mente capiamus'.

47. A. M. Gietl, *Die Sentenzen Rolands nachmals Papstes Alexander III* (Freiburg i-B, 1891),

233. This and similar utterances by twelfth-century schoolmen are gathered in a notable paper by L. Hödl, 'Die confessio Berengarii von 1059, eine Arbeit zum frühscholastischen Eucharistietraktat', in *Scholastik*, xxxvii (1962), 370-94.

48. Ed. R. Martin (Louvain, 1938), p. 211.

49. *PL* 192, 865. Alan of Lille (d. 1203) lays down that it is only 'by improper use of language that the body of Christ is said to be broken or ground with teeth', since that belongs to the *formae* of bread and wine. (*Theologicae Regulae* 108, *PL* 210, 679A; cf. *Distinctiones* 890C).

50. Odon Lottin, *Psychologie et Morale aux XIIe et XIIIe siècles* V (Gembloux 1959) p. 55, prints a text from Anselm of Laon (d. 1117): 'ut pueris solet tantum vinum dari, rusticis propter frequentiam populi panis' (a text which continues by explaining that only the outward species suffers fraction or grinding by teeth while 'dominicum corpus integrum remanet').

51. *Tractatus de fractione corporis Christi, PL* 166. 1341-8.

52. *De sacro altaris mysterio, PL* 217, 773-916.

53. Peter Martyr Vermigli, *Defensio doctrinae veteris et apostolicae de sacrosancto eucharistiae sacramento* (1559), pp. 225 f., hurls the Ego Berengarius of 1059 against Stephen Gardiner's disavowal that Catholic belief entails the presence of Christ's body 'in pane realiter, corporaliter, naturaliter'. Calvin (*Inst.* iv. 17. 12 f.) regards Ego Berengarius as the naked truth about transubstantiation which sophisticated schoolmen vainly tried to provide with a decent figleaf of qualifications. It did not occur to him that for Alexander III and Innocent III the

merit of transubstantiation was that it did not entail the 'sensualiter' theme of Humbert's formula.

54. In Netter's *Doctrinale Fidei*, 'De eucharistia' (vol. ii, ed. Blanciotti) Wyclif's dependence on Berengar is a leading theme. The text cited is at chapter 52 (ii. 341). For an erudite collection of authors who paired Wyclif with Berengar in the fourteenth century see Anne Hudson, *The Premature Reformation* (Oxford, 1988) p. 286 n. 47).

55. 'Nisi sane intelligas verba Berengarii, in maiorem incides haeresim quam ipse habuit.' This marginal note appears in the Glossa ordinaria of Johannes Teutonicus (*c.* 1216) printed in sixteenth-century editions of Gratian (not in Friedberg's edition) in comment on Ego Berengarius. In his vast commentary on Gratian of the fifteenth century, Torquemada (Turrecremata) comments ad loc. that in the schools it is a question 'whether the formula is erroneous or catholic'. Except figuratively it cannot be right to say that Christ's glorified body can be broken or eaten, for it is in heaven; nor that bread and wine are his body and blood whether before or after consecration. Christ's body cannot be broken or eaten 'sensualiter . . . nisi in solo sacramento'. Yet had the Confession been uncatholic, the immaculate apostolic see would never have approved it.

As the Council of Trent in February 1547 the French Franciscan Jean Consilii vigorously defended transubstantiation against the Protestant charge of innovation by the argument that before Berengar the term was not needed, and that although his Confession has words 'either false or exaggerated', that is all

explained by the gloss (*Conc. Trid.* v. 944. 27 ff.; 950. 38-41).

56. Luther, *Vom Abendmahl Christi, Bekenntnis*, WA 26, 442 f.

57. John Jewel, *Reply to M. Harding* (Works, Parker Society, 1845), i. 458 f. The influence of Martyr on Jewel was regretted by, for example, William Forbes Bishop of Edinburgh (d. 1634), *Considerationes modestae pacificae* (1658), *De eucharistia*, I, ii, 12 (Oxford 1856, p. 443). Among the Laudians, however, John Cosin's *History of Transubstantiation*, chapter 7, (admittedly a book marred by inaccuracies), is strikingly sympathetic to Berengar. Cosin's account of the Fourth Lateran Council lay wide open to the well-reasoned attack by Thomas Vane, *An Answer to a Libell . . .* (Paris, 1646). I owe the reference to Dr G. R. Evans.

58. Special interest attaches to the position of the Anglican John Johnson, *The Unbloody Sacrifice and Altar unveiled and supported* (1715, repr. Oxford 1847), for whom the spiritual presence of Christ's body and blood is necessary for the reality of the representative offering to the Father (vol. I, p. 263). This point was never made, to the best of my knowledge, in the controversies of early scholasticism. But it is implicit in Nicolas Cabasilas' *Expositio Liturgiae*, xxxii (*PG* 150. 440-1); E T by J. M. Hussey and P. A. McNulty (London, SPCK, 1960). In Lanfranc and twelfth-century schoolmen, the presence is real, the immolation symbolic.

59. Zacharias, *PL* 176. 508B; Caesarius iv. 56. Zacharias judged Berengar's offence to be his criticism of accepted Church usage, thereby presenting a challenge to authority. Sacramentology was in incoherent flux before the second book of

Ivo's *Decretum* gathered the conciliar canons and papal rulings to
give an authoritative guide to
Eucharistic belief and practice.
The canonistic movement in Ivo
and Gratian was to concentrate
in the Roman see the source of
ultimate juridical authority in
such matters.

60. *PL* 199. 1153-4.

Chapter 7: Full Communion with other Episcopal Churches

1. Among the provinces of the
    Anglican Communion, the pre-
    sent position is that there are
    differences of discipline concern-
    ing the admission of women
    priests to celebrate outside their
    own diocese or province. If
    fraternal relations between
    bodies in full communion are to
    be maintained, similar rules must
    evidently be in force in the wider
    context.

2. Reference should be made to the
    report of the English Arch-
    bishops' Commission, *Intercom-
    munion Today*, (CIO, London
    1968), which is a dintinguished
    analysis of the problem.

3. This position is censured in
    Article 28 of the 39 Articles of
    the Church of England, whose
    language is echoed in this
    sentence.

4. In many places relations are
    highly amicable, notably in
    regions where the uninitiated
    might not expect this, such as the
    diocese of Sydney.

5. For Duchesne's opinion, cf.
    Bruno Neveu, '*Mgr Duchesne et
    Son Memoire sur les Ordinations
    Anglicanes* (1895 ou 1896)',
    Journal of Theological Studies,
    n.s. 29, 1978, pp. 443-82. At a
    popular level it is still common
    for Roman Catholics to express
    the belief that, until such time
    as the see of Rome declares
    Anglican ministry valid, there is
    nothing but illusion in Anglican

faith in the reality of Christ's
presence and grace in the sacraments. One does not hear this, of
course, from theologians.

6. The Windsor (*Eucharistic Doc-
    trine*, SPCK, London 1971) and
    Canterbury (*Ministry and Ordi-
    nation*, SPCK, London 1973)
    statements have generally been
    welcomed, except by critics look-
    ing for the comfort of familiar
    formulae. The Venice statement
    (*Authority in the Church*,
    CTS/SPCK, London 1977) has
    attracted more vocal complaints:
    (a) from conservative Roman
    Catholics for its inductive rather
    than deductive approach to
    primacy; (b) from liberal
    Anglicans for its assumption
    that Anglicans believe in divine
    revelation; (c) from readers who
    have wondered why the four
    difficulties listed in para. 24 of
    the Venice statement are thought
    to constitute a sufficient obstacle
    to communion (if indeed they
    are). The suggestion that the
    statement does not uphold the
    supreme authority of Scripture is
    irreconcilable with the text of the
    document, unless supreme means
    exclusive.

Chapter 8: Justification by Faith: a perspective

1. *Table-Talk*, WA ii p. 138
    'Augustinus non recte intellegit
    articulum justificationis.'

2. There are provinces of the
    Anglican Communion where no
    mention is made of the Articles,
    and others (as in the United
    States, for example) where in a
    revised form they are printed as
    historical documents for ease of
    reference but no one is asked to
    assent to them. In the Church of
    England at ordination a can-
    didate declares his assent to the
    faith which is revealed in the
    Holy Scriptures and set forth in
    the Catholic Creeds and to which

the historic formularies bear witness—the Prayer Book, the Ordinal, and the Thirty-Nine Articles.

3. Some of the propositions from Quesnel condemned in the Bull 'Unigenitus' (1713) sound very like the kind of high Augustinian/Calvinist doctrine that some Evangelicals feel a debt to. The doctrine of the Bull is of great intricacy. It is not normally reckoned among the papal utterances to which the tag 'infallible' or 'ex cathedra' is to be attached. But I take it that Roman Catholics are the proper judges of the magisterial status of their own ecclesiastical documents. I sometimes find myself puzzled when Roman Catholics want to tell me what the doctrine of the Anglican Church is, and feel sure that Anglicans ought to exercise care in telling Roman Catholics which papal statements carry the supreme status. Here I think it sufficient to say that the Bull Unigenitus and the outcome of the Jansenist controversy illustrate the general consensus that an extreme Augustinianism denying free will and asserting irresistible grace is not characteristic of the Roman Catholic Church any more than of the predominant theology found in the Anglican Communion.

4. The theme of co-operation with grace appears in some things Catholics say about the place of the Blessed Virgin as model to the Church in faith, obedience, and holiness. I am not clear that there is inherent tension between Roman Catholic Marian dogmas and a biblical understanding of justification.

5. A pamphlet on the doctrine of Assurance by Michael Griffiths, widely current among Evangelicals in England, is careful to draw a distinction between proper confidence in the promises of God and the 'presumption' of claiming to possess a personal indefectibility as one of the elect, irrespective of neglect of the given means of grace. The author's concern is self-evidently identical with that of Trent.

Chapter 11: Newman, a man for our Time

The following abbreviations are used:

LD   *Letters and Diaries of John Henry Newman*, ed. C. S. Dessain et al. (Oxford University Press, 1961-84).

PPS *Parochial and Plain Sermons* (1868 edition): 8 vols.

VM   Via Media (1896 edition): 2 vols.

1. LD XXVI, pp. 299, 364.
2. J. H. Newman, *Autobiographical Writings*, ed. Henry Tristram (1956), pp. 254-5: 'How forlorn and dreary has been my course since I have been a Catholic! Here has been the contrast—as a Protestant, I felt my religion dreary, not my life—but as a Catholic, my life dreary, not my religion . . . I doubt whether I can point to any joyful event of this world besides my scholarship at Trinity and my fellowship at Oriel—but since I have been a Catholic, I seem to myself to have had nothing but failure, personally' (1863).

    Only the last decade, in a glow as Honorary Fellow of Trinity and then astonishingly a Cardinal, during which years he did nothing but say his prayers, was a time of recognition in the Church of his adoption. The sermons and letters before 1841 do not suggest that, prior to his loss of confidence in the Church of England, Newman found Prayer Book services dreary.

3. James Bryce, by upbringing an Ulster Presbyterian, in February 1875 when he was Regius Professor of Civil Law at Oxford,

called on Newman at the Birmingham Oratory, and found him 'not a priest in his manner—still an Englishman more than a R. Catholic' (LD XXVII, p. 238n). In the *Letter to the Duke of Norfolk* (1875) Newman wrote of there being 'no inconsistency in being a good Catholic and a good Englishman' (*Diff. Angl.* II, p. 177). A letter of 1866 from Manning to Monsignor Talbot in Rome complained of Newman's Catholic writings: 'It is the old Anglican, patristic, literary, Oxford tone transplanted into the Church' (Purcell's *Life of Manning*, 1896, II, p. 323). A letter of 1847 records how old Catholic families regarded the Oxford converts with 'cold curiosity' (LD XII, p. 19).

After 9 October 1845 English Protestants quickly brought the accusation that for many years past Newman had been a secret Romanist plotting against the Church of his baptism, and soon Henry Wilberforce was begging Newman to send a disavowal (LD XII, pp. 19-20). That in the 1830s Newman held Catholic doctrine concerning eucharistic presence and sacrifice, priesthood, apostolic succession, and (in the main) justification is beyond doubt. But he moved only slowly and with reluctance to the view that the Roman Catholic Church is, simply, the one authentic communion, all others being in schism or heresy or both. Episcopal denunciations of Tract 90 were causative in convincing him that only Rome taught and guarded Catholic truth. 'If all the world agrees in telling a man he has no business in our Church, he will at length begin to think he has none' (6 March 1842, *Keble Corresp.*, p. 187). A long time at Littlemore was required to convince him

that his motive for becoming a Roman Catholic was not mixed with anger at the English Church's dreadful treatment of him (passionately expressed in his sermon on the parting of friends). He could not justify himself in moving from one branch of the Catholic Church to another branch that might seem preferable. He had to feel convinced that 'Catholicism is a different religion' (LD XII, p. 224), and that Anglicans cannot be part of the Church if they do not condemn Adoptionists and Agnoetae, or if they fail to teach purgatorial fire and the need for clerical celibacy (ibid., p. 235).

4. Tract 38 (VM II, p. 20) and a letter of July 1834 (LD IV, p. 314) show Newman to have supposed that in 1530 the Diet of Augsburg approved the Lutheran Confession. On the recalling of the anniversary of his evangelical conversion, after his conversion to Rome, see LD XI, p. 252 of 24 September 1846.

5. *Lectures on (the doctrine of) Justification*, 3rd edn, p. 161. Newman's *Lectures on Justification* (1838) went through five editions in his lifetime (1840, 1874, 1885, 1890). I have discussed the argument of the book in the volume *Newman after a Hundred Years*, edited by I. T. Ker and A. G. Hill (Oxford 1990). A masterly study of Evangelicals is Boyd Hilton's *The Age of Atonement* (Oxford 1988).

6. Chap. 1; cf. LD XV, pp. 175-9. Spitting: LD XXII, pp. 217-18. His distaste for liberalism led him strangely to deny having even read Whately's *Logic* (LD XXVI, p. 164) to which he had actually contributed.

7. LD IV, p. 189. Newman (LD IV, p. 165) agreed with Whately on the unsuitability of Parliament for governing church matters.

8. R. Whately, *Letters on the Church* (1826), p. 174.
9. See Whately's *Romanism* (1878 edn), pp. 48-49; *Thoughts on Christian moral Instruction*, Charge, 1854, p. 13.
10. *Univ. Sermons* x, p. 200.
11. See W. J. A. M. Beek, *John Keble's literary and religious Contribution to the Oxford Movement* (Nijmegen 1959), and thereon Owen Chadwick's review in *JTS* ns 11 (1960), p. 429.
12. LD XXI, p. 378.
13. *Remains* I, p. 35, a note of 1 November 1826.
14. Froude, *Rem.* I, p. 379; a letter from Newman in Anne Mozley's edition, II, p. 403. Allusions to Scott's Novels are not infrequent in Newman's letters. In the *Letter to Jelf* written in defence of Tract 90, Newman claims to be blood-brother to Scott, Coleridge, and Wordsworth. He had certainly read more of Coleridge than he wished others to know (LD IV, pp. 256, 289; V, p. 53); see the splendid anecdote in Harold Anson, *Looking Forward* (1968), p. 63, recording Newman's saying to Acland that he could not read Coleridge because he did not live with Mrs Coleridge. (In general see H. F. Davis in *Dublin Review* 435 (1945), pp. 165-73.)
15. *Remains* II, pp. 383-411 = Tract 63. Newman in LD VI, p. 226; VM II, pp. 217f.
16. *Rem.* I, p. 336.
17. See Froude's letter to Newman of 4 March 1835 in LD V, p. 68; also *Remains* I, p. 363 of 8 April 1834. The same principle for interpreting the Articles is stated in Keble's sermon on Tradition (1836). It was an accepted Tractarian axiom substantially before Tract 90. Panic led the Hebdomadal Board to invite Convocation to approve a declaration that the Articles are to be subscribed in their original

sense and in that 'now to be proposed'.
18. LD VI, p. 18.
19. PPS I, p. 20, echoing Augustine, *Soliloquia*, i, 2, 7.
20. LD V, p. 40, March 1835.
21. VM II, p. 236. LD XXI, pp. 13-14 of 8 January 1864 records that, as an Anglican, Newman felt Protestants to be lax on purity. In Rome in 1847 he found the people unquestioning in faith, but dishonest (and dirty): 'They have not that *living* faith which leads to . . . sanctity' (LD XII, p. 24).
22. While Newman (according to the *Apologia*) looked back on this sermon, heard on the Sunday after his return from Sicily where he had nearly died, as the starting-point of the Oxford Movement, Isaac Williams (*Autobiography*, pp. 95-6) records that in the opinion of most people the sermon was 'indiscreet and fruitless'. The resemblance of Keble's character (hatred of humbug, playfulness, oddity, sensitivity to others, and severity) to that of St Philip Neri was among the factors leading Newman to become an Oratorian (LD XII, p. 25).
23. Letter to Faussett of 1838, VM II, p. 210.
24. LD VI, p. 61. All statements of a Via Media tend to become negative by stressing what is not to be said rather than what is.
25. VM I, p. 83.
26. Pusey (*Letter to the Bishop of Oxford*, 1839, p. 136) thought 'the miserable state of Roman Catholic countries' a consequence of withholding the cup from the laity.
27. Newman liked the statement of the (anti-Roman) Joseph Hall (1574-1656), bishop of Norwich: 'O blessed Mary, he cannot bless thee, he cannot honour thee too much, that deifies thee not' (cited

in LD XXI, p. 34, a letter of 1 February 1864). He was careful never to read *The Glories of Mary* by St Alfonso Liguori (*Diff. Angl.* II, p. 98).

The *Essay on Development* of 1845 sought to turn the edge of the Anglican arguments that late medieval centralization in the papal monarchy had left Anglicans more closely continuous with the ancient patristic Church than Rome, and the apostolic succession, even without universality of communion, was a sufficient guarantee of authenticity (cf. LD XI, p. 28).

28. Edward Norman, *The English Catholic Church in the Nineteenth Century* (Oxford 1984), p. 6.
29. The printed sermons sold well, and provided Newman with a steady income. Keble told Newman that reading them was 'the next thing to talking with you' (*Keble Corresp.* 1917, p. 217). The re-editing of PPS by W. J. Copeland (1868), who remained Anglican, led Newman to reissue his other Anglican works (LD XXVI, p. 293).
30. LD V, p. 32. (The letter is dated 27 February 1835.)
31. e.g. PPS I, pp. 32 ff. on those who admire biblical prose, though it contains much they themselves would not have said but which is suitable for the lower classes; or V, p. 42, 'A man of literature is considered to preserve his dignity by doing nothing.'
32. PPS III, p. 195.
33. *Diff. Angl.* I, p. 7; cf. PPS II, p. 289. The conclusion is not as compelling as Newman thought. Archbishop John Bird Sumner who gave this answer would have been regarded as heretical by a high Anglican for so speaking (so LD XII, p. 204; cf. XXV, p. 429). A heretical or ill-instructed

archbishop no more speaks authoritatively for the Anglican communion than a similarly disqualified pope, such as Honorius (condemned by the Sixth Ecumenical Council for heresy), on behalf of the Roman see. Newman can suggest that even a heretical pope, when speaking *ex cathedra*, could be protected from error as much as Balaam or Caiaphas (LD XXV, pp. 355f, of 10 July 1871). This reflects less a confidence in papal inerrancy than a faith that the universal Church will not be misled when not quite correctly instructed by bishops.

34. See, for example, on the Church PPS III, pp. 190ff., 206ff.; apostolic succession II, p. 401; IV, pp. 174ff.; priesthood II, pp. 300ff.; baptism II, p. 93 etc.; Eucharist II, p. 249; IV, p. 147; VI, pp. 136-141; frequent communion V, p. 28. A poetic passage on the sacraments in V, pp. 10-11; Immaculate Conception of BVM in II, p. 132.
35. PPS, IV, p. 36.
36. ibid., IV, p. 138.
37. ibid., VI, p. 108.
38. ibid., V, p. 183.
39. ibid., VI, p. 307.
40. ibid., VI, p. 80, esp. IV, pp. 12-13.
41. ibid., III, p. 13.
42. ibid., IV, p. 160.
43. ibid., V, pp. 288ff., 337.
44. ibid., V, p. 350.
45. See, for example, PPS V, pp. 288ff., 337; also polemically anti-Anglican statement in LD XII, p. 273 written in 1848 (the Anglican clergyman is gentleman, scholar, kindhearted father of the family, no saint). Denunciations of worldliness drew Anglican congregations at St Mary's; they were not well received in Rome in 1847 (LD XII, p. 13), where a critique of worldly Catholics was resented.

46. The custom was a consequence of requiring communicants for a celebration. A number of parish churches celebrated the Communion quarterly. Newman introduced an early communion each Sunday at St Mary's in 1837.

A letter of 1864 records that the wine customarily used for Anglican Communion services was called (ironically enough) 'Trent', and was laced with brandy, treacle and raspberry vinegar, so that it was unpleasant unless diluted with water (LD XXI, p. 77). This report goes strangely with Newman's hostile accounts of Anglican Communion services at which the remains of the wine were the excuse for a merry and profane party in the vestry afterwards (LD XII, p. 293 and elsewhere), such a scandal being treated as typical and characteristic.

47. PPS III, p. 310; VI, p. 188.

48. LD VI, pp. 42, 125. Anglo-Catholic borrowing of Roman ceremonial later seemed to Newman sectarian (LD XII, p. 157 of 19 January 1848).

49. LD VI, p. 89 of 1837.

50. LD VI, p. 139. On the Laudian custom of bowing at Jesus' name, PPS V, p. 19.

51. Ward's book, *The Ideal of a Christian Church* (1844), claimed the right to hold and teach every article of Roman Catholic faith and devotional practice and yet to remain in the Church of England. The ingenuity of the argument provoked anger. In February 1845 he was censured and deprived of his degree (given on the assumption that the recipient accepted the Thirty-Nine Articles); but at the same occasion in the Sheldonian a censure of Tract 90 was vetoed by the Proctors, evidently on the ground that Tract 90 expressed a legitimate position where Ward's book did not. Newman expressed gratitude, even though by that date his confidence in the Church of England had evaporated.

52. See the letter to the lawyer, E. L. Badeley, of 23 August 1844, printed in *Keble Corresp.* 1917, p. 327. On the incomprehensibility to Newman of Pusey's remaining an Anglican see the striking letter to Catherine Ward of 25 September 1848 (LD XII, pp. 268-75), cataloguing the Protestantisms of seventeenth century Laudians. Perhaps he did not believe in the Real Presence (LD XIII, p. 455)?

53. See Thirlwall's *Charges* I (*Remains literary and theological*, ed. J. J. S. Perowne, 1877), pp. 1-52. Thirlwall regarded the controversy about justification as one of words, involving no real difference of opinion; that about Scripture and tradition as more theoretical than actual; apostolic succession 'has been held by a large part of our best divines'. Newman's treatment of Article 22 could not be supported; but a denial of the general legitimacy of his position would be wrong. Thirlwall's *Charge* of 1848 (ibid., pp. 99-140) is a frontal attack on the *Essay on Development*, sharing J. B. Mozley's judgement that the presuppositions of that book are deeply sceptical. Newman was grateful for the *Charge* of 1842, offended by that of 1848 (LD XXVI, p. 235).

54. *Discussions and Arguments*, p. 343: 'England . . . the paradise of little men, the purgatory of great ones.' On Newman's long agony see above n. 3.

55. This question had disturbed him since Wiseman's article in the *Dublin Review*, quoting Augustine's triumphant sentence refuting the Donatist claim to be the sole survival of the true Church, the rest of Christendom

outside N. Africa being polluted: *Securus iudicat orbis terrarum*— 'the world judges that without the least anxiety'. The requirement of universality put a question mark against Anglicanism without vindicating Roman claims to be its embodiment. The argument's force was of course great if one believed the papacy to be occupied by Antichrist. And if one did not so believe, it became a question whether the separation of the sixteenth century could be justified.

56. LD XXVII, p. 138. Roman refusal to accept the validity of Anglican Orders (which Newman came to think doubtful) has tended to obscure the fact that far more vehement attacks came from Puritans who found Cranmer's Ordinal indistinguishable from the Pontifical.

57. Newman admired and liked Acton personally, and thought the excommunication of Döllinger cruel; but he did not share their difficulties with *Pastor aeternus*. No doubt that was not only because he had long held to the infallibility of the Church and to the propriety of seeing the pope as the organ and voice of decision in teaching authority, but also because he held that the interpretation of an *ex cathedra* utterance depends upon long study by the *Schola theologorum* and upon the sense in which it is ultimately received by the faithful. Newman did not envisage instant, unreflecting acceptance. The truth of a definition should be 'manifest', as stated in the ARCIC I *Final Report* A II 29, p. 95 (a text surprisingly criticized by the Congregation for the Doctrine of the Faith since the same doctrine is in the 1983 Code of Canon Law, 749, 3).

58. See the texts printed in Cuthbert Butler's *Life of Bishop Ulla-*thorne*, II, pp. 101-5, and in LD XXVII, pp. 401-11. It is part of the paradox of Newman that the view of the magisterium which converted him to Roman Catholicism was utterly uncongenial at Rome. He understood authority to lie in what Ian Ker has called a creative interplay between the magisterium and private judgement (*John Henry Newman: A Biography*, 1988, p. 523, quoting LD XX, pp. 425-6).

59. E. Burke, *Speech on the Acts of Uniformity* (1772).

Chapter 12: Newman's doctrine of Justification

1. The title in the first and second editions (1838, 1840) lacked the bracketed words. The copies of the first and third editions at the Birmingham Oratory have corrections in Newman's hand. The fourth and fifth editions appeared in 1886 and 1890. A French translation by E. Robillard and M. Labelle has a valuable introduction and notes by Robillard (Montreal, 1980).

2. For the Lutherans there is a reliable guide in R. D. Preus, *The Theology of Post-Reformation Lutheranism*, 2 vols. (St Louis and London, 1970-2). For a brief survey of the main Calvinist writers, see E. Bizer's introduction to his edition of H. Heppe, *Die Dogmatik der evangelisch-reformierten Kirche* (Neukirchen, 1958). The 1934 edition of Heppe's book appeared in an illegal but useful translation by G. T. Thomson (London, 1950); the first German edition is of 1861. There is useful matter in A. E. McGrath, *Iustitia Dei*, ii (Cambridge, 1986).

3. J. Davenant, *Praelectiones de duobus in theologia controversis capitibus* (Cambridge, 1631), 220-641, translated by J. Allport (London, 1844) under the title

Treatise on Justification, is both rigid and inconsistent. He refused to make any separation between justifying faith and hope or love, and insisted that good works are necessary for the justified and a 'moving cause' (but not a 'necessary cause') of salvation. The coherence of his language was immediately questioned by W. Forbes, *Considerationes modestae et pacificae*, i (posthumously published in 1658, reissued with translation in 1850 in the Library of Anglo-Catholic Theology). Much in Davenant is remarkably close to Trent, despite his strong Calvinism.

4. R. Boudens (ed.), *Conversations with Dr Döllinger* (Louvain, 1985), 254.

5. P. J. Spener, *Die evangelische Glaubensgerechtigkeit von J. Brevings vergeblichen Angriffen also gerettet, dass nechst gründlicher Beantwortung alles in dessen so genandten Glaubensstreits Anfang und Ende enthaltenen die heilsame Lehr von der Rechtfertigung des Menschen vor Gott erwiesen wird* (Frankfurt, 1684). The book runs to nearly 1500 pages. I have used the Wolfenbüttel copy of this rare volume, which is also in the British Library. The reprint of Spener's writings (Hildesheim, Olms, 1979-) has not yet included this massive work. The Evangelical background to Newman is well studied by T. L. Sheridan, *Newman on Justification* (Staten Island, NY, 1967).

6. Bull, *Apologia pro Harmonia*, VII. vii (Opera Latina; London, 1721), p. 668; trans. in Library of Anglo-Catholic Theology (Oxford, 1843), pp. 308-9).

7. Melanchthon's *Apology for the Confession of Augsburg* (1531) grants this point, ii. 40: 'Because to be justified signifies that the wicked are made righteous through regeneration, it signifies also that they are pronounced or reputed as righteous. For the Scripture uses both these ways of speaking.' Also iii. 40: 'It is generally admitted that justification signifies not only the beginning of renovation, but the reconciliation by which we are afterwards accepted.' McGrath's judgement (*Iustitia Dei*, ii. 126) is that the historical Luther (not Newman's caricature) occupied a position remarkably close to Newman's.

8. Newman used to say that he had rewritten the text fourteen times (14 Dec. 1869, *LD* xxix. 309). The experience of its composition was painful to a degree (*LD* xx. 169). Some Protestants came to suggest that Newman raised subtle and bewildering questions to drive the distressed to Roman infallibility; so an anonymous note in the *Christian Observer* (1854), 483.

9. *LD* vi. 186.

10. *LD* vi. 193.

11. *LD* vi. 212.

12. *LD* vi. 199.

13. *LD* vi. 221. J. A. Möhler's *Symbolik* first appeared at Mainz in 1832. The fifth edition appeared in English translation by J. B. Robertson (London, 1843). The book was immediately attacked by his Protestant colleague at Tübingen, F. C. Baur, to whom Möhler made the rejoinder *Neue Untersuchungen der Gegensätze zwischen der Katholiken und Protestanten, eine Verteidigung meiner Symbolik . . .* (Mainz, 1834). This had a second edition in 1835. The exchanges are a battle of giants.

14. G. S. Faber's writings included: *A Dissertation on the Prophecies that have been fulfilled, are now fulfilling or will hereafter be fulfilled relative to the Great Period of 1260 Years* (1807: 3rd

edn., London, 1808); *Remarks on the Pyramid of Cephrenes lately opened by Mr Belzoni* (London, 1819); *A General and Connected View of the Prophecies relating to the Conversion, Restoration . . . of the Houses of Judah and Israel* (1808; 2nd edn., London, 1809). *The Predicted Downfall of the Turkish Power: The Preparation for the Return of the Ten Tribes* (London, 1853)—evidently two works of vast historical importance for the genesis of Zionism; *The Primitive Doctrine of Election* (1836; 2nd edn., London, 1842).

15. *LD* vi. 229-33. Faber's letter to Newman of 12 Apr. 1838 assured him that he read with disgust and contempt the attacks on Newman: 'You and I may not always agree; but I think I can insure you from any such attacks, so far as I am concerned.' The outcome was otherwise. The adverse reaction of Samuel Wilberforce to Newman's thesis is studied by D. Newsome, 'Justification and Sanctification: Newman and the Evangelicals', *Journal of Theological Studies*, NS 15 (1964), 32-53.

16. G. S. Faber, *The Primitive Doctrine of Justification investigated relatively to the Definitions of the Church of Rome and the Church of England* (2nd edn., 1839), 409, 427.

17. *Apo.*, p. 169.

18. *LD* xiv. 333-4.

19. Much of what Newman knew is likely to have come through J. Milner's *History of the Church of Christ*, revised by I. Milner (Cambridge, 1795-1909), where Luther dominates the account of the Reformation and is given a pietist face.

20. Bull, *Examen Censurae*, XIII. vii (Opera Latina, p. 576; Library of Anglo-Catholic Theology, p. 149); id., *Apologia pro Harmonia*, VI. ii (Opera Latina, p. 576; Library of Anglo-Catholic Theology, p. 109); ibid. VII. xvi (Opera Latina, p. 673; Library of Anglo-Catholic Theology. p. 320).

21. M. Chemnitz's *Examen Concilii Tridentini* (Frankfurt, 1566) had many editions. There is a translation by F. Kramer, 2 vols. (St Louis, 1971-8). Johann Gerhard (1582-1637), after Chemnitz the greatest systematic theologian among the Lutherans, wrote *Loci theologici*, 9 vols. (Jena, 1610-22) and *Confessio Catholica*, 4 vols. (Jena, 1633-7) in which he cites passages from Catholic theologians in support of Lutheran theses; cf. id., *Bellarminius orthodoxias testis* (Jena, 1630). Newman may have learned something from Gerhard's controversial method when he cited Calvinist authors and Melanchthon to show their coincidence with Tridentine propositions. But this controversial technique was common, as in Cochlaeus and in Flacius's *Catalogus Testium*, and is as old as the Chalcedonian Definition of AD 451 in its string of phrases drawn from Cyril of Alexandria, designed to protect the citizenship rights of the school of Antioch.

22. *Apologia Confessionis Augustanae* (1531), ch. 4, sec. 73: 'by "faith alone" we exclude merit, not the word or sacraments as our opponents slanderously claim' ('Excludimus autem opinionem meriti, non excludimus verbum aut sacramenta, ut calumniantur adversarii').

23. Calvin's *Antidote* is printed in Corpus Reformatorum, vol. XXXV = Calvin, vol. vii (Berlin, 1868), 365-506. English translation in *Tracts and Treatises in Defence of the Reformed Faith*, iii (Edinburgh, 1851), reprinted

with notes by T. F. Torrance (Edinburgh, 1958).

24. J. C. Hare, *Vindication of Luther against his recent English Assailants* (2nd edn., 1855). His *Charges* to the clergy of his archdeaconry were reprinted in three volumes (Cambridge, 1856). The opinion that Tractarianism must logically lead to Rome was notoriously not held by Pusey, Keble, and J. B. Mozley. Y. Brilioth, *The Anglican Revival* (London, 1933), pointed out that many ex-Evangelical Tractarians were among those who became Roman Catholics; there were ex-Evangelicals who did not, of course.

25. Foxe, *Actes and Monuments*, ed. Pratt (London, 1853), iv. 259-322; Zwinglian anger with Luther at iv. 316-18.

26. Bull, *Harmonia Apostolica* (1669), I. iii. 3, defended in his *Examen Censurae*, X. i. W. Forbes, *Considerationes modestae et pacificae*, I. iv. 1 *init.* (4th edn. with English trans., Oxford, 1850), i. 300).

27. *Concilium Tridentinum*, V, ed. S. Ehses (Freiburg im Breisgau, 1911).

28. Bellarmine, *De Justificatione*, 5, 7 ((editio prima romana, 1840), iv. 886).

29. One bishop at Trent who found the subject bewildering uttered a heartfelt plea for simplicity: *Concilium Tridentinum*, v. 428, 27. I have summarized Seripando's role at Trent in the Turvey Abbey journal *One in Christ* (1984), 191-225. The classic monograph on Seripando is H. Jedin, *Girolamo Seripando* (Würtzburg, 1937; repr. 1984).

30. *Concilium Tridentinum*, v. 663 n.

31. R. Hooker, *Laws of Ecclesiastic Polity*, v, lxvi. 11 (ed. Keble (7th edn., Oxford, 1888), 254).

32. Richard Field, *Of the Church*, III, xi. app. ((Cambridge, 1849),

ii. 268-343).

33. Sessio VI, can. 32 (*Concilium Tridentinum*, v. 799),

34. Melanchthon's letter to Cranmer, about Jan. 1548, is epistula 4142 in *Corpus Reformatorum*, vi (Berlin, 1839), 801: 'Synodus Tridentia veteratoria decreta fecit ut ambigue dictis tueatur suos errores. Hanc sophisticam procul ab ecclesia abesse oportuit.' Melanchthon goes on to deplore no less the Protestant wrangle about predestination.

35. Chemnitz, *Examen Concilii Tridentini*, I. x. 4 (ed. E. Preuss (Berlin, 1861), 212-16).

36. J. Buchanan, *The Doctrine of Justification* (Edinburgh, 1867), 126-7.

37. Augustine, *De peccatorum meritis*, i. 18.

38. Id., *De Trinitate*, xiv. 23.

39. Id., *De Civitate Dei*, x. 22.

40. Ibid. xix. 27.

41. Id., *Contra duas Epistulas Pelagianorum*, iii. 19.

42. Id., *Contra Faustum Manichaeum*, xxxiii. 5.

43. *LD* vi. 228.

44. *LD* vi. 275.

45. S. Dessain, 'The Biblical Basis of Newman's Ecumenical Theology' in J. Coulson and A. M. Allchin (eds.), *The Rediscovery of Newman: An Oxford Symposium* (London, 1967), 100-22.

46. Newman stands much closer in sympathy to Augustine than does Jeremy Taylor, whom both would have found too inclined to Pelagianism. But the Eucharistic devotion of Taylor, his Catholic conception of the sacrifice of the Mass, and the coincident understandings of the verbal distinction and real identity between justification and sanctification, constitute a bond. Newman can hardly have failed to respond to Taylor's profoundly religious feeling. See now H. R. McAdoo, *The Eucharistic Theology of*

Jeremy Taylor (Norwich, 1988), for a masterly examination of Taylor's remarkable qualities.

Chapter 16: Romanticism and Religion

1. A. O. Lovejoy, *Essays in the History of Ideas*, Baltimore (1948), p. 252.
2. E. Benz, *Les Sources mystiques de la Philosophie romantique allemande*, Paris (1968).
3. H. Chadwick, *Lessing's Theological Writings*, London (1956).
4. See I. T. Ramsey's introduction to his edition of Locke's *The Reasonableness of Christianity*, London (1958).
5. R. Grimsley, *Rousseau and the Religious Quest*, Oxford (1968), p. 61.
6. G. G. Hough, *The Last Romantics*, London (1947).
7. A convenient anthology of Bushnell has been made by H. Shelton Smith, New York (1965).
8. J. H. Nichols, *Romanticism in American Theology*, Chicago (1961), and *The Mercersburg Theology*, New York (1966), containing excerpts from Schaff and Nevin.
9. E. G. Sandford (ed.), *Memoirs of Archbishop* (Frederick) *Temple by seven friends*, I, London (1906), p. 417.

Chapter 17: Royal ecclesiastical supremacy

1. David Wilkins, *Concilia Magnae Britanniae*, 4 vols. (London, 1737), III, 792-7. The text of the bull finally published in 1538 (ibid., 840-1) responded to the destruction of Thomas Becket's shrine at Canterbury in that year.
2. Matthew Parker, *Correspondence*, ed. John Bruce and Thomas Perowne (Parker Society, 1853), p. 110. In the 1560s Harding and Jewel had a sharp exchange about the degree of papal absolutism embraced by the great

canonist Hostiensis: see John Jewel, *The Defence of the Apology*, in *Works*, ed. John Ayre, 4 vols. (Parker Society, 1848), IV, 830-2. For Jewel it was axiomatic that the more extravagant the claims made for the papacy, the more improbable to reason and ungrounded in scripture or tradition they appear. Harding's 'Gallicanism' was dangerously credible. The passage is an early instance of the protestant insisting that the authentic doctrine of papal authority is extreme Ultramontanism, the Catholic minimising.

3. Reginald Cardinal Pole, *Pro Ecclesiasticae Unitatis Defensione* (Strasbourg, 1555), II, 42: 'sed audi aliam conclusionem, quam ego ex ipsis tuis verbis, quae contra Petri authoritatem proferes, inferam, primo ad confirmationem Petri authoritatis, deinde etiam regis: cuius quidem de authoritate nihil diminuam, cum Petro conservabo suam'. The Strasbourg edition was published in the protestant interest, with eight appended documents on papal authority, including pieces by Luther, Flacius Illyricus, Melanchthon, Bucer, Calvin and Musculus. The first English translation of 1560, by F. Wythers (*STC* 20087), was similarly published as a 'seditious and blasphemous oration' intended to discredit the conservative case. There are modern translations in English, by J. G. Dwyer (Westminster, Md., 1965), and in French, by N. M. Égretier (Paris, 1967).

4. Hooper's writings, and especially his hostility to wearing 'Aaronic' episcopal vestments at his consecration, made him a hero to the puritans, but a source of embarrassment to Edmund Grindal. Grindal, however, was able to report that Peter Martyr and

Henry Bullinger had regretted unguarded language in Hooper's work, *The Remains of Edmund Grindal*, ed. William Nicholson (Parker Society, 1843), p. 222 (Grindal to John Foxe, August 1556).

5. *The Later Writings of Bishop Hooper*, ed. Charles Nevinson (Parker Society, 1853), pp. 96, 79, 81. Many protestant texts of Edward VI's reign say alarming things about the moral disintegration of English society, a leap in the crime rate, and a slump in church attendance.

6. The major role played by apocalyptic in the Reformation age is well studied by Richard Bauckham, *Tudor Apocalypse* (Appleford, 1978), and K. R. Firth, *The Apocalyptic Tradition in Reformation Britain 1530-1645* (Oxford, 1979).

7. Hooper, *Later Writings*, p. 554: 'the see and chair of Rome . . . is indeed the very whore of Babylon that St John describeth in the Revelation of Jesus Christ, sitting upon a seven-headed beast, which St John himself interpreteth to be seven hills, and the children in the grammar school do know that Rome is called *civitas septem montium*, the city of seven hills'.

8. The assertion that the identity of the pope with Antichrist is no speculative conjecture but an article of faith was made by Gabriel Powel, *De Antichristo et Eius Ecclesia* (London, 1605), and was treated as a self-evident truth by Joseph Mede in the 1640s in works destined to exercise vast influence on Isaac Newton. Newton's editor, Horsley, dissented from the mathematician's axiom. In nineteenth-century England, scathing criticism of the papal Antichrist thesis came from the acid pen of the historian S. R.

Gardiner. At the popular level the belief remains tenacious. Hugo Grotius's *Annotata ad Vetus Testamentum* (Paris, 1644) and *Annotationes in Novum Testamentum* (Amsterdam, 1641-50) caused consternation to protestants by denying that correct exegesis could identify the papacy with Antichrist or the whore of Babylon. He outraged many to whom (as to the authors of the Westminster Confession adopted in Scotland) the exegesis was an essential, load-bearing axiom in justifying separation from Rome while simultaneously treating Anabaptists as schismatics. Henry More, *A Modest Inquiry into the Mystery of Iniquity* (Cambridge, 1664) and *A Plain and Continued Exposition of . . . the Prophet Daniel* (London, 1681), sought to answer Grotius with equal erudition. He feared that Anglican enthusiasm for Grotius had alarmed many into thinking the Church of England soft on popery. More regarded the Apocalypse as vindicating the Crown and Church of England, especially royal supremacy: see the folio edition of his *Theological Works* (London, 1708), p. 713. Richard Baxter, *The Grotian Religion Discovered* (London, 1658) warned that Grotius and some Anglican theologians such as John Bramhall were dismantling the defences against popery: G. F. Nuttall, 'Richard Baxter and *The Grotian Religion*', in D. Baker (ed.), *Reform and Reformation, Studies in Church History, Subsidia*, 2 (1979), 245-50.

9. Bramhall complained 'I am traduced as a factor for popery, because I am not a protestant out of my wits': John Bramhall, *Vindication of Grotius, The Complete Works of John*

Bramhall, 2nd edn (Dublin, 1677), ch. 5 at p. 624. It merits notice that in 1986 the General Assembly of the Church of Scotland formally resolved that it does not today accept, or require any assent to, the Westminster Confession's censures on the pope and the mass.

10. Cranmer's answer to Smith (*Cranmer on the Lord's Supper*, ed. John Edmund Cox (Parker Society, 1854), p. 378): 'What wonder is it then that the open Church is now of late years fallen into many errors and corruption, and the holy Church of Christ is secret and unknown? seeing that Satan, these five hundred years, hath been let loose, and antichrist reigneth . . .'. For Wycliffe see John Foxe, *Acts and Monuments*, ed. J. Pratt, 8 vols. (London, 1854-70; repr. 1877), II, 800; Thomas Netter Waldensis, *Doctrinale Antiquitatus Fidei Catholicae*, ed. B. Blanciotti, 3 vols. (Venice, 1757-9; repr. Farnborough, 1967), II, col. 127f. A remarkably early identification of the actualities of the tenth-century papacy with Antichrist occurs in the speech of Arnulf of Reims, written by Gerbert (later Pope Sylvester II!), at the council of S. Basle de Verzy in 991 (*Acta* in *PL* 139, 287-338; *Monumenta Germaniae Historica, Scriptorum*, 3 (Hannover, 1839), 658-86).

11. Foxe, *Acts and Monuments*, I, 5, thought the first evidence of the devil's release from prison was found in Pope Gregory VII. He also surprisingly records a view that the millennium of incarceration began with Constantine and ended with Wycliffe (ibid., I, 291).

12. Hooker remarks on Wycliffe's 'palpable error' in denying the propriety of endowments in the Church: Richard Hooker, *Of The Laws of Ecclesiastical Polity*,

ed. W. Speed Hill, 3 vols. (Cambridge, Mass., and London, 1981), III, 276 (VII. 22. 7). Tithes were for Wycliffe voluntary alms, not a compulsory tax: see Anne Hudson, *Selections from English Wycliffite Writings* (Cambridge, 1978), p. 147.

13. William Langland, *The Vision of William Concerning Piers the Plowman*, ed. W. W. Skeat (Oxford, 1886), I, 308, 127 (B X. 317, C VI. 169). In more modern editions such as Kane's the numbering of the lines is slightly different. The Kane-Donaldson edition of Langland is radically criticised by David C. Fowler, 'A New Edition of the B Text of *Piers Plowman*', *Yearbook of English Studies*, 7 (1977), 23-42.

14. Printed in *Fasciculi Zizaniorum*, ed. W. W. Shirley (Rolls Series, 1858), pp. 360ff. in Latin; the English text in Hudson, *Selections*, pp. 24-9, with commentary, pp. 150-5.

15. The anger of Thomas Cartwright on the subject shows that it cost less to die before the Reformation than after it. Instead of a sixpenny requiem, the clergy expected half-a-crown for a sermon: see John Whitgift, *The Defence of the Answer to the Admonition*, in *Works*, ed. John Ayre, 3 vols. (Parker Society, 1853), III, 378.

16. John Bramhall, *A Just Vindication of the Church of England from the Unjust Aspersion of Criminal Schism* (Dublin, 1677), II, 92, records 900 ducats—in a lengthy list of papal 'extortions', reinforced by a reference to Chaucer for the avarice in his time. Foxe, *Acts and Monuments*, II, 109 asserts that in 1504 the archbishop of Mainz paid 27,000 florins for his pall.

17. Parker, *Correspondence*, p. 419, anticipated by Latimer in a letter to Cromwell of 1537 and followed

by Aylmer, bishop of London. Ridley is found saying that truth is revealed to the English by God and the king (Foxe, *Acts and Monuments*, VI, 311). Haller's thesis that Foxe regarded the English as a uniquely elect nation is commonly dismissed today as an exaggeration. The thesis is, however, an exaggeration of an element certainly present in Foxe (e.g. *Acts and Monuments*, III, 142f), who was sure that national success and English protestantism were bound together in God's providence.

18. Hooper, *Later Writings*, p. 559. A similar doctrine is found in the *Decades* of Hooper's master, Bullinger.

19. See an account of the Oxford curriculum of 1552 in the letter from Conrad ab Ulmis to John Wolfius, printed in *Original Letters Relative to the English Reformation* (Parker Society, 1847), II, 459 (no. 219). He studied Aristotle's *Politics* in Greek, 6-7 a.m.; the *Digests*, 7-9; Peter Martyr on theology, 9-10; Melanchthon on logic at 10. After dinner, Cicero's *Offices*; Justinian's *Institutes*, 3-4 p.m., which were then memorised, 4-5; the evening spent in dialectical debates with other students. On the general background see John Barton, 'The Faculty of Law', in J. McConica (ed.), *The History of the University of Oxford*, III, *The Collegiate University* (Oxford, 1986), pp. 257-83.

20. *Acta Conciliorum Oecumenicorum*, ed. J. Straub (Berlin, 1971), IV. 1, 202, 12; the text is in *Sanctorum Conciliorum et Decretorum Collectio Nova*, ed. P. Labbe and N. Coleti, 23 vols., (Venice, 1728-33), VI, 197. For the role of the *sedes/sedens* distinction in Gallicanism, see A. G. Martimort, *Le Gallicanisme de Bossuet* (Paris, 1953), pp. 556-9.

21. *Acta Conciliorum Oecumenicorum*, IV. 1, 187, 22 and 188, 8-21.

22. Augustine, *c. litt. Petiliani*, II. 38. 132.

23. Augustine (*c. ep. Parmeniani*, II. 8. 15) regarded the Donatist doctrine of the bishop as indispensable mediator of grace as being 'intolerable' to Catholic ears. He also (*Sermo*, 99. 7-9) disliked the Donatist contention that the power of the keys in absolution and excommunication was wholly and without reserve delegated by God to the clergy. On succession, see *ep.* 53. Augustine did not, of course, regard succession as unimportant (e.g. *En. in Ps.* 44. 32).

24. Optatus, III, 3.

25. 'Sees': *De Doctrina Christiana*, II. 12. 25. 'See': *c. du. epp. Pelag*, II. 3. 5. *Ep. ad Catholicos de unit. ecclesiae*, 20. 55 has 'reges nostrae communionis'. In *c. litt. Petiliani*, i. 18. 20, 'per regum communionem' is a synonym for 'per ecclesiam catholicam'.

26. This set of canons became ascribed to the Council of Antioch of 341. Text in *Die Kanones der wichtigsten altkirchlichen Concilien nebst den apostolischen Kanones*, ed. F. Lauchert (Freiburg im Breisgau and Leipzig, 1896), p. 46.

27. This view, expressed by a member of one of the circus factions at Constantinople in the sixth century, is explicitly recorded, *Patrologia Orientalis*, ed. R. Graffin *et al.* (Paris, 1907-66; Turnhout, 1968), VIII, 175.

28. The classic discussion by U. Stutz, *Geschichte des kirchlichen Benefizialwesens* (Berlin, 1895; repr. Aalen, 1961) and his lecture *Die Eigenkirche als Element des mittelalterlich-germanischen Kirchenrechts* (Berlin, 1895); repr. Darmstadt, 1959, with

bibliography to 1955); recent literature is noted in R. Schieffer, *Die Entstehung des päpstlichen Investiturverbots für den deutschen König* (Stuttgart, 1981), p. 16. Among the most interesting of early documents is the Tivoli Register (Louis Duchesne, *Le Liber Pontificalis* (Paris, 1886), I, cxlvi ff) recording the benefaction of a Catholic Goth, Valila, an army commander, who built a church on his estate with endowment to maintain the clergy, lights, and repairs, while retaining himself a life interest in other properties given to the Church. A number of sixth-century Gallic councils resist attempts by landowners to withdraw priests on their land from episcopal control. An eloquent statement of the evils of lay domination is in Agobard, *De Dispensatione Rerum Ecclesiasticarum* (*PL*, 104, 236). Hincmar, however, was not so unsympathetic: see W. Gundlach, 'Zwei Schriften des Erzbischofs Hinkmar von Reims I', *Zeitschrift für Kirchengeschichte*, 10 (1889), 92-145.

29. The earliest instance of *beneficium* in our modern sense of 'benefice' has lately come to light among the new letters of Augustine found by Johannes Divjak. It is instructive that in the context the opulent lady who owned the land evidently exercised a veto over the nomination of a bishop for her tenants, but did not at this stage actually nominate. I have discussed this in 'New Letters of St Augustine', *Journal of Theological Studies*, n.s., 34 (1983), 443. Pope Celestine's maxim states the general custom of antiquity: 'Nullus invitis detur episcopus' (*ep.* 4, *PL*, 50, 434B). Leo I (*ep.* 167, *PL*, 54, 1203A) rules none could be bishop without election by clergy, assent of *plebs*, and

consecration by the provincial bishops, the metropolitan having a veto.

30. See, e.g., C. R. Cheney, *Pope Innocent III and England* (Stuttgart, 1976), pp. 121ff.

31. *Vita Sancti Anselmi*, ed. R. W. Southern (Oxford, 1972), p. 16.

32. Pope John X (*PL*, 132, 806).

33. *Sancti Aureli Augustini Epistolae*, ed. J. Divjak, *Corpus Scriptorum Ecclesiasticorum Latinorum*, 88 (Vienna, 1981), 22*. See Chadwick, above, n. 29, p. 446.

34. To the best of my knowledge the conscious distinction between 'ecclesia orientalis' and 'ecclesia occidentalis' is first explicit in Augustine, see Chadwick, above, n. 29, p. 428.

35. This formula was used by an English businessman at Bologna in February 1547 when his Italian hosts heard the news of Henry VIII's death and asked him for a defence of the English tyrant: see *The Pilgrim, a Dialogue on the Life and Actions of King Henry the Eighth by William Thomas*, ed. J. A. Froude (London, 1861), p. 32: the king, 'absolute patron of his private Christian dominion', acted as 'prince and apostle'.

36. Wilkins, *Concilia*, III, 764. There is trenchant matter on Justinian as model for Henry in F. W. Maitland, *Roman Canon Law in the Church of England* (London, 1898), pp. 93f.

37. Foxe, *Acts and Monuments*, VII, 618.

38. *Zurich Letters (i) 1558-79*, ed. Hastings Robinson (Parker Society, 1852), p. 19 (John Jewel to Peter Martyr, 28 April 1559); Jewel, *Defence*, in *Works*, IV, 1029ff. R. E. Rodes, *Lay Authority and the Reformation in the English Church, Edward I to the Civil War* (Notre Dame, Ind., 1982), writes perceptively

on St German and the lay lawyers, Erastian and Utilitarian, who saw the Church not as a sacrament of divine presence but as one of the institutions by which a Christian society could pursue its ends. To English pre-Reformation lawyers that was what it always had been.

39. I have tried to tell this story in my *Boethius* (Oxford, 1981), ch. 1.

40. St German's two *Dialogues* with his *New Additions* are edited by T. F. T. Plucknett and J. L. Barton, Selden Society, 91 (1974). There is also important matter in J. A. Guy, *Christopher St German on Chancery and Statute*, Selden Society Supplementary Series 6 (London, 1985), and in J. B. Trapp's Introduction in Thomas More, *The Apology*, ed. Trapp, *Complete Works*, IX (New Haven and London, 1979), xvi-xciii. See also G. R. Dunstan, 'Corporate Union and the Body Politic: Constitutional Aspects of Union between the Church of England and the Church of Rome', in Mark Santer (ed.), *Their Lord and Ours* (London, 1982), pp. 129-48.

41. Walter Ullmann, ' "This Realm of England is an Empire" ', - *Journal of Ecclesiastical History*, 30 (1979), 175-203.

42. Hincmar, *ep.* 19 ad Ludovicum III regem Balbi filium (*PL*, 126, 110f.). Hincmar's ecclesiology gets a sympathetic study from Yves Congar in the journal of the Spanish Dominicans, *Communio* (Granada), 1 (1968), 5-18.

43. Victor Martin's well-known book, *Les Origines du Gallicanisme* (Paris, 1939) contains much matter illuminating for the mind of Henry VIII, even though Henry is far from Martin's field of study. His treatment of Marsilius makes it unnecessary for the present essay to consider

the *Defensor Pacis* here, influential as the work was in England.

44. *LP*, C, 977.

45. F. Testa, *Capitula Regni Siciliae*, 2 vols. (Palermo, 1741-3), I, 576-7. The British Library and the Cambridge University Library possess this rare book (not the Bodleian). Foxe, *Acts and Monuments*, II, 465, pointedly noticed the powers of kings of Sicily to appoint bishops.

46. Foxe, *Acts and Monuments*, VIII, 20.

47. Matthew Paris's portrait of Innocent III is one of limitless avarice and hunger for power. The anti-clerical resentment over King John is mentioned by many writers: Foxe, *Acts and Monuments*, II, 331-2 is representative, and Robert Barnes (himself author of a papal history intended to prove the papacy Antichrist) waxed eloquent on poor John's humiliations. In his *The Supplycacyon of Soulys* (London, 1529; *STC* 18092-3), p. 8, Thomas More denied that King John had power to surrender sovereignty over England to the pope, evidently hoping to ward off the anticlerical barb. But its tenacity is shown by its recurrence in, e.g., John Overall, *The Convocation Book of MDCVI*, Library of Anglo-Catholic Theology (Oxford, 1844), p. 250.

48. Medieval popes took seriously the exhortation of 1 Timothy 5:8 that there was a duty to provide for one's household. I have drawn together texts from *Roberti Grosseteste Episcopi Quondam Lincolniensis Epistolae*, 3ed. H. R. Luard (Rolls Series, 1861), epp. 72, 124, 128, 131. Grosseteste's critique of the curia receives a masterly discussion from R. W. Southern, *Robert Grosseteste, the Growth of an English Mind in Medieval Europe* (Oxford, 1986), pp. 272ff.

For Wycliffe's appeal to his writings see ibid., pp. 298ff. The passage about the coronation unction (*Epistolae*, pp. 350-1) is reminiscent of Cranmer's very secular discourse at Edward VI's coronation on 20 February 1547, explaining the boy king how utterly insignificant this little ceremony is, reproduced in *Remains and Letters*, ed. J. E. Cox (Parker Society, 1846), pp. 126-7.

49. The effect on antipapal persons of the discovery that the Isidorian decretals were a forgery is never to be underestimated: see the stern words in, for example, Nicholas Ridley, *Works*, ed. Henry Christmas (Parker Society, 1841), p. 182; Foxe, *Acts and Monuments*, I, 279, 464.

50. Among many texts see, for example, Cartwright in Whitgift, *Works*, II, 441. Hooper regarded 'a mixed and mingled religion' as satanic, *Early Writings*, ed. Samuel Carr (Parker Society, 1843), p. 435 (1550). Bishop Richard Cox of Ely defended the prayer book and English ceremonial usages as modelled on St Paul's godly principle of being all things to all men, *Zurich Letters (i)*, p. 237 (Cox to R. Gualter 1571). In January 1559 Gualter had expressed to Queen Elizabeth his fears of 'an unhappy compound of popery and the gospel'. *Zurich Letters (ii), 1558-1602*, ed. Hastings Robinson (Parker Society, 1844), p. 5 (Gualter to Queen Elizabeth). A similar letter from Gualter to Richard Masters (ibid., p. 11) fears that a religion of 'mixed, uncertain and doubtful character' may one day facilitate a 'return to papistical superstition'.

The proposition in Article 19 of the Thirty-Nine Articles that 'as the Church of Jerusalem, Alexandria and Antioch have erred; so also the Church of Rome hath erred . . .' is strikingly anticipated in Cummian's letter (*c*. AD 632) describing the position of the British churches in the paschal controversy: 'Roma errat, Hierosolyma errat, Antiochia errat, totus mundus errat; soli tantum Scoti et Britones rectum sapiunt' (*PL*, 87, 974 D).

51. Foxe, *Acts and Monuments*, V, 127. Tyndale's accusation that the confessional had been abused, principally by the seduction of foolish women and the betrayal of political secrets, is an angry anticlerical commonplace of the age. For sorrowful Catholic pages telling the same story, see the lawyer Conradus Brunus (1491-1563) in his memorandum to the Council of Trent, printed in *Conc. Trid.*, XII, 404ff. A warning that as a whole Tyndale is less absolutist about royal power than some sayings in his *Obedience* suggest is given by W. D. J. Cargill Thompson, 'The Two Regiments: The Continental Setting of William Tyndale's Political Thought', in D. Baker (ed.), *Reform and Reformation, Studies in Church History, Subsidia*, 2 (1979), 17-33.

52. See *LP*, II, no. 1313 (p. 353), and Ullmann, ' "This Realm of England" ', pp. 175-203. L. G. Wickham Legg, *English Coronation Records* (Westminster, 1901), pp. 240-1, with facsimile, does not think Henry could have had his wish.

53. Wilkins, *Concilia*, III, 745. Tunstall thought the qualifying clause whereby the bishops accepted Henry as head of the Church 'so far as the law of Christ allows' failed to make it explicit that the qualification meant death to the proposition.

54. Luther in 1531 rejected Henry's divorce out of hand (*Weimarer*

Ausgabe Briefwechsel (Weimar, 1883ff), 6, 178-88, a letter to Robert Barnes), and his title 'head of the Church' in 1539 (WA Br. 8, 577-78, a letter to the elector John Frederick of 23 October 1539, concluding acidly 'Henry ought to be pope, as in fact he is in England'). The two letters are translated into English in Martin Luther, *Works*, ed. J. Pelikan *et al.* (St Louis, Mo., 1955), 1 (1975), 196, 205. Calvin, *Readings on Amos*, VII, 13 (*Opera Omnia* (Amsterdam, 1667), V, 223) tersely described Henry's claim as blasphemy, and goes on to express outrage at having heard Stephen Gardiner argue not from scripture or from reason, but exclusively from the will of the king, to rule against clerical marriage or communion in both kinds.

55. Foxe, *Acts and Monuments*, VIII, 53; also printed in Cranmer, *Remains and Letters*, pp. 214-15.

56. That Lever made the suggestion to the queen is stated by Sandys' letter to Parker, 30 April 1559, *Correspondence of Matthew Parker*, ed. John Bruce and T. T. Perowne (Parker Society, 1853), pp. 65-6. For Elizabeth's assertion of supremacy, see M. A. Simpson, *Defender of the Faith et cetera* (Edinburgh, 1978); N. L. Jones, *Faith by Statute*, Royal Historical Society, Studies in History (London, 1982), p. 32. Much in the writings of Professor D. M. Loades also bears on this question. If the application to the pope of the title supreme head was *ipso facto* to declare him a forerunner of Antichrist, as John Bradford thought (Foxe, *Acts and Monuments*, VII, 183), the same conclusion must also apply to the monarch.

57. Whitgift, *Works*, II, 239.

58. Whitgift, *Works*, II, 333-6. Foxe,

as this Cartwright/Whitgift exchange shows, is not easy to pigeon-hole in the variety of sixteenth-century English Church life. Though evidently strongly reformed in religion, often 'Swiss' in sympathy, he regarded the vestiarian controversy as a tragic squabble about trivialities (ibid., II, 750). Many passages uphold the right and duty of the sovereign to order the life of clergy in his realm, and vehemently attack the infringements and usurpations of papal power, especially by Gregory VII, Innocent III, and Boniface VIII. Yet he also evidently longed for a reformed see of Rome focusing the unity of 'sister churches' (ibid., II, 418), and was shocked at the spoliation of the Church of England by Henry VIII. Erasmian influence may be seen in his desire that the Apostles' Creed be the norm of orthodoxy (ibid., III, 103), his horror of elevating school opinions to articles of faith (ibid., III, 729), and his stern criticism of capital punishment for religious dissent (e.g. ibid., III, 99). Whitgift was not mistaken to see an ally in him; Foxe would not have liked his treatment of John Penry. Foxe disliked the title 'Book of Martyrs' already being ascribed to his work, and insisted that he wrote *Acts and Monuments of Things Passed in the Church* (ibid., III, 392).

59. J. J. Scarisbrick, *Henry VIII* (London, 1968), pp. 375-86.

60. Ibid., p. 351.

61. See *Visitation Articles and Injunctions of the Period of the Reformation*, ed. W. H. Frere and W. M. Kennedy (Alcuin Club Collections, 15), II, 2, 34. The Ten Articles, however, were agreed by Convocation in July 1536.

62. The Wittenberg Articles were discovered in Weimar early this

century and published by their finder, Georg Mentz, *Die Wittenberger Artickel von 1536* (Leipzig, 1905). Luther regarded these Articles as representing something of a compromise between his own position and that of the English divines, but one he could accept to help forward the Reformation (WA Br. 17, p. 383). An English translation of the Wittenberg Articles is given by N. S. Tjernagel, *Henry VIII and the Lutherans* (St Louis, Concordia, 1965), pp. 255-86.

63. Foxe, *Acts and Monuments*, V, 164. I am bound to think the protestantism of the Ten Articles exaggerated by D. B. Knox, *The Doctrine of the Faith in the Reign of Henry VIII* (London, 1961), and even by Professor Scarisbrick, *Henry VIII*, p. 438 ('blatantly heterodox'). What is no doubt true is that there was much left unsaid.

64. Foxe's verdict is again that in the Bishop's Book 'many things were slender and imperfect', *Acts and Monuments*, V, 87. He gives the names of the eight bishops responsible for its production (ibid., VIII, 11). Stokesley (London) and Gardiner (Winchester) could be relied upon to keep the protestantising sympathies of Latimer (Worcester) and Shaxton (Salisbury) in check. The preface signed by all the bishops in Convocation, headed by Cranmer, includes a declaration that 'without the power and licence of your majesty we acknowledge and confess that we have none authority either to assemble ourselves together for any pretence or purpose, or to publish any thing that might be by us agreed and compiled', *Formularies of Faith Put Forth by Authority during the Reign of Henry VIII*, ed. Charles Lloyd (Oxford, 1825, repr. 1856), p. 26. The declaration

presupposes that the king is pope of the English Church, and the bishops are only advisory on dogmatic questions, deriving from him their spiritual jurisdiction. Hooker, *Laws*, VIII. 2. 16, is much more nuanced, but grants that the limitations of regal power over the Church (apart from the self-evident lack of power of order and jurisdiction) have 'not hitherto been agreed upon with so uniform consent and certainty as might be wished'.

65. Ridley in 1555 remarked that Stephen Gardiner was 'thought to be either the first father or chief gatherer' of the King's Book: Nicholas Ridley, *Works*, ed. H. Christmas (Parker Society, 1841), p. 135. Gardiner himself denied having had a hand in the book (Foxe, *Acts and Monuments*, VI, 61; cf. VI, 124, which shows that the denial was regarded with incredulity), and affirmed that the master hand was Henry himself. The king's annotations on the Bishops' Book, printed in Cranmer, *Remains and Letters*, pp. 83-114, suggest that Gardiner may have been correct.

66. *Formularies of Faith*, ed. Lloyd, pp. 285, 248. The Greek rejection of universal papal jurisdiction was a frequent theme in protestant argument that such a degree of centralised authority lacks Catholic consent, e.g. Foxe, *Acts and Monuments*, II, 608; III, 700; VI, 255.

67. Paris, 1524; 2nd edn, Cologne, 1530. Crabbe's edition did not appear until 1538, and the margins of Cranmer's copy of Merlin were soon covered with his manuscript annotations.

68. John Rogers, on the protestant side, thought that the inconsistencies of parliament in consenting to the incompatible doctrines

of Henry VIII, Edward VI, and then Mary totally discredited its authority as a judge of the interpretation of God's word: Foxe, *Acts and Monuments*, VI, 603. That under Edward VI the magisterium was vested either in the young king or in parliament, even to the actual exclusion of the clergy, is evident from the pathetic plea of the clergy to Edward VI (Wilkins, *Concilia*, IV, 15) asking if they could please be consulted, whether by being given an actual voice in any laws governing religion 'or that at least parliament enact no religious laws without consulting the clergy in convocation'. Sir Simonds D'Ewes's *Journal, The Journals of All the Parliaments during the Reign of Queen Elizabeth* (London, 1682), on 14 Eliz. (22 May 1572) records the queen's pleasure that no bills concerning religion be received in parliament unless first considered by the clergy.

69. *The Papers of George Wyatt*, ed. D. M. Loades, Camden Society, 4th series, 5 (1968), p. 153.

70. Cecil held that the power of the crown is limited by the advice of the privy council (Foxe, *Acts and Monuments*, VI, 68). The oration of the protestant layman John Hales, submitted to Elizabeth in 1558 (text in Foxe, *Acts and Monuments*, VIII, 673-9), in effect pleaded for the reinstatement of the royal supremacy: 'The title touched the commonwealth and realm of England more than the king ... It was for the conservation of the liberty of the whole realm and so to exclude the usurped authority of the bishop of Rome.' In other words, royal supremacy meant in practice parliamentary control of the Church of England, or at least the negative proposition that the government of this Church could not make room for the pope.

71. *The Letters of Stephen Gardiner*, ed. J. A. Muller (Cambridge, 1933), p. 379 (no. 130). Foxe, *Acts and Monuments*, VI, 42-6, prints only about two-thirds of the text.

72. *Visitation Articles and Injunctions*, ed. Frere and Kennedy, II, 149.

73. See John Cosin, *Correspondence*, I, Surtees Society, 52 (1869), p. 147.

74. *The Huntyng and Fyndynge out of the Romische Fox* (Basel, 1543). *STC*, 24353 thinks it actually printed at Amsterdam by S. Mierdman. I have used the Bodleian copy (Tanner, 51).

75. How hostile was the English protestant reaction to Henry's dissolution of his 'pretended marriage' with Anne of Cleves may be seen in Richard Hilles's letter to Bullinger, Hastings Robinson (ed.), *Original Letters Relative to the English Reformation, 1531-58* (Parker Society, 1846-7), I, 205. Hilles is also eloquent on the execution of Barnes; ibid., I, 209f.

76. *LP*, XV, p. 484.

77. Luther (WA Br. 8, 577-8): 'Dr Anthony (= Robert Barnes) several times declared: Our king has no respect for religion and the gospel.'

78. William Wraghton (pseud.), *The Rescuynge of the Romishe Fox Other Wyse Called the Examination of the Hunter Devised by Steven Gardiner* ('Winchester', 1545). *STC*, 24355, assigns it to L. Mylius of Bonn. Foxe, *Acts and Monuments*, VII, 602, identifies the author as Turner, dean of Wells. His defence of 'supreme governor' is at fo. Cii. In 1555 Turner wrote under his own name *The Huntyng of the Romyche Vuolfe* (*STC*, 24356), written after Latimer's death but

before Gardiner's, i.e. in November 1555. This last work anticipates in content, verve and venom much that went into the puritan Admonitions to Parliament of 1571-2 and the Marprelate tracts.

79. Beza to Bullinger, 3 September (1566), *Zurich Letters (ii)*, 128, probably quoting the opinions of Perceval Wiburn: '. . . the papacy was never abolished in that country, but rather transferred to the sovereign . . . nothing else is now aimed at than the gradual restoration of what had been in any measure altered'.

80. In January 1555 Gardiner, Tunstal (Durham) and Nicholas Heath (Worcester) confessed expressly to John Rogers: in Henry VIII's time one could not say without pain of death that the king had no authority in spiritual matters such as forgiveness and authority to interpret God's word (Foxe, *Acts and Monuments*, VI, 593; cf. Bonner in ibid., VIII, 110). There is a parallel to the situation of the Henrician bishops in the Greek bishops who supported Chalcedon in the difficult times of the emperor Anastasius, 491-518. When the popes expressed the view that the Greeks had been guilty of grave compromise by holding communion with the patriarchs of Constantinople who (though some were Chalcedonian) were not acknowledged by Rome because of the Acacian schism they replied that they had kept their faith intact, and that to have withdrawn communion from the patriarchs would have brought expulsion and the surrender of their flocks to the wolves: Pope Symmachus, *ep.* 12 (*Epistolae Romanorum Pontificum Genuinae*, ed. A. Thiel (Braunsberg, 1867-8), pp. 709-17; Henry Chadwick, *Boethius*

(Oxford, 1981), pp. 181-3).

81. *The Huntyng of the Romysche Wolfe* (1555): 'When as Tunstal, Gardiner, Stokesay and the rest of the papists bare the swinge under king Henry the eighth, they suffered the kings and divers lords of the realm to put away and take as many wives as they list without any correction or admonition. If that they had done their duty, the virtuous lady Anne of Cleve had never been divorced and put away from the king her lawful husband . . . Henry with his covetous council took all the goods of the abbeys which belongeth for a great part as well unto Christ's church as the half of the goods of Ananias belongeth unto the Holy Ghost.' Turner omits to add that Bishop Latimer of Worcester, making the customary New Year's gift to Henry VIII, once gave him a New Testament wrapped in a napkin, inscribed 'Fornicatores et adulteros judicabit Dominus' (Foxe, *Acts and Monuments*, VII, 517). Turner was far from being the only protestant outraged by the deliberate ruthlessness with which Henry's dissolution of the monasteries enforced the annihilation of a major religious factor and a vast break with the past. See M. Aston, 'English Ruins and English History', - *Journal of the Warburg and Courtauld Institutes*, 36 (1973), pp. 231-55, at pp. 234ff.

82. That Oxford, especially Magdalen College, had its protestants in Elizabeth's time is clarified by C. M. Dent, *Protestant Reformers in Elizabethan Oxford* (Oxford, 1983), following Professor Patrick Collinson.

83. Foxe, *Acts and Monuments*, VI, 577f.

84. Ibid., VIII, 51f.

85. Parker, *Correspondence*, pp. 109-13 (16 March 1560).

86. Ibid., pp. 292-4 (24 December 1566).

87. Ibid., p. 479 (11 April 1575). Perhaps Cecil agreed with Sir Francis Knollys that bishops derive all spiritual authority, including superiority to presbyters, wholly from delegation by the crown, not from God by the commission in ordination: C. Cross, *Royal Supremacy in the Elizabethan Church* (London, 1969), p. 177. Knollys's view is an ultra-Caesaropapism analogous to the Ultramontane stance of Archbishop Castagna of Rossano (later, for a few days in 1590, Urban VII) submitted to the Council of Trent on 20 October 1562. Castagna held that bishops are the pope's vicars and derive all authority from him, including superiority over presbyters, so that no further justification, such as 'divine right', is necessary, *Conc. Trid.*, IX, 59, 18.

88. *Zurich Letters (ii)*, p. 358.

89. Hooker, *Laws*, III, 401 (VIII. 6. 9); cf. E. T. Davies, *Episcopacy and Royal Supremacy in the Church of England in the XVI Century* (Oxford, 1950; repr. 1978), pp. 132ff.

90. Wilkins, *Concilia*, IV, 374, cf. 611 for the text of a censure by the University of Oxford, 21 July 1683, upon the presbyterian and puritan view that 'the king's supremacy in ecclesiastical affairs . . . is injurious to Christ'. On the Hampton Court Conference see E. Cardwell, *Conferences Connected with the Revision of the Book of Common Prayer* (Oxford, 1840), pp. 202-3.

91. Whitgift, *Works*, II, 405; Hooker, *Laws*, VIII. 5. 10, 'the first institution of bishops was from heaven, was even of God, the Holy Ghost was the author of it.'.

92. See the abrasive message from the House of Commons to the Westminster Assembly of Divines, 30 April 1646, printed in *Minutes of the Sessions of the Westminster Assembly*, ed. A. F. Mitchell and J. Struthers (Edinburgh and London, 1874), pp. 448-55, showing that the parliament hated papal and royal supremacy, but enthusiastically upheld its own in matters ecclesiastical. Any suggestion that authority in the Church might have a divine sanction was anathema to the men who had executed Laud and were soon to kill the king.

93. (W. Allen), *A True, Sincere and Modest Defence of English Catholics* (Rouen, 1584), answering Burghley's defence of the government's harassment of recusants. A modern reprint is edited by R. M. Kingdon (Ithaca, NY, 1965). An excerpt is in Cross, *Royal Ecclesiastical Supremacy* (London, 1969), pp. 154-5. There is a vehement attack on the idea that a national Church ought to wait for a general council before taking crucial independent decisions, in *The Decades of H. Bullinger*, ed. T. Harding, 4 vols. (Parker Society, 1849-52), IV, 116f.

94. Among the critics of James I's defence of the oath of allegiance, the learned and witty tracts of the Jesuit Martin Becan (in his collected *opuscula*, 5 vols. (Mainz, 1610-21)) are outstanding. James's best defender was Lancelot Andrewes.

95. Cranmer, *Remains and Letters*, 2 vols. (Oxford, 1833), I, 116.

Chapter 18: The status of Ecumenical Councils in Anglican thought

1. Tertullian, *de Ieiunio*, 13, 6 'Aguntur praeterea per Graecias illa certis in locis concilia ex universis ecclesiis, per quae et altiora quaeque in commune tractantur, et ipsa repraesentatio

totius nominis Christiani magna veneratione celebratur.'

2. Ignatius of Antioch, *ad Ephes.* 1; *ad Magn.* 2; *ad Trall.* 1.

3. Cyprian, *Ep.* 55, 5 'Ac si minus sufficiens episcoporum in Africa numerus videbatur, etiam Romam super hac re scripsimus ad Cornelium collegam nostrum, qui et ipse cum pluribus coepiscopis habito concilio in eandem sententiam . . . consensit.'

4. See, for example, Pope Celestine I, *Ep.* 18, 1 (Migne P. L. 50. 506 A), in his letter to the Council of Ephesus (431). The Latin text is edited by Schwartz in *Acta Conciliorum Oecumenicorum (ACO)* I, ii, 1, p. 22; the Greek version in *ACO* I, i, 3, p. 55. After citing Matt. 18, 20, he continues: 'quanto magis eum (*sc.* spiritum sanctum) nunc interesse credamus quando in unum convenit turba sanctorum?' The argument first occurs in Ignatius, *ad Ephes.* 5, 2.

5. On the sacred number 318, derived from the number of Abraham's servants in Genesis 14 (in turn derived from the numerical value of the Hebrew letters of the name Eliezer), see M. Aubineau in *Revue d'Histoire ecclésiastique* 61 (1966), pp. 5-43, and my remarks in the same volume, pp. 808-811.

6. It is worth noting in passing that the title 'ecumenical synod' is first applied to Nicaea by Eusebius of Caesarea, *Vita Constantini* iii, 6 (cf. also the chapter title in the index at the head of book iii, p. 72, 11 ed. Heikel), and that the title was not his invention. Eusebius happily borrowed for Christian use a phrase already current for the worldwide brotherhood of Dionysiac actors. See, for example, P. Oxy 2610, s. iii; P. Oxy 2476 (A.D. 289); BGU 1074 (A.D. 275).

Eusebius' idea was quickly taken up by Athanasius (*de Decretis* 4; *ep. ad Afros* 2-3) and so became common parlance. See *J.T.S.* April 1972, p. 132.

7. The notion that the emperor's assent conferred binding force upon a conciliar decision was a natural assumption made on legal analogy. Its earliest theological occurrence may be seen in the implications of Eusebius of Caesarea's letter to his Church, when he recalls that after he had declared his faith the emperor Constantine himself had affirmed its orthodoxy. The doctrine that Constantine conferred authority on the Nicene creed by his ratification is first found in Marius Victorinus, *adv. Arium*, ii, 9 (see the fine edition and commentary by Henry and Hadot in Sources Chrétiennes). The first appearance of the notion that authority was conferred on the Nicene creed by papal ratification is harder to trace. Damasus, *ep. Confidimus*, denies authority to the council of Ariminum of 359 on the ground that its decisions lacked Roman approval (Theodoret, *H. E.* ii, 22, 9; the Latin from cod. Veronensis LX (58) best edited by Schwartz, *Zeits. Neutest. Wiss.* 35 (1936), pp. 19-20), but falls short of saying that the Nicaenum possesses authority because and insofar as Pope Silvester ratified it. Pope Julius I claimed that the Greek bishops at Tyre had no right to depose Athanasius of Alexandria without reference to Rome (Athan. *Apol. c. Ar.* 35), which Socrates (*H. E.* ii, 17, 7) and Sozomen (*H. E.* iii, 10, 1) understand to mean a claim that conciliar decisions are invalid without Roman approval rather than a simple assertion of the right to participate in decisions where Rome is

properly concerned. If Siricius *ep.* 6, 3 (P. L. 13, 1165) is insinuating the notion of papal ratification of Nicaea, he does it obscurely. Explicit statements come late in the fifth century with the Roman synod of 485 (Felix, *ep.* 11, 4, ed. Thiel p. 255) and the forgeries of the time of the Laurentian schism (see Duchesne, *Liber Pontificalis* I, pp. cxxxiii ff.). For astringent criticism of the idea of imperial ratification see Maximus Confessor's dispute with Theodosius of Caesarea (P. G. 90, 145-48).

8. See A. M. Ritter, *Das Konzil von Konstantinopel und sein Symbol* (1965), pp. 173 ff. The council of Chalcedon was reacting against the deliberate ignoring of the council of Constantinople of 381 at the council of Ephesus under Dioscorus of Alexandria in 449, whose silence on the subject provoked sharp comment in Theodorus Lector's history: ed. A. Papadopoulos-Kerameus in *Zhurnal Ministerstva Narodnago Prosveschcheniya* 333 (1901), p. 12 no. 18. G. C. Hansen, *Theodoros Anagnostes* (1971), p. 99.

9. The council of Constantinople (381) made decisions so unwelcome to Rome that its admission to the Roman canon of general councils seems first to have been won, after a sustained campaign by the ecumenical patriarch, only under Hormisdas in 519 (*collectio Avellana* 145 = Hormisdas, *ep.* 47), unless its possible recognition is implied by Gelasius' letter to the bishops of Dardania, *Avellana* 95 = Gelasius, *ep.* 26, 2 ed. Thiel p. 394.

10. E.g., the pro-Chalcedonian petition addressed to the emperor Anastasius by Theodosius and Sabas from the Judaean desert in 516, Cyril of Scythopolis, *Vita S.*

Sabae 57, ed. Schwartz p. 58. Similarly the petition to the emperor Justin from Jerusalem, Antioch and Syria, which Justin sent on to Pope Hormisdas in 520 (printed among the letters of Hormisdas, *ep.* 129, ed. Thiel p. 944).

The important article by R. Devreesse, 'Le cinquième concile et l'oecumenicité byzantine,' *Misc. G. Mercati* III = Studi e Testi 123 (1946), pp. 11-15, shows that later Byzantine texts give the title 'fifth council' to any of the synods summoned under Justinian's authority— that of 536 against Severus, the edict against Origen, and the council of 553. He also prints an excerpt from the tenth century Paris codex, Coislin. 120, fol. 31 (part of a note on the 'six ecumenical councils'), in which ecumenical synods are distinguished from local synods by the fact of being called by emperors and of including invitations to all bishops of the empire.

11. Irenaeus, *adversus Hoaereses* iii, 11, 8.

12. Greg. Magn. *Registr. ep.* i, 24 (MGH I p. 36, 17).

13. *Liber Pontificalis, Vita Sergii* (ed. Duchesne I, 372, 19-20) 'decepti subscripserant.'

14. The Acts of the council of 692 do not survive apart from the canons and the address to the emperor Justinian II, in which the council claims to supplement the work of the fifth and sixth councils. At the Second Council of Nicaea the patriarch Tarasius affirmed that the Quinisext canons were produced four or five years after 680 by the same bishops as those who had met for the sixth council (Mansi, xiii, 219; Labbe viii, 877, 880), an assurance intended to answer the scepticism of some about the authenticity and authority of the

canons. Pope Hadrian I defended the Seventh Council before the hostile Frankish bishops by saying that the Seventh Council had been able to cite the authority of the Sixth Council (viz. Quinisext, canon 82) to prove that at that time images were being venerated (P. L. 98, 1264A).

15. Fritz' article 'Quinisexte' in *DTC* conveniently notes precisely which canons pass into Gratian.

16. Anastasius Bibliothecarius' translation of the Acts of the Seventh Council is prefaced by severe warnings against canons which the Greeks pretend to have the authority of the Sixth Council (Mansi xii, 982; Labbe viii, 675).

17. Hincmar, P. L. 126. 360A.

18. Gratian I, xv, 1, 6. (Their authority like the 4 gospels, I, xv, 2).

19. Gratian I, xvi, 8.

20. Gratian I, xvi, 6-9.

21. See Friedberg's edition I, p. xx.

22. Gratian I, xvii, 1, 1.

23. *Summa Theologica* III, 25, 3-6. Thomas's normal conciliar canon is of six councils Gratian (I, xvi, 8) says that the Popes confirmed 8 councils.

24. Basil, *de Spiritu Sancto* 29, 72. The appeal to the precedent of patristic tradition appears in Eusebius of Caesarea's defence of his subscription to the Nicene creed (in his letter to his church), when he remarks that though *homoousios* is not in scripture, the term has been used by certain orthodox writers. For the development of florilegia see T. Schermann, *Die Geschichte der dogmatischen Florilegien vom 5/8 Jh.* = TU, N. F. 13, 1 (1904); M. Richard's study of Chalcedonian florilegia in Grillmeier/Bacht, *Das Konzil von Chalkedon: Geschichte und Gegenwart* I (1951), pp. 721-748, and his masterly survey,

'Florilèges grecs', *Dict. Sp.* 5 (1962), 475-512.

25. *De Spiritu Sancto* 18, 45.

26. There is a masterly study of the English writers of the sixteenth century by S. L. Greenslade, 'The English Reformers and the Councils of the Church,' in *Oecumenica: Jahrbuch für ökumenische Forschung* 1967, pp. 95-115 (with summaries in French and German). This study is explicitly limited to the sixteenth century writers included in the Parker Society edition, and does not extend to the main seventeenth century theologians whose position is probably more characteristic of the 'main stream' of Anglican thought.

27. 'Iam vero conciliis, potissimum generalibus, tametsi ingentem honorem libenter deferimus, ea tamen longe omnia infra Scripturarum canonicarum dignitatem ponenda judicamus: sed et inter ipsa concilia magnum discrimen ponimus. Nam quaedam illorum, qualia sunt praecipua illa quatuor, Nicenum, Constantinopolitanum primum, Ephesinum, et Chalcedonense, magna cum reverentia amplectimur et suscipimus. Quod quidem judicium de multis aliis quae postea celebrata sunt ferimus, in quibus videmus et confitemur sanctissimos patres de beata et summa Trinitate, de Jesu Christo Domino et Servatore nostro, et humana redemptione per eum procurata, juxta Scripturas divinas multa gravissime et perquam sancte constituisse. Quibus tamen non aliter fidem nostram obligandam esse censemus, nisi quatenus ex Scripturis sanctis confirmari possint. Nam concilia nonnulla interdum errasse, et contraria inter sese definivisse, partim in actionibus juris, partim etiam in fide, manifestum est. Itaque legantur concilia quidem

cum honore atque Christiana reverentia, sed interim ad Scripturarum piam certam rectamque regulam examinentur.'

28. *Opera Omnia* (Paris, 1620), I, 744 A.

29. F. X. Funk, 'Die Berufung der ökumenischen Synoden des Altertums', in his *Kirchengeschichtliche Abhandlungen und Untersuchungen*, i, pp. 39-86 (with further controversy on the subject in vol. iii, pp. 143-49 and 406-439).

30. Observe F. Dvornik's implication that the status of the Eighth Council against Photius, accepted by the West, rejected by the East, is diminished by the fact that the Papacy did not number it among general councils until 200 years afterwards (*The Photian Schism*, p. 444).

31. The Anglican and Orthodox traditions are probably closest to one another in the common character of their thinking about Reception in relation to conciliar authority. For a recent restatement of the Roman Catholic view see A. Grillmeier, 'Konzil und Rezeption', in *Theologie und Philosophie* 45 (1970), pp. 321-352, esp. p. 345 (the hearing church does not contribute anything to the validity or obligatoriness of the decision). A valuable and sympathetic study of the question is given by W. Küppers, 'Reception, prolegomena to a systematic study', in *Councils and the Ecumenical Movement* (World Council of Churches Studies, no. 5, Geneva 1968).

32. The classic passage is *de Baptismo* ii, 3, 4.

33. J. N. D. Kelly's magnificent textbook, *Early Christian Doctrines* (1958, several later editions), cannot continue beyond Leo and Chalcedon. I do not mean to suggest that this is a fault in the book; nor that there are not other books of the first quality on the period after 451, among which it must suffice here simply to mention J. Meyendorff, *Christ in Eastern Christian Thought after Chalcedon* (Washington D.C., 1970). Several of the questions touched on in this paper are well treated in H. K. Margull (ed.), *Die ökumenische Konzile der Christenheit* (Stuttgart, 1961), translated by W. F. Bense as *The Councils of the Church* (Philadelphia, 1966).

Sources

The papers collected in this volume have previously been published in the following places:

1. Episcopacy in the New Testament and the early Church: from *Lambeth Conference 1978 Preparatory Articles, Today's Church and today's World* (CIO, London).

2. Ministry and Tradition: from *Teologia del Sacerdocio* 21 (Burgos, Aldecoa, 1990).

3. The Vindication of Christianity in Westcott's Thought: Westcott Memorial Lecture (Cambridge University Press, 1961).

4. Ego Berengarius: from *Journal of Theological Studies* ns 40 (1989), published by Oxford University Press.

5. The Lambeth Quadrilateral in England: from *Quadrilateral at One Hundred*, edited by J. Robert Wright (Forward Publications, Cincinnati 1988).

6. Truth and Authority: Westminster Abbey Lecture 1981 (SPCK).

7. Full Communion with other Episcopal Churches: from *The Churchman* 95 (1981).

8. Justification by Faith, a perspective: from *One in Christ* 1984 (Turvey Abbey).

9. Lima ARCIC and the Church of England: from *One in Christ* 1984.

10. Ecumenical Stocktaking: from *The Tablet*, February 1992.

11. Newman's significance for the Anglican Church: from *Newman a man for our time* edited by David Brown (SPCK 1991).

12. Newman's doctrine of Justification: from *Newman after a Hundred Years*, edited by Alan Hill and I. T. Ker (Oxford University Press, 1990).

13. Newman's Sacramental Faith: from *The Tablet*, 13 August 1990.

14. Paul VI and Vatican II: from *Journal of Ecclesiastical History* 41 (1990).

15. Why Music in Church? Church Music Society Lecture 1981.

16. Romanticism and Religion: from *The Future of the Modern Humanities* (Publication of the Modern Humanities Research Association, 1969).

17. Royal Ecclesiastical Supremacy: from *Humanism, Reform and Reformation*, edited by B. Bradshaw and E. Duffy (Cambridge University Press 1989).

18. The Status of Ecumenical Councils in Anglican Thought: from *Orientalia Christiana Analecta* 195 (Rome, 1973), essays in honour of Georges Florovsky.

19. Making and Remaking in the Ministry of the Church: from *The Making and Remaking of Christian Doctrine* (edited by Sarah Coakley and David A. Pailin, Oxford University Press, 1993).

Index

Abbaudus 57
absolution 61, 163, 185, 250
Acontius 280
Acton, Lord 161, 168, 286, 300
Adelmann of Liège 51
Agobard 308
Alcuin 44, 55
Alexander VI, Pope 242
Alfonso Liguori 298
Alger of Liège 42ff., 52ff.
Allen, W. 254
Amalarius of Metz 54
Ambrose 37, 274
Ames, W. 73
Anglican-Methodist conversations 71
Anglican orders 91
Anastasius, librarian 261
Andrewes, L. 112
Anselm 18, 46, 55, 74, 144, 237f., 278
Apostles 2ff.
Apostolic Canons 13
Aquinas 74, 94, 131
ARCIC 64, 90-93, 135ff., 143-153
Aristotle 35f., 42f., 94, 204
Articles, Thirty-nine 116f., 128, 159, 174, 244, 250, 263f.
    Tract 90: 165, 190
assurance 99f., 115f., 164, 179, 184
Athenagoras, patriarch 89
Augustine of Hippo 12, 14, 17f., 36, 40ff., 50, 53, 55, 65, 79, 94, 99ff., 131ff., 141, 160, 181, 183, 206ff., 237f., 269f., 274

Baptism 13, 125f., 131f., 136
Bagot, R. 166
Baius, Michael 133
Bandinelli, R. 56
Barnes, Robert 251
Basil 262f.
Baur, F. C. 25f.
Becan, M. 315
Bellarmine, R. 54, 98f., 123, 266
Benson, A. C. 19, 285

Benson, E. W. 20
Berengar 33-60
Bernard 74, 94, 103
Beza, T. 251
Bishops 61ff., 87, 139, 279
Blennerhasset, Lady 192
Boethius 43f., 207, 290
Bonaventure 94
Boniface VIII, Pope 242
Bramhall, J. 161, 165, 231
Bright, W. 21
Brooke, Z. N. 50
Bryce, J. 295
Bucer, M. 98, 106f., 126
Buchanan, J. 181
Bull, G. 103, 124f., 132, 159, 167, 171f., 185f.
Bullinger, H. 244, 250f.
Burke, E. 15, 168
Burnet, G. 63
Bushnell, H. 224

Caesarius of Heisterbach 47, 59
Calvin 35, 98, 171, 177
Cano, Melchior 266, 287
canon, NT 2, 16
Cartwright, T. 246
Cassander, G. 123, 171
Cassels, W. R. 29, 286
Cervini, M. 93ff., 179
Chemnitz, M. 114
Chrysostom, John 44
Clement of Rome 4f., 9
Clement VII, Pope 229, 241
Coleridge, S. T. 222
Concord, Formula 113f., 155, 170
confirmation 9
Congar, Y. M. J. 199, 269
Consilii, Jean 293
Constance, council 275
Contarini 106f.
Cosin, J. 249, 274
Councils, general 78, 253, 258-269, 316
Cranmer, T. 231, 244, 252, 255
Credner, K. A. 25
Cromwell, Thomas 246f.

Cullen, P. 188
Cyprian 7, 12f., 111, 258

Davenant, J. 122, 128, 171, 180
Davenport, C. 121
Deacons 3f., 139
decretals, false 261
Dessain, S. 185
Didache 4
dispensations 238f.
Döllinger, J. J. 171, 189
Donatism 10, 12, 135, 167, 209, 235f.
Driver, S. R. 20, 285
Duns Scotus 291
Duprey, P. 199
Durandus of Troarn 42f., 49f.

Eck, Johann 107
Edward VI 230
Eisengrein, M. 115
Elizabeth I 246, 251, 275
Erasmus 95
Erskine, T. 181
Eucharist 33-60, 88, 152f.
  sacrifice 130, 136f., 184
Eugenius IV, Pope 276

Faber, G. S. 174f., 310
Ferdinand the Catholic 242
Field, R. 180, 265
Filioque 89f., 151, 278
Fisher, John 229
Flacius 43
Florence, council 35, 94, 247, 257, 275f.
  purgatory 105
florilegia 262f.
Florus of Lyon 56
Forbes, W. 112, 118, 122f., 131, 178
Foxe, J. 178, 242, 252, 275, 287, 311f.
Froude, H. 63, 158f., 168
fundamentals 146f., 279

Gardiner, Stephen 119, 247ff, 251f., 257, 275, 312
Gerhard, Johann 171, 175, 302
Gerson 276
Gladstone, W. E. 167
Gnostics 9
'God is English' 232, 275, 307
Gore, C. 21
Gorham, G. C. 66
Gratian 58, 261
Gregory the Great, Pope 260
Gregory VII, Pope 44ff.
Grindal, E. 253
Gropper, J. 106-108
Grosseteste, R. 243
Grotius, H. 231, 305
Guest, Edmund 117, 120
Guitmund of Aversa 44f., 56

Hales, John 313
Hampden, R. D. 162
Hampton Court conference 254
Hare, J. C. 178
Harnack, A. 115
Henry VIII 229ff., 274, 314
hierarchy of truths 198
Hincmar 241, 261, 288, 308f.
Hitzig, F. 27
Hoadly, B. 155
Honorius, Pope 260, 268, 298
Hooker, R. 72f., 121f., 128f., 152, 154, 159, 171, 180, 253, 265
Hooper, John 117, 230ff., 304f.
Hort, F. J. A. 19
Humbert, Cardinal 18, 33f., 39f., 144, 278
Huygens, R. B. C. 286

icons 261ff.
Ignatius of Antioch 8f.
imputation 102ff., 116, 118f., 124f., 129, 170, 179, 182
'indifferent' (adiafora) 280
Innocent III, Pope 57f., 243, 262
Innocent IV, Pope 243
intercommunion 85f.

Irenaeus 16, 28, 260, 272
Ivo of Chartres 50, 290

James I 254f.
Jansen, C. 133
Jerome 9, 99, 236
Jewel, J. 59, 239, 304
John, St 5, 39
John of Damascus 237
John Paul II, Pope 144
Johnson, John 293
Julian of Eclanum 114
justification 93ff.
    formal cause 110, 118, 156, 173
    in Newman 156f., 170-186
Justinian 233f., 239

Kant, I. 21f.
Keble, J. 154, 158f., 192
Kerularius, M. 18
keys, power 2, 111
Kierkegaard, S. 222f.
Knox, A. 174, 184
Knox, J. 254
Küng, H. 281

Lanfranc 37ff.
Langland, W. 232
Lardner, N. 25
Laud, W. 74, 266
Laynez, Diego 108
Lee, Prince 22, 24
Leo I, Pope 147, 268
Lessing, G. E. 219f., 236
Liddon, H. P. 20, 285
Lightfoot, J. B. 19ff.
Lima 135ff.
Locke, J. 220
Lollardy 231ff., 243f.
Lovejoy, A. 217
Lumen Gentium 197f.
Luther, M. 33f., 58f., 65, 94ff.,
    175, 243, 310f.

Mabillon, J. 51
Macy, G. 287
Malines conversations 70

Manning, H. E. 154, 161, 167,
    169
Marcion 16
marriage 238f.
Martyr, Peter 292
Mary, St 82, 140f., 147f., 161,
    191, 195, 200f., 282
Maurice, F. D. 20
Mazochi, L. 107, 116
Melanchthon, P. 37, 95, 98, 101,
    106f., 109, 123, 126, 156, 171,
    176, 185, 279, 301
Möhler, J. A. 173, 222
Montague, R. 121
Montanism 16
Morley, John 29
music 203ff.

Netter, Thomas 50f., 58, 266, 288
Newman, J. H. 15, 77, 126f.,
    154-193, 225f.
Nicaea, Council (325) 7, 13, 258f.
    Council (787) 261ff.
Nicholas II, Pope 33ff.
Nicolas Cabasilas 293
Nicolas of Cusa 266
Non-jurors 155
Novatian 13

Oecolampadius 35, 287
Oetinger, F. C. 219
Old Catholics 70
ordination 6f., 12f., 149, 151f.,
    190

Paley, W. 281
papacy 81, 169
    antichrist 66, 107, 169, 181,
        231, 243, 255, 305f.
Parker, Matthew 230, 232, 252
Paschasius Radbertus 47
Pastoral epistles 4
Paul III, Pope 107, 242
Paul VI, Pope 89, 92, 194-202
Paul of Samosata 13
Petau, D. 124
Peter, St 149

Peter Lombard 56, 94, 100
Pighius 106
Philips, Gerard 196ff.
Photius 261f.
Pius IX, Pope 158, 282
Pocock, N. 63
Pole, R. 93, 105, 229f., 242, 245, 304
predestination 96ff., 113f., 127, 166
Prynne, W. 74
purgatory 104f., 128, 247
Pusey, E. B. 159, 162, 165, 190, 200

Quesnel, P. 133
Quinisext 260

Ramsey, A. M. 71
Ratisbon, colloquy 106
Ratramnus 36, 47, 278
Ratzinger, J. 196f.
reception 271
revelation 280f.
Ritschl, A. 26
Robert of Melun 56
Romaine, W. 171
Rousseau, J. J. 220f.
Routh, M. J. 154
Runcie, R. A. K. 150
Rupert of Deutz 52f., 57
Ryle, H. E. 22

St German, C. 240
Sanday, W. 20, 285
Sarpi, P. 93
satisfaction 111
Schleiermacher, F. D. E. 222f.
Schwegler, A. 27
Seripando, G. 106ff., 130, 179f.
Sidgwick, H. 23, 28
Soto, D. 115
South India Church 71
Spener, P. J. 172
Spinoza 219f.
Stapleton, Thomas 100, 267
Stephen, Pope 12

Stillingfleet, E. 72
Suarez, F. 123
substance 34ff., 42ff., 138, 152
succession 9f., 15, 149, 307
Sumner, J. B. 298
'Supernatural Religion' 29
Symmachus, Pope 240
Syropoulos 94

Tait, A. C. 66
Taylor, Jeremy 124, 171f., 186
Temple, F. 226
Thirlwall, C. 30, 166, 299
Thorndike, H. 154, 166, 266f.
Three Chapters 234
tradition 12f., 157, 272f.
transubstantiation 33-60, 138f., 157, 165, 192, 266, 287
Trent, council 93ff., 179f., 264
Tunstall, C. 241, 245, 310
Turner, W. 250f.
Tyndale, W. 244f., 310

Ullmann, W. 240
Unigenitus 294
unilateral decisions 270-284

Vazquez, G. 100, 123
Vega, A. 115
Vercelli, council (1050) 39
Vigilius, Pope 234, 239, 259f.

Walter of St Victor 59
Ward, W. G. 165
Waterland, D. 125
Wesley, John 134, 155
Westcott, B. F. 19ff.
Westminster Confession 170, 181
  assembly 315
Whateley, R. 157f.
Whitgift, John 73, 246, 254
Wiburn, P. 253, 314
Wilberforce, H. 163
Wilberforce, W. 160
Willebrands, J. G. M. 200
William of St Thierry 55
Wiseman, N. 167

Wolsey, T. 248f.
women priests 18, 82f., 90, 139,
    150, 270ff.
Wyclif 33ff., 231, 306

Zacharias of Besançon 59
Zahn, T. 24
Zwingli 35, 58, 97, 220